AN EPITOMIZED

HISTORY

OF

THE MILITIA

(The "Constitutional Force")

TOGETHER WITH THE

ORIGIN, PERIODS OF EMBODIED SERVICE,

AND

SPECIAL SERVICES

(*INCLUDING SOUTH AFRICA, 1899-1902*),

OF

MILITIA UNITS EXISTING OCTOBER 31, 1905.

COMPILED BY

COLONEL GEORGE JACKSON HAY, C.B., C.M.G.,

*Late Commanding 3rd Battalion, The Prince of Wales's Own
(West Yorkshire Regiment).*

The Naval & Military Press Ltd

Published by

The Naval & Military Press Ltd
Unit 10 Ridgewood Industrial Park,
Uckfield, East Sussex,
TN22 5QE England

Tel: +44 (0) 1825 749494
Fax: +44 (0) 1825 765701

www.naval-military-press.com
www.nmarchive.com

In reprinting in facsimile from the original, any imperfections are inevitably reproduced and the quality may fall short of modern type and cartographic standards.

CONTENTS.

PART I.

Chap.			Page.
I.	General		1
II.	Origin, etc.		10
III.	Territorialism, etc.		21
IV.	Composition of the Force		28
V.	Pay and Emoluments		36
VI.	Discipline, etc.		40
VII.	Weapons		50
VIII.	Equipment, etc.		53
IX.	Commissions of Array, Assizes of Arms, Acts of Parliament, etc.	1122 to 1539	60
X.	Muster Returns, 1539—Henry VIII.		63
XI.	Acts, etc., 1542 to 1588 Spanish Armada Assembly, Harleian MSS.		88
XII.	Acts, etc., James I., 1603, to Chas. II., 1661		97
XIII.	Origin of Militia, Scotland		107
XIV.	Strength of Welsh Militia 1684, etc. Militia Returns, 1697, Egerton MSS.		110
XV.	Acts, Orders, etc., 1698 to 1786		136
XVI.	Origin of Militia, Ireland, etc.		146
XVII.	Acts, etc., 1793 to 1795. Volunteering from Militia to Line. Increase and Decrease of Force. Supplementary Militia, Local Militia, etc. The Ballot Act.		148
XVIII.	Strength of Force at various periods. Type of Men obtained 1803. Substitutes, etc. Numbers furnished to Regular Army, etc.		162
XIX.	Epitome of Services		168
XX.	Introduction to Origin, etc., of Units		184

PART II.

	Page.
Origin, Embodied periods, and Services of Units existing Oct. 31st, 1905.	185
Index	187

CHAPTER I.

NAMES OF THE FORCE AT DIFFERENT PERIODS—IMPORTANCE OF TRADITION—CONTINUITY AND POSITION—RÔLE OF THE CONSTITUTIONAL FORCE—THE "POWER OF THE COUNTRY" AS A MILITARY LIFE BUOY—OFFICIAL DOCUMENTS, ETC., BEARING UPON THE PATRIOTISM OF THE PEOPLE AND THEIR FORCE—THE CHORD OF SENTIMENT AND SYMPATHY.

What can better indicate the great age of the Constitutional Force of defence, than the coincidence that the interesting details of its remarkable career interwoven with trials and thrilling triumphs of the Country during many centuries, should have passed out of the general knowledge of all classes of people.

This obvious wastage of Tradition, with possibilities detrimental to the continued patriotism of the people, and spirit of the heterogeneous army now required for obtaining the safety of the country and welfare of Empire, would appear to create an opportunity for inviting National interest in the history of that parent military force, whose units in far off days were led by Kings on the field of battle, and in later times have been the means of providing a reserve strength on many occasions of National danger.

As a tribal combination in remote ages, arising out of the natural instinct of the people to defend all that was dear to them, the "Fyrd" for many centuries, "Posse Comitatus" or power of the Country in Norman times, followed by quaint views, Assizes of Arms, musters of "Trayned men having abiliments of war to serve the Lord their King," Militia by name in several forms, and Trained Bands, the Constitutional Force of England can claim to have fulfilled in one form or another for near two thousand years, that highly honourable duty of bearing arms and rendering service, which in far back ages rested upon all the people.

A Prize Essay of the American Military Service Institute has, in effect, placed before the world, that tradition tends to create esprit defined as a common spirit, effacing personal interests and individualities, impelling cheerful and efficient performance of duty, also that by keeping in memory the record of customs and deeds well performed, tradition becomes advantageous when antiquated methods which have outlived their usefulness are not allowed to block the progress of constantly changing and improving ends.

It goes on to say that the French have adopted an expression, "Esprit Militaire," for general use, distinct from the limited application of Corps Esprit. The authority Hoenig says, elaborate preparations, the best arms, and skilful manoeuvres are only means to an end, as victory depends almost invariably on the Esprit of an Army and Nation. The people must possess National Spirit to develop the esprit of their troops, whilst the army as a complete machine, all branches working harmoniously together for one common end, requires to be increased in strength by the sense of public sympathy and support, and those sentiments of pride which come from past history.

These extracts from an admirably expressed Essay on Esprit, seem to present, when considered in relation to Tradition, a conclusive reason for keeping alive and in the memory of the people, the impressive and instructive annals of such a Force as that of the People have contributed to the Military and other records of the country.

"The Times," with all its vast accumulated knowledge, following the exercised power of research, has stated that the antecedents of the Militia, now representing the Constitutional Force, form a complete thread in the nation's Military history throughout many centuries. "The Broad Arrow," representative of the Service Press, describes the Militia as being the only legal Military defensive force of the country with a permanent existence, whilst the "St. James's Gazette" and other journals have, with educational exactness, referred to historical incidents associated with the force of the people, which must be laid under contribution in compiling the annals of this peculiar institution of the country. The position of the country, whether viewed geographically or as an Empire with the flag of freedom and justice planted in every part of the world, its people imbued with a characteristic disposition to enjoy the blessings of peace and safety, and ruled over by a Sovereign mindful of the requirements of his kingdom and peaceful wishes of his loyal subjects, creates a unique combination of circumstances which necessitate the maintenance of an Army composed of several branches under different obligations of service.

This collected and collated narrative of events, which can only at present be traced out piecemeal in the voluminous archives of the State and gleaned from occasional pages of ancient and other histories, or necessarily in part referred to in those valuable works that have at periods dealt with varied matters relating to the country, its military customs and antiquities, is not intended to be alone pleasant reading to those who are or have been connected with the Constitutional Force.

Although any concentration of the annals of a force having such a far distant origin, and of incidents culled from the Press and published digests of the services of units, cannot, from its character as a work of compilation, aspire to any novelty of description, it is hoped that "Esprit Militaire" resulting from the circulation of tradition will tend to expand that sympathy and support between the people and all branches of the Army, which in the permanent interest of the State it has been implied should always prevail in any country requiring to preserve peace, prestige, and prosperity.

If in laying bare to view an abridged general history of "the Constitutional Force," along with all that is known of the origin of existing units, their periods of embodied duty and special services performed, including a succinct account of the doings of those Militia Battalions and units that, beyond their obligation of service and representing the Constitutional Force, voluntarily took an active and material part in the great South African War, produces no other effect, it will place the State in possession of concentrated details that may be of value for purposes of reference, and preserve to the Force, districts, and units, what in the past have so often been lost or accidentally destroyed.

Whilst the leading organ of the Press has with privileged freedom pointed out that the strength or weakness of the country appears to have been often reflected by the condition of its Constitutional Force, it will not come within the scope of any work of this nature to criticise either the dynastic, political, or financial exigencies which may have occasioned changes seeming to be remarkable, nor can any problems of defence be introduced.

The rôle of the Constitutional Force has been in all times and under every form of Government, theoretically that of an emergency force, both before and after the formation of a regular branch of the Army. Scott's History of the British Army says:—

> "It was the feeling of dependence on the part of Sovereigns on an army of free citizens that induced them to engage mercenaries. They found that they could possess no real power without them, and the supply of foreign garrisons and castle guards at home made an absolute requirement for more continuous service."

King Canute is said to have kept a body guard of several thousand mercenaries; whilst Lord Macaulay remarks, in his

History of England: "King Charles II., fearful of his safety, surrounded himself with regular troops."

The expediency of what took place in 1661, and its effect upon the country, are not, however, matters forming any part of the history of the People's force. According to Hume's History of England, the Militia then numbered 160,000 men, reputed to be in a high state of efficiency and discipline—as the result of Cromwell's able administration.

At the time of this very important Military epoch in the nation's history, created by the formation of a branch of the Army for continuous service, the Constitutional Force was and had been in many centuries the only army of the country, out of which we know that armies were raised by impressment and otherwise for the oft recurring foreign expeditions, so largely filling along with disturbances and fighting at home the numerous volumes of England's early history.

After 1661, and the prospect of the Militia being called upon to make sacrifices and render service became apparently reduced, this ancient force of the people, which in the previous seventeen hundred years had so often fought for their country, became the expansile reserve strength of the nation, as in the early Norman age when William the Conqueror re-modelled the army of his kingdom.

To what extent this peculiar force has responded to the oft-repeated demands upon it since the introduction of a standing branch of the Army, and the manner in which those representing the people have performed multifarious duties at home and beyond the sea arising out of the grave necessity of situations involving "imminent national danger," are to be found irrevocably recorded in the Annals of the Houses of Parliament, whose Acts and Resolutions have often indicated the appreciation of ruling Sovereigns and gratitude of the nation. Whilst it may be said that this "Power of the Country" has been typical of a national military life-buoy—collapsible when not wanted, yet reliably buoyant on all occasions of actual danger—the force would appear to have aptly demonstrated the value of ancient customs and tradition.

The history of tribal units, bandes, companies and larger organised bodies of the armed people, at times embracing the whole of the able-bodied people "assessed to armour," represents an accumulation of interesting data, and incidents connected with the liability to render service and of duties performed, which seem to be a valuable asset of the nation in the form of tradition worth keeping before all classes of the people, along with the records of those tidal waves that since the latter part of the eighteenth century have carried on their crests from the Constitutional Force tens of thousands of trained men to augment the regular branch of the Army at critical moments in the nation's life.

Historians have passed down for contemplation how Queen Elizabeth, addressing her "Milecia" assembled to resist the Spanish Armada in 1588, strengthened them by touching and quaint expressions of sentiment when "placing her chief strength and safeguard in the loyal hearts and good will of her subjects." If it be politic to foster and stimulate "public sympathy and support, and those sentiments which come from past history," the old Constitutional Force of England has among its records the sentiments of Sovereigns and appreciation of others since the days of "Good Queen Bess" that should, under any circumstances, always find a place in any history of the Force. We can find that King Charles II., though remembering the fate of his ancestor and fearful of his own safety, abolished the Feudal System of Norman times, and reorganised under the Acts of Parliament which he confirmed, the ancient Force representing his people. Lord Macaulay says: " by solemn acknowledgment of both Houses of Parliament it was admitted that the King, by ancient Constitution of the Realm, was the sole Captain-General of the Force."

Passing on to more recent times, there are many official documents interesting to the people and those who carry arms for their country.

In 1756 Parliament decided that "a well ordered and well disciplined Militia was essentially necessary for the safety, peace and prosperity of the kingdom," and at recurring intervals thoughts and utterances bearing upon the ceaseless patriotism of the people, elasticity and zeal of their force, are to be found and can be quoted without endangering the progress "of constantly changing and improving ends."

A Horseguards Circular, 1799, of His Royal Highness the Duke of York, says:—

"Having witnessed the brilliant success which has already attended the efforts of His Majesty's arms in Holland, and for which the country is so much indebted to the distinguished gallantry and zeal of the first volunteers from the Militia," etc.

In 1802 His Majesty King George III., through the

Secretary of State for War, expressed "the truly meritorious zeal of the Militia and public spirit under all the trying occurrences which had arisen to call forth their loyal exertions during the long and arduous contest in which we have been engaged."

His Royal Highness, by Horseguards Circular, 1811, described the Force "as being a never failing resource on every occasion of difficulty and danger."

In 1814 His Royal Highness the Prince Regent, in the name of His Majesty, took the opportunity, on peace being declared, to convey to the Constitutional Force by Horseguards Circular his approval of "The gallant and patriotic spirit displayed by the Force, which at most critical periods of the war was the means of reinforcing the disposable force of the country—a measure which essentially contributed to its military renown by placing the British Army foremost in those Confederate bands that resisted the unbounded ambition and overwhelming power of the late ruler of France, and by their bravery and discipline, under the direction of Divine Providence, rescued that country from tyranny and oppression and restored to Europe the blessing of peace."

Her Majesty the late Queen Victoria communicated to the Militia, after the Crimean War in 1856, "the high sense she entertained of their conduct, zeal and spirit which had been manifested while they had been embodied," etc.

The Field Marshal Commanding-in-Chief also at the same time expressed "his acknowledgments for their zeal and discipline; that they had not only performed every duty which fell to their share with the cheerful obedience of good soldiers, but they had in large numbers gallantly volunteered into the Line at the most critical period of the War, and by thus reinforcing the British Army before Sebastopol had essentially contributed to its success, whilst several regiments having volunteered their services for Mediterranean garrisons liberated an equal number of regiments of the line to proceed to the Crimea." In coming down to still more recent times, it would be discourteous not to keep in memory the opinion held and expressed in South Africa by the distinguished late Commander-in-Chief, Field Marshal The Rt. Hon. Earl Roberts, etc., on the occasion of his re-embarkation for England, as promulgated by War Office Circular, Jan., 1901, to embodied Militia units at home :—

"The work of guarding the lines of communication is one that is often apt to be passed unnoticed. I have appreciated the arduous duties performed by the Militia, and I thank all for the very great assistance rendered."

No reference to incidents associated with the obligation of service fulfilled by the people, and services rendered by the Constitutional Force would, however, be acceptable without some mention of the many thanks accorded by the Sovereign and Houses of Parliament at times when they were impressed with the value of what had been done for the common weal. The speech made by Lord Castlereagh, as Secretary of State for Foreign Affairs, in the House of Commons, November 13, 1813, requires notice in detail, forming, as it does, one of the bright stars illuminating the history of the Force, and an example of its life-buoy character when required for use. Lord Castlereagh said, when referring to the one hundred thousand men given by the Militia to the Regular branch of the Army for active service in the Peninsula :

" We could not have kept possession of Portugal, or have sent forces to co-operate in the deliverance of the Peninsula at large, and taken up that menacing position on the frontiers of France which our Army now occupies; we should have been shut up within the bounds of our insular policy, and could not have set that glorious example to other nations, or borne our share in the general exertions which have been made for the deliverance of Europe. Parliament ought always, therefore, to bear in recollection that it is to the Militia we owe the character we at present enjoy in Military Europe, and that without the Militia we could not have shown that face which we have done in the Peninsula."

There should be also kept in memory one of the last speeches made by the great Duke of Wellington in the House of Lords, when he spoke in the highest terms of the services rendered by the Militia in the "War of Freedom."

In bringing to a conclusion this limited selection of memorable occasions in modern times when "esprit effacing personal interests" were strikingly in evidence, it would be, perhaps, interesting to support those sentiments expressed by quoting some statistical details of the continued "love of country and pride of race" which were practically demonstrated during the prosecution of the Crimean and great South African wars. We have it recorded upon the authoritative statement of a late Inspector General of Auxiliary Forces that about fifty Militia battalions offered their services for the front during the Crimean War, and that several regiments went beyond the sea to garrison Gibraltar and other Mediterranean stations; whilst 14,000 of the best Non-Commissioned Officers and Men of the Militia (as Militia Reservists) served in South Africa to augment their affiliated Line Battalions. Besides this, 1981 Officers and 40,000 Men were contributed to the regular branch of the Army during the prosecution of the war, and, in addition, sixty complete Militia Battalions—comprising 1691 Officers and 43,875 N.C. Officers and Men—volunteered for and took part in the campaign, also ten Battalions at garrisons in the Mediterranean, Egypt, and elsewhere abroad.

Although the noteworthy achievements of this ever-available force for contingencies during near 2,000 years (which in principle and effect has been "the chord of sentiment and sympathy between the people and the Army, in touch with local enthusiasm and local interests") are to be found to some extent securely preserved among the archives of the State, the foregoing quoted references of some of the later obligatory and voluntary duties efficiently performed reflect the immeasurably more responsible position which the Constitutional Force filled as the only army in earlier centuries. Whilst it is not possible to notice within the limited space of an epitome all that might be of academic value and locally interesting, nor deal exhaustively with the many volumes of ancient history and the innumerable Militia Acts of Parliament for "placing the country in a posture of defence," etc., every effort has been made to extract in brief from these and other sources, general historical works, regimental records, State, county, official and privately owned documents, whatever information appeared to be of general interest, which should be drawn together and kept safe for the benefit of the State, Districts, and Corps.

With reference to the introductory observation that the annals of the Constitutional Force had passed out of the general knowledge of all classes of the people, the writer would venture to emphasise this by saying that it was his experience (during near a quarter century in command of a Battalion and about forty-five years' connection with the Force), when lecturing to crowded audiences composed of different classes in life, upon the history of all branches of their territorial regiment, the peace and safety of the Empire and kindred subjects; also on occasions of closer contact with the actual recruit-giving classes, to find the deepest interest taken in the annals of battalions, and a wish in evidence to acquire far more information about the diversified and fascinating antecedents of the general Army of the State, than could be imparted at such times.

In now attempting to satisfy that local wish—in respect of the force of the people—and a wish doubtless animating all sections of the community throughout the country—it has been thought tactful to pass on quickly from the tempting zone of comment to the more convincing haven of facts and incidents likely to find a place in the thoughtful minds of a patriotic and practical people.

CHAPTER II.

DERIVATION OF THE WORD "MILITIA"—DEFINITION OF THE FYRD-ROMAN ORGANIZATION FOR DEFENCE—THE MILITARY SYSTEM OF KING ALFRED—INTRODUCTION OF THE FEUDAL SYSTEM—DEFECTS MADE GOOD BY THE POSSE COMITATUS—THE BANDE OR COMPANY AS THE TERRITORIAL UNIT OF ORGANIZATION—"FRAME OR MODEL OF THE MILITIA" IN 1644—ABOLITION OF THE FEUDAL SYSTEM—RE-ORGANIZATION OF THE FORCE OF THE PEOPLE.

There are probably few persons who would wish to exact any metaphorical wandering on the shores of Ancient Britain for the purpose of tracing out exactly the kind of paint, skins, and feathers that comprised the uniforms of the people's army in remote ages, nor for any complete list and description to be presented of all the wondrous weapons for destruction and defence borne by successive generations of the People's Force.

In any consideration of the origin of "The Constitutional Force" it becomes desirable, if not altogether necessary, owing to the efflux of time and paucity of details given by historians in their references to the means of defence in the early ages, to fully appreciate what is known of military service by the people in the days of early Britain, ancient Rome, and the Saxon ages. It seems to be of import to compare one with the other their respective systems and observe the continuity of principle and organization which characterised the bearing of arms by the people in those times and in after years, coupled with the semblance of some of the regulations and quaint customs incidental to service and defence, which appear to have prevailed in many ages.

The first General known to have commanded a combined Force of the British people is usually said to have been Cassivelaunus, selected by the Chiefs about the year 54 B.C. to be the Generalissimo of their Army to oppose Caesar's second Roman invasion. His headquarters appear to have been in the neighbourhood, and probably about the same site, which afterwards formed the Roman city of Verulanium.

Those who have visited St. Albans will know that about that place many characteristic remains exist of ancient British defences. It is stated that Caesar pressed the Britons under Cassivelaunus back on their stronghold, and eventually took it by storm.

Historians observe that there is no doubt but that the ancient Britons had a good military organisation, though wanting in tactics, and that every able-bodied man was held liable to serve under his recognised Chief. They were armed with lances, spears, bows and slings, and are reputed to have possessed great nobility, making use of saythed chariots, also being fleet of foot, were good at rearguard actions, and harassed Cæsar's legions effectively.

Little information has reached us about the territorial areas represented by the tribes, or the organisation of the people as soldiers into larger units for command, nor the name by which these tribal soldiers of early Britain were known. The Force of the people has borne so many names during its long career that it has become like Shakespeare's rose, of little practical value, except that the more modern designation of Militia—" Milecia " in Queen Elizabeth's reign—suggestively connects the Force with the period of the Roman occupation of Britain, and indirectly with the days of early Britain, the Tribal laws of all the people liable to render service being similar in both early Britain and ancient Rome. Sir Francis Palgrave says, "Ancient Rome, in levying her soldiers, required each tribe to furnish one thousand mille, or milemen, and whoever was of that number was called a Miles," meaning soldier, and from this it has been generally agreed that the familiar name, " Militia," was derived. Another name, "The Fyrd," associated with the Force of the people in many early centuries, is, according to the Royal Berkshire Militia History, Anglo-Saxon, with the double meaning of peace and freedom, an appropriate title for those not constantly engaged in the art of war. Palgrave goes on to state, "From earliest times to which our documents reach we find the Fyrd appearing as a general armament of the people, comprehending every rank, though under different obligations and penalties." The late Mr. Davidson, Clerk of the Peace for Oxfordshire, in describing the soldiers of the people, or Miles, in the historical records of his County Militia, quotes the best definition of them that has ever appeared: "They combined the character of defenders, contribute to the prosperity of the country, are connected with their fellow-subjects, and interested in the support of the laws and good government of the Kingdom." Although Palgrave used the Anglo-Saxon word, Fyrd, which appears to have continued in use until about the time of the Norman King Henry I., 1100 A.D., his outline of the obligation of the people as soldiers agrees with what we know prevailed in earlier days than those of the Anglo-Saxons, notably in early Britain, and probably during the Roman occupation.

It has never been determined how long the simple Military Tribal organisation of early Britain lasted, but it is more than likely that the Romans would continue a territorial system which resembled that of their own country. We have evidence still remaining that they constructed defensive works, and as a great military power it is probable that they improved the training of the people for defence and war. Historians record that minute instructions were in force for the management and control of the Roman Miles; they had to assemble fully armed on the ringing of the great bell of the Capitol at Rome. This custom existed in England in the time of Henry III., 1230 A.D. The records of the 6th Battalion Royal Fusiliers, City of London Regiment, compiled by Colonel Helpman, include that:—

"The Mayor of the City was obliged to keep a select body of armed men always ready to muster, fully armed, on the tolling of St. Paul's bell."

The Militia History, County of Southampton, by Colonel Lloyd-Verney, refers to a similar practice in 1651 A.D., when invasion was expected on the South Coast: "The Centenors had to raise their Companies for the hindrance of landing by raising the gare and ringing of church bells, and repair to their rendezvous"; whilst we find in later times that the armed people of the Constitutional Force were gathered together by the firing of beacons on occasions of "alarme," and it will be interesting to know that still more recently "Signals of alert on the Coast for troops by means of flags by day, lanterns by night, were discontinued as interfering with the private signals of His Majesty's cruisers."

The Romans are said to have been in the habit of recruiting their armies out of countries conquered, and also that they defined the tribal areas of Britain for the purposes of government and defence. Camden's Brittainia, quoting from Tacitus, says: "The Romans, according to ancient custom, divided the countries they had subjugated into districts under kings or chiefs, that these might be their slaves," or subservient to their rules and requirements.

Colonel Percy Groves, in his sketch of the Royal Guernsey Militia, says that in 347 A.D. there were military chiefs in the island appointed by the Romans.

The Roman organisation of their troops into units under centurions, out of which legions for battle were formed, requires no explanatory comment. Colonel Helpman, with all the advantages of research among the City of London records, states that in the 5th century and after the Roman occupation, "a well regulated system of military service is met with, the kings having a method of raising and training troops by calling upon each district to furnish a certain number of men officered by their natural chiefs."

The attention given to the Forces of the country by King Alfred the Great in 871 A.D, embracing and continuing from Anglo-Saxon to Saxon times that service of all the people (probably originating in pre-historic ages), along with a system of division into local units, and provision for the formation of larger bodies and armies on occasions, thereby interesting all classes of the people in the defence of their country and certain members in the responsibility of command, would appear from the remarks made by most writers in effect ("seeing the germ of a valuable system, it was developed by variations suitable to the times") that the changes initiated were such in extent as usually follow periodic reorganisations, rather than the introduction of any new principle. Grose describes the Saxon system as follows:

"All qualified to bear arms in one family were led to the field by the head of the family, and every ten families made a Tything commanded by the Borse-holder, ten Tythings constituting a Hundred under the Chief Magistrate of the Hundred, and several Hundreds a Trything, and the Force of the County or Shire commanded by the Heretoch or Duke, under the supreme command of the King's Lieutenant or General whose office lasted only during any war."

Groves states that in the 9th century the Forces of the Island of Guernsey were under the command and administration of Centeniers, Vingteniers and Dixeniers.

Although in the earliest known times there existed organised tribal and territorial liability of all the people to bear arms as soldiers, there is no evidence that the whole of the people were ever called upon to do so simultaneously. Some writers refer to numbers being left at home to till the soil. It would not be of any practical value to follow all the numerous unexplained limitations of age affecting those held liable to serve at different times. At some periods all between 15 and 60 years were physically good enough, or necessary for the purposes required. The area organisation into units, and out of which large bodies were assembled for special purposes, is a subject bearing upon the origin and continuity of the Force. Beyond the insight given into the general methods adopted in the Tribal days of early Britain, ancient Rome as rulers of the country, and throughout the Saxon ages, many details will be unfolded in the process of dealing with incidents of those times.

The Normans, after conquering the country, continued the Saxon Fyrd as the Military Force of the nation until the introduction of their Feudal Law about twenty years after William the Conqueror had ascended the Throne, when the national Force of all the remainder of the people, or Fyrd, became more essentially a reserve for extreme emergency, though it is evident that this "Power of the Country" was drawn upon by the Normans and in several following centuries, by impressment and otherwise, to complete armies for the prosecution of foreign wars. It may be noted, as an example of what was imposed upon the people in olden times and conduced to the gradual growth of that freedom in after years now enjoyed by all classes, that in the reign of King Edward III., 1327 A.D., the impressment of men out of the Constitutional Force for expeditions beyond the sea had become such a scandal in the country as to cause Parliament to interfere, an Act being passed "forbidding the practice and providing that men for the King's service must be properly enlisted and paid," though it appears that the exigencies of the country in 1596 A.D. obliged this Act to be forgotten. "Troops being urgently required to march to France, soon after Easter Day, one thousand men were impressed for service in London by closing all the church doors during Divine service and taking the numbers from among the congregations," whilst it is recorded that ten thousand men were in the reign of King James I. forced to serve in Ireland, and in 1643 A.D., August 10, an Act of Parliament was passed which makes it clear that even at this later date the troubles of the country and requirements of the King obliged resort to the convenient and economic method of raising men by impressment. This Statute "authorised the Country Committees to impress whatever soldiers should be needed," the King for his army adopting the same plan.

Before leaving the Norman Age, and the effort made by William the Conqueror to remodel the Military Force of his Country upon a different basis than had existed from the earliest known times, we should notice the disposition evinced by some historians to ignore or put in shadow the People's Force, or "Power of the Country," during Feudal times.

The Norman Conquerors naturally favoured the military method of their own land, though during the many years before its introduction into England, between the time when Duke William claimed and ascended the Throne by right of conquest as King William the First of England, until the passing of the Military Tenure Law, the ancient Fyrd, comprising all the people of every rank as soldiers, or liable to serve as such, continued to be the sole Army of the country, nor when the Feudal Law was accepted were those not embraced in this Class Levy exempted from rendering service.

It is not proposed to review all the details of the complicated regulations, defects, and ingenious evasions of the Feudal System initiated in England at Sarum on the now familiar Salisbury Plain. The Levy then created touched only a class of the people, and retained the power to call upon the great Force of all the remainder, which we know by military history was often availed and eventually proved to be a valuable means of restraining the power obtained by great noblemen under the Feudal Law.

At a Council of the Nation assembled at Sarum 1086, it was resolved "That every free-man be in readiness to take the field against the foe of the Nation anywhere."

This has been described by some writers as "patriotism, not compulsion, a nation of free-men living under the laws which they had made and were adapted to the times."

Blackstone says, "All the great landowners submitted their lands to the yoke of military tenure, became the King's vassals, and did honour to his person." Other Historians have told us how this came about. "The Country was threatened by Denmark, and the King, unable previously to obtain acceptance of his views, and the Fyrd neglected, brought over for defence a force of Normans who, being quartered on the landowners, conduced to their approval of the Feudal Law."

This history is not concerned in the Military Tenure system beyond what will show that the ancient Force retained for occasions of emergency did perform under the new order of things what exceeded its obligation and made good the grave defects which existed under the Feudal Law.

The duty of the Military Knights under Tenure Law was intended to provide for the military requirements of the

King and Country. They had to follow the King with their retainers whenever called upon to do so. That of the Posse Comitatus or remainder of the people to assemble and serve as soldiers when required to suppress disorder in their territorial districts, or elsewhere in the country to repel invasion. We have now to observe how the People's Force became contributors to the military history of England during Feudal times.

Scott and other eminent writers unite in saying that the period of service which had to be performed under Military Tenure Law was so limited as to detract from the fighting value of the Force, that the schemes propounded for evasion of liability, payment of "shield money" and other devices all militated against the value of the Feudal System. For example, fines for "not proceeding on service with the King," "To avoid crossing the sea with the King," etc. Grose tells us what happened at the Siege of Avignon, 1226, and at Anger, 1230, both in France: "The right of the Feudal soldiers to claim discharge after forty days promoted the break-up of the armies under King Henry II.," but payments appear to have been also exacted from the General Levy. The Knights and their forces were chiefly mounted, the people's force serving as foot soldiers. We find it recorded that in 1093 "William Rufus levied 20,000 footmen for service in Normandy, and on their arriving at the seaside for shipment he caused his treasurer to offer that in order to save the nation the cost of so many men going, and themselves the peril, as many as would should pay ten shillings and go home again."

Hume, in his history of England, gives a scathing description of the Feudal Forces, which reflects very clearly how the emergency force of the nation came to be requisitioned for the battles of the country during Feudal times. "The military tenants, unacquainted with obedience, inexperienced in war, holding rank in the troops by birth and not merit, composed a disorderly and feeble army, and during the few days they were obliged to remain on service under their tenures constituted a cumbrous and dangerous machine which came gradually into disuse."

We find that while pecuniary supplies were often exchanged for military service, the Barons and Knights even entered into engagements to provide the numbers of men wanted. The Feudal Laws were finally abolished by King Charles II. in 1660.

Leaving the Norman age, we find during some centuries, until the permanent formation of regiments for administrative purposes, some quaint references to Bande or Company Units. In Plantagenet times, about 1150, the South Devon Militia History, by Colonel Fisk, has it that "those arrayed for service were formed into squads of twenties and companies of one hundred, commanded by Vintenors and Centenars, these being at times massed in thousands," after the practice of ancient Rome and in the Saxon ages.

At later dates, and probably in earlier periods, the organised local bandes or companies representing the Constitutional Force and defensive land power of the country appear to have intensified their territorial character by bearing the names of the localities in which they were raised, sometimes along with those of their leaders, and were often assigned particular duties in schemes of defence. The Isle of Wight Light Infantry history mentions that in 1341 A.D. "The men of Ryde and sacred Quarr under the Lord of Knighton, New Church and adjacent Hamlets under the government of its own bailiffs, one bande being given the duty to guard the fair undercliff and rocky heights, another ranging their stout hearts to defend the cliffs and downs," etc. The Ordonnances of King Richard, 1385, will be given in detail hereafter, but in this connection of organised units (the bande or company) it is opportune to quote how they are referred to as being the unit of that day.

"The gain of arms (meaning plunder) only having the benefit of quarters under the banner or pennon of arms of a Captain." "Those who make themselves Captains shall be drawn and hanged." This has reference to the improper raising of forces for other purposes than the King's use.

In 1539 A.D., when King Henry VIII., wishful to know the strength of his kingdom, ordered a muster of those having abiliments of war, each hundred of a county furnished its contingent. By Council Order, 1544, A.D., "to raise and carry on war with France, an invasion by the French being momentarily expected, the Lords Lieutenant of counties were authorised to appoint chosen captains to train the men."

At the historical assembly of the forces of the Kingdom 1588 A.D., in the reign of Queen Elizabeth, to oppose the threatened attack by the Spanish Armada, we find the returns rendered by "ye County Lieuftenants of the able trayned and furneshed men reduced into bandes under Captaines and how they were soarted, with weapons in a readiness with convenient armour, furniture and other accessories."

In 1625 A.D., by "a true noate of the strength of the Island of Wight taken by Sir John Oglander Lieutenant, and by him delivered to the Counsell," we still have evidence of the bande or company as the organised unit.

The return includes "the names of Captaines as they are to take place and be ranked when they shall appear in the field with their companies and in all meetings on martial business," but in 1628 A.D. we meet with evidence of the introduction of permanently organised larger bodies. "A difference having arisen about precedence upon several pretences, an order was issued that the two Lieutenants of the Isle of Wight should command one of each division, "according to their convenience to be appointed to either of the divisions, leaving that to be accommodated by themselves with their own comodities expecting that upon all muster and other occasions for the souldiers ryseinge one of them bee in the head of the troopes of each Division."

Towards the middle of the same century, taking the Royal Berkshire Regiment as typical of others, their annals compiled by Miss Thoyts explain that the companies were raised in separate districts of the county and bore the names of the places where the men were drawn from, the heraldic device of leaders being in the colour of their respective companies. Miss Thoyts also remarks on this page of her book that the national uniform was scarlet, except in Tudor days green and white, and red white and blue in the reign of Queen Mary from the combined arms of England, Scotland and France.

The permanent organisation of bandes or companies into regiments for administrative and all other purposes, which has continued into the present day, appears to have taken place early in the seventeenth century. Groves says: between 1625 and 1630 A.D. the orders in Guernsey were issued to the Captaynes and several companies, but that early in this century the companies were formed into three Regiments and the rank of Colonel established.

Whilst we know that provision had always existed for massing the smaller organised units of the armed people, it will be interesting to keep in memory that larger districts than represented by bandes had the claim to perform special duties. It is recorded that the men of Kent were entitled to meet the enemy first and those of London to guard the king's body.

Firth, in his history of the Civil War, 1642 A.D., says

"there was no real territorial system though certain regiments had an original connection with counties."

Although this statement assured a previous local connection of the Constitutional Force, it might create an impression that territorialism ceased as an institution of the country on the outbreak of the Civil War. The explanation is not far to seek; Guizot's history of the Revolution says: "The counties were covered by warlike confederations supporting one side or the other, who received from the King or Parliament, according to their views, commissions for their leaders and power to levy soldiers, impose taxes, and adopt other measures for success." It may be added that in those troublous times, causing general disorganisation, when soldiers together with the people held individual opinions upon the situation, freely acted upon and apparently without restraint, some of the old regiments forming the army of the country would be defected and hastily refilled whenever and wherever required, whilst we know that many new ones were formed for the purposes of the Civil War regardless of either system or ancient custom.

It is recorded that in this struggle the units of some counties fought against each other. Gardner's history of the Civil War speaks of an Ordinance in 1642 for the formation of several associations of counties to unite their forces into armies, and in 1644 Parliament ordered the committee of both kingdoms to consider the state and condition of all the armies and forces, and submit "a frame or model of the whole Militia." Firth describes "this new model of Cromwell's army" as follows:

"Each county had its garrison raised by the county committee, each grouped in associated counties with each their major-general and their field army, the new model being at first only one of several armies in the service of Parliament. The various counties had previously each a separate army. By gradual process these either disappeared or were absorbed into the new models."

This comprehensive concentration of the forces of the country dating prior to the introduction of any standing branch of the army, and reflecting the more crude organisation of the "Power of the Country," as a means of defence in earlier times, appears to be matter which should be included in any history of that force whose original regiments or corps played an important part in the civil war of the 17th century, nor will it be without interest to observe that the "new model of Cromwell's army" formed a basis for years to come.

In this new army, regiments of foot were composed of ten companies, not all of equal strength.

        The Colonel's company numbered ... 200
        ,, Lt.-Colonel's ,, ,, ... 160
        ,, Major's ,, ,, ... 140

the remaining seven being each of 160. This system of field officers commanding companies lasted until 1800. After 1778 the subaltern of the colonel's company ranked as a captain. In 1648 there was an ordinance for " settling the Militia of the severall Counties of the kingdom and dominion of Wales and Town of Berwick." On the restoration of King Charles II. to the throne, and his recognition of the "Power of the Country," the reform of the constitutional force retained both regimental units and county territorialism. Most writers consider that the regulations introduced at this period and at the great reorganisation of the force of the people in 1661-2, when King Charles II. abolished the Feudal System, established details which though at varying intervals subjected to developments and changes in harmony with "ever changing and improving ends," still form the basis of those conditions under which the Militia serves as an emergency force of the country.

CHAPTER III.

TERRITORIALISM OF THE FORCE—RE-ORGANIZATION OF 1756—LAND DIVISIONS OF THE COUNTRY IN SAXON AND NORMAN AGES—BOROUGHS IN CONNECTION WITH THE PEOPLE AS SOLDIERS—THE ROMAN WALL, ETC.—ADMINISTRATION AND CONTROL OF THE FORCE.

It is noteworthy as regards territorial areas and the existence of Militia in Scotland that King Charles II., in a letter June 10, 1661, to the Lord High Commissioner of Scotland upon the subject of the Militia of that country, referred to the " Militia of our severall counties," the proportion to be locally set down for each shire.

In 1715 the Act "for ordering the forces of Great Britain called England" speaks of "Tythings and other places within the Hundreds of Counties." After this date, for many years, the military lifebuoy of the country was happily seldom wanted, and it is no part of the duty of any would-be historian to deal with its condition for want of repair.

The next important change brought about was the re-organisation of the force in 1756, under Pitt's scheme and Act 30 Gro : II. c. 25, which created what has been known as the "quota" of men due by counties for the Militia, the ballot being put into force where necessary. Lords Lieutenant were again in evidence with their Deputy Lieutenants in dealing with the organisation and control of the ancient force within the boundaries of their jurisdiction. At this time less than eight companies constituted a battalion, and over seven a regiment, the Lord Lieutenant in each county being in supreme command, with one field officer on his staff. The force of Ireland was similarly organised in 1793-32, Geo. III., c 22, and Scotland in 1798-37, Geo. III., c. 103. It is recorded by Colonel Raikes in his history of a West Yorkshire regiment that up to 1852 regiments in that county were still raised out of wapentakes, or hundreds, which takes us back very forcibly to the practice in Saxon ages.

Between 1756 and 1881 we find, except in the period of repose between the end of the great French wars and Crimean days, many changes in the general march of progress. Territorialism, a method of early Britain and associated with the "Force of the People" for over nineteen hundred years, was applied in 1881 to other branches of the Army, and the whole of the Infantry forces of the State were so arranged as to form a "composite machine for one common end," though with different obligations, and all under the system of voluntary enlistment, requiring "public sympathy and support and those sentiments which come from past history."

The imitation of old centuries by new ones in the creation of territorial areas and measures associating them with the general military resources of the country, make it not without interest and possibly instructive to study briefly what has been said by writers on the subject of the land divisions of the country.

Scott has it that "our English counties present a curious mixture of Saxon and Norman systems. In Saxon England "shire" signified a district or division presided over by the Shire-reeve or Sheriff, and larger areas by the Earldorman or Elder-man, the same as Senior or Senator among the Romans. In later times the great provinces of the country were under a single Earl. In Edward the Confessor's reign, after 1042, the whole kingdom is said to have been at one time divided among five Earls." Kemble states that it was not then a title of rank, but distinctive appellation the same as those which attached themselves to distinguished chiefs. Scott explains "that after the Norman Conquest, 1066, the ancient titles held by leaders of the Force of the People were discontinued and the chief men of counties were styled Counts for a time, and their Vice-Comes Viscounts, which has always been Englished by the old Saxon word Sheriff. When counts or earls disappeared the sheriffs became the head men of counties." It is not of material consequence for the purpose of this work to fix exactly when counties, shires and smaller areas were created. Johnson's Dictionary includes, that in Saxon times there were intermediate divisions between shire and hundred, known by local names such as sokes, lathes, rapes, etc., though all were subdivided into the Saxon Hundred or Wapentake," the latter name finding a place in history by reason of its court.

In Edward the Confessor's reign (1042-1066), at stated intervals the elder sort met the king at this public court, and alighting, touched his spear, so confirming a common interest intended to imply a public league or unity of purpose. This court figures often as being linked with the Constitutional Force, its name as an area continuing in some counties until quite recent times, and associated with recruiting for the the Militia.

Fisk refers to hydes of land in Devonshire of about one hundred acres as being connected with the raising of troops. At one time five hydes furnished one soldier—one providing the man and the others four shillings each for his pay when on duty. He remarks, as an example of the inequality of this contribution, that Exeter, though a large place, found only one man on the basis of five hydes. It is important to note that the whole of the people were not then bearing arms. The Encyclopedia Britannica (8th edition) has chronicled that King Alfred divided the country into shires. Mr. A. Ballard, in his recently-published and interesting History of Boroughs, in effect associates these with the people as soldiers. He says "that some places, such as Canterbury and Rochester, were walled places from the earliest Saxon times, and, following Professor Maitland, he adopts the view that such places were strongholds for refuge and possessed garrisons, the neighbouring people using them for safety when necessary. Edward the Elder in the beginning of the tenth century secured his conquests in the Midlands by the creation of boroughs—a deed of 904 speaks of the erection of a Burg at Worcester for the protection of the folk.

Contrast is often said to imply relation. The Roman Wall across Northern Britain, and Peel Houses (some of which remain), into which the people fled and defended themselves when incursions were made, affords matter for contemplation. Prior to the Saxon age we have to remember the seven separate kingdoms of the Anglo-Saxon Dynasty soon following after the districts into which the country had been divided by the Romans after they conquered the tribal areas of early Britain. Passing on to the more complex subject of the administration and control of the force of the people, there is no doubt but that the force of the country in Roman times was regulated by the military governors of districts appointed by the Romans, and that their successors had a similar system until the formation of the seven kingdoms of the Anglo-Saxon Heptarchy, when each separate kingdom controlled its own force of the people and on similar lines to those which afterwards prevailed in the Saxon age, King Alfred developing and improving what he found to be the army system of his kingdom.

Blackstone says: "In the time of our Saxon ancestors the Duke or Heretoch held unlimited power in the leading and regulating of armies and were elected by the people in full assembly, so giving an interest and power to repress any opposition in harmony with the old Saxon law that any officer entrusted with power should be subject to the vote of the people themselves. In later times the power passed into the hands of great noblemen, whom all writers imply were thus unintentionally given the means of rebellion, which history shows were frequently used.

In King Canute's time, 1017, the Heretochs appear to have been appointed by the king, and not the people.

Palgrave remarks about the Saxon Fyrd that it evidently included all the force of the country, and to King Alfred is given the credit of being able to introduce a rotation of duty leaving certain numbers to follow their civil occupations. He also states that the Levy in Saxon times was assembled by the king's royal bann, sometimes with the consent of the "Witena-gemote," or as Chambers' Encyclopedia calls it, the National Council of England in Anglo-Saxon times, by which the King was supposed to be guided in all his main acts of government. Each kingdom had its own Witeganemot before the union of the several kingdoms in 827, after which there was one for the whole country. It was composed of bishops, earldormen of districts and a number of the King's friends and dependants, the King's thanes.

When the House of Normandy ruled England the Force of the People ceased to be the only army of the country and became essentially a reserve force for pressing necessity, instead of an emergency one for all purposes. Palgrave says the Sheriffs retained power to raise the Posse Comitatus composed of those between fifteen and sixty years of age, peers and spiritual men excepted, to preserve the peace and repel invasion.

The warlike Plantagenets who followed are recorded as having instituted commissions of array to muster the people, appointing persons of position in each county to act as arrayers, with arbitrary power to raise men and money for military purposes.

In the time of the House of Lancaster, in 1403, we have clearly established by Act 4, Henry IV., c. 13, the king's right to control the forces of the country, and in the following year under the potent influence of threatened invasion the power of arrayers was more fully defined and enlarged. This included the training and arraying of men at arms, and for all other able-bodied ones to arm themselves. This enactment indicates that only a limited number had been bearing arms.

It is interesting to observe that "the godliness of defence" or of bearing arms caused at this period and at other times the Sunday afternoons to be used for assemblies and training.

When Henry V. reigned, there is quaint evidence that the sheriffs were concerned in the management of the Constitutional Force as in Saxon ages, and we get an insight into the value of archers. Fisk quotes that the sheriffs were "ordered to collect feathers from the wings of geese, plucking six from each goose, for the use of bowmen." "As a cherished weapon of might the battles of Cressy, Poictiers and Agincourt testify to the terrible skill with which the bow could be used."

The last of these commissions of array is said by Rymer to have been in 1557 with the advent of Lords Lieutenant. There is some confusion of dates as to when these county officials were actually appointed; some writers give the date as being about 1545, but the precise date is not important. Lt.-Col. Holden, in his History of the Worcestershire Militia, says "the power of mustering remained in the hands of sheriffs until 1549., 3 Edward VI." The Act of 1557, however, appears to make it clear that the sheriff's power as chief controlling officer of each county force had then ended, lords lieutenant by the Act being the persons authorised to call musters, and given stringent powers in respect of false returns, the making away with arms and armour required to be in possession, etc. In dealing with offences, captains and deputy-lieutenants disposed of smaller cases.

Strype's Annals describes the change as follows : " Lords Lieutenant were empowered to be the King's Lieutenant within their respective counties for levying men and to fight against the king's enemies and rebels, and to execute upon them martial law, and subdue all invasions and insurrections," etc. This variation in the method of raising troops and control of the force reverting as it did to what was analagous in the early ages when the Heretoch held similar powers, must be regarded as an epoch in the history of the National force.

The orders issued to Lords Lieutenant appear to have reflected both the past and future. The Archæologia gives some details of the regulations then promulgated :

"To muster men, armour and horses, to appoint to everie Capten the number he should leade, to deliver to him the names and dwelling places of his number, and to order everie Capten to take often musters and views of his band seeing them harnessed with weapons and armour convenient, to appoint places of rendezvous, to look to places where an enemy is likely to land, break bridges on his landing, etc., and carry out the Statute of the last Session in the 4 and 5 yrs of their Majesties Raignes."

The commissions of Lords Lieutenant were at first issued yearly.

Grose says in 1572 the Justices of the Peace for each county with special Commissioners were instructed to muster the whole male population over sixteen years of age, registering their places of residence, and occupation, and the kind of service suitable to each, and that all were sorted into bands of 100 footmen, the Commissioners deciding who out of the number should be subsequently trained.

In 1574 the importance attached to the office of Lord Lieutenant is best indicated by extracts from a letter addressed by Queen Elizabeth to the Lieutenant of Devon, Cornwall and the City of Exeter, quoted by Fisk from Archaeologia: "requireth most earnestlie her said cosen immediatelie with all speede to renew such good orders as by him were last yere taken upon musters," "upon experience had she perceaveth that for the juste and necessarie defence of the realme, the late laws either wanting sufficient provision, or ells the interpretacion thereof is so by sondrie persons construed to their privat ease and relief of charage, which in many is more regarded than the care of the Commonwealth," therefore " she requireth her saide cosen to prescribe all who had been undervalued to be better and more amplie furnished either with horse, gelding, corselet, bowe, bill, handgonne," etc.

In 1588, among other duties of Deputy Lieutenants, they kept the beacons in repair, and Captains reported to these officials any irregularity in the keeping of armour. The Muster Master acted as an adjutant, inspecting and reporting to the Deputy Lieutenants anything amiss; this official for each county was in existence 1629. The Acts 13, 14, 15, Charles II. re-established the authority of Lords Lieutenant in connection with the defence of the country, with power to assemble men for yearly training, and in other matters propounded regulations which doubtless aimed at improving the efficiency of the force and convenience of the people.

Captain Raikes, in his history (3rd. West York. Light Infantry), replete with statistical county information, deals concisely with the continuity of Lords Lieutenant in respect of their jurisdiction over the Militia by stating "that they were inseparably associated from the reign of King Henry VIII. until Feb., 1872, when by an Order in Council the jurisdiction was re-invested in the Crown," but there were periods, nevertheless, when their powers were weakened, if not suspended, certainly during the Commonwealth. Whilst in 1756, after a long period of repose for the force and people, measures being urgent for the defence of the realm, we find Lords Lieutenant instructed to introduce the ballot where necessary as a permanent provision for providing the fixed quota of men due from each county. At this time and for some years Deputy Lieutenants granted discharges from service in the National Force. In 1803 the Home Office representing "Internal Defences" exercised a limited control, and all correspondence relating to the Militia was addressed to the Secretary of State, Home Department. It may be mentioned that at an exceptional training of the forces in 1831, after another enfeebling rest consequent on the previous long succession of wars, during which many regiments of the force had been continuously embodied and employed for upwards of twenty years, the Lieutenants of counties in exercising their power, etc., ordered and directed Justices of the Peace to issue commands to the Chief Constable, petty constables, etc., to provide "sufficient carriages and horses to convey the arms, clothes, accoutrements, etc., with all able men to drive the same, and to provide quarters for the men on march from headquarters to place of training and exercise."

After 1872, although the Constitutional Force units retained their county territorialism, in name, they were controlled by the War Office, and with the exercise of still greater powers in 1881, when a territorial system was generally applied to the whole of the infantry forces of the Army.

CHAPTER IV.

MILITARY CHARACTER OF THOSE BEARING ARMS IN DIFFERENT AGES—ORDINANCES OF 1646 AND 1648.

With regard to the military character of those bearing arms in different ages, the greater number have been at all times foot soldiers, as usual in the composition of armies, but the value of mobility was evidently known to the early Britons, some of the tribal soldiers being trained in the use of chariots.

Historians describe the Anglo-Saxons as chiefly footmen. Grose states that there were two classes of infantry, the heavy ones having skin helmets, oval shields, long broad swords and spears, the others carrying bills, spears and battle-axes; the javalin with which Angle-Saxons are reputed to have been experts being also in use. The horse and foot were alike uniformed in tunics to the knee, without sleeves, and they wore leg bands, the chiefs only wearing armour.

In Norman times the general levy, composed of all the people (other than those who were Feudal knights and their vassals, who were sometimes mounted) formed the infantry of the army, joined by those vassals who were archers. Under the Plantagenets, the Assizes of Arms and Statutes regulating the means of defence were numerous. It will be found by the details given at a later stage that the laws of the country necessarily created a contingent of mounted men, those who must ride to carry the heavy defensive equipment of the day; every man between fifteen and sixty years of age was at this time assessed to armour, and " to have in his house harness for to keep the peace " according to his estate and degree. The scale of arms and armour was based upon income or value of effects. This ingenious system obliged the wealthy to provide themselves with very complete armour in the cause of defence, the nature of which caused them to be cavalry.

Scott remarks that the Statute 27, Edward I., 1298, was important. It required for the first time that armed or barbed horses should be provided in the levies, whilst in the reign of King Edward III. Grose refers to a type of cavalry in a Statute which calls them "hobblers," (light horse) as not to be used for the king's service except at the king's wages when they go out of their counties, nor without common consent and grant of Parliament. He also describes the Plantagenet unit of mounted troops to have been small bodies under officers named constables. Scott draws attention to the "Bill for Great Horses," 33, Henry VIII., c 5, as curious. The object of this "sumptuous law to restrain extravagance and promote the supply of horses for the defence of the realm" makes the subject one of importance." Noblemen and other subjects having parks should breed and increase the number of horses for defence, and other persons temporal whose wife, not being divorced nor willingly absenting herself, shall wear any French hood or bonnet of velvet with any habiliment "past or egge" of gold, pearl, or stone, or any chain of gold about her neck or in their partletts, or in any apparel of their body, shall keep or sustain one stout trotting horse for the saddle; and if the wife of any person, except as before, wear any velvet in the lining or other part of her gown other than the cuffs or purflets of such gown, then her husband shall find one trotting horse." In 1585, by the Talbot papers, Lords Lieutenant were to exercise in martial feats those reduced into bands and take view of horsemen, fifty horse being the number for a captain and one cornet, clad in cassocks of one colour.

In 1587 the provision for organising companies of foot soldiers into larger bodies carried with it seven hundred horsemen to each larger body of 500 foot, though in 1588 no explanation has ever been ventured of the remarkably small percentage of mounted men furnished by counties at the great Spanish Armada muster of that year; each county then sent, according to the certificates returned, many footmen, "trayned" and otherwise, with some horse soldiers under the heads of "Launces, Lighthorse, and Petronelles." It is equally strange that mounted men should have carried at this time a kind of gun, whilst the infantry were still chiefly armed with bills, swords, daggers, and bows. In the great civil war of the seventeenth century we find cavalry much in evidence, but the disorganisation which arose in the normal strength and composition of county foot regiments by the raising of new regiments on the sides of both King and Parliament, and records incomplete and mixed owing to the nature of the struggle, make it impossible to trace with accuracy all the original county regiments and define their composition. The difficulty is intensified by finding that regiments in this war were bearing, or appear in military histories, under the names of their commanders, many of whose names have since disappeared. An extract from an Ordinance of 1646 and also a copy of an Ordinance 1648 although embracing other matter than the subject under notice, may be here introduced as giving us general information about the Army of those times:—

From King's Pamphlet E 296.

ORDERS ESTABLISHED.

The 14th of this present January, 1646, by
His Excellency
Sir Thomas Fairfax,
For Regulating the
Army
and
For the Soldiers paying of Quarters, and fair
behaviour in the Countreys:
Published by special command from
His Excellency Sir Thomas Fairfax.

At a Counsel of War held at Northampton, Thursday the 14th of Jan. 1646.

Orders set down and agreed upon, to be presented to the General for the better regulating of the Army in discharging of quarters, and otherwise.

I. That all Members of this Army from the fourth of this instant January for such time as they have or shall have pay, and orders to discharge their quarters, shall pay for the same at the several rates hereunder expressed, except they can in any particular finde themselves or their Horses cheaper. And above these respective rates, none shall be compellable to pay until the Counsel of War, or Superior Authority shall give other order, but at these rates the respective Landlords are to finde those that are or shall be duly quartered upon them, and at these rates every one shall discharge his Quarters weekly, and at their remove shall make even for any odde days less than a week.

The Rates to be as followeth, viz.:

Each Trooper mounted, to pay for his Diet, and Hay for one Horse, Ten pence per diem.

A Trooper unmounted, for Diet Six pence per diem.

A Dragooner mounted, for Diet and Hay, Nine pence per diem.

A Dragooner unmounted, for Diet, Five pence per diem.

Officers of Horse or Dragoons not in Commission, viz., Trumpeters, and Corporals of Horse, Sergeants of Dragoons, and Chyrurgions Mates, Sadlers and Farriers of Horse, and all Servants of Horse-Officers, to pay the same rates as Troopers.

Drummers and Corporals of Dragoons, and Dragoon-Officers men, to pay the same rates as Dragoons.

Each Gentleman of the Life-Guard, to pay for his own and his servants' Diet, Sixteen pence per diem.

He that hath no servant to pay for his own Diet, Twelve pence per diem.

Gentlemen of Captain Knights Troop, for their own Diet, Nine pence per diem.

For their men as Troopers.

All that have Horses to pay for provender (unless they can buy cheaper) at Six pence per peck.

Each Foot Soldier, as also Corporals and Drummers of Foot, Four pence per diem.

Sergeants of Foot, Six pence per diem.

All Commission-Officers of Horse, Foot and Dragoons to pay for Diet as they can agree with their Landlords.

From King's Pamphlet E 474

An
Ordinance of the
Lords and Commons
Assembled in Parliament
For the Setling the Militia
In the severall Counties, Cities, and Places within the Kingdome of England, Dominion of Wales, and Towne of Berwick upon Tweed.

Die Sabbathi, 2 Decemb. 1648.
Ordered by the Lords Assembled in Parliament,
That this Ordinance be forthwith printed
And published.
1648.

" And be it further ordained, that the said Commissioners shall have further power and authority to settle and order the Militia of the said Counties, Cities, and places respectively, according to the authorities, powers, and instructions herein after granted, limited, and expressed. That is to say, that the said respective Commissioners, or any five or more of them shall hereby have full power and authority to send forth their Warrants to all Constables, Headboroughs, Tythingmen, or to use all other lawful means as they shall think fit; whereby to enforme themselves of all such persons within the respective Counties, Cities and places, as are able to find or bear Armes; and what Armes, Horses, weapons, and instruments of warre they or any of them already have been or are charged to find or bear, and thereupon the said respective Commissioners or any five or more of them shall hereby have full power and authority to charge any persons with Horse or Foot Armes, having a respect to the Limitations and Proportions hereafter mentioned: that is to say, that no person shall be charged by the Commissioners aforesaid with any Horse and Horse Armes, unless the persons so to be charged have a yearly Revenue of one hundred and fifty pounds, above all charges and reprises, or two thousand four hundred pounds in money or other estate equivalent thereunto; nor with any Dragoon Horse and Armes for a Dragoon Horse, not having fifty pounds yearly Revenue, or five hundred pounds in money or personal estate, at the least; nor with any whole Foot Armes, unless the said person have a yearly Revenue of twenty pounds *per annum*, or two hundred pounds in money, or other estate equivalent thereunto; and also the said respective Commissioners, or any five or more of them shall hereby have full power and Authority to charge such other persons who are not able to find Armes to bear the same for such other particular persons who shall be charged therewith, or for the general service of the County, allowing them reasonable pay for the same, not exceeding for a Horseman two shillings, for a Dragoon one shilling six pence, for a Foot souldier eightpence *per diem*."

There are copies of letters of the Council of State during the Commonwealth, in existence, establishing that Militia Regiments had troops of cavalry at this period.

In September, 1651, an Official Letter to Berkshire says, "We have received yours from Wallingford concerning the horses of the Militia Troops who charged and did good service at the battle of Worcester."

From the same authority, August, 1655: "The Militia troupes of Horse of the Counties of Oxford, Bucks, Herts,

Berks, Hants, Sussex, Kent, Cambridge, Suffolk, Norfolk, Rutland, are to be reduced to eighty in each troupe."

When the Constitutional Force of the kingdom was re-organized, after the restoration, and Act passed, 13 Charles II., c. 3, "Ordering out all the forces in the several Counties," Regiments appear to have included a body of Light Horse furnished by the Peers and others charged according to their estates.

A curious anomaly existed. The regulations caused some landowners to be liable for the fractional part of a horse. No explanation is available as to how this difficulty was overcome, but it appears that in some Counties, possibly all, a custom prevailed of considering a number of footmen equivalent to a horseman.

In "the progress of His Grace the Duke of Beaufort through Wales," 1684, most of the Militia Regiments paraded contingents of mounted men. The records of the Northumberland Light Infantry Militia, compiled by Major Adamson, show, that in 1697, each £3 2s. 6d. in the book of rates, found, or, he says, ought to have done so, a Light Horse, presumably with a man, and that the Regiment numbered 102 horse, 297 foot, as the establishment, eleven of the former being wanting.

The Egerton MSS. Militia Returns of 1697, preserved in the British Museum, give in detail the strength and composition of most of the Militia units in England and Wales. These are valuable documents.

In the reign of King William III. such regiments included bodies of horse. It will be found by the observations made on the condition of the Force in each county (Egerton MSS.), in respect of evasions to render service, etc., that they take us back to what existed in Feudal and other early ages. Also that the remarks were quaintly expressed and remarkable in character. In one county it was noted that near twenty horses were provided by Papists and non-jurors; in another that the Church Clergy are not charged for their spiritual estates, but for their temporal, etc., etc.

According to returns of the strength of the English Militia in 1712, there were 7,450 horse included, whilst in Statute II., King George I., c. 14, it is interesting to note that armour for horsemen was then discontinued, the arms being a broadsword, case of pistols with 12-inch barrels and a carabine, and it is recorded that in the Monmouth rebellion, 1745, Lumley's Horse, among the Militia, "did good service."

There is no mention of mounted Militia troops in the reorganization of 1757, but it would appear by the Berkshire records that they existed in a somewhat different form. An advertisement in the "Reading Mercury" of 1798 refers to a provisional troop as belonging to or being attached to the Militia Regiment of that county, and probably to others, as in earlier times. Mounted Militiamen were apparently discontinued towards the end of the eighteenth century or earlier, as a large force of "Yeomanry" was employed in Ireland during the rebellion of 1798. It is noteworthy, that mounted troops under the title of Imperial Yeomanry have lately been formed under Militia regulations, though, as a distinct branch of the force, and with a territorial connection. The Artillery branch is necessarily of more modern creation. Groves has it that among the earliest occasions of the use of artillery by the English (obviously employing men of the Constitutional Force as gunners) were the campaigns of Edward I. in Scotland, and Edward III., at the capture of Berwick, 1333. It is also stated that at the battle of Worcester 1642, Charles II. had some field guns constructed of leather. In 1549 each parish and company in the Isle of Wight possessed its gun (this being probably the custom at other exposed places) and they appear to have been kept in the Churches. When invasion was expected the voluminous instructions issued May 17, 1651, included "That each centenor take care that the parish guns belonginge to the severall companies be kept complete, and provided with sufficient wheeles and carriages togeather with necessarie stores of powder, bullets and case shott."

In Guernsey, 1682, the "Parish Cannon" were served by invalids.

"Battalion Guns" at a later date were manned by selected men, at one period each company of a regiment was required to have a team of trained men.

In 1802 most regiments had brass six pounder field pieces.

During the South African War Militia infantry battalions at home and abroad were temporarily furnished with machine guns. It is difficult to determine when Militia Garrison Artillery units were first formed. In 1855 there were thirteen corps of Artillery, which had previously been Infantry, and others have since been raised at different periods as Artillery on the augmentation of this branch. Field Artillery has been still more recently added, though we find field guns served by the infantry in the Channel Islands 1755. The Engineer and Submarine Mining portions of the Constitutional Force have been of later creation, the former in 1877, and Submarine Miners in 1878, and chiefly formed out of Militia Artillery or Infantry corps, nor is it possible to deal minutely with the Medical branch.

CHAPTER V.

PAY AND EMOLUMENTS OF THE CONSTITUTIONAL FORCE SOLDIER—SUBSTITUTES—GRATUITIES FOR SPECIAL SERVICE, ETC.

To present a complete statement of the pay and emoluments of the people as soldiers of their country at various periods during so many centuries, might be the means of providing a fascinating study for some readers, but to produce any reliable chronological details would impose a deeper research than the archives of the State and military histories can be expected to have recorded.

The value of money, conditions of soldiering, and the military requirements of the country have been so frequently changed, that no looking back to frame a comparison between ancient, mediaeval, and modern ages, in respect of the mercernary side of bearing arms, could have any practical value.

It is certain that in early times and for some centuries, service by all the people was an obligation resting on them as a birthright, probably under some unwritten law of remote ages, and without either pay or reward, let us believe for love of country. The earliest mention of daily pay for soldiering is to be found in the feudal times. Scott says that after the limited gratuitous period of service of the Feudal Levies had become exhausted, the only remedy for prolonged service was "a daily rate of pay," but this was not always optional to the king, nor convenient, for want of money. It is probable that when any of the General Levy, or Posse Comitatus, were taken or induced to go on foreign expeditions, they received some pay or consideration for doing so, though it is recorded that impressment was at times prevalent.

Grose, as an unimpeachable authority, has many references to the emoluments of soldiering, and there are some scattered details in other works. It will sufficiently indicate the changes that have occurred if one or two of them are here recorded. Grose and others state that in the days of Edward I., 1272, each constable (an officer of horse) received on march or duty one shilling per diem, and when with a horse one shilling and sixpence: each vintenar (a petty officer) fourpence, and foot soldiers twopence each. Martyn's history of Thetford quoted by Fisk, period Edward III., 1336, states that two men chosen to go into the army against Scotland were paid £1 for the two (probably bounty) and cloth for the tailor into two gowns 6s. 11d., besides some other items. The shoeing of two horses cost at this time fourpence.

Captains, however, appear to have been well paid about 1585. The archives of Northamptonshire disclose that Captain Burnaby was paid £25 "for trayning at Daventry, five dais at £5 his own allowance," and 8d. per day for 150 men, besides other items for waggoners carrying armour, and allowances to the captains for "cerariage" of their armour.

Any attempt to deal exhaustively with this subject up to the days of the proverbial soldier's shilling would involve the consideration of stoppages and allowances, and so introduce matter which might be controversial in respect of what the soldier actually received in different ages; for instance, in 1795 we find that by custom, owing to the high price of bread and meat, a soldier had to pay for about half the cost of his ration, amounting to near fourpence per diem beyond what was called the "camp stoppage," until the practical interest taken by King George III. caused the excess to be a charge in the public accounts. Then, again, we know that crimping irons at one time formed part of a soldier's kit, but there are no details of the expense imposed upon soldiers "for cleaning their heads of long hair once a week with bran," nor the cost to them of producing "natural pigtails which had to be cued and appear grey but no powder to be on the face," etc.

The emoluments of soldiering in the Constitutional Force have not, however, been entirely derived from official sources; we find in 1759 that the Lincolnshire regiments in recognition of their rapid forced march to Liverpool on the occasion of Thurot's French squadron threatening the town and port "the Noblemen and Gentlemen Officers in the two regiments were admitted as Freemen of the Borough and Corporation without fees, with a liberal present in money to the two Regiments and leather breeches to each man."

Between 1811-13, service in Ireland was popular, though of an arduous character, both owing to excise patrol duty.

The records of the 3rd Royal Scots disclose that during the year 1813 the regiment received from the Excise £1,045, whilst an Irish Militia regiment was paid £403 16s. 9d. in 1811 for the destruction of 236 stills, etc., and for four months' similar work in 1812, £576 15s. 2d.

In 1813 men on furlough who obtained good recruits were granted an extension of leave.

It is difficult to determine when "bounty" for service in the "Constitutional Force" was first introduced. Sums were paid in early times which partake of that character, but this method for inducing men to serve for a payment regulated by the ordinary law of supply and demand, stimulated by the exigency of the situation, appears to have very firmly established itself at the end of the 18th and beginning of the 19th centuries, when large sums were also paid to Militiamen for passing into the standing branch of the Army for general service.

At a later date bounty became a retaining fee for a fixed number of years' obligation to come out for yearly training, and embodied service on occasions of emergency involving national danger.

Beyond these sources of remuneration for bearing arms in the National Force, there have been the payments received for substitutes, a relic of remote ages. In one county it is stated that upwards of £60 was paid at the end of the 18th century. The Official Returns, Whitehall, 18 March, 1808, show that "The sum fixed by each County or Riding in England and Wales as the Average Bounty for Substitutes" varied in England between £16 1s. 0d. Rutland, and £40 11s. 10d. Northumberland, whilst in Wales the cost ranged from £16 Montgomery to £44 Anglesea.

In these returns for the two countries 3,129 men were principals and 22,956 substitutes who had benefited to the extent of some hundreds of thousands of pounds from those who ought to have served. At this time associations or companies assured persons against the operations of the Ballot Act. When the Act was suspended in 1830, one company existed with a capital of £750,000, which for a yearly premium provided its policy holders with substitutes when drawn for service.

Before bringing to a conclusion this "quid pro quo" side of bearing arms in the Constitutional Force for service when required, it should be brought into this concentration of details that in 1814 and 1816 subalterns who were serving when their regiments were disembodied after the Napoleonic age (during which many regiments had been continuously employed for upwards of twenty years) received a disembodied allowance: Lieutenants 2s. 6d. per diem, Ensigns 2s., Surgeons' Mates and Assistant Surgeons 2s. 6d. if they had not the financial qualification for the rank of captain. These payments appear to have continued until 1852, during a period when regiments were only assembled on three or four occasions for annual training. In 1835, Sept. 11th, by Order in Council, those belonging to the Permanent Staff were "to die out."

In 1820 we find by the Treasury Book records that the Militia contributed twelve pence in every pound to the support of Chelsea Hospital fund, presumably deriving some benefit. At this time sergeants received one shilling per diem and the like amount for subsistence, corporals 8d. and 8d., and privates 6d. and 6d.

When Militia battalions were disembodied after the Crimean war, surgeons and assistant surgeons received the equivalent of one year's pay, subalterns six months', non-commissioned officers and men fourteen days'.

It is noteworthy that the gratuity granted to officers for compensation during the South African war (beyond the ordinary pay and allowances of the army) took the form of a payment to all ranks of officer of £100 for any period up to one year's service, and at the rate of £100 per year for longer duty if abroad (or £50 if in the United Kingdom) in addition to the special war grant according to rank paid to those who served in South Africa, and one half of this allowance to others who proceeded beyond the sea to foreign stations.

The special compensation to N.C. officers and men for the sacrifices they had suffered being on this occasion also based on their length of embodied service and liberal in character.

By Army Order, May 1st., 1902:

"On disembodiment in lieu of all Militia Bounties (except Reserve and Special Service Sections) pay, rations, and messing allowance for 42 days, plus seven days for each month or further period beyond six months of embodied service, also gratuity of one pound for each year or portion of a year of embodied service under certain limitations as to absence, sickness, etc.

Militia in South Africa after one year's service received on the basis of at least 126 days' pay and allowances, besides thirty shillings bounty instead of twenty—up to two years' service, and twenty shillings after two years'."

CHAPTER VI.

DISCIPLINE — PUNISHMENT FOR DESERTION — ORDONNANCES OF WAR — EFFICIENCY OF CROMWELL'S ARMY—ABOLITION OF LOSS OF LIFE OR LIMB IN PEACE TIME BY JAMES II.—"CAT-O'-NINE-TAILS" AND MARTIAL LAW — PUNISHMENTS BROUGHT INTO LINE WITH THOSE FOR OFFENCES IN CIVIL LIFE.

Passing on now to a brief notice of some of the peculiar methods adopted for stopping evasion from service, the maintenance of descipline, and punishment of desertion, etc., apparently in all ages inseparable from the bearing of arms, it is pleasant to find by the nature of the punishments imposed a gradual advance in the civilization and character of the people as soldiers. The early Britons are reported to have lacked discipline. We have no record of how they endeavoured to enforce it. It may be considered certain that the stern and exacting character of the Romans in the management of their troops at home, and in all their martial operations, extended to Britain whilst they were in occupation of the country.

The late Colonel John Davis, A.D.C., in his history of the 2nd Royal Surrey Militia, remarks that in Anglo-Saxon times all were obliged to fight. If a landowner remained at home he forfeited all his lands, and for failure of duty was fined sixty shillings and the Churl thirty shillings for the like offence as the "Fyrdwite," the arms being adapted to a scale of wealth applicable to the whole of the people. The Churl was not the lowest rank. We find by Stubbs' Select Charters (thanks to the researches made by Mr. Berry-Potter, who compiled a history of the Volunteer Force) that in King Ethelred's reign, 866, there was an ordinance which makes clear the importance of Fyrd service in those days. "This is the Ordinance which King Ethelred and his 'Witen' ordained as frith-bot (meaning an amendment of peace) payment to atone for breach of peace for the whole nation at Woodstock in the land of the Mercians according to the law of the English. "Chap. 28—if any one without leave return from the fyrd in which the King himself is, let it be at his own peril of himself and all his estate, and he who also returns from the fyrd let him be liable to CXX. shillings."

In Norman times the "Posse Comitatus" was bound to

attend upon summons for the military defence of the country under pain of fine and imprisonment.

King Henry II., 1181, adopted other methods of dealing with those liable to bear arms and armour, and probably initiated the excessive flogging of after years. Blackstone says that the Act passed enforcing the provision of arms and armour by every man according to his estate and degree, and empowering musters, arming, and exercising of all the inhabitants of districts, also for making it illegal to sell or pawn arms or armour which should be in possession, enjoined the justices that "the King would punish corporally in their limbs and not in their goods or lands any who were without their arms."

Grose observes that the Ordonnances of War and martial regulations of our early kings give great insight into military history, the earliest to be relied upon being those of King Richard I., 1189, "for the government of those going by sea to the Holy Land," and the "Constitutions to be made in the Army of our Lord the King" of King John, whose reign began 1199. He held that these latter were apparently calculated to facilitate the supply of the Army with necessaries which it seems were exposed in the churchyards for sale by the churchwardens, under the eye of the superintendents or chief men of the Church. If they were absent, the persons taking goods elsewhere had to deposit the value in the church. Grose suggests that in times of war or insurrection the country people brought in their goods to the churches as a place of safety and sanctuary where no one would dare to take them by force.

It may be added that there is evidence of churchyards being used as places of assembly and for purposes of drill at different periods, and we have already referred to cannon stored in the churches.

Scott concludes that in 1205, when King John was abroad in France with an expedition, every man at home capable of bearing arms was called upon to serve or be ready to do so in defence of his country under pain of forfeiting any lands he might own, and if not a landowner, of becoming a slave for ever with all his posterity and paying a yearly poll tax of fourpence. This record is of import as showing that all classes of the people were liable to render service.

In 1213 of the reign all historians refer to the culvertage or "turntail tax." Scott says about it "that it subjected those liable to serve and be present with the King to forfeiture of all property and perpetual servitude for failing to do so, and that although not intended to apply to the posse comitatus whose duty was in case of internal commotion or actual invasion and in no case out of the kingdom, pretexts were easily invented to induce the county forces to relinquish this privilege. This limitation of obligatory service was afterwards confirmed by Acts of Edward III., 1327, with the addition of words "urgent necessity." Most writers remark that it was always possible to assert that emergency had arrived.

The regulations of King Richard II. of about five hundred years ago show in such a conclusive and quaint way the organization and customs of the Army, and the character of discipline to be upheld, that they are given in detail. The translation by Grose from the old French in which they are in, is adopted :

"These are the Statutes, Ordonnances, and Customs, to be observed in the Army, ordained and made by good consultation and deliberation of our most Excellent Lord the King Richard, John Duke of Lancaster, Seneschall of England, Thomas Earl of Essex, and Buckingham, Constable of England, and Thomas de Mowbray Earl of Nottingham, Mareschall of England, and other Lords, Earls, Barons, Banneretts, and experienced Knights, whom they have thought proper to call unto them; then being at Durham the 17th Day of the Month of July, in the ninth Year of the Reign of our Lord the King Richard II.

I. *Firstly*. That all manner of persons, of the nation what state or condition they may be, shall be obedient to our lord the king, to his constable and mareschall, under penalty of every thing they can forfeit in body and goods.

II. *Item*, that none be so hardy as to touch the body of our lord, nor the vessel in which it is contained, under pain of being drawn, hanged and beheaded.

III. *Item*, that none be so hardy as to rob and pillage the church nor to destroy any man belonging to holy church, religious or otherwise, nor any woman, nor to take them prisoners, if not bearing arms; nor to force any woman on pain of being hanged.

IV. *Item*, that no one be so hardy to go before, or otherwise than in the battail to which he belongs, under the banner or pennon of his lord or master, except the herbergers, whose names shall be given in by their lords or masters to our constable and mareschall, upon pain of losing their horses.

V. *Item*, that no one take quarters, otherwise than by the assignment of the constable and mareschall and the herbergers; and that after the quarters are assigned and delivered, let no one be so hardy as to remove himself, or quit his quarters, on any account whatsoever, under pain of forfeiture of horse and armour, and his body to be in arrest, and at the king's will.

VI. *Item*, That every one be obedient to his captain, and perform watch and ward, forrage, and all other things belonging to his duty under penalty of losing his horse and armour, and his body being in arrest to the mareschall, till he shall have made his peace with his lord or master, according to the award of the court.

VII. *Item*, that no one be so hardy as to rob or pillage another of money, victuals, provisions, forage, or any other thing, on pain of losing his head; nor shall any one take any victuals, merchandise, or any other thing whatsoever, brought for the refreshment of the army, under the same penalty; and any one who shall give the names of such robbers and pillagers to the constable and mareschall, shall have twenty nobles for his labour.

VII. *Item*, no one shall make a riot or contention in the army for debate of arms, prisoners, lodgings, or any other thing whatsoever, nor cause any party or assembly of persons, under pain (the principles as well as the parties) of losing their horses and armour, and having their bodies in arrest at the king's will, and if it be a boy or page he shall lose his left ear. Any person conceiving himself aggrieved shall make known his grievance to the constable and mareschall, and right shall be done him.

IX. *Item*, that no one be so hardy as to make a contention or debate in the army on account of any grudge respecting time past, or for any thing to come; if in such contest or debate any one shall be slain, those who were the occasion shall be hanged; and if any one shall proclaim his own name, or that of his lord or master, so as to cause a rising of the people, whereby an affair might happen in the army, he who made the proclamation shall be drawn and hanged.

X. *Item*, that no one be so hardy as to cry "havok," under pain of losing his head, and that he or they that shall be the beginners of the said cry shall likewise be beheaded, and their bodies afterwards be hanged up by the arms."

[Grose says "Havok" was the word given as a signal for the troops to disperse and pillage, as we learn from the following item in the droits of the marshall, Vol. I., p. 229, wherein it is declared that in the article of plunder all the sheep and hogs belong to such private soldiers as can take them; and that on the word havok being cried, every one might seize his part; this probably was only a small part of the licence supposed to be given by that word.]

XI. *Item*, that no one make the cry called "Mounté" (raising a false alarm) or any other whatsoever in the Army, on account of the great danger that may thereby happen to the whole army; which God forbid! and that on pain, if he be a man at arms, or archer on horseback, of losing his best horse; and if he be an archer on foot or boy, he shall have his left ear cut off.

XII. *Item*, if in any engagement whatsoever an enemy shall be beat down to the earth, and he who shall have thus thrown him down shall go forwards in the pursuit, and any other shall come afterwards and shall take the faith or parole of the said enemy, he shall have half the said prisoner, and he who overthrew him the other half; and he who received his parole shall have the keeping of him, giving security to his partner.

XIII. *Item*, if any one takes a prisoner, and another shall join him, demanding a part, threatening that otherwise he will kill him (the prisoner), he shall have no part, although the share be granted to him; and if he kills the said prisoner, he shall be in arrest to the mareschall, without being delivered till he has satisfied the party, and his horses and armour shall be forfeited to the constable.

XIV. *Item*, that no man go out on an expedition by night or by day, unless with the knowledge and by the permission of the chieftain of the battail in which he is, so that they may be able to succour him should occasion require it, on pain of losing horse and armour.

XV. *Item*, that for no news or affray whatsoever that may happen in the army, any one shall put himself in disarray in his battail, whether on an excursion or in quarters, unless by assignment of his chieftain, under pain of losing horse and armour.

XVI. *Item*, that every one pay to his lord or master the third of all manner of gains of arms; herein are included those who do not receive pay, but only have the benefit of quarters, under the banner or pennon of arms of a captain.

XVII. *Item*, that no one be so hardy as to raise a banner or pennon of St. George, or any other, to draw together the people out of the army, to go to any place whatsoever, under pain, that those who thus make themselves captains shall be drawn and hanged, and those who follow them be beheaded, and all their goods and heritages forfeited to the king.

XVIII. *Item*, that every man, of what estate, condition, or nation he may be, so that he be of our party, shall bear a large sign of the arms of St. George before, and another behind, upon peril that if he be hurt or slain in default thereof, he who shall hurt or slay him shall suffer no penalty for it; and that no enemy shall bear the said sign of St. George, unless he be a prisoner, upon pain of death.

XIX. *Item*, if any one shall take a prisoner, as soon as he comes to the army, he shall bring him to his captain or master, on pain of losing his part to his said captain or master; and that his said captain or master shall bring him to our lord the king, constable, or mareschall, as soon as he well can, without taking him elsewhere, in order that they may examine him concerning news and intelligence of the enemy, under pain of losing his third to him who may first make it known to the constable or marschall; and that every one shall guard, or cause to be guarded by his soldiers, his said prisoner, that he may not ride about at large in the army, nor shall suffer him to be at large in his quarters, without having a guard over him, lest he espy the secrets of the army, under pain of losing his said prisoner; reserving to his said lord the third of the whole, if there is not a partner in the offence; and the second part to him that shall first take him; and the third part to the constable. On the like pain, and also of his body being in arrest, and at the king's will, he shall not suffer his said prisoner to go out of the army for his ransome, nor for any other cause, without leave of the king, constable, and mareschall, or the commander of the 'battalion' in which he is.

XX. *Item*, that every one shall well and duly perform his watch in the army, and with the number of men at arms and archers as is assigned him, and that he shall remain the full limited term, unless by the order or permission of him before whom the watch is made, on pain of having his head cut off.

XXI. *Item*, that no one shall give passports or safe conduct to a prisoner or any other, nor leave to any enemy to come into the army, on pain of forfeiture of all his goods to the king, and his body in arrest and at his will; except our lord the King, Monsieur de Lancaster, seneschall, the constable, and marshall; and that none be so hardy as to violate the safe conduct of our lord the king, upon pain of being drawn and hanged, and his goods and heritage forfeited to the king; nor to infringe the safe conducts of our said Lord of Lancaster, seneschall, and mareschall upon pain of being beheaded.

XXII. *Item*, if anyone take a prisoner, he shall take his faith, and also his bacinet, or gauntlet, to be a pledge and in sign that he is so taken, or he shall leave him under the guard of some of his soldiers under pain, that if he takes him, and does not do as is here directed, and another comes afterwards, and takes him from him (if not under guard) as is said, his bacinet or right gauntlet in pledge, he shall have the prisoner, though the first had taken his faith.

XXIII. *Item*, that no one be so hardy to retain the servant of another, who has covenanted for the expedition, whether soldier, man at arms, archer, page or boy, after he shall have been challenged by his master, under pain that his body shall be in arrest until he shall have made satisfaction to the party complaining, by award of the court, and his horses and armour forfeited to the constable.

XXIV. *Item*, that no one be so hardy to go for forage before the lords or others, whosoever they may be, who mark out or assign the places for the foragers, if it is a man at arms he shall lose his horses and harness to the constable, and his body shall be arrested by the mareschall, and if it is a valet or boy, he shall have his left ear cut off.

XXV. *Item*, that none be so hardy as to quarter himself otherwise than by the assignment of the herbergers, who are authorised to distribute quarters, under like penalty.

XXVI. *Item*, that every lord whatsoever cause to be delivered to the constable and mareschall the names of their herbergers, under penalty, that if any one goes forward and takes quarters, and his name is not delivered in to the constable and mareschall, he shall lose his horses and armour."

There were other ordinances in the reign of Henry V., 1413 to 1422, of a very voluminous character and, in the spirit of the times, with heavy and painful penalties, but they largely applied to ecclesiastical matters, conditions for loot and the keeping of women from the army. Grose also refers to some orders given by Henry VII. before the battle of Stoke in 1487, and to the unique pamphlet of regulations issued by Henry VIII., when with his army at Calais prior to the capture of Tournay. These were "emprynted" and are amongst the Loseley manuscripts. Although of rare value, they are couched in such language as not to be useful for the purposes of this book. It should be noted that these ordinances are believed to have been the first printed ones.

In 1640 there were Articles of War by the Earl of Northumberland for King Charles I., and by the Earl of Essex for the Parliamentary forces; these latter contained upwards of ninety paragraphs, eleven being on religion and moral duties, framed in a severe spirit, "soldiers being punished almost brutally on the slightest infraction of them."

Some writers speak of the iron will and stern discipline of Cromwell, but history records that his army, largely composed of the Constitutional Force of the Kingdom was in a high state of efficiency and discipline. In 1672 the liability under Charles II. for not finding a horse soldier was £20 and footman £5. The lenient spirit of King James II., as reflected by his Army Regulations, does not appear to have placed him in the position of a successful military reformer. The Train Bands which he raised as a species of Militia seem to have been (except in the case of those belonging to London) wanting in discipline and efficiency when fighting side by side with the county units of the old Constitutional Force.

It is noteworthy, however, that his ordinances, numbering sixty-four, ended with the merciful wish to prevent punishment extending to the loss of life or limb in peace time. Grose considered that many of the Articles of James II. really formed the basis of those existing in 1801.

Raikes has it that in 1757 punishments for absence and disobedience were awarded by Justices of the Peace on the scale of 1st offence fine 2s. and "set in the stocks for an hour"; 2nd offence fine 4s. and four days to the House of Correction; 3rd offence fine 6s. or one month; drunk on duty fine 10s.

In 1761 the Berkshire Annals record that £100 was the fine for not serving or providing a substitute. The age at this period was 18 to 45 years and for a term of three years' service. Parish officers could choose volunteers, if preferred, instead of obtaining men by ballot. No articled clerk or poor man with three children born in wedlock could be compelled to serve.

A punishment awarded for high treason of Militiaman at this date will interest those who collect the gruesome customs of bygone ages: "To be drawn upon a hurdle to the place of execution on Wednesday 30th September next and then and there severally hanged by the neck, to be severally cut down and have their entrails taken out and burnt before their faces; to have their heads severed from their bodies and their bodies afterwards severally divided into four parts, and their heads and quarters disposed of at His Majesty's pleasure."

In 1768 King George III, men for not joining their regiments were punished by a fine of £20 or six months in gaol or until paid, and the penalty for desertion after receiving the Militia bounty was the same.

The effect of considerable bounty payments in 1787, and feebleness of the law to detect frauds, are matters worthy of note, although it may be improbable that history will ever repeat itself in this form.

> "Thomas Hodgson aged twenty-six when convicted of robbery and executed for it, confessed to having enlisted forty-nine times into regiments in England, Scotland, and Ireland under different names, often doing so to different recruiting parties of the same regiment, and seldom staying more than a day or two before deserting; he was convicted three times for desertion and whipped once for it; he obtained three hundred and ninety-seven guineas in bounty money and fifty-seven guineas by robberies."

At this time deserters were still liable to a fine of twenty pounds or six months' imprisonment, and by the king's order it was read at the head of every regiment that "All deserters from the Militia would be sent to the East Indies or Coast of Africa for life."

Advertising became the medium for recovering deserters. "Two belonging to Lord Craven's company of foot commanded by Lord Paget were advertised for in a Reading paper, five guineas being the reward for each recovery."

The punishments for army offences in 1795 are usually referred to as heavy, disobedience and absence receiving five hundred lashes, and four to five hundred being the ordinary sentences for misdemeanour. In this year one regiment records five hundred lashes with the "cat-o'-nine-tails," by drummers of the corps, for being drunk, quarrelling in Barracks and knocking down a corporal. Southey wrote that in 1807 "the martial laws of England are the most barbarous which in this day exist in Europe, offenders sometimes being sentenced to one thousand lashes, a surgeon standing by to feel the pulse during execution, and determine how long it could be continued without killing." The numbers up to five were counted "between each lash."

In 1814 the Militia was brought under the Articles of War and regulations in force for the regular branch of the Army.

Coming to 1853 we find a continued advance towards better treatment of soldiers and lighter punishments, in harmony with the changed tone of the country and those undertaking its military requirements. The Mutiny Act was altered to stoppage of one penny per day for eighteen months instead of six months' imprisonment for enlistment by Militiamen into the Line without the sanction of their commanding officers; after years brought a succession of changes, all tending to bring the lot of a Militia soldier (in respect of punishment for his offences) into line with those in civil life, all alike being "interested in the laws and good government of the kingdom."

CHAPTER VII.

Interest of Soverigns in the Weapon of their Day—The Bow as a Cherished Weapon of Might—The Fire Arms Age—Associations for Promoting Proficiency in the use of Arms, Etc.

The practical interest taken by ruling sovereigns to promote enthusiasm and proficiency in the use of the weapon of their day must in all times be gratifying pages in the history of the Constitutional Force.

The principle of bearing arms by the people in defence of their country having come down from far distant ages, it will be in keeping with a work of this character to observe some of the arms that have been borne by them.

Whilst no effort of description can rival the great museums formed for the study of the many remarkable weapons of destruction produced by inventive skill in successive ages, and an epitome cannot attempt to embrace all that might be considered of importance, two trusted weapons representing ancient and modern times have been selected as being identified with the safety and progress of the nation.

When we look back to the early ages we find weapons in use which ofttimes have contributed to the prestige of the country and formation of Empire.

The bow is frequently mentioned in military history since its introduction by the Normans until superseded by "Pikemen wearing bright armour and gonners having coats of mail with helmets." It was an important weapon in the hands of the English. We have in evidence the battles which have been won by its aid, and the vast destruction its expert use caused at those of the Standard, Cressy, Poictiers and Agincourt. Writers have said that its habitual use for general purposes on the Scotch and Welsh marches, when the people were combining the duties of husbandmen and emergency soldiers, and suddenly required to defend themselves, their property and country, was the means of providing fearless soldiers to handle their cherished weapon of might.

In the reign of King Richard I., 1189, a select body of archers was sent to the war of the Crusades. The statute of Winchester, 13, Edward I., 1285, speaks of the bow as the arm "of all the other sort," or national weapon for the bulk of the people. This enactment, which in part was intended to facilitate the arming of the people for defence, says: "bows and arrows out of the forest and in the forest bows and bolts." Scott describes this curious difference between in and out of the forest as having for its object the prevention of poaching the King's deer, there being in use at this period two kinds of arrow, "pile or ball headed and barbed ones," the former useless for poaching purposes. He quotes Blount's Tenures in support of this opinion: "The Foresters shall not carry in the wood of Roger de Torney any barbed but piled arrows."

Fisk gives the price of bows and arrows in the time of King Edward III., 1327, as one shilling and sixpence for a painted bow and fourteen pence for a sheaf of twenty-four steel pointed arrows. By Hollingshed's Chronicles, London in 1355 sent five hundred archers for the army going to France. In 1406 King Henry IV. instituted regulations for the manufacture of arrows,—all heads were to be stamped with the maker's name under a penalty. The plucking of geese by sheriffs under the order of King Henry V. has been already mentioned. King Henry VIII. is reputed to have taken great interest in archery, and that county archery clubs were numerous.

The Act 33, Henry VIII., required "the inhabitants of all towns to keep their butts in repair."

> "Every man under sixty years of age to use and exercise shooting with the bow, fathers and masters instructing their sons and servants and providing bows and arrows for their use. None under twenty-four years of age were to fire at a standing mark, or a less distance than eleven score yards under penalty of six shillings and eight pence for each shot."

Grose directs attention to the encouragement given by King Edward VI., 1547. There is an entry in the King's journal, "One hundred of the Archers of the Guard shot before him at an inch board divers of the arrows pierced it through."

The Devon records state, however (and it is strange), that anything in the shape of a bow drill does not appear to have existed until the "invention" of one William Neade in the time of King Charles I., which was ordered to be used at all trainings. To conclude this treatise on the bow it may be interesting to remember that the yew trees in churchyards are reputed to have originated out of a Royal Command, to ensure a supply of suitable wood for the making of bows. We know that in later times walnut trees were planted in favoured places for making gun stocks.

Moving onwards to the great revolution in the means of defence created by the introduction of fire-arms, embracing through many centuries, quaint and cumbrous weapons supported by forked rests, carrying twelve bullets to the pound, and in turn the matchlock, fusil, flint and steel, and percussion cap ages, and barrels at one time five feet in length followed by rifles of many and varied types, we find in the reigns of the late Queen Victoria and His Majesty King Edward VII. reflections of that same interest in the weapon of the day which characterised the sovereigns of earlier ages.

In these times there are associations initiated by officers past and present of the Constitutional Force, which have for their object the creation and fostering of an interest in the rifle, together with proficiency in its use.

In 1887 the officers of Lancashire founded the Red Rose Club, with the Right Hon. the Earl of Derby, K.G., as patron, which awards prizes for musketry.

In 1890 a combination entitled the Militia Rifle Association, originating out of the Militia Eight Club, a child fathered by Lieut.-Colonel Holden, was formed to embrace the whole Constitutional Force of the United Kingdom. In 1898 Her late Majesty Queen Victoria presented a large silver-gilt challenge cup for the best shooting battalion; whilst in 1902 His Majesty King Edward VII. contributed a valuable challenge cup for company officers firing and making the best average in the annual course.

In 1894 the Yorkshire White Rose Club came into existence, patron at a later date H.R.H. the Prince of Wales, to encourage emulation among the ten county Militia units and their interest, etc., in gun practice and musketry, a large number of valuable challenge cups being accumulated.

Besides these larger associations, there are several others of importance. Staffordshire has its inter-regimental challenge cup, etc. for the four Militia units of that county, and many regiments possess their trophies to engender a taste for the use of the rifle.

Reverting to 1619, "England's Trainings" gives some insight into the musketry of those days, and describes what was held to be requisite for good shooting: "The souldier if he bears a peece must first learn to hold the same and plant the great end on his breast with a gallant and souldier-like grace; he that means to be accompted a forward and perfect good shot by continuall exercise, must be so ready that in all particular points touching his peece, powder, match, bullets and the use of them, that he neither be to seeke nor grow amazed," etc.

It should be mentioned that in 1759 butts were kept in order, and prizes given, out of the regimentally-accumulated funds derived from punishment fines and penalties.

CHAPTER VIII.

EQUIPMENT OF THE CONSTITUTIONAL FORCE SOLDIER—ARMOUR, ETC.—THE HEAD COVER IN DIFFERENT AGES—CRIMPING IRONS, POWDER, AND THE CUE—BADGES AS CONNECTING LINKS WITH THE ANCIENT PARENT MILITARY FORCE OF THE COUNTRY.

We now come to a branch of the great historical tree of the force which, having been subjected during two thousand years to many loppings and much grafting, appears to have passed through more changes than the tree itself in the process of obtaining the peace and safety of the country.

The gods of fashion and invention, apparently moving hand in hand with those responsible for the outer preparation of the people as soldiers, have left us with an overwhelming collection of quaint records relating to curious garments and ingenious armour which can only be partially dealt with.

It will be observed that the head covering in all ages has often caused anxiety to reformers as being, it would appear, of primary importance for efficiency, and sympathy will doubtless be extended to all whose lot it may have been to present the Constitutional Force soldier in such apparel, etc., as would best suit the period, his duties as an emergency soldier, and the pocket of the nation.

Writers of ancient history say that the inhabitants of early Britain (and it should be remembered that all were liable to render military service in those days) were clothed in the skins of wild beasts, though some coast dwellers holding communication with the outer world were more civilised; but we have little information as to the distinctive martial attire adopted by the tribal levies when called upon to serve. There is, however, no reason to suppose that the war kit was of an extensive character.

The equipment of the People's Force throughout near twenty centuries seems to have been divided into the skin, iron, leather, and cloth ages, with some kind of material partaking of the nature of cloth in favour between the skin and iron periods, and there was the picturesque military costume of the Stuart times.

The helmets of skin, hair outwards, worn by the heavy infantry in Saxon days, reproduced to some extent in later ages, and regarded with pride by certain units and branches of our present Army, together with the Highland costume probably originating out of the Saxon tunics to the knee, with leg bands, must necessarily be a source of interest to the parent military force of the country.

At times, coats of mail, and armour of many types, formed the war covering of certain numbers of the Constitutional Force.

The Statute of Armour was repealed by King James I., though iron skull caps and some form of armour continued in use until well after the middle ages.

In 1154 the head covering was of iron and leather, and coats of mail, though many of the lowest class were more simply protected.

A protection for the body stuffed with hair or wool and covered with leather was introduced in 1181 for use by the lower sort of those required to be in possession of armour.

In 1336 cloth had evidently established itself. The Devon records speak of "gowns for soldiers made by the Taylor."

Armour in 1488 was composed of small pieces of iron sewn on leather and covered with cloth, and in 1512, when an army was raised to oppose French invasion, an ordinance by Henry VIII. required "everie man to have a cap to put his sculle in price 8d. the pece."

1539 produced costumes for special occasions.

The Wriothesley Chronicles describe a great muster in London, when "Coates of cloth of gold and velvet were worn and jerkins of white cotton and buffe leather, hose of white satten, etc."

Twenty marks appears to have been the cost of equipping for active service those county troops in 1544 who were sent to help in the French war.

The troops of 1553 provided by the county of Berkshire to aid King Phillip and Queen Mary wore blue coats with red crosses, costing six shillings and fourpence each (the material is not stated) and their weapons (bills) eighteenpence each, paid for by the inhabitants. In 1581 Pikemen were attired in "coates of broade blue with a coarslet." Archers in blue cassocks with white facings, jerkins of buff or deerskin, and iron scull caps lined with red cloth. Grose says the majority of the infantry had "Cassokes" of some motley or other "grene collar" or russet, the cavalry wearing red cloaks, all paid for out of stoppages. By State Papers Queen Elizabeth, 1585, we find that 4,000 imprest men of nineteen counties for the expedition to the Netherlands cost for cote money four shillings per man!!!

Scott remarks that in 1588 "there was great deformitie in the apparell and armors worn very uncomlie uneasilie."

In 1598 it cost £3 per man to arm and apparel 2,000 men levied from London, Kent, Essex, Sussex, Middlesex and Surrey for the rebellion in Ireland.

When the London troops in 1599 mustered in Greenwich Park for review, it is recorded that "the Pikemen were in bright armour, Harquebusses in coats of mail with helmets, Harbordiers in German rivets, led by wardens of the City Companies mounted, and dressed in black velvet, with Ensigns in white satin faced black sarsnet and rich scarves."

In 1601 the men levied for service in Flanders received forty shillings each for their apparel on embarkation. Those armed with Calivers in 1603 were uniformed in a combination of armour and leather, with iron-ribbed leather helmets.

The statutes of armour were in the reign of James I. repealed, though iron skull caps and some form of armour were retained for musketeers, and cassocks still in favour.

In 1625 we find that coats cost about sixteen shillings each, and at the siege of Gloucester, the red and blue regiments of London are mentioned, besides the Train-bands in blue, yellow, green, orange, white and red. The heads of pikemen were encased in helmets of leather with some iron protection, and feathers at the top.

The difficulty of clothing soldiers in 1642 was so great that King Charles I. impressed tailors. The colour of certain regiments in 1643 will interest all rifle units. Colonel John Hampden's regiment, which fought at Chalgrove, was clothed in green, and called the "Green Coats," reputed to be one of the best in the Parliamentary army.

1648 provided the musketeers, who carried cumbrous weapons on forked rests, also armed with long swords, and there was the picturesque costume of Stuart times, a slouched hat with drooping feathers, balloon trousers to the knee fastened with large bows of ribbon, hose and shoes also bearing bows of considerable size.

Pikemen in 1649 were protected with back, breast and head pieces of iron, and leather was still largely used to complete their efficiency.

In 1685 we read of red and yellow "liveries," and boots or shoes being worn indiscriminately.

1689 still had confidence in "coats of armour," flexible and otherwise, the fashion in head pieces being a skull cap of basin form.

1715 brought the abolition of armour for horses, whilst Holberdiers and half Pikemen officers were in 1727 made soldier-like by three-cornered hats and coats to the knee worn fastened at the top only.

1759 caused the long red coats in fashion to be hooked back in the skirts and expose a red waistcoat, the skirts of coat being lined with the colour of the facings, the hair was cued, a three-cornered hat with cockade, and gaiters black or white appear to have been optional. At this date it is recorded that the insufficiency of clothing provided was of such serious import on embodiment that colonels were authorised by Royal Warrant, Oct. 23, to supply their men with the several articles usually furnished to other regiments.

Although it is not chronicled that the scant costumes of remote ages had been revived, it appears that breeches and waistcoats were in 1760 not found by the Government.

By Royal Warrant, G.R. Court of Kensington, "The embodied Militia being in great want of clothing our Royal will and pleasure is, that such monies for the clothing of the current year shall be paid to our trusty and well beloved—the Colonels of Regiments—at the rate of £3 10s. 0d. for Sergeants, £1 15s. 0d. Corporals, and £1 10s. 0d. for Drummers and Private men."

A quaint mitre shaped cap worn at this date can be seen in the Museum of the Royal United Service Institution.

The Hampshire records contain a rather explanatory order: "Geaters well blacked, Buckle Garters clean and white." The cap assumed another form in 1794, becoming a true half circle worn across the head, with bows at each end, and the initials of regiments on the front.

Militia officers were at this time authorised to wear a blue undress with red collars and cuffs. In 1796 long coats were abolished, and in 1797 coloured feathers were introduced to distinguish companies—red and white in the body of the Unit, white for Grenadiers, and green for Light Infantry.

1798 brought the Supplementary Militia into existence, and they had issued to them by colonels who received an annual allowance for the purpose, coat, waistcoat, breeches, hat with feather and cockade, stock, etc. It is recorded that the accoutrements of tanned leather were supplied by the Ordnance Department to those wishing for them, but being of such bad quality and unlikely to last the twelve years, most regiments took the allowance and paid the difference for buff ones.

Gold lace and epaulets were at this time worn by the officers in some regiments, and silver by others. In 1799 the hair of both cavalry and infantry was cued, except flank companies, those without sufficient hair being supplied with false queues to save the expense of stuffed tails, etc. The hat at this period was of cocked hat type, with flaps to turn down.

Having now to pass into a century replete with changes, and which in number exceed what can be herein brought together, it may be thought satisfactory to keep in memory those only which attained some historical importance, and a few others entitled to notice. There was the characteristic swallow-tailed coatee worn in 1814, so attractive to artistes; displaced in 1855 by the double-breasted tunic, which in turn gave way two years later to a single-breasted creation of the modern type. There was also the truly historic "shell jacket," in which so many of the eighteen thousand Militiamen fought at Waterloo, one finding its way into the museum of that place; whilst the celebrated painting of a square at Quatre Bras, by Lady Butler, "repelling an onslaught of the finest cavalry of France on that memorable day," shows the Constitutional Force soldiers fighting in their Militia kits. The jacket disappearing along with the tunic for N.C. officers and men at a later date, were replaced by cloth frocks for N.C. officers and kersey frocks for the men.

The blue undress of officers appears to have had a vicarious existence; originating in 1794, it passed out of favour (as a frock coat) in 1857, to be re-introduced in 1902, the interval being represented by a braided blue cloth patrol jacket, which in its turn gave way to a plain one of serge. There was also in 1874 a red serge lasting for about a year. The sash forming an attractive feature in the uniform of the Constitutional Force officer appears to have passed through a century of unrest. In 1803 it was round the waist, in 1857 on the shoulder, and in 1902 had dropped to the waist again.

We find in 1855, by W.O. Circular of July, that "off reckonings," or the allowance made to colonels for the clothing of their regiments, were discontinued.

The innumerable changes of this century in the matters of gold and silver, leather, steel and brass, feathers and tufts, epaulets and wings, braid and buttons, present an accumulation of details which cannot claim to be noteworthy in detail, but it may be mentioned that in 1803 "love ribbons" were on the swords of officers attending funerals, and it is important to bring into these records that in 1852 and 1881 the uniform of the Force, including also the Artillery and other branches, were assimilated to that of the regular branch of the Army except as to silver lace, etc., in 1852, gold lace following in 1881.

In 1811 Militiamen passing into the regular branch of the Army took with them their clothing, except greatcoats. No record is available of the date when this apparently economic regulation was cancelled.

The efficiency of the Force in many ages having caused attention to the head covering, it is necessary to observe some of those flights of fashion in the 19th century which dawned with a somewhat remarkable "cocked-hat." This protection for the head appears to have been abolished during the year and replaced by what is described as a "cap" with tuft and cockade.

In 1814 "bearskins" for the Grenadier companies of regiments were reproduced, whilst during the remainder of the century we find the chaco both tall and short, helmets in blue and khaki, caps round and long, the Glengarry and field service, taking their turn in protecting the head of the "Constitutional Force" soldier.

In connection with martial apparel it would form an interesting study to trace the origin of badges associated with the Constitutional Force. We find that some distinctive ones have been in use from early times, whilst in 1881 all territorial regiments (then composed of several units under varied obligations of service) not in possession of such a badge were assigned a national one, the English regiments receiving the rose, Scotch the thistle, Irish the shamrock, and Welsh the dragon.

There is little doubt but that some of the badges in use at different times formed connecting links with the ancient parent military force of the country; for instance, the three Saxon swords and five crowns of the 6th Middlesex Regiment, the "Stafford knot." Captain Troughton, in his records of the 4th Battalion, N. Staffordshire Regiment, explains that this was the badge of the ancient Norman Barons de Stafford, the first of whom was a companion of William the Conqueror.

The mediæval rose—either red, white, or united—is interesting to many regiments; we have it indicated by the annals of the County of Southampton Militia that "the red rose surmounted by the Crown and Garter became connected with that County, and its Forces, out of presentation by King Henry V. to the trained bands of the County, afterwards called Militia, in recognition of their proceeding with him to France and being at the battle of Agincourt."

There is also the white horse of some regiments, which as a badge appears to have been originally black until 1122, when its colour was changed to white upon the conversion of its holder to Christianity and as an emblem of the pure faith.

Tradition associates the oak leaf with King Charles, etc.

CHAPTER IX.

STATUTES, ORDERS IN COUNCIL, ETC. DEALING WITH THE "CONSTITUTIONAL FORCE" FOR DEFENCE, ETC. — THE "WITENA-GEMOTI," COMMISSIONS OF ARRAY, ASSIZES OF ARMS, ACTS OF PARLIAMENT.

When we approach and consider the countless Ordinances, Statutes, Orders in Council, etc., which have dealt with the "Power of the Country" as a means of defence—the only army for all purposes in some centuries, and a reserve in others originating with William the Conqueror—it becomes apparent that the information obtainable from these sources, drawn together and arranged chronologically, only requires to have interwoven the usual details incidental to the bearing of arms for an unimpeachable and continuous history of the Constitutional Force throughout many centuries. There were regulations of the Army in Saxon times initiated by kings or their council, the "Witena-gemoti." References have been made to some of those which are mentioned by historians, and to the known methods of earlier and later dates.

Before making a selection from the many Statutes which have engaged the attention of Parliaments after King John gave the country in 1215 a Constitution to protect its rights and privileges, it is necessary for the purpose of these annals to notice the system of military service by the people under the first "Commission of Array" of King Henry I., 1122, and the first "Assize of Arms," for which the country was indebted to the care of King Henry II. in 1181.

We have it stated in Stephen's Commentaries of the Laws of England that Commissions of Array were "the sending into every county officers in whom the King could confide, to muster and array or set in military order the inhabitants of districts;" whilst Lingard's History of England says, with reference to the Assize of Arms:

"It was distinctly a return to the old military system, it gave new life to the fyrd, the ancient Militia which had never gone out of use, each man was to have the arms which befitted the amount of his property, and it was by a jury that the liability of each man was to be ranked in such and such a class, the schedule was to be read in open court, and all were obliged to swear that they would provide themselves with the arms against the next feast of St. Hilary, to be faithful to King Henry the son of the Empress Matilda, and to keep their arms for the King's service and with fidelity to the king and kingdom."

In now bringing into evidence some of the numerous Acts of Parliament — which from the preambles, it would appear, often reflected the military condition of the country and its state of emergency—we find that an epitome of certain Acts which were passed at important epochs relating to the military service of the people, together with a few brief references to official utterances, will sufficiently indicate the gradual development of the "Constitutional Force" and the uses to which it might be put.

After the first Assize of Arms, there was another of some importance—that of

1252, when 36, Henry III., authorised changes in the property qualification regulating the scale of arms and armour.

In 1285—13, Edward I.—came the celebrated Statute of Winchester, under which "all men of every rank and degree between fifteen and sixty years of age were to keep in their houses harness for to keep the peace."

Stephens says, "to provide a determinate quantity of such arms as were then in use." All were assessed to armour on a scale according to the value of their lands, goods and incomes. The masses of the people (those with less than forty shillings yearly) were to be armed with bills, knives, and other less weapons, and all the others "that may" with bows and arrows." The Views of Arms and Armour (the more wealthy having the latter) were held twice yearly by constables appointed by the Hundreds as under the Assize of Arms, 1181.

Grose and others direct attention to the stringent regulations against the selling, pawning or parting with arms. No Jew could have in possession any coat of mail, nor were any arms to be carried out of the country unless by permission of our Lord the King.

The following Acts, etc., now claim our special attention :—

1298, 27, Edward I., was a Statute which introduced armed horses into the Levies, Scott remarks, for the first time in England.

1327, Act 1, Edward III., empowered the King to require all men "to arm as in the time of his progenitors Kings of England, for service in their shires and sudden coming of strange enemies into the realm," another Act being passed to check the practice which appears to have been in vogue of "taking men for the Royal Forces engaged in foreign wars."

1336, Act 9, Edward III., was to stop "the finding of men at arms and archers other than those which hold by such service except by consent and grant of Parliament."

1352, Act 25, Edward III., "to prevent the sending of men out of the Kingdom and at any rate out of their shires but in case of urgent necessity."

1386, 9, Richard II., Ordinance made at Durham to regulate the discipline of the Army.

1403, Act 4, Henry IV., confirmed the right of Commissioners of Array to control the Forces of their Districts.

1404, Act 5, Henry IV., an invasion being feared, "to empower the Commissioners of Array to raise and drill all men at arms and require all other able-bodied men to be armed according to their substance."

1406, Act 7, Henry IV., to regulate the making of arrows and require heads to be stamped with the maker's name under a penalty.

1413, 1, Henry V., an Ordinance by the King at Mans, chiefly providing for the safety of the Church, and payment by soldiers of one third loot to their Captains—and another Order in this year to the Sheriffs of Counties to collect the feathers from geese for the archery purposes of their troops.

1513, 5, Henry VIII., Articles of War issued by the King when in France with an expedition, which are said to have been the first ever printed.

1539, 30, Henry VIII., provided for the great muster, by virtue of a Royal Commission issued March 1, of "all harnessed and furnished men in Counties, and other able bodied persons fitt for warre."

These quaint returns indicating the strength and condition of the Constitutional Force, or Army of the Country, in 1539 are given in the next chapter as taken from "the letters and papers of the reign of Henry VIII.," arranged by James Gardiner.

CHAPTER X.

STRENGTH AND CONDITION OF FORCE, 1539—ASSEMBLY OF "ALL HARNESSED AND FURNISHED MEN" BY COUNTIES AND OTHER ABLE-BODIED PERSONS "FITT FOR WARRE."

RETURNS OF MUSTER 30, HENRY VIII, 1539.
Of "All Harnessed and Furnished Men and Others Fitt for Warre" in England and Wales.

M. 1.
BEDFORDSHIRE—8 April, 30 Henry VIII.:—

	Archers.	Billmen.	Pairs of harness.
Bereford Hundred	44	130	20
Stoddon Hundred	32	122	12
Wylly Hundred	67	179	24
Bedford Town	75	97	12

The Commissioners:—Lord Mordaunt to harness 20 men.
St. John to harness 50 men.
Harding to harness 2 men.
Fitzhugh to harness 2 men.

M. 2.
CORNWALL—
"The book of musters of the King's Grace's tenants and tinners of his manors within written and of the stannaries of Blakemour and Fowymour, as by the same more plainly appeareth."

Cornwall—Parishes and Manors of Stoke Clymslond:
177 names of the King's tenants and the tinners—
Calstoke or Calste—113.
Ryllatom—113.
Leskerde—111.
Stannary of Fowymour—471 tinners.
Stannary of Blakemour—764 tinners.
Lordship of Dyndagyll (Tintagel)—48 names of tenants and residents.
Parish of St. Tawyn—28 names of tinners.
Manor of Hellston in Fryg—124 names of tinners.

M. 3.

DERBYSHIRE—12 April, 30, Henry VII.—

High Pekk Hundred:
  Archers with horses—harness 64, without 148, billmen with horse and harness 300, without 612.

Derby Town, 16 April, 30, Henry VIII.:
  Archers with etc., 10, without 56, billmen with, etc., 39, without 126.

Scarresdall Hundred, 14 April, 30, Henry VIII.:
  Archers with, etc., 64, without 74, billmen with, etc., 321, without 684.

Worsworth Wapentake and Hertyngton Soke, 8 April, 30, Henry VIII.:
  Archers with, etc., 38, without 96, billmen with, etc., 129, without 361.

Appulte Hundred:
  Archers with, etc., 26, without 108, billmen with etc., 98, without 255.

Morleston and Litechurche Hundred:
  Archers with, etc., 79, without 197, billmen with, etc., 61, without 482.

Repton and Greslay Hundred:
  Archers with, etc., 28, without 47, billmen with, etc., 53, without 154.

M. 4.

DEVONSHIRE—10 April, 30, Henry VIII.—

Robourght Hundred	181 names
Tavistocke Hundred	137 ,,
Lifton Hundred	387 ,,

M. 5.

DORSETSHIRE—10 and 11 April, 30, Henry VIII.—

Lyme Regis Borough	96 names
Whytechurche Hundred	343 ,,
Gotherthorne Hundred	198 ,,
Bemyster Hundred	321 ,,
Halestoke Hundred	32 ,,
Redehone Hundred	73 ,,
Tollerford Hundred	171 ,,
Colyffordtre Hundred	320 ,,
Uggescombe Hundred	323 ,,
Liberty of Frampton	192 ,,
Borough of Weymouth	64 ,,
Borough of Melcombe Regis	45 ,,

Liberty of Portland	54 names
Liberty of Wyke	16 ,,
Liberty of Pudelhynton	45 ,,
Liberty of Alton	33 ,,
Manor of Delysshe	21 ,,
Hylbourne of Delysshe	10 ,,
Pudeltowne Hundred	199 ,,
Totcombe Hundred	227 ,,
George Hundred	211 ,,
Borough of Dorchester	248 ,,
Modbarugh Hundred	116 ,,
Hundredeslearugh Hundred	115 ,,
Egerdon Hundred	108 ,,
Yettemyster Hundred	156 ,,
Shurbraune Hundred	409 ,,
Brownshall Hundred	103 ,,
Muton Buckelon Hundred	247 ,,
Rede Lune Hundred	177 ,,
Gyllyngham	32 ,,
Ore	20 ,,
Shaston Borough	129 ,,
Muthercome Tithings	44 ,,
Myllton	16 ,,
Haselor Hundred	161 ,,
Russhemore Hundred	55 ,,
Borough of Wareham	115 ,,

M. 6.

ESSEX—18 . . . 30, Henry VIII.—

Barstable Hundreds ... ... 917 names
(One of them with a "wepyn called an halywater sprynkyll")

Final totals, viz.:—"Parsons, vicars, chantry priests and curates charged with armour and artillery at these musters 19, gentlemen at these musters 5, archers, besides three priests that be good bowmen 301, bylmen 524, aged men 57, and widows 9, charged with armour 66, gunners 1, town harness, viz.:— 3 harness, 2 jacks, 1 bow, 1 salet. There be at this muster 301 able men, but not of sufficient substance to furnish themselves with harness or weapon."

Belye and Polomershe Townships ... ... 48 names

M. 7.

TOWN OF GLOUCESTER—1 March, 30, Henry VIII.—
The Hundreds of Dudston and King's Barton
    within the county of the town of Gloucester   635 names

M. 8.

GLOUCESTERSHIRE—31 March, 30, Henry VIII.—

Bollowe Hundred	379 names
Breavelle Hundred	478 ,,
Bledeslowe Hundred	290 ,,
Duchy of Lancaster	246 ,,
Weysbury Hundred	222 ,,

"Figures representing the numbers of able men are inserted at the end of each rotulet and section. By these it appears that the total able men are:—Botlowe 263, Breavelle 227, Bledestowe 161, Duchy of Lancs. 125."
"2 Weysbury 95."

Barkeley Hundred	886 able men
Tewxbury Hundred	348 ,, ,,
Tylbolston Hundred	62 ,, ,,

M. 9.

HEREFORDSHIRE—

"Certificate addressed to the King by some of the Commissioners . . . and by this book certify all archers and billmen and persons who though not able for war possess 'abilaments of war.' . . . Giving under headings of the hundreds and townships the names of the men . . . and after each man's name his harness and weapons (e.g., 'horse and harness for himself,' 'a salet, a glaif, and a gorget,' a gleif and dagger,' 'a dagger,' etc."

Hundred of Radlow	610
Hundred of Grymer	405
City of Hereford	346
Hundred of Huntyngton	316
Hundred of Stretford	443
Hundreds of Wigmore, Wolfey and Leominster (Sir Edw. Crofte 40 pair of harness, Thos. Monyngton 6 pair)	916

"With the note:—The hundred of Wigmore was lately part of Wales, and newly united to Herefordshire, the inhabitants are unable to have more habiliments of war than above expressed."

Hundred of Webbetre	413
Hundred of Ewyaslacy	213

M. 10.

HERTFORDSHIRE—Friday before Palm Sunday, 30, Henry VIII.—

THE CONSTITUTIONAL FORCE.

Hertford town ... ... 86 names of archers and billmen
(Note . . . "a good many more names appear in the harness lists.)

Musters in Hertford Hundred.

(Giving under township lists of names, singly or in groups, of persons who find "horse and harness," followed by lists of archers and billmen.)

Contents: — Hertford town (Thos. Harteswell, Nic. Nores, Thos. Myners) 80 names of archers and billmen, Hertyngfordbury 34, Bayford (Thos. Knyghton) 21, Berkehamsted Parva 12, Essynden 20, Broxburne (John Cook, Wm. Apryse) 25, Hoddysdon (Ric. Braughing, Hen, Burrel) 68, Amwell hamlet in Hodesdon 12, Cheshunt Strete 93, Waltham Crosse 74 (two of them Dutchmen), Wormsley 22, Brekynden Holde 28, Amwell 32, Stansted Thele (John Flemyng, serjeant at arms) 10, Stapullforde 14, Bengehoo 29, Tewyng 21.

500

Hertyngfordbury ... ... 34 names
The rest amount to 480

M. 11.
LEICESTERSHIRE—18 March, 30, Henry VIII.
Melton Mowbray ... 61 names of archers and billmen.
Other places amount to 575.
Goscotte Hundred—17 March, 30, Henry VIII. ... 552

M. 12.
LINCOLNSHIRE, LINDSEY.—
Wapentake of Hyll:
Total harnesses 49½, able men 104, archers of the best sort 17, of the mean sort 16, billmen of the best sort 20, of the mean sort 50.

	Total Harnesses.	Able Men.	Archers (best.)	Archers (mean.)	Billmen (best.)	Billmen (mean.)
W. of Candyshowe	115	482	97	22	174	187
Soke of Bollyngbroke	62½	—	40	26	96	252
(Horses 12)						
W. of Calcewath	120	—	58	61	81	243
W. of Yerburghe	—	—	34	112	62	129
(Almain rivetts, coats of plate and brekendyns 110)					jakes	120
W. of Haverstowe (No totals—in all 209.)						
S. of Horncastle	—	—	9	38	49	160
(Total almain rivetts, etc., 40)					jakes	13

	Total Harnesses.	Able Men.	Archers (best.)	Archers (mean.)	Billmen. (best.)	Billmen. (mean.)
W. of Gartree	112	—	15	56	120	293
						jakes 29
W. of Wraggoe	—	—	12	64	30	194
(Almain rivetts, etc., 62)						
W. of Aslakhoo (No totals given)						
W. of Lawres	78	360	45	—	—	—
W. of Well	29	—	24	30	19	120
(Horse 24)						
W. of Walschecroft ...	—	510	71	71	470	470
(Horse 20)						

M. 13.

NORFOLK.—

Only totals given—202 archers of both sorts, 519 billmen of both sorts, whereof 163 archers and 246 billmen are "sufficiently harnessed."

M. 14.

NORTHAMPTONSHIRE—31 April, 30, Henry VIII.—

Fallesley Hundred	325
Newbottelgrove	170

Hundreds of Norton Wardon and Sotton—6 May, 31, Henry VIII.—Archers 200, billmen 300, harnesses 100.

Corbye Hundred	754
Willibroke Hundred	253

Spelloo Hundred—Total archers 27, billmen 54, harnesses 23.

Wymersley Hundred—Total archers 59, billmen 77, harnesses 44.

Gyllsborough Hundred	269	93	176	44
(all "sodyars")				
Rothewell Hundred	107	26	81	—
(all "sodyars")				
Hyghem Ferrars Hundred				94
Hawfordes How Hundred				78
Hokeslowe Hundred				161
Orlyngher Hundred				68
Pokebroke and Navesforde Hundred ...				158
Nassaburgh Hundred				244

M. 15.

NORTHUMBERLAND—27 March, 30, Henry VIII.—

The 4 wards in Northumberland of Thos. Horsely, Gilb. Myddyton, Robt. Brandlyng, Thos. Baater, and 4 of Jas. Lawsone—1,047, and 64 names of mariners who lacked their fensible array at muster and promised to provide it, and 110 of poor men unable to buy harness.

Cokdale and Part of Bamborough ward.—17 and 18 April, 30, Henry VIII., 1340, and Reedsdale 188, all able men, with horse, harness and spears, "beside all the foot thieves."

Caldmarton Heath Muster ... ... 490 (17, 18, 20 April,
Mylfeld Muster ... ... 261 30, Henry VIII.)
Braxhill Muster? (21 Apr.)... ... 704
and 75 other persons.

The total of able men—Numbers not filled in; the number of Scots in the whole number is 231.

View of musters taken by Sir Reynold Carnaby, Sir John Fenwyke, and John Swyneborn, 19 April, 31 (sic) Henry VIII.

Sir Reynold Carnaby's servants—19 names (one of them a priest)

Lewis Ogle's (Bailiff of Hexham) servants—3 names.

Yngorve's servants 19 names (three of them "footmen with spears").

And 2,513 names, and North Tyndell "thieves" 391, all with horse and harness.

Fletham Moor Muster—21 April, 30, Henry VIII.—442 (27 of them Scots). And 14 able men with horse and harness.

M.16.

NOTTINGHAMSHIRE—24 March, 30, Henry VIII.—284.
"of the which persons aforenamed we have prepared and made in readiness 31 persons, that is to say 21 bows and 10 bills, in harness and horsed, at all times to serve our sovereign lord the king."

North Clyde, part of Barssett Lawe Wapentake, 24 March, 30, Henry VIII.:

Total harness 107, archers 270, billmen 480.

Brokestowe Wapentake:

Total harness 154, billmen 300, bowmen 200.

Totals of both Wapentakes, i.e., harness 261, etc.

Rysclyf Hundred:—342.

M. 17.

OXFORDSHIRE—Certificate dated 25 April, 30, Henry VIII.—No numbers given.

M. 18.

SHROPSHIRE—31 March, 30, Henry VIII.—

Muster of "the one part of the Hundred of Bradfort":
  Total billmen 617, bowmen 117.
Muster for half the Hundred of Bradford:—1,012 names.

M. 19.
  SOMERSETSHIRE—

Hundred of Stone and Cattyssagsshe ...	626
Hundred of Jyngsberg	386
Hundred of Southpetherton	393
Hundred of Abdyke and Bulstone	708
Hundred of Crukern	267

and, besides, in Henton St. George, Hugh Poulett, Knt. wt. 40 harness, 30 bills, 20 bows, etc., 30 servants to Sir Hugh, and 5 tenants and 9 others.

M. 20.
  STAFFORDSHIRE—1 March, 30, Henry VIII.—

Cutleston Hundred	1,304
Pyrehill Hundred	1,102
Other places	1,563
Seysdon Hundred	577

  A muster roll—of which the heading is torn, leaving only the concluding words of each of the 5 lines, viz.: "Bassytt," "and com," "the Kinge's subjectes," "hundred within the cowntye," "Stafford"—giving the names of 29 archers who have horse and harness, 152 having various items of harness detailed, 103 having no harness, and a like arrangement of billmen in lists of totals.—537

Offelaw Hundred—27 Apr., 31, H. VIII. ...	911	,,
Offelaw Hundred in another hand	335	,,

  In another hand, with notes by John Vernon:—A number of lists without any headings, each subdivided as "with horse and harness," "with some habiliments of harness," and "without horse and harness," viz.: 1st list 78, 2nd 85, 3rd 77, 4th 55, 5th 79, 6th 170. Burton 168. Typton 55.

M. 21.
  SUFFOLK—

Rysbrydge Hundred—9 and 11 April, 30, Henry VIII.:
  Totals:—161 archers, 178 billmen, 68 bows, 79 bills, 79 harness, 21 horses, 48½ sheaves of arrows.
Wyllfford Hundred:
  Totals:—Harness 58, archers 56, billmen 180.
  Muster taken at . . . , 20 April, 30, Henry VIII. for Looes Hundred—179.

Woodbridge—17th April, 30, Henry VIII.—85
Threadling Hundred—141.
Cosford Hundred—530.

M. 22.

SURREY—27 March, 30, Henry VIII.—

	Total archers.	Billmen.	Harness.
Hundred of Blackheath	85	167	80
Hundred of Tanrigge	109	281	61
Hundred of Raigate	109	283	76
Hundred of Wotton	31	166	138
Hundred of Wallyngton	—	232	56

M. 23.

SUSSEX—8 April, 30, Henry VIII.—

City of Chichester:

Bowmen with harness 20, billmen with harness 25, gunners "with handgonnes, powder and pellattes for them" 8, bowmen without harness 15, billmen without 50, "aliens" billmen without harness 18.

Eststret:—Upper ward 28 (1 Frenchman, lower ward 37 (3 Dutchmen and 1 Frenchman), ward without Estgate 19 (1 Dutch and 1 French), Palent 56 (12 aliens). Suthestret:—Upper ward 18, lower ward 14. Westret:—Upper ward 34 (aliens, one of them a gunner), lower ward 30 (1 Breton and 1 French). Northestreet:—Upper ward 30 (3 aliens), lower ward 30 (6 aliens, 5 of them gunners). Vyntre Ward and Litill London, 12. Men of the clergy within the close, viz.: the dean has 6 able men, the archdeacon 4, and Dr. Trobleffeld, residentiary 2.

Chichester Rape:

Earl of Arundel's servants 123, all harnessed.
Earl of Southampton's servants 183, all harnessed.
Lord Lawarr's servants 57, all harnessed.

	Bowmen.	Billmen.	Harness
Estborne Hundred	95	124	22
Dumford Hundred	86	131	40
Westborn and Syngleton Hundred	115	193	54
Boseham Hundred	46	124	26

Men charged with harness not yet ready—30 pair.

	Bowmen.	Billmen.	Harness. Pair
Boxer Hundred	49	65	28
Stokebridge Hundred	49	40	35
Manwood Hundred	73	83	63
Aldwyke Hundred	46	51	19

Men in these 4 hundreds charged with harness having none ready—35 pair.

	Bowmen.	Billmen.	Harness.
Hundreds of Avysford Polyng and boro' of Arundel (7 & 8 Apr, 30 H. VIII.)	122	339	101
Rutherbrigge Hundred	194	352	116
Esewrithe & Bury Hundred	210	472	96
Byrtford Hundred	63	110	55
Steyning & Bramboro' Boro's. Hundred	19	26	13
Steyning Hundred	24	48	31
Eswrith Half Hundred	17	31	17
Sir Wm. Shelly's Servants	8	4	—
Sir Rd. Sherley's Servants	4	5	—

Totals for the whole Rape of Hastings:

    Bowmen 450, billmen 681, bows 518, sheaves of arrows 448, whole harness 322, jacks and coats of fence 102, bills and exes 848, salets 202, horsemen's harness 6, swords 225, daggers 443, horses 27, spears 6, odd harness *nil*.

Longbrege Hundred—30, Henry VIII.:

    Bowmen 32, billmen 33, "almen ryvetes" 15, "brygedyns" 1, "jakkes and cotes of fence" 24, bows 38, sheaves of arrows 35 and 6 arrows, bills 70, "sallettes" 52, "splyntes" 19 pair.

	Bowmen.	Billmen, etc.
Grensted Hundred	22	34
Hartefelde Hundred	38	48
Lokksfeld Hundred	93	312
Retherfeld Hundred	37	83
Ruschmonden Hundred	41	103
Tottnour Hundred	10	39
Flexborowe Hundred	10	16
Alciston Hundred	17	22

	Bowmen.	Billmen, etc.
Dyll Hundred	10	31
Willingdon Hundred	14	29
Bourn Hundred	14	19
Sheplake Hundred	18	33
Perkgate Hundred	1	—

M. 24.

WILTSHIRE—1 March, 30, Henry VIII.—

(Musters taken thereupon by Lord Hungerford and John Bonham.) (Giving under tithings lists of archers and billmen followed by a note of the harness there.)

Melksham Hundred	73
Bradford Hundred	146
Warmyster Hundred	150
Wesbery Hundred	73
Aldewarbury Hundred	186
Chaltre Hundred	211
Frustefeld Hundred	52
Wonderdyche Hundred	74
Downton Hundred	164
Damesham (for the South part)	130
Camdon and Cadworth Hundred	250

Certificate of Edm. Mompesson, Barth Husse, and Chas. Bulkeley, of Musters within the City of New Tarum.
(Giving under the several wards lists of archers and billmen and of persons assigned to have harness in readiness.)

Contents:—Ward of the Market, 199 names of archers and billmen, and 41 of those assigned to have harness. W. of the Mede, 79 and 12 (among them John Goodale, bailiff, and John Abarowe, gent.). W. of Martyn, 169 and 39. W. of the New Strete, 145 and 49. In the said city are 10 archers and 10 billmen, well harnessed, ready "at the King's commandment to the sea."

Certificate of John Erneley, Chas Bulkeley, and Wm. Button.
"The division of the whole shire" of Wilts,
The Muster (Giving under tithings, etc., lists of archers and billmen, followed by the names of those assigned to have harness, and the harness.)

Contents:—

Ambresburye Hundred. Tithings	220
Swanborough Hundred	480
Potterne and Cannynges Hundred	432
Elstubbe and Everley Hundred	228

Certificate of the view of able men, archers and billmen, taken 10 April, 30, Henry VIII., by Sir Hen. Longe, John Hamlyn, and Wm. Stumpe, commissioners assigned by the King's commission to them and others, of the hundreds of Northe Damerham, Chyppenham, Callm Mallmesbury, and Wharwelldown.:—

Totals for each Tithing—

North Damerham Hundred	102
Chippenham Hundred	521
Callm Hundred	163
Wharwelldowne Hundred	192
Malmesbury Hundred	290

"This is the certificate of Sir William Essex, Sir Anthony Hungerford, and Sir John A. Brygges, and William Stompe, commissioners for the musters before them, taken of the hundreds and towns," etc. (Giving under headings of Townships lists of the "archers" and "bills," followed by a list of the individuals or groups who furnish harness. No numbers except the totals.)

	Archers.	Billmen.	Harness.	Horses.
Kynworthstone Hundred	9	180	66	10
Kyngbrygge Hundred	70	194	56	15
Selkeley Hundred	170	160	63	10
Rammesberg Hundred	42	100	52	30
Hyghworth, Crykkelade, and Staple	35	51	92	10

M. 25.

WORCESTERSHIRE — Westm., 27 March, 30, Henry VIII.—

(Giving under the several wards a list of names, each described as a "bowman" or a "billman," and with the harness any of them possess noted.)

Wards of All Saints 79 names, St. Martin 57, St. Nicholas 39, St. Clements 23, St. Peter's 73 (St. Andrews) 83 (?), The High Warde 90.

Certificate of John Dyngley, George Wylloughby, Wm. Sheldon, and Wm. Cokesey, commissioners, amongst others, for views and musters in Worcestershire, assigned to the hundred of Blakynhurst, Easter Term, 31, Henry VIII. (Giving under each town or township the names of the able archers and billmen (and one "horseman") and the number of horses and harness expected of the town; for instance, "These townships be limited in horse, harness, and artillery for a archer" or "in harness and artillery for a archer and harness for a billmann").

Blaykynhurst Hundred: archers 159, billmen 185, horsemen 1, horses 6, harness 25.

Similar certificate for the hundred of Oswaldstow, Worc. (Giving the names of able archers and billmen and the harness which the townships, and some individuals, will furnish; for instance "This town will horse, harness and furnish one archer" or "These townships have horse, harness, with artillery to one archer") In the following abstract names in in parentheses before the figures are those of gentlemen.)

Contents:—[Commencement lost] Parish of (Ke) mesey Ric. Mucklow, gentleman) 39 names (Mucklow and Anth. Aylworth will furnish 3 harness), Tyberton 14, Hyndlyppe 7. (Thos. Solley 2 harness), Warmedon 9, H . . . 12, (Nich. Flytte 1 harness), Wytley Parna 19, Odyngley 6; Claynes 31, and Whitston tithing therein 11, in all 42 (of whom Ant. Wood and several others furnish harness); Specheley and Cudley Bethnall and Wittinton and Bradicot (Ric. Sheldon will furnish 1 harness) 26, Wolverley 20 (Roger Holbarow and two others 1 harness), (S)toltun with its members, viz., Wolfeirton Magna (et Parve) cum muknill 21 (John Bradford 1 harness), Hownyd Morton and Hatfield (Wm. Gower 1 harness) 12, Hertilburg (Ric. Connysbye 1 harness) 38 (Thos. Best and others 1 harness). Parish of Stoke Prior 13, Hanbury justa Wyche with its members 37, Holfaste and Estynton 8 (Giles Bryggys 1 harness), Alchurche 45 (Robt. Porter and six other important persons furnish harness) Kenwicke 1 (i.e., Edm. Evet, who says he is charged to find an able person under his landlord, Sir Humph. Stafford), Ridmersley parish 23, Rypple parish 34; Herdwicke Breadon, Westyncott, Kynsham 22 (Thos. Mills and another aged man find harness), Mytton (Wm. Reid, with 5 servants and harness) 10 (Humph. Davys will furnish harness), Norton in Breadon 15, Hill Crome 8, Velys (Earl's) Crome 10, Crome Debitot 9, Parish of the Berow 23, Pendock 11, Welland and Little Malvern (John Russell Esq., and John Russell, his son, furnish harness) 32, Opton upon Severn 26, Elmeley Castle (Edm. Raynesford) 20, (Geo.

Weloughby furnishes harness), Overbury, with its members, 18, Fladbury Hill, More and Weyer Pedle 32, Cleve Priors and Hervyngton (Thos. Busshell finds harness) 15, Leggebarowe 13, Throkmerton (Thos. Middlemore Esq., finds harness) 14, Stoke and Bradley, Hableuche, and Rowslenche 30, Cutliston Priors and Iccombe 5, Byshampton 12, Rynghtiswesborn, a member of Braedon parish, 5, Inkebarowe with its members 70 (Geoff. Markham 1 harness) Evinlode and Dalysforde 16. Blockeley and Upton le Olde 20 (Robt. Palmer and Ric. Walgrove 2 harness), Draycote Northewicke juxta Bickley 8, Paxforde and Dorne 9, Hangyngaston 4, Charlton Cropthorn and Netherton (Wm. Dyngley, Esq., being aged, finds harness) 21, Blackwell 7, Shypston under Stowre (Wm. Sheldon 1 harness) 26, Tredyngton with its members except Blakwell and Calton, 29, Calton (Wm. and Humph. Jevetts) 4.

Total "of able men in the said hundred of Oswaldeslowe" 1,203. (N.B.—This figure gives us 230 more than are accounted for in the above abstract, and suggests that about four leaves are lost at the commencement)—whereof 535 are archers and 668 billmen (These are further classified as horsed and harnessed; but the numbers are lost by mutilation). Signed: John Russell, Sen.

Another leaf of the same (found apart), beginning with the memorandum that Arnold Gower, gent., and Ric. Fermour, aged man, will each furnish an archer, and that the "said parish" will furnish 2 men [Name of parish lost.], 28 names, some of them mutilated; "this parish will horse, harness, and furnish an archer." Hodynton 6, Hallow 32.

Fragments of two other leaves of the same, viz.:—

Beginning with the names of 6 archers and 3 billmen, but the name of the township to which they belong lost, followed by the note: Thos. Ludlowe will horse and harness himself and servant. (Township of St. John's), names of 11 archers and 14 billmen. "Adhuc" the township of St. John's 9 billmen, with note that John . . . . and Wm. Gower, Esq., provide horse and harness. The parish of St. John's in the country, names of 8 archers and 17 billmen.

Another smaller fragment in the same hand, having on the one side the word ". . . nford" in the margin, with the names of Ric. Habyngton, gent., John Ketilbye, gent., and 8 others archers," opposite it. On the other side 8 names of billmen and the note, "This parish will horse, harness, and furnish—one archer."

THE CONSTITUTIONAL FORCE. 77

Similar certificate for Halfshire hundred, Worc., made by Sir Gilbert Talbot, Walter Bloute, Thomas Evance and Ralph Sheldon, commissioners, in April, 31, Henry VIII. (Giving under the townships the names of the able archers and billmen, the names of those, mostly aged and impotent, who "will harness a man" and the number of harness furnished by the township. No indications given of the rank of the persons named.)

Kydderminster 52 names (Ric. Averey, Thos. Wilcocks, the Vicar, and 11 others will harness men), Wytton 9 (Edw. Ensall finds harness, Oldyngton 2, The Leye and Norton [?] 2, Trympley and Horeston 8, [Blank] 8 ("this village will horse and harness a man"), Blakester and Netherton 3, Haburley 4, Wannerton and Horcot 2, Frawyshe 2, Polkeston 4, Commerton and Agbarow 2, Over Mitten 7, Kyngeford 1, Stoone 14, Chaddesley 45 (Wm. Newman and 3 others find harness), Elmeley Lovet 19 (Ric. Poler and 3 others find harness), Cradeley 11 (Wm. Wall and John Hormour, harness), Dudley 20 (Ralph Selee and 8 others, harness), Olde Swynford 20 (John Bradley and 9 others), Ludley 5, Pedmore 19 (John and Thos. Bradeley and Thos. Holt), Churchill 5, Hugley 11 (Roger Jeston and 4 others), Droyte Wych 67 (John Butler, Sen., and 9 others), Wychebolde 30 (Ric. Dethicke, jun. and sen., and 4 others), Elmebridge 14 (Edm. Pursill), Sallwarppe 29 (John Trymnell and John Thommys), Churche Leach 7, Kyngeton 12 (John Wolmer), Crowle 15 (John Horneyblow and 2 others), Doverdale 6 (Wm. Brace), Hampton 13 (Thos. Wythe), Russhecke 15 (Wm. Newport), Hadsore 4 (Chr. Barnesley), Bromesgrove 31 (Humph. Daffye and 5 others); the following "Yeldes" members of Bromesgrove: Flokebury 9 (Wm. Wilke and 3 others), Burneford 4 (Wm. Burneford), Shepley 10 (John Brace) [Name lost] 5, [Name lost] 13 (Wich Burnesley and Harry Folke), Woodecote 8, Moseley 8, Hedley 21, "these said V. Yeldes of Kynges Norton be appointed to furnish X. men with horse and harness." [Name lost] 14 (John Watkyns, Ric. Saunders and 2 others), [Name lost] 23 (John Lane and Thos. Lewes), Coston Hacket 2 (Wm. Beke), Northefylde 28 (Harry Norton and 17 others), [Name lost] 14 (George Walshe and 3 others) . . . oveley 8, Belbroughton 16 (John Apen, or a Pen, and 4 others), Cokesey 2 (John Wylkes), Upton Warren 7 (Wm. Horton and John Palmer), . . . [Name lost] 40 (Auth. Hanbury and John Taylor of Byshopt . . . and another). Totals of able men, archers and billmen, "horses to serve the King's grace," and harness, but the figures lost by mutilation.

M. 26.

YORK AND AINSTEY—

Certificate of musters taken 24 and 25 April, 31, Henry VIII., by Robt. Elwald, Mayor of York, Hen. Hayson, Geo. Gayle, Wm. Harryngton, John North, Wm. Dogeson, Robt. Halle, and John Shadlok, aldermen; Peter Robynson and John Bean, sheriff's commissioners of the city, allotted according to the King's commission. (Giving under headings of the parishes, or other divisions, the names of the men able for war, arranged as horsed and harnessed, and not horsed and harnessed, each kind being further sub-divided into archers and billmen. In some cases a further division is made of parcel harnessed, i.e., having horses but no harness, harness but no horses, or incomplete harness.

Borothom Ward :—Parish of St. Michael in the Belfrey (Robt. Elwald, mayor, John Elwald, his son, Miles Newton, Percival Selby, Hen, Faux, Ralph Pulleyn, alderman) 17 names of the mayor's officers and servants and 136 other names. Men of war dwelling within the Cathedral Close : The Lord Dean's servants 33 (one of them a spearman), servants of Wm. Clyff, treasurer of York, 11, of Geoff. Downes, chancellor, 5; of Dr. Clyfton, sub-dean, 4, of Mr. Edw. Kellet, chaunter, 5; of John Good 7 (one a servant of Mr. Ashton). Parishes of St. Martin's in Connyngstreet (Mr. Wm. Wright, alderman; Mr. Reynold Beisley) 65, St. Wilfred's 20, St. Elyns in Stayngaite 72, St. Olyff and part of the said parish of St. Martin in the Belfray 54.

Monk Ward : — Cryst parish in Connygarth (Wm. Harryngton and Robt. Halle, aldermen, Robt. Man, merchant) 51 (one of them with a hand-gun and powder), the Trinities in Gooderomgait (Geo. Gayle, alderman) 21, St. John de Pyke (Tristam Tesh, Esq.) 25, All Hallows in Prisholme 4, Our Lady in Ladythorp 4, St. Maurice without Monkhouse 20, St. Samson's (Wm. Dogeson, alderman) 60, St. Andrew's (Edmond the surgeon) 8, St. Cuthbert's 4, St. Elyns upon the Walls 17, St. Saviour 23.

Wallmegate Ward and Castlegate	487
Wynth Ward and Northstrete	286
Wapentake of Aynsty	397
[Same writing as Wallmegate and Mynyth Wards]	394

A set of totals in the same hand :—Total of "the aforesaid archers" horsed and harnessed 196, billmen horsed and harnessed 281, able men having "some part harness" and no horse 91, having horse and no harness 16 horses, archers having neither horse nor harness 492, billmen having neither horse nor harness 851, handguns 4. Total of all the said persons, 1,885.

Liberty of St. Mary's Abbey.

A declaration of the number of able men to serve the King under the Lord Privy Seal within the liberties of St. Mary's Abbey, York, now in charge of Matthew Boynton, deputy steward, as appears by indentures and bills assigned by the bailiffs of the several lordships. The indentures are dated 13 and 14 April, 30, Henry VIII., and the bailiffs bind themselves to be ready on "lawful warning each to bring a fixed number of men; total of bowmen, billmen, and footmen 342. The lordships and numbers and Spawnton 100 and Normanbie 21, and the townships Hornesey 29, Hornesey Bekke 44, Garford 28, Dighton 16, Popleton 24, Harton 30, Myton 20, Overton 10, Clyfton 20, Fulforthe 8, and Cottingwith 30.

M. 27.

YORKSHIRE—EAST RIDING—

Musters taken in the East Riding of Yorkshire, viz. :—

Within the liberties of Howden, 13 April, 30, Henry VIII., before Sir Peter Vavasour and Wm. Thwaytes, commissioners thereunto assigned. (Giving under each township the list, (1) "persons able to serve the King with sufficient horse and harness" and (2) "persons able to serve the King having neither horse nor harness".)

Contents :—Howden, Yorkflett, Ellerkar, etc., etc.

Total of persons able to serve the King with horse and harness 81; without harness 408.

In the Wapentake of Bukcrosse, 16 April, 30, Henry VIII., before Sir Marm. Canstable, sen., and Wm. Constable, commissioners. (Making no division of harnessed and not harnessed, etc., etc.)

Ryllyngton, Yeddyngham, Estheslerton, Westheslerton, etc., etc., 709.

In the wapentake Betwixt Ouse and Darwent, 18 April, 30, Henry VIII.

Total of persons with horse and harness 137, without 791
Wapentake of Dykryng 1,149

Wapentake of Holderness, taken April 14, 30, Henry VIII.
South "balery" 2,162
North "bayllery" 908

Musters taken in the Wapentake of Harthill [date lost] 3,014.

M. 28.

YORKSHIRE—NORTH RIDING—

Note recording that the Lords Scrope and Latimer and the other commissioners for the musters in the North Riding of Yorkshire assembled at York, 20 March, 30, Henry VIII., and there allotted themselves by division. And John Pulleyn, "allotted by division at the city of York," 12 March, 30 Henry VIII., to view the King's subjects within the wapentakes of Hangeste and Halykeld. N.R. York, to be ready in armour of war when called upon 613.

West Sanfield, in the Wapentake of Halykelde—322.

Certificate of musters taken at Richmond, N.R. Yorks., 8 April, 30, Henry VIII., before Lord Scrope of Bolton, Marm. Wyvell and Wm. Zauckard. Total: Archers horsed and harnessed 357, billmen ditto 295, spearmen ditto 8, archers not horsed or harnessed 242, billmen ditto 478; in all 1,380.

Musters taken on Bagley More nigh Thresk, N.R. Yorks., 9 April, 30, Henry VIII., before Sir Roger Lassells, Robt. Meynell and Jas. Fox, justices, by virtue of the King's commission, "of the wapentake of Byrdford and the liberties of Byland and Newburge, to them assigned and allotted by division had and made amongst the said commissioners."

Total of archers 248, billmen 140, able men (as well archers as billmen) without harness 412.

Certificate of musters taken on Middleham Moor, N.R. Yorks, 9 April, 30, Henry VIII., by John Lord Scrope, etc.

Totals:—Archers horsed and harnessed 455, billmen 326, archers without horse and harness 286, billmen 377, spearmen 7; in all 1,451.

View and musters at Pickering, N.R. Yorks., 13 April, 30, Henry VIII., before Sir Ralph Eurye, the younger, etc.

Total of archers horsed and harnessed 180, billmen ditto 111, archers not horsed and harnessed 360, billmen ditto 366.

Musters taken on Semer Moor, Yorks., 17 April, and at Gisburghe, Yorks., 18 April, 30, Henry VIII., before Sir Jas. Strangways, etc., etc.

Totals:—Archers horsed and harnessed 389, billmen 313, archers and billmen without horse or harness 753; in all 1,455.

Musters taken of the inhabitants within the liberty of Allertonshire, N.R. Yorks, by Sir Jas. Strangways, etc., 342.

"Musters taken of all men, able and not able, within, the liberties of Whittley and Whittley Strand by Gregory Conyers, etc, 1025.

Musters taken at Barton Crosse in Rydall Wapentake, N.R. Yorks., by Sir Nich. Fairfax, etc. Sum total "of the whole ridding" 267 with horse and arms, 911 without.

M. 29.

YORKSHIRE—WEST RIDING—

Certificate of musters taken on Aldeffeilde Moor, W.R. Yorks., 24 March, 30, Henry VIII., before Sir Wm. Malory, John Pulleyn, etc., etc.

Totals:—Archers harnessed 33, billmen 53, archers not harnessed 133, billmen 136; in all 355.

Certificate of musters taken on Ripon Common, W.R. Yorks., 26 March, 30, Henry VIII., before Sir Wm. Malory, John Pulleyn, etc., etc.

Totals:—Archers harnessed 49, billmen 97; archers not harnessed 158, billmen 270; in all 574.

Musters taken at Wyke, 26 (March), 30, Henry VIII., by Sir Wm. (Gascoygne), the elder, etc., etc.

Total archers horsed and harnessed 156, billmen 160, archers parcel harnessed 68, billmen 130, archers having no harness 152, billmen 320.

Certificate of musters taken at Harrowgayte More, Yorks, 27 March, and at Folyfate Rygg, Yorks., 31 March, 30, Henry VIII., before Sir Wm. Malory, John Pulleyn, etc., etc.

Totals:—Archers harnessed 158, billmen 169; archers "parcel harnessed" 15, billmen 140; archers without harness 256, billmen 503.

Certificate of musters taken on Feryngesby Moor, W.R. Yorks., 29 March, 30, Henry VIII., (1539) before Sir Wm. Malory, etc., etc.

Totals :—Archers harnessed 45, billmen 48, spearmen 10; archers not harnessed 130, billmen 149; in all 382.

The muster of archers and others on horse and foot, with their names and the diversity of their harness, in the wapentake of Staynclif, commonly called Craven, and in the forest of Boolande thereto adjoining, W.R. Yorks., before Sir Thos. Tempest of Bracewell and John Lambart of Colton, commissioners thereto assigned by division among all the commissioners, taken 27 and 28 March and 1 April, "and divers other times and sundry places."

Total able men in Craven, 2,610.

Total able men in Boolande, 503.

General totals concluding that all the able men viewed are 3,141.

Certificate of Sir John Dawnay, Sir Hen. Everyngham, and Chas. Jakson, commissioners, assigned with others by the King's commission dated 1 March, 30, Henry VIII., of musters in the Wapentake of Osgetcrosse, W.R. Yorks. (being assigned thereto by division made among all the commissioners at York, 19 March), taken at Pontfrett 31 March, 7 and 15 April, at Gray Stones in Barnesdayle, 31 March and 9 April, at Wentbryg, 26 April, and at Snayth 8, 10 and 20 April, 30, Henry VIII.

Total with horse and harness : 3 spears, 355 archers, 383 billmen. Without horse or harness : 175 archers and 573 billmen.

Muster of the wapentake of Yewercrosse, W.R. Yorks., taken at Gray Mere Stone on Bentham More, 1 April, 30, Henry VIII., by Sir Marm. Tunstall and Ric. Redman, 1,254.

The muster of archers and others on horse and foot, with their names and the diversity of their harness in the liberties of Bradford, W.R. Yorks., before Sir Robt. Nevyll, etc., etc., taken 13 and 18 April, "and divers other times."

Total of able men 405. (Totals of various arms not given.)

Musters taken in the wapentake of Barkston, W.R. Yorks., 17 April, (30), Henry VIII., before Wm. Babthrop, etc., etc.

Total able to serve with horse and harness : 150 archers and 166 billmen; without horse or harness : 460 archers, 1,379 billmen.

WESTMORELAND AND CUMBERLAND—

(Giving names of all the gentlemen within the shire of Westmoreland. 64.)

(Names of all the gentlemen within the shire of Cumberland. 114.)

Musters in Wales

ABERGAVENNY—

"These musters were taken for the town and lordship of Burgavenny," 31 March, 30, Henry VIII., by George Herbert, steward there, by virtue of the King's letters.

Total: able bowmen 132, glaythes 493, long spears 42; "unable" bowmen 71, glaythes 307, spears 60.

ANGLESEY AND MERIONETH—

County of Anglesey—1,228 men, of whom 620 harnessed, 114 with coats of fence only, and the residue unharnessed.

Hundreds or commotes of Dyndathwy—104 names of archers and billmen harnessed, and 100 billmen not harnessed; Mernay 84 and 120, Mallth 93 and 58, Lliwen 100 and 48, Turkelye 84 and 187, Talbolyon 100 and 100; corporate towns of Bewmares 100, all harnessed; Wyburch 33, all harnessed.

County of Merioneth—1,886 men, of whom 420 harnessed, the "residue without harness, weaponed with bills, spears, elm bows and arrows, clubs and staffs." Within the hundreds of Pentlyn and Ederneon 50 horses, but in all the other hundreds no horses meet to serve the King.

Hundreds or commotes of Estem—299 names of men sworn to do service at an hour's warning. Ardudny 646 (among the 25 inhabitants of the town and franchise of Hardelegh), Talepont 400, Penllyn 319, Edermeon 322.

Lordship of Brecknok—Wallia 141 names, Pennederyn and Stradvollte 129, the Forreste 187, Glytarvey 60, Commote 285, Offic. Angl. 274, Offic. de Llywell 101, Villa Brecon 397, Lordship of Crughoell 320. Additional list headed "Hothny Slade," 121 names.

Bromfeld, Yale and Chirkeland—Book of the able men mustered by Edw. Almer, deputy steward of the lordships of Bromfeld, Yale and Chirkeland, upon letters of the King and his commissioners in the marches of Wales, dated Ludlow, 20 March, 30, Henry VIII.

The Holt town 94 names, Raglar de Marford (Sir Roger Puleston, "not able") 276, raglar de Wrixham 388, Wrixham town (John Puleston, sen.) 134, Yale raglar 210.

Total harness 511, being 58 Almen rivettes and 453 jacks; horses 25, archers 232, bills 601, spears 304, remainder, "having neither harness nor weapons nor of power to buy any," 374.

Carmarthen—Commotes of Iskennen, 144 names (including Sir Morgan, vicar of Landobie), Cornowgland 84, Cloygo lordship 38, tenants of Ric. More's land 33, commote of Kydwelle 30.

Kermerdynshire—Total 3,865, whereof 753 harnessed and 184 nags.

(Cardiganshire?)—Total 2,858, whereof 609 harnessed and 184 nags.

Pembrokeshire—Total 1,166, whereof 139 harnessed. (No nags mentioned.)

Lordship of Haverford West—Total 454, whereof 43 harnessed. (No nags.)

Carmarthen, Glamorgan and Pembroke—The muster of the lordship of Llanymthenery before Thos. Johns, Esq., farmer there, in April, 30, Henry VIII.

Total—703 names, 30 horses and nags; 68 of the names belong to Llanymthenery town.

Similar muster of Llanesdurn lordship. In all 123 names.

Similar muster of Langharn. In all 290 names, 21 horses.

Similar muster of Emlyn. In all 256 names, 27 nags.

Similar muster "Thomas Jonez, Esq.—is tenants in Pembrokeshyr and within the lordship of Haverford West and Dews Land," in April, 30, Henry VIII. In all 380 names, 4 nags.

Carnarvonshire—The county of Carnarvon, 2,429 men inhabiting therein, whereof 729 harnessed, and the residue "without any harness, weaponed with bills, spears, clubs or staves. And as for any horsemen there be none within the said county able to do the King service."

Commote of Iscorvay—347 names of men sworn to do the King service, besides the town of Carnarvon. Town and franchise of Caernarvon 92. Commotes of Uchgorvai 213, Ucharp 200. Evionedd 407, Issaphe 318, Nanconwy 200, Dynllayn 160, Gafflogio 170, Kemttmayn 254.

Cours—Names of able men, harness, etc. (in the lordship of Cawrse) "mustered by . . . . . 127.
(Mutilated.)

Cilgerran—The parish of Cleday 54 names, also 12 under the heading "Llylredyn," Penrytth 20, Llanvyhangell 22,

Llankolman 8, Manerdyvye 44, Kylgarran (parish and town) 49, Brydellt 23, Llantowt 22.

Note that "I, William Vachan," will make ready 4 archers and 4 long spears, and besides have four of my sons horsed and harnessed. Also that I have taken the ability of all parsons, vicars and priests, within "the same lordship of Kylgarent," and of all widows.

Denbigh—"The book of the musters of John Salesbury, Esq., steward of Denbighland.

Totals—Footmen, without harness, 901; bowmen, without harness, 241; billmen, 880, of whom 511 have thick coats and 97 "saletts and skolles and none other harness." There are 24 billmen in the steward's household with harness, and as many horsemen and footmen as he can make when called upon.

Dewddwr and (Pool)—Muster roll for Doyddwr, giving the names of 22 "horsemen harnessed," 15 "archers harnessed," 36 archers with bows and swords or bows only, 15 footmen harnessed, 40 with glaives and swords only, and 97 with glaives only.

Similar muster roll (mutilated, and name of the first place lost), "archers harnessed, viz., cotes, sculles and swordes," 16 names (rather mutilated); archers having bowes, arrows and swords, 29; Llannerchudol, archers harnessed *ut supre* 7, with bows and swords only 22, with bows only 5; ciertre, 34 names in all, arranged as in the preceding, Stradmercell 50, Mochaunt 35, Arechen Iscoid 21, Plasy Dinas 22, Mechen Dinas 22, Mechen Uchoid 71, Villa Pole 24.

Flint—Heading and name of the first place lost, all except initial letters, followed by 25 names visible and space for 21 lost; township of Weppreye, 6 names lost and 27 visible; townships of Golstyn 12, Kelstertyn 12, Lleprog Vaur and Lleprog Vaughan 14, Koet y Kya 4, township of Caervallogh 41, Lychtyn 36, Yeflo 42. Parish of Llanglassa—Trelogan 9, Putyn 21, town of Axton 28, Kelstan 10, Gulgrey 5, Grovant 30, Gwespr 22. Parish of Halywell—211. At Denbigh 58. Parish of Whitforde—253. Parish of Kilken—1,413. Signed, Roger Brereton, Schreyff of Flyntchyre.

Glamorgan—Musters of Landaff by Sir Rice Manxell. Landaff 52 names, Whitchurche 25, Elley 14, Urleton 11, Kayre 12, Merther Mawer 4. "Here followeth the musters of Sir Rice Manxell's servants and tenants within Glamorgan and Gowher. Servants, 39 names; Glamorgan 49, Gowher 147.

Hawarden and Mohuntes Dale—Mustered Sir Wm. Stanley, Steward. Hawarden 256, Mohuntesdale 337.

Kynleth Owen and Stannage—Mustered by George Cornewall, owner of the lordships.

Arranged in sets of harness: Kynlett Owen 22 sets, 52 names (7 of them horsemen). Stannage 7 sets, 16 names, in horsemen.

Monmouth—

Town of Newport—(Wm. Morgan with 8 horses, George Morgan with 2, John Harry Kemmyshe with 3) 109 names. Wentlogg—Parish of Barlege (Wm. Morgan John) 118, of St. Meleins 48, Marsefylde (Thos. Lewes) 66, [blank, perhaps to be taken as part of the preceding] 26, Coydkernew 17, Seint Bredis and Teland 23 and 20, St. Wolowe 35, 73e 8, Riska 19, Malpas 16, Hesstllis 19, Maghen (Roland Morgan) 29, Menythis tolowyne 104, Bedwelltee 39, Bedwes 26.

Kydwelly—Parishes of Llanedi 36, Llangenyd 7, Llanenlly or Llunnelly 78, St. Ismaell 50, Penbre 59, Llannen 43, Llangyndeirn 69, Llandyvayloe 66, Llangwnvor 31, Kydwely 75.

Mowthon—Muster taken by Ric. Mitton, lord of the same.

Names of 12 able horsemen, 12 able bowmen, and 26 able billmen, each with a note of his harness and weapons.

Nerberth—Muster of all the King's tenants and subjects dwelling within the lordship of Nerberth, taken by Jas. Williams, steward, 30 April, 30, Henry VIII. In all 144 names.

Powis—

Kerion or Kereygnion 283 names, Llannerchudol 62, Cierto 46, Stradmercell 130, Mochaunt 145, Mechen Iscoid 67, Plas y Dinas 54, Mechen Uchoyd 114, Villa Pole 54.

List of horsemen in the above places, viz.: 14, 6, 8, 17, 23, 6, 6, 17, and 14 names respectively.

Presteign and Builth—

Town and lordship of Presten 146 persons, whereof 10 horsemen furnished, 22 footmen harnessed, and 60 able men with gleyves. Lordships of Norton, Kynghton and Knocklas 137, whereof 4 horse, 14 foot and 52 with gleyves. Town and lordships of Radnor (Radnor Foren and Radnor Bridge) and Glandestry 288, whereof 13 h., 36 f., 80 g., 40 "maris pyckes," and 93 able men without weapons. Lordships of Millenethe 437, whereof 13 h., 36 f., 164 g., 34 m. Lordships of Gwerthronyon 262, whereof 15 h., 40 f., 92 g., 29 m.

Lordship of Buylth 820, whereof 32 horsemen furnished, 100 footmen harnessed, and 160 "able men, every man with his morice pyk."

Lordship of Cantercelyff 428, whereof 15 h., 80 f., and 140 "able men every with his gleyf." Town and lordship of Glynburch and the Haye 153, whereof harnessed men 34, able men with gleyfs ready 50.

Ruthin—Harnessed men—Ruthyn 23 names, commotes of Dogg 56, Llanugh 33, Collwn 45. Unharnessed—Archers 183, billmen 286.

Uske, Caerleon, and Treleck—Musters before Sir Wm. Morgan, steward. Sir Wm. Morgan himself with 40 servants, "upon geldings and round nags"; Thos. Morgan Esq., with 6 servants upon geldings; Harry Lewis of Seint Pere "himself and two demilances with VI. archers a horseback"; also the names of twelve other gentlemen with one or two servants each, and 3 other gentlemen and 31 yeomen without servants, all furnished with halberts and gleves; in all 112. Names "of them that hath part of their harness lacking for the rest" (after each name: "a coat, salet, and a gleve," "a coat and a halbert," or the like) 177. Names of the 80. Then the names of 672 persons without any general heading, but after each name the words, "a salet and a halbert," or "a halbert," or "a gleve," or the like, among them being included 10 mariners of Carllion "that were presented to serve the King in the ship called the Trinity of Caerllyon."

The parishes or towns to which these belong total 1,108.

Thornebury Hundred — 369 able men. "No general totals are given, but it appears by addition that the total number of harness is 306, and of horses 189."

Kyssgatt Hundred—409 able men.

CHAPTER XI.

Acts of Parliament 1542 to 1588—Spanish Armada Assembly of "Able Trayned and Ffurnished Men," Etc.

Returning to the Acts of Parliament, we find that in—

1542, Act 33, Henry VIII., regulated and encouraged archery for the defence of the kingdom, and an Act for "great Horses" was passed to oblige the breeding and keeping of them for the defence of the realm.

1547, Act 2, Edward VI., restricted the sale of horses, armour, and arms.

1549, Act 9, Edward VI., appointed Lords Lieutenant for Counties, for the organising and controlling of the forces, in place of Commissions of Array.

1553, Act 1, Mary I., repealed the Statute of Winchester, the arms, etc., which had become obsolete.

1557, Act 2, Mary I., defined the duties of Lords Lieutenant "To call musters of men, arms and horses; fine for absence forty shillings, prevention of false returns, making away with arms and arms, and power to deal with offences of Captains and petty Captains when assembled under Deputy Lieutenants, to appoint places of rendezvous, attend to the razing of the beacons, look to places where the enemy may land, break bridges, cut trenches, and throw down trees in the event of invasion," etc.

1558, by Act 5, Mary I., all temporal persons having estate of £100 or upwards were to keep six horses for demi-lances. Scott says, three of them at least with steel saddles and sufficient harness and weapons requisite for demi-lances, and ten light horses able for light horsemen, also certain armour—forty pikes, thirty long bows, thirty sheaves of arrows, thirty steel skulls, twenty black bills, classified according to incomes from one thousand marks down to possession of goods £10, etc., etc.

The Bill for Great Horses, 33, Henry VIII., was also repealed in this year.

1587—An Order in Council required Deputy Lieutenants "to especially supply horsemen for defence of the realm."

1588, Act 30, Elizabeth, granted power to impress men for the Militia and there was "the great muster to resist invasion by the Spanish Armada," with "abstract of the certificates returned from ye Lieuftenants of the able trayned and furneshed men in the severall Counties: upon letters from the Lordes reduced into bandes under Captaines, and howe they were soarted wt. weapones: in Aprille an dom 1588."—Harleian MS.S.

Sussex—
Ablemen	7572		Trained	2004
Sussex ffurnished	4000		untrained	2001

	untrained		Trained.		
Cat.	682		Cat.	360	
Musk.	237		Musk.	600	
Corst.	282	2001	Corst.	600	2004
Bowes	588		Bowes	180	
Bills	212		Billes	264	

	Launces	200
Horsemen	Lighthorse	204
	Petronells	30

Surrey—
Ablemen	8552		Trained	1522
Surrey ffurnished	1900		untrained	372

	Launces	8
Horsemen	Lighthorse	98
	Petronels	29

Berks.
Ablemen	3120		Trained	1000
Barkeshir ffurnished	1900		untrained	930

	Launces	10
Horsemen	Lighthorse	95
	Petronelles	2

Gloucs.—
Ablemen	14000		Trained	3000
Gloucestershire ffurnished	4000		untrained	1000

	Launces	20
Horsemen	Lighthorse	180
	Petronelles	35

Essex.—

Ablemen	6340	Trained	2000
Essex ffurnished	4000	untrained	2000

(No Horse—MS. torn away.)

Hants.—

Hampshire
Ablemen The Ld. Marquiss 4747 ffurnished 4037
Ablemen The Earl of Sussex 3944 ffurnished 2678

Trained	806
Untrained	1672

(No Horses given.)

Norf.—

Ablemen	6340	Trained	2200
Norfolk ffurnished	4400	Untrained	2000

Horsemen
{ Launces 80
Lighthorse 321
Petronells 374
Petronells of the Justices 53 }

Suff.—

Ablemen 4239 (No trained or untrained given)
Suffolk Total 3892
(No "ffurnished" given) (No Horse given)

Kent.—

Ablemen	10866	Trained	2958
Kent ffurnished	7124	Untrained	4166

Horsemen
{ Launces 64
Lighthorse 80
Petronell 84
Argolets 300 }

Lincs.—

Ablemen	6400	Trained	1500
Lincolne ffurnished	2150	Untrained	650

(No Horsemen given.)

THE CONSTITUTIONAL FORCE. 91

Lancs.—
    Lancashire ffurnished   1170

    Horsemen { Launces   20
                  { Lighthorse   50

Cheshire.—
    Cheshire ffurnished   2189

    Horsemen { Launces   30
                  { Lighthorse   50

Oxford—
    Ablemen   94564   Trained   1164
    Oxenford ffurnished   1144   Untrained   3400

    Horsemen { Launces   23
                  { Lighthorse   103
                  { Petroneles   32

Devon—
    Ablemen   10000   Trained   3661
    Devonsheire ffurnished   6200   Untrained   1650

    Horsemen { Launces—they find none but, instead, 200 muskets.
                  { Lighthorse   150
                  { Petroneles   50

Dorset—
    Dorsetshire   Trained 1500   Total 1359
                      Untrained 1800

    Horsemen { Launces   120
                  { Lighthorse   90
                  { Petroneles   40

Derby—
                             Trained   400
    Ablemen   1600
    Darbyshir ffurnished   600   Untrained   200
  besides 100 furnished for Ireland.

    Horsemen { Launces   18
                  { Lighthorse   50
                  { Petronele   12

THE CONSTITUTIONAL FORCE.

Staff.—
  Ablemen   1910   Trained   400
  Staffordshire
  ffurnished   100   Untrained   200

              Horsemen { Launces   28
                       { Lighthorse   50
                       { Petroneles   26

Cornwall—
  Ablemen   1760   Trained   1500
  Cornewall   Untrained   2100

              Horsemen { Lighthorse   96
                       { Launces   4
                       { Petronelles —

Hunts.—
  Huntingdon   Trained and untrained 400

                        (No Horse given.)

Bucks.—
  Ablemen   2850   Trained   600
  Buckingham
  ffurnished   600

              Horsemen { Launces   18
                       { Lighthorse   83
                       { Petroneles   20

Somerset—
  Ablemen   120000(sic)   Trained   4000
  Somersetsheir
  ffurnished   4000

              Horsemen { Launces   50
                       { Lighthorse 250
                       { Petroneles   60

Wilts
  Ablemen   7400   Trained   1200
  Wiltshire
  ffurnished   2400   Untrained   1200

              Horsemen { Launces   25
                       { Lighthorse 100
                       { Petronelles —

Cambridge—
- Ablemen 1000 Trained 500
- Cambridgscire
- ffurnished 1000 Untrained 500

Horsemen { Launces 50
Lighthorse 40
Petronelles 80 }

Northants.—
- Northampton Trained 600
- Untrained 600

Horsemen Launces 1900—00
Lighthorse 80

Notts—
- Ablemen 1800 Trained 400
- Nottingham
- ffurnished 1000 Untrained 600

(No Horse given.)

Herts—
- Ablemen 3000 Trained 1500
- Hertfordsheir
- ffurnished 3000 Untrained 1500

(No Horse given.)

Shrops.—
- Ablemen 1200 Trained 600
- Shropshire
- ffurnished 1200 Untrained 600

Horsemen { Launces 28
Lighthorse 165 (?)
(This is very faded and the number of petron. is quite gone.) }

Denbigh—
- Ablemen 1200 Trained 400
- Denbighe
- ffurnished 600 Untrained 200

Horsemen { Launces —
Lighthorse 30
Petroneles 30 }

Flint.—
- Flintsheire ffurnished 300
  - Trained 200
  - Untrained 100
  - Horsemen { Launces —; Lighthorse 30; Petronelles — }

Carmarthen—
- Ablemen 704
- Carmarden ffurnished 704
  - Trained 300
  - Untrained 404
  - Horsemen { Launces —; Lighthorse 15; Petronelles 10 }

Radnor—
- Ablemen 400
- Radnorshire ffurnished 400
  - Trained 200
  - Untrained 200

(MS. torn away) horse and petronelles.

Anglesey—
- Anglesey 1108 men.
  - Horsemen { Launces —; Lighthorse 17; Petroneles — }

Worcs.—
- Worcestershire Able and ffurnished 600
  - Trained 600
  - Horsemen { Launces 17; Lighthorse 83; Petroneles 10 }

Montgomery—
- Montgomery Furnished 600
  - Trained 300
  - Untrained 300
  - Horsemen { Launces 1; Lighthorse 19; Petronelles 30 }

THE CONSTITUTIONAL FORCE.

Pembroke.—
   Pembroke
   Ablemen and furnished 800   Untrained nos. not filled in.

Horsemen { Launces —
             Lighthorse —
             Petroneles 30

Middlesex—
   Middlesex
   Trained and furnished 10,000

Horsemen { Launces 19
             Lighthorse 65
             Petroneles —

Anno 1588 Certificate of the Forces of London. Whereof { AbleMen 20,000
                                         Armed 10,000
                                         Trained 6,000
                                         Untrained 4,000

Muskets 1000
Pikes 2000
Calivers 2400 } 6000
Bills 600

(Where Note appears in 2nd Abstract the MS. has faded and figures disappeared.)

"The abstracts of the nombers of evrie sorte of the armed men in the Counties through ye Kingdom." Taken ano 1588.

Counties	Ablemen	Armed	Trained	Untrained	Pioners	Launces	Lightors	Petronels
Sussex	7,572	4,000	2,000	2,000	50	20	204	30
Surrey	8,552	1,892	1,500	372	200	8	098	29
Barkshire	3,120	1,900	1,000	900	115	10	95	2
Oxenford	4,504	1,164	0,000	120	30	30	150	40
Gloucestre	14,000	4,000	3,000	1,000	300	20	180	35
Essex	0,000	4,000	2,000	2,000	600	50	200	00
Northampton	1,240	1,200	0,600	0,640	080	20	080	00
Southampton	0,000	2,478	0,806	1,672	1,000	00	000	00 374
Norfolke	0,000	4,400	2,300	2,100	0,000	80	082	055
Suffolke	0,000	4,239	2,000	2,239	0,000	80	230	084
Kente	18,866	7,124	2,958	4,166	1,077	70	230	000
Lanckeshire	0,000	1,170	1,170	0,000	0,000	64	265	000
Cheshire	0,000	2,189	2,189	0,000	0,000	20	050	091
Lincoln	6,400	2,150	1,500	0,650	0,630	30	050	037
Dorset	0,000	3,330	1,500	1,800	000	23	130	000

THE CONSTITUTIONAL FORCE.

Counties	Ablemen	Armed	Trained	Untrained	Pioners	Launces	Lighters	Petronels
Devonshire	10,000	6,200	3,660	2,550	600	120	000	022
Derbishire	1,600	1,000	0,400	0,600	060	000	150	026
Stafforde	1,900	1,000	0,400	0,600	100	008	050	020
Buckingham	2,850	0,600	0,600	0,000	600	008	050	000
Cornwalle	7,766	3,600	1,500	2,100	000	004	096	060
Somerset	2,000	4,000	4,000	0,000	1,000	050	250	060
Wiltshire	7,400	2,400	1,200	1,200	0,000	015	100	010
Cambridge	1,000	1,000	0,500	0,500	0,000	014	040	080
Huntingdon	0,000	0,400	0,400	0,000	0,009	019	065	000
Midds	0,000	1,000	0,500	0,500	0,000	020	060	000
Hertfordsh	0,000	3,000	1,500	1,500	0,200	020	060	000
Nottingham	2,800	1,000	0,400	0,600	100	020	060	020
London	17,883	10,000	6,000	4,000	000	000	000	020
Some Total of the English shirs	111,513	80,875	44,727	35,989	7,133	823	2,823	563

The Abstract of the nombers of everie sorte of the armed men in the marches of Wals and the Englishe shires annexed.

Salop		1,200	600	600	700	28	70	00
Denbyhe	1,200	0,600	400	200	160	00	30	100
Flintshire		0,300	200	100	200	00	03	030
Carmarden		0,704	300	400	300	00	15	10
Radnor	1 500	0,400	200	200	100	00	14	00
Anglesey		1,120	000	000	100	-	17	-
Worcestre		0,600	600	000	-	17	8-	-
Mongomery		0,600	300	300	050	01	19	30
- broke		0,800	800	8-	396	00	-	30
-		63-4	340	-	—6			
					48,147			

CHAPTER XII.

ACTS, WARRANTS, ETC., 1 JAMES I. TO 15.—CHARLES II.—ORDINANCE, PUTTING FORCE IN POSTURE OF DEFENCE.—ABOLITION OF FEUDAL SYSTEM AND TRAIN-BANDS.

In 1603, Act 1, James I, repealed the old Statutes of Armour, and abolished the keeping of arms. In future arms were to be lodged in stores.

1605, 3, James 1.—Muster of armed men throughout England and Wales, by virtue of Royal Commission dated Augt. 21 (taken from Military MSS., Royal United Service Institution. See Raikes' History, 1876.) Produced "16345 pyoners, 935 demi-lances, 6777 high horses besydes what the Noblemen, Earls, baronnes, lords, Abps., Bishops and prelatts of England can make, which is supposed to be about 20,000 armed Men and 4000 Horses."

1614, Act 11, James I., ordered a general muster of Horse and Foot after harvest time.

1615, Act 12, James 1., suspended the command of the Militia by Lords Lieutenant, and ordered a re-organisation of the Army, and a force to be raised having the character of Militia, but under the name of Train-Bands, intended to supersede the old county forces, and to be composed of 160,000 men between the ages of sixteen and sixty.

It would, however, appear from what took place in the following reign, and when the Civil War broke out, that the organization of the ancient Constitutional Forces of counties had continued for emergencies, and a nucleus was in existence for completion of the county regiments in 1641.

1625—Charles I. appointed a Committee or Corps of Armourers to repair arms, inspect magazines, etc.

1629 By Order in Council, "The Militia to be put on a better footing, Lords Lieutenant to fill up all vacancies for officers, muster horsemen with their arms, etc.," and Muster Masters were appointed "to keep the Train-Bands to their duty."

When we get near the middle of the 17th century the "Constitutional Force" appears to have entered upon twenty years of unrest, and passed through times of much importance in its history.

A Warrant issued by the King, May 15, 1640, indicates the state of the country, and duty which the people as soldiers were called upon to perform.

"To suppress, slay, kill destroy, and apprehend all such persons as should be tumultuously assembled," etc.

In 1641, Parliament found it necessary to prepare the Militia for eventualities, and on Feb. 12th we find, by Rushworth's "Historical Collections," fit persons appointed to be entrusted with the Militia for the several counties and places of England and Wales; whilst in 1642 an Ordinance was issued for forming the county forces into those associations of counties referred to by Gardiner and others as "separate armies," and bearing a remarkable resemblance to to the tribal divisions of early Britain, kingdoms of the Saxon age, and the more lately re-organised commands of the United Kingdom for all branches of the Army.

According to "Calender of State Papers Domestic" at this period and in following years, there were many votes and resolutions of Parliament affecting the strength, etc., of the Militia as being practically the only army of the country. We find remarkable efforts used to encourage its territorial usefulness for the supply of those required to bear arms—some counties "thanked for their forwardness in furnishing their proportions of the levies," others written to upon their "backwardness," and to some "urging expedition," etc.

At this time the committees of both kingdoms were actively controlling the county forces; for example, Aug. 16, 1644, there is the entry: "the 1000 men of Kent are to continue as a Regt.," and from what follows we obtain some information in respect of the separate armies of associated counties and how these were maintained. "The rest of the recruits of that Association of Counties are to go into the recruits, the charge to be proportionate to all the Counties." It would appear from this disposition of those levied that while these separate armies existed, the territorial organisation had become one of several counties, though the ancient county area was retained as convenient for collecting the levies.

There is also another entry, making it clear that Horse Militia formed part of those to be furnished, and that financial difficulties were not the military trouble of any particular age. Out of the £2,000 to be paid, "the Middlesex squadron of Horse to receive their three months arrears." It may be here stated that in 1648, when the fortifications of Farnham Castle were demolished, "the lead, iron, timber, and glass were taken by the Officers and Men of the Militia and sold, the proceeds being appropriated as part of the pay due to them.

In 1644 there is to be found in "King's Pamphlet, E. 193," an Ordinance dated Feb. 15th for the raising and maintaining of special forces for the defence of the kingdom under Sir Thomas Fairfax, Knight, as Commander-in-Chief, but as this appears to have been an additional force raised out of certain counties for service only during the continuance of the war, it did not affect the system which prevailed for providing the general army of Parliament.

The maintenance of this special army was "to bee Taxed, Leavied, and paid" by certain counties named, nineteen being included in the list for £53,386 0s. 6¼d. monthly while the war continued.

1648 produced another Ordinance which refers distinctly to the Militia, and we give it in detail from "King's Phamplet E 474":—

DIE SABBATHI, 2 DECEMB, 1648.

An Ordinance for the setling the Militia in the severall Counties, Cities, and places within the Kingdom of England, Dominion of Wales, and Towne of Berwick upon Tweed.

"The Lords and Commons Assembled in Parliament finding it necessary, that the Severall Counties of the Kingdoms of England and Dominion of Wales, and Towns of Berwick, be put into a posture of Defence, for the preservation and safety of the King, Parliament, and Kingdome; Do Ordaine, and be it hereby Ordained by the said Lords and Commons, That for the Setling of the Militia in the Kingdome and Dominion aforesaid, and Towne of Berwick, The persons hereafter named, shall be Commissioners for the severall Counties, Cities, and places for which they are hereby respectively appointed Commissioners:" [We omit the names of the Commissioners, but include the list of places as indicating those which presumably had Militia Forces at this date.]

"Bedford, Berks, Buckingham, City of Bristol, Cambridge and Isle of Ely, Chester, City of Chester, Cumberland, Cornewall, Darby, Dorset, Devon, City of Exeter, Dureme, Essex, Gloucester, City of Gloucester, Huntington, Hereford, Hartford, Kent and City and County of the City of Canterbury and Cinque Ports, Leicester, Lancaster, Lincolne, City of Lincolne.

Middlesex, Nottingham and Towne of Nottingham, Northampton, Norfolke, City of Norwich, Northumberland, Towne of Newcastle, Towne of Berwick upon Tweed, Oxford, Town and County of Poole, Rutland, County of Southampton, and Towne and County of Southampton, Sussex, Staffordshire and City of Litchfield, Shropshire, Surrey, Sommerset, Suffolke, Wilts, Warwick and for the City and County of the City of Coventry—Worcester, City of Worcester, Yorke, City of Yorke, Towne and County of Kingston upon Hull, City of Westminster, Hamlets of the Tower, Westmoreland, Carnarvon, Flynt, Merioneth, Montgomery, Radnor, Carmarthen, Denbigh, Pembrooke, Cardigan."

COPY OF ORDINANCE.

"The Commissioners shall severally and respectively have power to assemble and call together all and singular persons within the said respective Counties, Cities places, as well within Liberties, as without, that are meet and fit for the warres, and then to traine, exercies, and put in readinesse; or cause to be trained, exercised and put in readinesse; and them after their abilities and faculties to cause to be arranged and weaponed: and to take care, or cause to be taken, the muster of them in places most for for that purpose; and to lead, conduct and imploy, or cause to be led, conducted, and imployed, the persons aforesaid arrayed and weaponed, for the suppression of all Rebellions, Insurrections, and Invasions, that may happen within the severall and respective Counties, Cities and places. And shall have further power and authority to lead, conduct, and imploy, or cause to be led, conducted and imployed the persons aforesaid arrayed and weaponed, as well within their said severall Counties and places, as within any other part of this Kingdom of England, or Dominion of Wales, for the suppression of all Rebellions, Insurrections, and Invasions that may happen, according as they from time to time shall receive directions from the said Lords and Commons assembled in Parliament," etc.

And be it further ordered that the said respective Commissioners or any five or more of them shall hereby have full power and authority to assemble, muster, and array all such Horse 'nd Foot forces within the said respective Counties; and to forme and put them into Companies, Troopes and Regiments, and to nominate and appoint Colonels, Lieut. Colonels, Majors, Captaines, and other Officers of Warre, and to grant Commissions unto them under their Hands and Seales, authorising them respectively to traine and discipline according to order of Warre the respective Horse or Foot forces, and to lead and conduct them within the said respective counties; And with the said forces to oppose, seize, secure, disarme, kill and slay all such persons as shall raise or cause any tumults, insurrections, or invasions, or leavy any force against the Authority of Parliament, for the suppression thereof, according to such Orders as they shall from time to time receive from the said respective Commissioners, or any five or more of them, or from both Houses of Parliament, and to lead and conduct them out of the said respective Counties for the purposes aforesaid, if they shall be ordered and commanded by both houses of Parliament, and not otherwise.

And it is further ordained, That the said respective Commissioners in their generall meeting, or any seven or more of them, at the said generall meeting, shall hereby have full power and authority to charge and raise by way of assessment such summes of money for the providing magazines of Ammunition, and for defraying such other incident charges as shall be requisite for carrying on of the said Militia, and not otherwise. And in case of non payment of such summes which shall be so assessed, the same to leavy by way of distresse and sale of the goods of such as shall refuse or neglect to pay the same, rendring to the party the overplus of the said distresse if any be.

And be it further ordained, That the said respective Commissioners, or any five or more of them, hereby have full power and authority to impose a fine, not exceeding forty shillings, to be leavied as is aforesaid on every person who shall be charged to finde or serve on horse or dragoon; and 20 shillings on every foot souldier for every day that they shall make default of their aforesaid service; the said fines to be imployed towards the provision of Arms and Ammunition for the severall Counties Cities, and places respectively, where or in the several defaults shall be made, or to imprison their persons by the space of ten dayes and not longer; unlesse such just and reasonable cause shall be shewed to them, for which they shall think fit to remit the said penalty, And also the said respective Commissioners or any five or more of them, shall hereby have full power and authority to disarme all Papists and Delinquents, and all such as shall raise or cause, or endeavour to raise or cause any tumults, insurrections, or invasions; and to secure and imprison their persons, for the prevention and suppression thereof, if they shall find it needful so to doe; And to put the Armes of Papists and Delinquents into the hands of such well-affected persons as they shall think fit; And to cause all such, who being charged with any Armes, shall refuse to serve in their own persons, or whom the said respective Commissioners, or any five or more of them shall think not fit to serve in their own persons, to deliver such armes as shall be charged on them to such persons as the said respective Commissioners or any five or more of them shall think fit to serve with the said Armes: And to cause them to pay to such as shall so serve with their Arms such reasonable sallary as they shall think fit and appoint, not exceeding the respective Proportions aforesaid: And for default of payment thereof to levy the same as is aforesaid, or to imprison their persons as is aforesaid if they shall find it needful so to doe.

And it is further ordained by the said Lords and Commons, That if any person or persons shall find him, or themselves agrieved at any Assessment set on him or them as aforesaid, and shall make complaint thereof, within six days after demand made of the money assessed, the said Commissioners, or any two of them shall have hereby power and authority, to relieve such person or persons so agrieved, if they shall find upon examination just cause so to doe; And also the said Colonels, Lieutenant Colonels, Majors, Captaines and other Officers and persons, whom the said Commissioners shall employ in the said service, shall bee obedient and assistant to them in the execution of this Ordinance, And what they or any other persons whatsoever, shall act or doe according to this Ordinance, or in pursuance thereof, they shall be saved harmelesse, and indempnified for the same by authority of Parliament.

And it is ordained, That all and every the said Comisssioners, and all such Colonels, Lieutenant Colonels, Majors, Captaines, and Officers of Warre, whom they shall nominate and appoint, shall before they enter upon the execution of their said respective Offices and trusts, take the national League and Covenant, whereby their good affection to the Parliament and Kingdome may appear, and that they may thereby be engaged to pursue the same; provided that all persons whatsoever, who have beene in Armes since these late Wars against the Parliament and Kingdome, or have voluntarily contributed Money, Horse, Plate, or Armes against the Parliament or their adherents, and all persons who have not voluntarily contributed money, Horse, Plate, or Armes, for the service of the Parliament or Kingdome, or who have not constantly adhered to the same, from the beginning of the late Wars, be and are hereby disabled to act, or execute anything in or by this Ordinance, either as Commissioners, or as Commissioned Officers under them. Provided that no Commissioner in this Ordinance named for a County shall act by vertue hereof, unlesse hee have an Estate in the said County, chargeable with an Horse and Arms, at the least, by vertue of this Ordinance; so as this extend not to the Commissioners named for Cities, and Counties of Cities, or to such Corporations, who have distinct Militia's setled by this Ordinance.

And be it ordained by the said Lords and Commons, And it is hereby ordered and ordained, That no person or persons, whatsoever, shall raise or keepe up any of her Forces of Horse or Foot, or in other way or manner than is directed and appointed by this Ordinance, unlesse he or they shall have order and direction for the same from both Houses of Parliament; or shall erect, make, hold or keep up any Garrison or Garrisons in any County, City or place within the Kingdome of England, or Dominion of Wales, but by the authority aforesaid; provided, That this clause or anything therein contained, shall not extend to the Forces under the command of Thomas Lord Fairefax, according to the present establishment of the Army, not to any Garrison or Garrisons, which shall be recovered, or taken from the enemy; provided further, that nothing herein contained, shall extend to the disbanding of any Forces now raised by both, or either House of Parliament, or by authority, order, or direction from them, or either of them.

And it is also ordered and ordained, That the Forces lately raised by Commissioners in the severall Counties, and to be raised by vertue of this Ordinance, shall be ordered, directed, and disposed by the respective Commissioners in the respective Counties, Cities, and places aforesaid; provided also and be it ordained, That this Ordinance shall continue for one whole yeare, from the twentieth day of September, 1648, and no longer.

Jo. Browne, Cler. Parliamentorum."

We obtain from this Ordinance a great insight into the regulations affecting the "Constitutional Force" at this date.

In 1650 there was an Act placing the Militia of each County under Commissioners, subject to the Council of the

State and with very great powers. This system continued during the Commonwealth, and according to all historians the Force was maintained in a highly efficient state. Officers were required to possess a property qualification.

In 1651 the Commissioners were authorised to impress ten thousand men for service in Ireland.

With the restoration of King Charles II. we again enter an important epoch in the history of the Force.

In 1660 the days of the worn-out Feudal system, which had been practically out of use for some centuries, and altogether in abeyance during the Commonwealth, was abolished. King Charles II., recognising the principle and expansive value of the ancient force representing the people, caused it to be re-organised and made efficient for the future purposes of his kingdom, when forming a standing branch of the Army.

The Train-Bands (except London) were abolished in 1663, and the King interested himself in the Militia of Scotland. All writers are agreed that Acts 13, 14, 15, Charles II., furnished the basis upon which the "Constitutional Force" rested until 1757—though at periods during those years allowed to be in a state of "repose." It must, however, for all time be interesting to look back upon some of the provisions, etc., of those Acts which more immediately touched the force and people. We find, according to Act 13, Chas. II., from Statutes of the Realm, that

"THE SOLE RIGHT OF THE MILITIA WAS IN THE KING,"

"Forasmuch as within all his Majesty's realms and dominions, the sole and supreme power, government, command and disposition of the Militia, and of all forces by sea and land, and all forts and places of strength is, and by the laws of England ever was, the undoubted right of his Majesty, and his royal predecessors, kings and queens of England; (2) and that both or either of the houses of parliament cannot nor ought to pretend to the same; nor can lawfully raise or levy any war offensive or defensive against his Majesty, his heirs or lawful successors; and yet the contrary thereof hath of late years been practised, almost to the ruin and destruction of this kingdom; and during the late usurped governments, many evil and rebellious principles have been instilled into the minds of the people of this kingdom, which may break forth, unless prevented, to the disturbance of the peace and the quiet thereof."

Among the provisions of this Act were:

"The Militia and land Forces to be exercised as usual; Lords-Lieutenant, Deputy Lieutenants, Magistrates, etc., who had been acting under their powers during the Civil War were to be indemnified; the over charges of counties for military purposes adjusted; subjects not to be compelled to serve out of the Kingdom; and Lords Lieutenant, their Deputies, and Officers, had to take the oath of allegiance and supremacy," etc.

Act 14, Charles II., was passed:

"FOR ORDERING THE FORCES IN THE SEVERAL COUNTIES OF THIS KINGDOM."

Recited "that the government of the Militia is in the King," etc., "The King to issue Commissions of Lieutenancy, who were empowered to grant Commissions to Officers, etc., with power to the King to displace them.

Persons not having £100 per Annum Real, or £1200 of Personal Estate not liable to find Horsemen.

In case of Invasion, etc., soldiers to be furnished with one month's pay in advance. Lieutenants authorised to inflict fines up to 5s. or up to twenty days Impt. in the case of soldiers not doing their duty. Persons not appearing to serve imprisonment for five days or a penalty. Horseman not exceeding 20s., Footman, 10s. Power to the King to raise £70,000 monthly in one year, and so on for three years in case of apparent danger, to be levied by Lieutenants of Counties.

Persons allowed to find substitutes and substitutes required to serve. Persons listed deserting, or being exchanged, or quitting the service without leave. Penalty £20, and if no Distress Imprisonment not exceeding Three months.

Subjects exempted from marching out of the Kingdom.

By Act 15, Charles II.

"FOR THE BETTER ORDERING OF THE FORCES IN THE SEVERAL COUNTIES OF THIS KINGDOM."

We learn that "Every soldier enlisted was required to pay not exceeding one shilling if a Horseman, 6d. for a Footman, to the Muster Master of the County. Lieutenants and Deputies were to summon and continue trained Forces on Duty as long as convenient, in lieu of the days appointed by the Statute 14, Chas. II., and may be so kept for fourteen days. Lieutenants and Deputies were to dispose of the Fourth Part of the month's assessment amongst inferior Officers, etc., etc.

CHAPTER XIII.

MILITIA OF SCOTLAND, 1661.—ORIGIN OF FORCE.—ARCHERY.—WAPPENSCHAWING, ETC.

With reference to the action taken by the Sovereign to organise the Militia of Scotland, we are indebted to the well-known authority, Mr. A. Ross, of Edinburgh (through Colonel Menzies) for information extracted from the Parliamentary History of Scotland, which explains very concisely the re-organisation of the ancient force of the country.

"Letter from King Charles II. to the Estates of Parliament dated from Whitehall 10th June, 1661, addressed to the Lord High Commissioner the Earl of Middleton."

"We send you a list of those whom wee think fit to intrust with the Militia in our severall counties of that our Kingdom both for horse and foot, leaving to you to proportion the numbers, and wee desire a draught of such a commission as shall be convenient to be given to every one of them, wee have also thought fitt to intrust you with the command of them as our general and have sent you a warrant for a commission to be past our great seale."

In November 23, 1663, "the numbers of the Militia were settled at 20,000 foot and 2000 horse to be raised in the proportions set down in the Act for service within the three kingdoms."

November 16, 1669.—"The constitution of the Militia, scale of pay, limits of time, and places of service etc. were settled."

May 8, 1685, an Act was passed obliging persons to accept office laid on them, under which it was enacted, "that if any of His Majesty's subjects within this his ancient Kingdom shall refuse to be an Officer in the Militia, etc., laid on them by the King or Council, they shall be fined."

June 4, 1685.—"Our Sovereigne Lord with the consent of his estates of Parliament considering that it may be for the ease of the people to have the ordinary rendezvous of the Militia discharged unless extraordinary occasions should otherwise require therefore they discharge all rendezvous of the Militia in all times coming during His Majestie's Royall Pleasure, and until his pleasure be so declared that no leaders nor assistants shall be lyable for furnishing or contributing to buy or maintain horse or foot on that account; and they recommend to the Secret council to take such courses for disposing of the Militia arms in the respective Shyres as shall seem most expedient for his Majesty's service wt prejudice alway's of the continuance of the former and present constitution of the Militia during the present rebellion."

March 18, 1689.—"The Committee for securing the peace of the Kingdom is recommended to select officers for the Militia of the Shires and the Militia to be in readiness for securing the Protestant religion and the laws and liberties of the Kingdom."

The following curious Warrant was granted May 3, 1689: "The Committee of Estates doe grant warrant to the Commissionars of Militia in the Shyre of Berwick to quarter upon the persons appoynted by them who are deficient in the outreick of the eighteen horses and one halfe appoynted by the Act of the Estates to be raised by that Shyre."

With regard to the origin of the Militia Force of Scotland, there are numerous evidences in history that for years anterior to 1661 bodies of local troops existed which were akin to the Militia of later times, and out of which armies were formed. It will have been noticed that in 1661 His Majesty expressed himself as if a Militia force existed.

According to early Scottish history, the national forces were territorial in character. Colonel Thos. Innes, in his History of the Royal Aberdeenshire Highlanders Militia, replete with interesting references to the forces of his country in far back centuries, says, "names have changed and the forms of weapons in the progress of military art, but in substance the levying, embodying, drilling, and preparation for service is much the same as in the days of the Stuarts; we can recognise in early corps the lineal predecessors which territorial regiments now represent."

It appears that from remote periods the Sovereign was empowered by Statutes to require all persons between sixteen and sixty years of age to be ready furnished with proper arms according to their condition in life, and prepared to march with so many days' provisions whenever wanted.

In 1424, James I., the value of a man's estate, rent or goods, regulated the available military strength of the country, and it was ordained "that all men busk themselves to be archers frae they be twelve years of age," and "there be bow-marks specially near to the paroche Kirks," the penalty for non-attendance at archerie being a sheep. "If the laird did not raise the said paine the Scheriff or his ministers should raise it to the King."

"Wappenschawing" took place in each shire four times a year, all who came being enrolled for service with the "manner of their arms," and captains were chosen in each parish by the Sheriff, the King's Commissioner, to muster their companies on holydays before noon.

We find that in early times the clans of the Highland districts rendered service under traditions of their own, they gave their services to the Sovereign only as it pleased their chieftain to require, whilst in the Lowlands the forces furnished to the Crown were mostly under the Feudal tenure system—estates being held subject to providing for the military requirements of the King. In 1643 and 1647 changes were made. In the latter year there was a regularly organised and paid force in the character of that which had previously existed during wars, an organised reserve force being also available to suppress intestine commotion, repel invasion, and recruit the paid branch of the Army, all fencible persons being divided into regiments, foot companies, and horse troops. The shires provided arms and ammunition.

In 1649, Feb. 28, the Estates of Parliament "ordain the whole shires and burghs within the kingdom to raise and put out" the quotas for each county—the total number being 13,400 foot and 5,440 horse.

In 1650, the numbers and proportions were changed to 18,514 foot and 2,581 horse.

After the restoration of King Charles II., the proceedings of the Scottish Parliament, and strength, etc., of the Force have been already referred to.

James II. suspended the trainings of the Militia in Scotland. In 1797, under an Act of the British Parliament, 6,000 men were to be raised, and the Militia Force re-organised on the basis of the Militia Acts of England, the numbers being increased to 8,000 in 1802, with power to raise 4,000 supplementary men in case of invasion, etc. Volunteering from the modern Scottish Militia to the Line on occasions of grave emergency began in 1805, with the same patriotic result obtained in other parts of the Kingdom. Since 1802 the quota of men to be found by counties, and strength of regiments in later times, have been determined by the exigency of the times and Parliament.

CHAPTER XIV.

MILITIA TAX 14, CHAS. II.—LEVY OF MEN FOR FOREIGN WAR.—MILITIA OF WALES.—RAISING MILITIA, 6 WILLIAM AND MARY.—MILITIA RETURNS, 1697, ETC.

Reverting to the Militia Tax clause of Act 14, Chas. II., in respect of the £70,000 in a year that might be levied by the Sovereign, "State Papers Domestic" contain copy of a letter dated January 29, 1664, from King Charles to Lords Lieutenant, which somewhat clearly records the character and extent of service attaching to the Militia obligation at that period, and the continued connection of Sheriffs with the Force.

"The plots and conspiracies of the last year compelled its raising, and the experience of another year proves that the restless spirits who have been pardoned excite fresh disorders and require the often summoning of the Militia, they are therefore required to raise £70,000 for one month, etc., and paid to the Sheriffs of Counties by them to be disbursed for the said purposes only." From a further entry, the country being engaged in foreign war and requiring aid, we gain some knowledge of the method adopted for maintaining the forces required.

"A competent number of men are to be levied out of the divers Countries of our realm, voluntarily or by press, making choice of those that are able and sufficient for the wars, and the arms being extraordinary instead of apparel and arms, to levy after the rate of £3 10s. a man, whereof 40s. for apparel and 30s. for arms."

1684—Charles II., in the attention given to the Force at this date it is recorded that to allay the public feeling which prevailed, the King undertook to withdraw all commissions held by Papists, and in this same year we find, according to Dinsley's "Account of the Progress of His Grace the Duke of Beaufort through Wales," some details of the strength and organisation of the Militia in Wales.

The Militia of Denbighshire consisteth of 5 Companies of Foot and one Troop of Horse, commanded by Sir Richard Middleton as Captain.

The Militia of Flintshire consisteth of 5 Companies of Foot, Sir Roger Mostyn, Bart., Captain.

The Militia of Caernarvonshire consisteth of three companies of Foot and one Troop of Horse.

The Militia Foot of Caernarvonshire form three compleat Companies.

The Militia of Isle of Anglesey consist of one Troop of Horse, commanded by Bulkeley, Esq.; as Captain And four Companyes of Foot.

The Militia of Merionethshire consists of one small Troop of Horse, commanded by . . . . as Captain. And two Companies of Foot.

Wednesday, Aug. 6, 1684. His Grace the Duke of Beaufort, accompanied with the Earle of Worcester, Sir John Talbot, and other persons of quality, took a view of the Militia of this County (Brecknock) in a meadow near the Town, where they were drawn up to exercise, and made several close and laudable Fireings.

It consists of one Troop, commanded by a Captain, Lieutenant, Cornet, and Quartermaster; and 5 Companies of Foot, commanded by a Colonel, Captains, Lieutenants, and Ensigns.

The Militia of Caermarden County consists of one Troop of Horse, and one Regiment of Foot, consisting of . . . Companies, commanded by Sir Rice Williams, as Colonel.

The Militia of Cardiganshire, consisted of one Troop of Horse, commanded by . . . . and three Companies of Foot.

The Militia of Penbrokeshire, which made their parade August the 11th, 1684, in . . . . near Haverford West, before his Grace the Duke of Beaufort, were one Troop of Horse, consisting of . . . men, commanded by . . . . Captain, ... Lieutenant, . . . Cornet, ... Quartermaster—And one Regiment all of Firelocks, commanded by . . . . . Colonel, ... Lieutenant-Col., ... Major.

The Militia of Glamorganshire, maketh one Regiment of Foot, consisting of . . . . Companies, commanded by the Right Honourable Charles Earle of Worcester as Colonell, - . . . . as Lieutenant-Col. . . . as Major, ... Captains . . . . Lieutenants, ... Ensigns.

And one Troop of Horse, commanded by the Right Honourable the Lord Arthur, second son to his Grace the Duke of Beaufort, as Captain; Sir Richard Basset as Lieutenant; . . . . . as Cornet; . . . . as Quartermaster.

Monmouthshire Militia maketh one Regiment of Foot, commanded by the Right Honourable Charles Earl of Worcester as Colonel; . . . as Lieut.-Col.; . . . . as Major.

And one Troop of Horse, commanded by the sayd, Earl of Worcester, son and heir-apparent to his Grace the Duke of Beaufort.

1685.—James II.—We learn from a debate in the House of Commons that Local Forces received careful consideration, and that fearing a renewal of Papacy, great excitement prevailing, the Militia was called out and warned to be ready for active service.

The Articles of War by King James have already been referred to, and the lenient spirit in which they were framed.

1695—Act 6, William and Mary, "for raising the Militia of the Kingdom for the year."

This Statute gives such a remarkably clear insight into the system which had prevailed since 13. 14 Charles II., and the organisation provided for in 1695, together with the method of payment of such troops, that an epitome of the Act is given from "the Statutes at Large."

"Whereas by an act of parliament, made in the thirteenth and fourteenth years of the reign of his late majesty King Charles the Second, instituted, An act ordering the forces in the several counties of this kingdom, it was (amongst other things) enacted, That in case of invasions, insurrections, or rebellions, whereby occasion should be to draw out the soldiers mentioned and appointed in and by the said act into actual service, the persons charged by the said act with horses, horsemen, and arms, should provide each their soldier respectively with pay in hand not exceeding one month's pay, as should be in that behalf directed by the respective lieutenants of the several counties, and in their absence, or otherwise by their direction, by their deputies, or any two or more of them: For repayment of which said monies, and for satisfaction of the officers for their pay during such time, not exceeding one month, as aforesaid, as they should be with their soldiers in such actual service, it was thereby declared, that provision should be made for the same by his said Majesty, his heirs and successors, out of his or their public treasury or revenue: Nevertheless it was thereby further provided and advanced, as aforesaid, that no person who should have advanced his proportion thereof, should be charged with any other like month's payment, until he or they should have been reimbursed the said month's pay, and so from time to time, the said month's pay by him or them last before provided and advanced, as aforesaid: And whereas upon the invasion of the coasts of this kingdom by the French it was found necessary, for the public defence and safety, to draw out the said soldiers into actual service, and to charge the said persons to provide each their soldier respectively with pay in hand, although the month's pay, by several of them before that time provided and advanced, was not, nor could be, reimbursed: And whereas the like occasion may possibly happen during the present war:

Power given to raise the Militia notwithstanding the month's pay formerly advanced be not paid

II. Be it therefore enacted by the King's most excellent majesty, by and with the advice and consent of the lords spiritual and temporal, and the commons, in this present parliament assembled, and by the authority of the same. That if at any time before the five and twentieth day of April, which shall be in the year of our Lord one thousand six hundred ninety and six, it shall be found by his Majesty for the defence and safety of this kingdom, to draw out the said soldiers into actual service, and the same shall be declared or signified to the respective lieutenants or deputy lieutenants, and the lord warden of the cinque-ports, two ancient towns and their members, or in his absence his lieutenant or lieutenants, in pursuance of such orders from his Majesty, notwithstanding that one or more months' pay, before that time advanced, be not reimbursed, to raise and draw out the said soldiers into actual service, and to cause the persons charged as aforesaid to provide each their soldier with pay in hand, not exceeding one month's pay, in such manner as if all the pay before that time advanced and provided had been fully reimbursed and paid. E.X.P."

1697—By an Act, the Regular Forces were reduced, and the Constitutional Force to be made more useful by re-organization, regular trainings, etc.

The "Militia Returns" of 1697, from Egerton's MSS., are given in detail, as being reliable information upon the strength, etc., of Regiments in those Counties which find a place in these valuable documents.

COUNTY OF BERKS.—The Duke of Norfolk, Lrd. Lieut.

	No. of Men.
Coll., The Duke of Norfolke.	
Lieut. Coll., Paul Coulston, Esqr., 10 Comp.	977
Capt. Lieut., Edmund Sayer, Esqr., 3 Troops	175
	1152

COUNTY OF BEDFORD.—Duke of Bedford, Lord Lieut.

Horse, 2 Troops—Sir Rowland Alston, Barrt., Capt.	119
Foot one Regiment in 5 Companys } Edw. Lord Russell, Coll. Sir John Burgoyne, Bart., Lieut. Coll.	420
	539

Returns.

The Militia is in good condition.

The Lord Stafford has an Estate of 400 per ann. not charged. The Lord Ashburnham was charged formerly for a Horse for Brogborough Parke and part of a horse for Beckerings Parke. His Lordp. has since purchased in a Lease of Great Parke from ye Executors of ye E. of Alesbury worth about 400 p. ann. He now furnishes but one horse therefore we conceive him uncharged for Beckerings park and Great parke, both about 700 p. ann.

The Earle of Kent about 10 years since purchased at Clophill about £300 for wch he is not charged.

The Countess Dowager of Kent by the old Muster Rolls stands charged with 4 horses. She now sends only 3 and wee hear she has made Several Purchases since she was first charged.

Great part of the Estate late the Lady Wentworths being formerly in the hands of Mr. Wild and other Morgagees of the late E. of Cleveland and now in the possession of Sr. Robt. Howard & Mr. Northee is not charged so the whole of that Estate being about £2000 p ann. finds but one horse.

Wee conjecture some other Estates are not charged of which we have not due information.

COUNTY OF BUCKINGHAM.—The Earle of Bridgewater, Lord Lieut.

One Regiment of Foot ⎫ William Cheyne Esqr. Coll.
  in 10 Companys   ⎭ Roger Chapman Esqr. Coll.   820
Horse 3 Troops   Sr. Denis Hampson Bart. Capt. 177
                                            997

Returns.

That having informed themselves as well as they could by consulting the Muster Book and otherwise they could not find out any Estates chargeable towards the Militia that were not charged, except my Lord Montagues Estate at Winwood. That all the Arms were good at the last muster in 1695.

COUNTY OF CUMBERLAND AND WESTMORELAND. The Earle of Carlisle Lord Lieut.

One Regiment of Foot⎫ Sir Daniel Fleming Kt. Lt. Coll. 537
  in 7 Companys   ⎭ Sir George Fletcher Bart. Coll.
Horse one Troop   ...Andrew Huddleston Esqr. Capt. 70
                                            607

COUNTY OF CHESTER.—The Earle of Rivers Lord Lieut.

Totl. of the Regiment⎫ Earle of Rivers Coll
  in 7 Companys   ⎭ Samuel Daniel Lt. Col.   ...929
Horse 2 Troops   ...Sir Thomas Belloe Capt.   ...104
City of Chester one foot company 120
                                          1153

Returns.

That this County is high charged to the Militia.

The reason is that when Charles Earle of Derby and William Ld. Brereton were in joint Com Lord Lieuts. by reason of some contention betwixt themselves this County was raised to a higher charge proportionately to others and has continued so ever since.

Near 20 of the Horse are provided and sent in by Papists and Nonjurors.

That the Militia of the City of Chester wants regulating wch. Company was antiently under the Command of the Coll. of the County Regiment.

The Lord Huntingdon has lands in the County in right of his wife, but refuses to send in the men usually charged on the lands till he be charged by his Peers.

They know not of any lands besides in the County that are uncharged to the Militia.

COUNTY OF CAMBRIDGE AND ISLE OF ELY.—The Duke of Bedford Lord Lieut.

5 Companys foot	677
3 Troops of Horse. William Sayer, Esqr. Capt.	151
	828

Returns.

That the Militia is in the condition it used to bee.

They know of no others excused in the County which by Law are chargeable, but the Clergy, who have always been excused.

In the Isle of Ely the Militia are full and in good order.

The Lords Torrington, Sidney and Effingham are charged to Horse, but refuse to pay by reason they are not assest by their Peers.

CO. DEVON.—The E. of Stamford, Ld. Lieut.

Six Regiments

Col. Earl of Stamford	7 Companies	710	men
,, Sr. Francis Drake, Bart.	6 ,,	860	,,
,, Sr. Wm. Davy	8 ,,	840	,,
,, Sr. Walter Yonge, Bart.	8 ,,	850	,,
,, Saml. Roll, Esqr.	6 ,,	800	,,
,, John Arscott	6 ,,	860	,,
		4920	,,
3 Troops Horse Capt. Sir John Ellwill		236	
		5156	,,

DARTMOUTH INDEPENDENT COMPY.—Capt. John Whitson, 60 horse.

Exeter Regiment.—

Col. ... Earle of Stamford ... 8 Companies ... 480 men

Dissenting Ministers } not charged for Personal Estate.
Church Clergy ...

Church Clergy not charged for their Spiritual Estates, but for their Temporall.

Councellors at Law ⎫ residing within this City, not charg'd
Drs. of Physick ... ⎭ for Personal Estate.

Plymouth Regiment.—
Major—Mayor ... ... 5 Companies 467

The number of Militia within this Town may bee more or less as the number and Quality of the Inhabitants may bee; for Persons are Assessed in Towns as heretofore and not strictly for Estates; viz. one Man's arms £50 p ann or £600 Personal Estate. If soe one Quarter of this Number could not bee assess'd.

Total No. of Companies 55 ... Total No. of men ... 5927
„ Troops 3 „ horse ... 236
                                                    ─────
                                            Total   6163

MILITIA IN CO. OF DERBY.—D. of Devonshire, Ld. Lieut.
Capt ... Henry Heveningham 140 horse ... 2 troops
   No Coll. mentioned.
Capt. John Adderley ... ... 130 men
  „ Ralph   „   ...   ... 140 „
  „ John Every   ...   ... 130 „
  „ Henry Gill   ...   ... 124 „
                           ─────
   Total of Foot ... ... 524 „
       „ Horse 140
                         ─────
              Total   664

Returns.

That they are not able to give the Account required of the said Persons and Estates, there having been no Survey taken of them these 30 years last past, since when several Estates have been alienated, some of which have been sold by those chargeable with Foot to those chargeable with Horse, by reason whereof the Foot have been lost and no encrease made of the Horse. And some sold by those chargeable with Horse, to others chargeable with the Like, and no Surcharge upon the Purchaser for the same, to supply such Share and Proportion with which the Seller was charged, which has reduced the Militia to a less number and occasioned great disorders both in the Troops and Companies, which they say Cannot be reformed without a new Survey of the Estates chargeable.

MILITIA IN CO. OF ESSEX.—Earl of Oxford, Ld. Lieut.

The Blew Regt. of Foot.

Col. ... Evan Loyd ... ... 8 Companies ... 1004 men

3 Regiments of Foot out of this Regimt. 90 men are to be detach'd as Grenadiers.

The E. of Oxford's Regt. of Foot.

Col. ... Earl of Oxford ... 8 Companies ... 1130 men

The Green Regt.

Col. ... ———— ... ... 8 ,, ... 936 ,,

Total 3070 ,,

Horse 4 Troops.

Four Troops Capt. Sir Francis Nasham, Bart. 250 horse
           Men 3070

Total of Both 3320

Returns.

That they had formerly taken such care to charge the whole County, that they can find no Estate uncharged save that wch. the E. of Montagu holds in right of the Duchess of Albermarle, and hath not been charged since the Duke's decease who was Lord Lt. of the County; and wch. they cannot meddle with he being a Peer.

MILITIA IN CO. GLOUCESTER.—Lord Dursly, Ld. Lieut.

Col. ... Ld. Dursley ... ... 6 Troops ... 243 Horse

White Regt. of Foot.

Col. ... Sir John Guise ...10 Companies ... 583 Men

Green Regt. of Foot.

Col. ... Sir Ralph Dutton, Bart. 8 Companies ... 534 ,,

Blew Regt. of Foot.

Col. ... Sir Tho: Stephens ... 9 ,, ... 551 ,,

Red Regt. of Foot.

Col. ... Maynard Colchester ... 9 ,, ... 531 ,,

Total of Men 2199
,, Horse 243

,, Both 2442

THE CONSTITUTIONAL FORCE.

Returns.

Noblemen not charged.—
Duke of Beaufort ...2000 p ann in Majr. Codrington's troop
Earle of Essex ...1000 ,, Lt. Col. Barker's ,,
Ld. Weymouth ...1200 ,, ,, ,, ,,
Lord Brooke ... 600 ,, Capt. Carter's ,,

MILITIA IN CITY OF BRISTOL.—Ld. Dursley, Ld. Lieut.

Coll. ... Charles Bartley, Esqr. 10 Companies ... 727 Men

MILITIA IN CO. HERTFORD.—E. of Essex, Ld. Lieut.

Col. ... Earl of Essex ... 10 Companies ... 1025 Men
   Horse 3 Troops
Capt. Henry Gore, Esqr. ... 1 Troop ... ... 60 Horse
,, John Charlton, Esqr. ... ,, ... 62 ,,
,, Gilbert Hookate, Esqr. ,, ... 61 ,,

                      Total of Horse 183
                      ,, Foot 1025

                      ,, Both 1208

Returns.

Peers of the Realm chargeable for Horse in the said County and not yett charged.
   In Capt. Gore's Troop.—
E. of Portland... 4
E. of Salisbury 1
Bp. of London 1
   In Capt. Charlton's Troop.—
E. of Bridgewater 1
E. of Essex 3
Marq. of Carmarthen ... 3
   In Capt. Keates Troop—
E. of Salisbury ... ... 5 } Total 19.
D. of Bedford 1

MILITIA IN CO. HUNTINGDON.—Ld. Lieut., E. of Manchester.

Horse 1 troop Capt. Heneage Montague Esqr. ... 72 Horse
Col. Robt. Apreece Esqr. ... 5 Companies ...390 Men

                  Total of both ...462

Returns of the Deputy Lieut.—
   Earle of Montague not charged for his Estate at Coppingford and Winwick of 300 £ p ann.

Lord Rockingham not charged for his Estate at **Great Gidding** and **Lutton** of 600£ p ann and upwards.

MILITIA IN CO. KENT.—Earl of Romney Ld. Lieut.

Regt. of the Lath of Sutton at Hone.

Col. Sr. Stephen Leonard, Bart.	6 companies	614 men
	1 troop	55 horse

Regt of the Lath of St. Augustine.

Col., Henry Oxenden, Esqr. ...	7 companies	705 men
	1 troop	56 horse

City of Canterbury.

Col., Henry Lee, Esqr.	... 4 companies	303 men

Regt. of the Lath of Aylesford.

Col., Sir Philip Boteler, Bart. ...	7 companies	785 men
	1 troop	70 horse

Regt. of the Lath of Shipway.

Col., Sir Wm. Honywood, Bart.	7 companies	669 men
	1 troop	50 horse

Regt. of the Lath of Scray.

Col., Sir Francis Head	... 6 companies	474 men
Total	...37 ,,	3550 men
,, ...	... 4 troops	231 horse
,, of both ...	3781	

Returns.

Lath of Sutton at Hone.

We believe all are charged that are by Law chargeable, the Peers and Nobility excepted.

Lath of St. Augustin.

Wee know not of any persons here uncharged except the Peers of the Realme.

Lath of Aylesford.

All persons estates within this Lath are moderately charged according to the Act of Parliament and know of none that are not charged except the Peers.

Lath of Shipway.

We certify that all estates of Deputy Lieuts. except officers, and all other Persons except Peers of the Realm by Law chargeable, are duly charged.

Lath of Scray.

To return an Account of Defaulters and what their Estates ought to find is impossible, the dep. Lts. not having mett to hear defaulters of this Regt.; this 5 or 6 years, by wch reason it is allmost a 3d. part less than it was.

MILITIA IN E. AND W. PORTS OF CINQUE PORTS.—E. of Rumney Ld. Warden.

Eastern Ports.—(Sandwich, Ramsgate (St. John Bapt. and St. Peter's), Fordwick and Feversham).

Col., Vice Admirall Alymer ... 8 companies   866 men

Western Ports.—(Dover Towne, Dover peere, Folkstone, Hyth, Romney, Tenterden, Lydd, Rye, Winchelsea, Hasting, Peavensy, Seaford).

Col., The Hon. Sr. Basil Dixwell	12 companies	1092 men
Eastern Reg.		866
Total of both		1958

MILITIA IN CO. PALATÍNE OF LANCASHIRE.—E. of Macclesfield, Ld. Lieut.

Col., Earl of Maclesfelld	... 8 companies	548	men
Col., Roger Kirkby ...	... 8 companies	592	,,
Col., Sir Ralph Ashton	... 6 companies	461	,,
		1601	,,
	3 troops	150	horse
	Total of both	1751	

MILITIA IN CO. LEICESTER.—Earl of Rutland, Ld. Lieut.

Col., John, Ld. Roos ...	... 3 troops	175	horse
Col., Richard Lister ...	...6 companies	609	men
	Total of both	784	

Returns.

The Militia of this County is in a very good posture and condition, and so appeared to us at the last Generall Muster. And wee believe there are no persons or Estates chargeable, but what are charged, except some of the Peers in this County.

The Peers who have estates in this County and shew horses in the Militia are the D. of Devonshire, my Ld. Ferrars, my Ld. Jeffreys, and yr. Lordpp.

There are some other Peers who never showed a Horse since my Lrd. yr ffather or your Lordp. were Lord Lieuts.

MILITIA IN CO. LINCOLN.—Earl of Lindsey, Ld. Lieut.

For the Parts of Kesteven.
Col., E. of Lindsey ...	... 3 companies	384 men
Capt., E. of Lindsey ...	... 1 troop	94 horse
	Total of Both	482 (sic)

For the Parts of Holland.
Major, Reuben Parke ...	... 4 companies	435 men
Capt., Sir John Oldfield	... 1 troop	86 horse
	Total of both	521

In Lindsey Coast.
Col., Charles Dymocke Champion of England	} 8 companies	545 men
Capt., Sir Edw. Asycough	... 1 troop	62 horse
Capt., Matthew Lister ...	... 1 troop	91 horse
		153 ,,
	Total of both	698

Total of all Foot	1494
Horse	333
	1827

Returns.

For Kesteven and Holland.
They know of no Estates but what are charged.
For Lindsey Coast.
Not having had any Muster nor the Weeks tax raised this 6 years must of necessity be much out of order.

MILITIA IN CITY OF LONDON.—Lord Mayor, etc.

Orange Regiment.—
Col., Sr. Robert Clayton	... 8 companies	1221 men

White Regiment.—
Col., Sr. Wm. Ashurst	... 8 companies	1412 ,,

Green Regt.—
Col., Sr. Wm. Hedges ... 8 companies 964 ,,
Yalow Regt.—
Col., Sr. Thos. Stamp ... ... 8 companies 989 men
Red Regt.—
Col., Sir Thomas Lane ... ... 8 companies 1046 men
Blew Regt.—
Col., Sir Owen Buckingham ... 8 companies 1130 ,,

Total ... ...48 companies 6770 ,,

Returns.

We humbly represent That all the Six Regts. of Train'd Bands of the City, are very well compleated, and in good condition, all able men and well appointed, and of great affection to his Maty. and the Government.

Edward Clarke ... Lord Mayor.

MILITIA IN CO. MIDDLESEX.—D. of Bedford, Ld. Lieut.
County Regt.—
Col., Rd. Shoreditch, Esq. ... 6 companies 603 men
Red Regt.—
Col., The Hon. Phillip Howard 10 companies 1400 ,,
Esqr.
Blew Regt.—
Col., John Bond Esqr ... ...10 companies 1358 ,,

26 companies 3361 ,,

County Troop.—
Capt., Sr. Chas. Gerrard, Bart. 1 troop 85 horse
Westminster Troop.—
Capt., Anthony Rowe, Esqr. ... 1 troop 46 horse
2 troop 131 horse

Total of Both 3492

Defaulters ... ...County Regt. 46
Red Regt. 177
Blew Regt. 205

(sic) 423

Peers charged with Horse wh. do not send.—
D. of Norfolk   Ld. Brodnall
D. of Beaufort   E. of Peterborough

D. of Grafton	E. of Dorset
E. of Falconbridge	E. of Suffolk
Ld. Willoughby	Lady Bellasis
E. of Leicester	D. of Ormond
E. of Craven	D. of Newcastle
E. of Montague	E. of Berkeley
Lady Arlington	Ld. Osullton
D. of Somerset	E. of Salisbury
D. of Devonshire	E. of Essex.
Mary of Normandy	E. of Radnor
Ld. Wharton	E. of Gainsborough

MILITIA IN CO. NOTTINGHAM.—D. of Newcastle, Ld. Lieut.

Col., John, D. of Newcastle	6 companies	400 private soldiers
Capt., Sr. Scroope Howe	1 troop	60 horse
Capt., Rd. Taylor	1 troop	120 horse
		400 foot
	Total of both	520

Returns.

The Lieutenancy being very small there are few Persons and Estates within the same, but what are charged towards the Militia as the Law directs. But care shall be taken, that such as are not now Contributors to the Militia shall be charged, as soon as the Deputy Lts. who are Members of Parliament return from the session.

MILITIA IN CO. NORFOLK.—D. of Norfolk, Ld. Lieut.

Blew Regiment. ?

Col., Sir Jacob Ashley, knt.	7 companies	817 men

Yellow Regt.—

Col., Robert Walpole, Esq.	7 companies	734 men

Purple Regt.—

Col., Edmund Wodehouse	7 companies	826 men

White Regt.—

Col., Sr. Richard Berney	7 companies	688 men

Lynn Regis.—

1. Capt., Sr. John Turner, Kt.	2 companies	250 men

Yarmouth.—

1. Capt., John Robbins	4 companies	536 men

Norwich.—

Col., Duke of Norfolk ...	... 6 companies	681 men
Col., Duke of Norfolk ...	... 6 companies	335 horse
	Total of Foot	4532
	Total of both	4867

Returns.

The Estates are charged as the Law directs.

MILITIA IN CO. OXFORD.—Earl of Abingdon, Ld. Lieut.

Col., Ld. Norreys	... 8 companies	742 effective private men
Capt., Henry Bertie	... 1 troop	130
	Total of both	872

Returns.

The Militia within this Lieutenancy are in as good a Condition as the Militia is capable off, and may in a little time be made very fitt for service, whenever his Mats. hath occasion. And I doe not know of any Estates in the County that ought to be Contributory to the Militia, which are not charged either to Horse or Foot.

MILITIA IN RUTLAND.—Lord Sherard, Ld. Lieut.

Capt., Millesburne Sill, Esqr. ...	1 company	93 men
Capt., Bennet Sherard ...	.. 1 troop	53 men
	Total of both	146

Returns.

All Estates in the County are charged to the full.

MILITIA IN CO. STAFFORD.—Ld. Pagett, Ld. Lieut.

Capt., — Ward ...	... 5 companies	500 men
Capt., — Lane ...	... 1 troop	60 horse
Capt., — Kinnersly ...	... 1 troop	60 horse
		120
	Total of both	620

Returns.

They know of none but what are either Finders, Maintainers or Contributors to Horse or Foot.

MILITIA IN CO. SALOP.—E. of Bradford, Ld. Lieut.

Col., E. of Bradford ...	... 8 companies	1050 men
Capt., Rd. Corbet ...	... 1 troop	40 horse
Capt., Rogr. Owen ...	... 1 troop	42 horse
Wm. Fosbroock—Provt. Marchl.		82 horse
Rd. Cromton—Muster Mar.	Total of both	1132

Returns.

When the Militia was first settled in ye County of Salop after King Charles his Resturation severall Farms, part of Gentlemen's Estates were leased out to tennants for Lives, and were charged towards ye Maintenance of Foot and ye Tenants contributed accordingly, while their Landlords at the same time were charged for their Demesnes and rackd Lands to the finding of horse; since which time severall of those Farms having falne out of lease the owners have taken from contributing to the foot, by vertue of a Clause in ye Āct for ye Militia which said that noe person shall bee charged with the finding both of horse and foot in ye same County, by which means ye Foot have been much lessened, and the Estates are falne out of Lease not all charg'd; but upon a review of ye settlement of ye Militia in a little time will bee. These are all the estates that are uncharged in that County except that of the Lord Jeffreys which hath bin of late years purchased there.

The souldiers are for the most part well clothed and their arms are in good order.

MILITIA IN CO. SOMERSET.—D. of Ormond, Ld. Lieut.

Bridgewater Troop.—		
Col., Nathaniel Palmer ...	... 1 troop	51 horse
Wells Troop.—		
Lt. Col., John Hunt ...	... 1 troop	55 horse
Bathe Troop.—		
Major., Edw. Baker ...	... 1 troop	55 horse
Crewkorne Troop.—		
Capt., Wm. Hilliard ...	... 1 troop	55 horse

Taunton Troop.—
Capt., ——   ... ... 1 troop   53 horse
                         ─────   ─────
                         5 troops   269 men

Bridgewater Regt. out of 8 Hundreds.
Col., Sr. John Trevillian   ... 8 companies   724 men
Wells Regt. out of 8 Hundreds.
Col., Edward Berkeley ...   ... 8 companies   726 men
Bathe Regt. out of 8 Hundreds.
Col., ——   ... ... 8 companies   547 men
Crewkhorne Regt. out of 9 Hundreds.
Col., Namy Henly   ...   ... 8 companies   787 men
Taunton Regt. out of 9 Hundreds.
Col., Sr. Fr. Warr   ...   ... 8 companies   650 men
                                             ─────
                                             3434 men
Regt. of Horse 5 troops   269 men
                                             ─────
Total of both   3703

Returns.

That to the best of their knowledge there are none at present chargeable to the Militia of this County by Law but who are charged to the same, ffor they do not believe the parishes out of which the men comes will hardly sufferr their neighbours to escape scot free and they to bear the Burthen.

MILITIA IN CO. SUSSEX.—Earl of Dorset, Ld. Lieut.

Eastern Part.—
Col., Sr. William Thomas   ... 9 companies   830 men
Western Part.—
Col., Sir John Fagg, Bart.   ...10 companies   783 men
Chichester Co.—
Capt., Rd. Torrington ...   ... 1 company   120 men
                                             ─────
                                             1733 men
Capt., John Morske   ...   ... 1 troop   55 horse
Capt., John Miller   ...   ... 1 troop   50 horse
                                             ─────
                                             105
Total of Foot 1733

Total of both   1838

Returns.

As to the Militia in the 3 Western Rapes, they know of no Persons or lands but what are charged unless it be the lands of officers in the Militia.

Sir Wm. Thomas says the Number of his Regiment is much lessned wch. is occasioned by the increase of Horse.

MILITIA IN CO. SUFFOLK.—Ld. Cornwallis, Ld. Lieut.

Red Regt.—

Col., Anthony Crofts	... 6 companies	460 men including officers
White Regt.—		
Col., Sir Phillip Parker	... 7 companies	509 men
Blew Regt.		
Late Col., Sir Phillip Skipton	... 8 companies	657 men
Yellow Regt.—		
Col., Sir Thos. Bernardiston	... 8 companies	660 men
Ipswich.—		
Capts., Manning and Neeves	... 2 companies	181 men
	31 companies	2467 men
Col., Ld. Cornwallis ...	... 4 troops	208 horse
	Total of both	2675

Returns.

This is according to the Muster roll in 1692, since which time they have not been call'd together.

MILITIA IN CO. SURREY.—D. of Norfolk, Ld. Lieut.

Col., D. of Norfolk ...	... 9 companies	1209 men
The D. of Norfolk's Troop.—		
Capt. Lt., Sigismond Stidolfe	... 2 troops	132 horse
Militia of Southwark.—		
Col., D. of Norfolk	... 6 companies	910 men
	Total of Foot	2119 men
	Total of Horse	132
	Total of Both	2251

Persons having estates in the Burrough or Precincts yt do not find to foot, under pretence that they furnish Horse in the County, viz.

	p ann		p ann
E. of Salisbury	1600	Mrs. Howland	300
D. of Albermarle	2000	John Hether, sen., Esqr.	600
Sr. Henry Blunt	1000	John Hether, junr.	400
Sr. Robert Clayton	600	John Bennet	600

MILITIA IN CO. SOUTHAMPTON.—D. of Bolton, Ld. Lieut.

Col., Duke of Bolton	6 companies	366 men
Col., Marqs. of Winchester	6 companies	435 men
Col., Henry Compton	6 companies	399 men
Col., ( )	5 companies	371 men
Capt., Duke of Bolton	2 troops	120 horse
Col., George Rodney Bridges	6 companies	448 men
Col., Henry Dawley	5 companies	440 men

Winchester Independent Co.

Capt., Ld. Wm. Paulet	1 company	150 men

Southampton Independent Co.

Capt., John Smith, Esqr	1 company	200 men
	Total of Foot	2809
	Total of Horse	120
	Total of Both	2929

Returns.

They assure that all Person's Estates within the County, which by Law are chargeable are already charged to Horse or Foot.

MILITIA IN THE ISLE OF WIGHT.—Ld. Cutts, Governor.

East Meaden Regt.—

		Files	Spare men
Col., Ld. Cutts	8 companies	732	70
	Both	802	

West Meaden Regt.—

Col., David Urry	8 companies	750	104

Independent Co. a Cowes.

Lt., Joseph Burton	1 company	16	96
	Total No. in the Files		1578
	Total No. of Spare men		174
			1752

Returns.

All the Militia are well arm'd and fitt for service.

The Men call'd Spare men are such as attend the Feild pieces, and take the arms from any of the listed Men, when dead or superannuated.

There are no other persons chargeable towards the Militia, this being the Antient Constitution of this Island, and is preserved to them by an Act of Parliament made in the 13th and 14th of King Charles the Second Entit. An Act for ordering the forces in the severall Counties of this Kingdom.

MILITIA IN CO. WARWICK.—E. of Northampton, Ld. Lieut.

Col., Sir Charles Shuckbury ...	6 companies	585 men
Capt., Sir Wm. Underhill ...	3 troops	174 horse
Coventry	1 company	40 men
,, ...	1 troop	7 horse
Total of Foot ...	7 companies	625
Total of Horse ...	4 troops	181
Total of both		806

Returns.

The Estates they find are charged as the Law requires them, having been lately another troop added; it being thought more for his Matys. service to have 3 troops of Horse in the County than 2 as formerly.

The Militia of Coventry consists of 40 foot and 7 horse, wch. as there is occasion is to be joined with the County of Warwick.

MILITIA IN CO. WILTS.—E. of Pembroke, Ld. Lieut.

Red Regt.—Sarum Division.

Col., Sr. Thos. Nampesson ...	6 companies	543 men

Blew Regt.—Marlebrough Division.

Col., Edward Webb	6 companies	749 men

Greene Regt.—Devizes Division.

Col., Henry Chivers	6 companies	514 men

Yellow Regt.—Warminster Division.

Col., Henry Bainton	4 companies	432 men

Company of New Sarum.

Capt., George Clement, Esqr....	1 company	128 men
	23 companies	2366 men

Col., Thos. Penruddock ... 4 troops   232 horse
                    Total of foot   2366

                    Total of both   2598

Returns.

That they always take care to full charge every body.

MILITIA IN CO. AND CITY OF WORCESTER.—D. of Shrewsbury, Ld. Lieut.

Capt., Ld. Herbert of Cherbury. 2 troops   120 horse
Col., D. of Shrewsbury ... ... 7 companies   786 men

                    Total of both   906

Returns.

All persons within the County chargeable are charged.
At the last Muster they appeared full and in good Order.

MILITIA IN N. RIDING CO. YORK.—D. of Leeds, Ld. Lieut.

Richmondsh. Regt.
Sr. Chr. Wandesford, Col. ... 7 companies   326 men
Cleeveland Regt.
Sr. Thos. Pennyman, Col. ... 6 companies   300 men
Bulmer Regt.
Late Coll., Sr. Bar. Bourcher ... 5 companies   276 men
Bulmer Troop.
Capt., Sr. Wm. Robinson ... 1 troop   56 horse
Cleeveland Troop.
Capt., Sr. Wm. Hulster ... 1 troop   57 horse
Richmondshire Troop.
Capt., John Hutton, Esqr. ... 1 troop   62 horse

   Total of Horse   ... 2 troops   172 (sic)
   Total of Foot   ...18 companies   903

   Total of Both   1077

Returns.

This is a true list of the Militia within our riding according as they were last mustered. Wee know of none not charged to the Militia, except the Peers, who are not chargeable by us.

MILITIA IN E. RIDING, CO. YORKS.—D. of Leeds, Ld. Lieut.

Col., Marqs. of Carmarthen ...	8 companies	679 men
Capt. Sir Rd. Osbaddeston, Knt.	2 troops	128 horse
	Total of Both	807

Returns.

They were mustered in May (96) and appeared in very good Order, and now that they are Impowered to receive their contributions, we cannot doubt of their entire obedience whenever his Matys service shall require it.

The Lord Howard and the Countess of Winchelsey have each of them £500 p ann in the East Riding, but have not for many years past sent their horses.

MILITIA IN W. RIDING CO. YORK.—D. of Leeds, Ld. Lieut.

Col., Ld. Fairfax	6 companies	544 men
Col., Sir Henry Goodrick, Bart.	6 companies	528 men
Col. (dead) Sir Mich. Wentworth Knt.	6 companies	520 men
Col., Marqs. of Carmarthen ...	7 companies	520 men

This is the City of Yorke Regiment. 4 companyes whereof 2112 men are raised in the city and 3 in the Ayncitty, and encrease and decrease according to the Number of the Inhabitants.

Capt., Thos. Ld. Fairfax	3 troops	213 horse
	Total of Foot	2112
	Total of Both	2325

Duke of Norfolk
Duke of Devonshire
Ld. Archbp. of York
E. of Strafford
E. of Scarsdale
E. of Huntingdon

E. of Thanett
E. of Bridgewater
E. of Holdernesse
Ld. Visct. Wharton
Ld. Visct. Lonsdale

These Lords not having been of late charged by their Peers, do not send in their Horse.

Duke of Someset ...	1	E. of Burlington ...	... 2
Mary of Hallifax ...	4	E. of Radnor ...	... 3

These usually send in their number of Horse.

THE CONSTITUTIONAL FORCE.

Returns.

Upon the last charge and since, the number of Horse has been advanced, by reason whereof, the Number of Foot has been something diminished, and upon that alteration there are severall small estates within the severall weapentakes of the West Riding which did contribute to Foot, and are at present uncharged. The Deputy Lts. of the parts aforesaid reserving them to supply such Persons, as upon complaint shall be adjudged to be Overcharged.

MILITIA IN N. WALES.—E. of Macclesfield, Ld. Lieut.

Montgomery.—
Col., Sr. John Price, Bart.	1 company	364 men
Horse—Capt., Matthew Price, Esqr.		56
		420

Denbigh.—
Col., E. of Macclesfield	1 company	500
Horse—Capt., John Doulben		62
		562

Flint.
Col. Sir Roger Puleston	1 company	250 men
Horse Capt. Owen Barton		25
		275

Merioneth and Carnarvon.
Col. Hugh Nanny, Esqr.	1 Company	530
Horse Capt. Symon Lloyd, Esqr.		48
		578

Anglesey.
Col. ... Arthur Owen, Esqr.	1 company	250
Horse Capt. John Hill, Esqr.		26
		276

Total of Foot	1894
,, Horse	217
,, Both	2111

THE CONSTITUTIONAL FORCE.

MILITIA IN MONMOUTHSHIRE AND S. WALES.—E. of Pembroke, Ld. Lieut.

Monmouth.
Col. Sir John Williams, Bart.	7 companies	490
Capt. Nicholas Arnold	1 troop	55
		545

Glamorgan.
Col. ... Sir Edward Mansel, Bart....	9 companies	483
Capt. ... Martin Button	1 troop	40
		523

Carmarthen.
Col. Rowland Gwyn, Esqr.	341 men
Capt. Thos. Cornwallis, Esqr.	40
	381

Cardigan.
Col. Lord Lisburn	142 men
Capt. John Lewis, Esqr.	60
	202

Pembroke.
Col. Sr. Thos. Stepney, Bart.	456
Capt. Arthur Owen, Esqr.	36
	492

Brecknock and Radnor.
Col. Edw. Price, Esqr.	505
Capt. Sir Edw. Williams	48
	553

Total of Foot	1927
,, Horse	224
,, Both	2151

Returns.

The Deputy Lieuts. of the severall Countys return, that they allways take care to full charge every body as the Law directs.

Militia of the Tower Hamlets.—Ld. Lucas, Govr.

Tower Hamlets.
1st Regt.
Col. ... Lord Lucas ... ... ———
2nd Regt.
Col. ... Sir Henry Johnson ... ... ———

Lord Lucas having perused the Lists of each Captain in these two Regiments, finds he may modestly and safely engage and promise his Majesty—2000—able and effective Men duly qualified and fitt to serve him on any occasion.

CHAPTER XV.

ACTS AND ORDERS, 1698 TO 1786.

In 1698, by Order of the House of Commons, regularly paid troops were further reduced, and in 1699 regulations were introduced to improve the Militia.

In 1704 there was an Act for drawing out the Militia in 1705, and it is recorded that the month's pay advanced for the previous year had not been repaid to counties. There was also an Act to prevent mutiny, desertion, and false returns, and an Act for the paying and clothing of the Militia.

1714, Act Geo. 1. abolished armour for horses, and made some change in arms. etc., the most remarkable being the introduction of muskets for infantry with barrels five feet in length, and bayonets, Lords Lieutenant at a later date being authorised to determine the length to be issued convenient in their respective commands.

Grose has it that at first bayonets were only used by Cavalry and Grenadiers.

In 1755—28, Geo. II.—an Act was passed to embody the Militia in case of Colonial as well as domestic rebellion.

It would appear that between 1714 and 1755 votes were only taken for the Militia in 1734 and 1745, and we are therefore unable to trace what strength and state of efficiency were relied on by Parliament in 1755 to satisfy this possible call to render service.

In 1756 there came the great revival initiated by Pitt, which resulted in the passing of an Act—30, Geo. II.—in 1757 for "The better ordering of the Militia Forces in the several counties of that part of Great Britain called England."

The Preamble explains in forcible language the urgent necessity for this addition to the Statute Book.

"WHEREAS A WELL-ORDERED AND WELL-DISCIPLINED MILITIA IS ESSENTIALLY NECESSARY TO THE SAFETY, PEACE, AND PROSPERITY OF THIS KINGDOM," Etc.

As this Act marked another re-organisation in the history of the ancient Force of the People, resulting in services rendered which were of vast import to the nation, we are constrained to record somewhat fully the provisions made by the Act for producing that expansiveness and efficiency which reflected the value of this great power of the country.

We find the Lords Lieutenant of Counties again empowered to organise and assemble their forces, and the chief command reposed in them. Deputy Lieuts. and Colonels were to have incomes of £400 per annum, or be heirs to twice that amount; Lt.-Colonels and Majors £300; Captains £200; Lieutenants £100; and Ensigns £50 per annum; whilst officers might be promoted for merit on extraordinary occasions, but none higher than Captains. Power was reserved to the King to displace officers at his pleasure. A certain number of officers were to be discharged at the end of each four years.

An adjutant from the King's Forces was appointed to each regiment, and Sergeants out of the Army, who were to be entitled to the benefits of Chelsea Hospital.

Alehouse keepers, etc., were disqualified from being Sergeants.

The number of private men to be raised in each County was defined.

Three officers were allowed to 80 private men, and constables made returns of all men between the ages of 18 and 50 years who were liable to serve. Deputy Lieutenants settled the lists of those able to serve, and caused them to be chosen by lot.

Persons chosen were enrolled for three years, or provided fit substitutes.

Persons refusing to serve were fined £10, and at the end of three years liable to serve again.

Dep. Lieuts. met occasionally, and on the Tuesday before Michaelmas to grant discharges to those entitled, and to fill up by lot all vacancies.

Persons changing their residence to give previous notice to the Dep. Lieut. or be liable to fine of 20s.

No substitute to be excused from serving.

Private men serving for themselves exempted from several duties and offices.

Those serving for three years were liable to serve again in rotation.

If Quakers chosen refused to serve or provide substitutes, Dep. Lieuts. were to provide same and levy the expense by distress.

Sundays not to be used as days for exercise.

If the numbers raised were insufficient to be regimented, they were to be formed into battalions, and in both cases exercised for four days in Witsun week annually.

Smaller bodies to be exercised as shall be thought fit by the Lord Lieutenant.

(It will be noticed by these two provisions that the importance of "all the year round" company exercise was recognised, and the exercise in larger bodies confined to four days in each year.)

Commissioned Officers were to attend the exercise of companies and half companies.

Captains had charge of the arms and clothes, etc., of their companies, churchwardens providing chests.

Names of men absent from exercise were reported to a Justice, who might fine for the first offence 2s., and for the second offence 6s.; whilst drunk on duty forfeited 10s.; and disobedience, 1st offence 2s. 6d., 2nd 5s., and for the third and every other offence, 40s.

Selling, pawning or losing arms, clothes, etc., carried a forfeit of £3, and for neglecting to return them smaller fines.

The absence from annual meeting entailed a fine of 10s. per diem, whilst N.C. Officers neligent, disobedient or insolent forfeited any sum not exceeding 30s.

We find at this period the first use of the letter "M" applied to the Force.

Muskets were to be so marked, and the name of County, etc.

In case of invasion or rebellion, etc., the King had power to draw out and embody the Militia and put them under the command of General Officers, and they were to receive like pay as the King's Forces, be subject to like rules and articles of war, and, being maimed or wounded, equally entitled to Chelsea Hospital.

Private men not appearing or refusing to march to forfeit £40.

Officers and Private men, when called out to their annual exercise, to be quartered on public-houses, etc.

Militia not liable to march out of the Kingdom.

Fines and penalties not otherwise provided for, to be paid to the Clerk of the Regiment and made a common stock, to be applied in erecting butts, providing powder and ball, and in prizes to the best workmen, etc., etc.

NUMBERS TO BE FURNISHED BY COUNTIES.

Bedford.—Four hundred.
Berks.—Five hundred and sixty.

Cambridge.—Four hundred and eighty.
Chester, with the city and county of Chester.—Five hundred and sixty.
Cornwall.—Six hundred and forty.
Cumberland.—Three hundred and twenty.
Derby.—Five hundred and sixty.
Devon, with the city and county of the city of Exeter.—One thousand and six hundred.
Dorset, with the town and county of the town of Poole.—Six hundred and forty.
Durham.—Four hundred.
Essex.—Nine hundred and sixty.
Gloucester, with the city and county of the city of Gloucester, and the city and county of the city of Bristol.—Nine hundred and sixty.
Hereford. Four hundred and eighty.
Hertford.—Five hundred and sixty.
Huntingdon.—Three hundred and twenty.
Kent, with the city and county of the city of Canterbury.—Nine hundred and sixty.
Lancaster.—Eight hundred.
Leicester.—Five hundred and sixty.
Lincoln, with the city and county of the city of Lincoln.—One thousand two hundred.
For the Tower Division in the County of Middlesex, commonly called the Tower Hamlets.—One thousand one hundred and sixty. And for the rest of the County of Middlesex.—One thousand six hundred.
Monmouth.—Two hundred and forty.
Norfolk, with the city and county of the city of Norwich. Nine hundred and sixty.
Northampton.—Six hundred and forty.
Northumberland, with the town and county of the town of Newcastle-upon-Tyne, and the town of Berwick.—Five hundred and sixty.
Nottingham, with the town and county of the town of Nottingham.—Four hundred and eighty.
Oxford.—Five hundred and sixty.
Rutland.—One hundred and twenty.
Salop.—Six hundred and forty.
Somerset.—Eight hundred and forty.
Southampton, with the town and county of the town of Southampton.—Nine hundred and sixty.
Stafford, with the city and county of the city of Litchfield.—Five hundred and sixty.

Suffolk.—Nine hundred and sixty.
Surrey.—Eight hundred.
Sussex.—Eight hundred.
Warwick, with the city and county of the city of Coventry.—Six hundred and forty.
Westmoreland.—Two hundred and forty.
Worcester, with the city and county of the city of Worcester.—Five hundred and sixty.
Wilts.—Eight hundred.
For the West Riding of the County of York, with the city and county of the city of York.—One thousand two hundred and forty.
For the North Riding of the said county.—Seven hundred and twenty.
For the East Riding of the said county, with the town and county of the town of Kingston upon Hull.—Four hundred.
Anglesea.—Eighty.
Brecknock.—One hundred and sixty.
Cardigan.—One hundred and twenty.
Carmarthen, with the county borough of Carmarthen.—Two hundred.
Carnarvon.—Eighty.
Denbigh.—Two hundred and eighty.
Flint.—One hundred and twenty.
Glamorgan.—Three hundred and sixty.
Merioneth.—Eighty.
Montgomery.—Two hundred and forty.
Pembroke, with the town and county of the town of Haverford West.—One hundred and sixty.
Radnor.—One hundred and twenty.

1758 produced an explanatory Act—31, Geo. II. An epitome of the Preamble is given from "The Statutes At Large," together with those clauses which materially concern the Force and People.

"An act to explain, amend, and enforce an act made in the last session of parliament, intituled, An Act for the better ordering of the militia forces in the several counties of that part of Great Britain called England."

PREAMBLE.

Whereas several doubts have arisen, and difficulties have occurred, in carrying into execution an act passed in the last session of parliament, intituled, An act for the better ordering of the Militia forces in the several counties of that part of

Great Britain called England: and whereas it has been found, that some farther provisions are necessary, in order to enforce the execution of the said act; be it therefore enacted by the King's most excellent majesty, etc., etc.

Direction to appoint the officers of the militia before the second meeting of the deputy lieutenants in their subdivisions.

Repeal of the clause in the former act prescribing that there shall not be more than 3 officers to 80 private men, and so in proportion.

Power to captains to appoint corporals and drummers, and displace them; and, with the approbation of the lieutenants, to appoint serjeants out of the militia-men to fill up vacancies; and the colonel or commanding officer of the battalion may, upon complaint to the captain, remove such serjeants.

Where commissions have not been issued, or accepted of, the lieutenant to advertise a meeting of persons qualified and willing to act as officers in the Militia fo rthat county or place; where they are to deliver in their names, and rank they are willing to serve in; and if at such meeting, or within one month after, a sufficient number of persons duly qualified shall not be found to accept commissions, the lieutenant is, by like public notice, to suspend all further proceeding, till March following, when like summons and notice is to be given, and the provisions in the former and this act, are then to be carried into full execution.

The names of persons intended for officers are to be certified to his Majesty, before the commissions be granted them; and if he shall signify, within a month, his disapprobation of any such, no commission is to be granted to such persons.

Lists of the inhabitants between 18 and 50 years of age, distinguishing each person, to be made by Constables to the Deputy Lieutenant.

Copy of the list to be affixed on the door of the church on the Sunday before the return is made.

Deputy lieutenants, assisted by the justice on the day of the returns, after hearing particular grievances, are to amend the lists; and the number of men of each hundred, etc., is to furnish is to be ascertained, and such number is to be chosen by lot, out of the said lists. A meeting is then to be appointed to be held within three weeks after, and orders issued for summoning the men chosen to appear thereat; the men to appear accordingly, and be sworn and inrolled, to serve 3 years; or provide proper substitutes; who are to be sworn, and sign on the roll their consent to serve for the said term; on penalty of £10, and being liable to serve at the end of 3 years.

Persons that are free of the waterman's company not liable to serve.

Deputy lieutenants and parish officers to be continued in the lists, and liable to serve.

Deputy lieutenants are annually to transmit to the lieutenant true copies of the roll for their respective subdivisions; and a general meeting for forming and ordering the militia, to be held within three weeks after.

The lists of two or more parishes may be united, and proceeded on, as if they had been returned for one parish.

Parishes may offer, and deputy lieutenants may accept volunteers; in which case, so many men only as shall be wanting of the quota of such parish are to be chosen by lot of the lists.

If such volunteers shall not appear at the next meeting, and serve; the church-wardens are to find other persons to serve in their stead, or forfeit £10 a man.

Application of the penalty, churchwardens to be reimbursed the same out of the poor rate.

The oath; to be administered by the deputy lieutenant.

Discharges may be granted, and vacancies filled up, at any meeting of the deputy lieutenants in their subdivisions.

A vacancy upon the death of a substitute; or his entering into the King's service; or upon his promotion in the militia; or upon his discharge for just cause; to be filled up by lot.

The privy council upon receiving the corrected lists ordered to be transmitted to them, are to settle the quota of men to serve for each country, according to the proportion the returns for each county bear to the whole number to be raised throughout the kingdom; and are forthwith to transmit accounts of the numbers so settled, to the respective lieutenants; and if the number shall be greater than was required by the former act, a general meeting is to be held, and the additional men are to be then chosen by lot; and if less, a proportional number is to be discharged by lot.

Where the number to be raised in any county, shall be unequally or erroneously apportioned, amongst the hundreds or divisions thereof, the lieutenant and deputy lieutenants are to make a new and more equal distribution; and raise, and discharge men conformable thereto.

Persons tampering with constables to make false returns, or to erase the name of any person out of their lists, forfeit £50.

Militia men exempted from statute work; and from serving any parish office; and from being pressed into the King's service; and substitutes, having been in active service, are equally entitled, with Militia men to retain their regimentals at the end of three years' service.

Militia man falling sick on a march, or at the place of annual service, is to be provided for by an order from the magistrate, or justice of the place; and the expense thereof to be reimbursed by his proper parish.

Every militia man to receive one guinea upon being ordered out into actual service.

Weekly allowance to be made to the distress'd families of militia men in actual service which is to be reimbursed out of the county stock.

Fines for not serving to be applied in providing substitute in such person's room.

Surplus to go into the regimental stock.

The exercise in half and whole companies not confined to Monday, and the day left open to be appointed as shall be found best for the service; so as the men be exercised in half companies recited.

The lieutenants may change the exercise from two days in a harvest month, to the Tuesday and Wednesday in Easter week.

Militia men to be furnished where they are quartered at a certain rate, viz.

Subalterns at 1s. and private men at 4d. per diem.

Power to the captain, when the militia is called into actual service, to augment his company with volunteers, with the consent of the lieutenant.

A commission officer being a justice of the peace, may upon his own view, punish a militia man guilty of any offence punishable by the recited act.

Lieutenant of the Tower impowered to appoint deputy lieutenants, and grant commissions, and regiment the militia of the said hamlets, as the Act of 13 and 14 Car. 2. directs; and raise trophy money for defraying incident charges; and appoint a treasurer of the said monies, who is to account yearly upon oath.

The said accounts to be certified to the justices at their sessions; and no warrant to be issued for raising trophy money, till the preceding year's accounts are settled.

Provisions etc. in the recited act with respect to Co. Northumberland, extended to Berwick upon Tweed and the number of men to be chosen by lot to serve for the said town, to be in proportion to the number appointed for the other hundreds, etc., within the said county.

Clause in the recited act relative to the militia in the isle of Purbeck repealed; and the militia thereof for the future to be in proportion to the number appointed for the other hundreds, etc. in the county of Dorset."

1760.—By Royal Warrant Court of St. James's, December Seventeenth, "Twelve pence out of every shilling to be contributed by the embodied militia to the support of Chelsea Hospital."

1761.—Act. 2, Geo. III., authorised Parish officials, subject to the approval of two Deputy Lieutenants, to select volunteers instead of taking men by ballot. No articled clerk, apprentice or poor man with three children, etc., to be compelled to serve. Age 18 to 45 for three years' service, and penalty £100 for not serving or providing a substitute.

1771.—By G.O. each Regiment when embodied was to have a Light Infantry Company and Band.

1779.—Act. 19, Geo. III., augmented the Militia by raising Volunteer Companies for service during embodiment, the men to receive the same pay, bounty, etc., as the Militia, and be subject to Militia regulations.

At this time vacancies were filled by ballot, the numbers being apportioned to Parishes by Lords Lieutenant and Deputy Lieutenants.

The property qualification of Officers was enforced, and up to one third were discharged every four years under exemption from serving as privates or having to find substitutes. All able bodied persons fit to serve were liable, except Peers, Members of Universities, Clergymen, Constables, apprentices and Seamen. The annual Training took place in two periods of fourteen days, or one of twenty-eight days determined by Lords Lieutenant.

1786.—Act. 26, Geo. III., amended and reduced into one Act the Militia laws, the Force being described as—

" Essential to the constitution of the Nation and found to be capable of fulfilling the purposes of its institution, and through its constant readiness on short notice for effective service has been of the utmost importance to the National defence of the Kingdom of Great Britain."

This Statute increased the property qualification of Officers. The existing quota of men was confirmed. The names of Officers, etc., to appear in the " London Gazette."

Lieut. Colonels Commandant to have the rank of Colonel after five years' service, etc., etc.

CHAPTER XVI.

Origin of Militia, Ireland, Etc.

1793.—Act. 33, Geo. III., reorganized the Militia of Ireland, amended and reduced into one Act the laws relating to the Militia, and fixed the quotas of men to be furnished by the different Counties in Ireland, formed into Regiments and under conditions similar to those prevailing in England.

It would be here desirable to record the apparent origin of the Irish Militia.

In early times the territories of Ireland had their means of defence, organized on much the same lines as Saxon England.

Litton Falkiner explains in his fascinating " Illustrations of Irish History" that "by an old law the Septs, and men in one Town or County, were formed into armed Associations, choosing their chief head or Captain as most fit to defend them." At one period " divers kind of foot use divers kind of arms, the Galliglasses armed with marions and halberts, the Kerne and some of their footmen with weighty iron mails and jacks, and assail horsemen aloof with casting darts, and at hand with the sword."

It appears in the " Records of the Waterford Artillery " by Major Wheeler Cuffe, and from Smith's " History of Waterford," that this town had in 1584 an armed force of 300 shot and 200 billmen, as also had some other places.

In 1641 the principle of compulsory service between 18 and 60 years of age was adopted in Ireland. Falkiner in his Chapter on the present Irish Guards, has it, that two Dublin Regiments of Militia were raised for defence in 1660 one for duty within and the other without the City, sometimes referred to indifferently in the Assembly rolls as the Guards of the City and that a Militia 24,000 strong had been raised.

Captain Hore in his researches for completing an exhaustive History of County Wexford found the Militia, or a force of that character, in existence in 1667.

We find that the Irish Militia took part in the Wars of King James II., 1685, and of King William III., 1690, and it is recorded that the Militia of Ireland was called out by Queen

Anne in 1702. At a later date there were Volunteer Associations, in character Militia, which on occasions performed duty, and out of which we find that Militia Regiments were formed.

In 1793 the Irish Parliament consolidated the Militia laws, the Force was reorganised and its quota fixed at 21660, each County being required to have its Regiment or Force.

The Records of the Royal Longford Militia refer to the changes of 1793 in words which speak for themselves.

"The State of Ireland in 1792 was most disturbed, midnight marauding to obtain arms, and local risings, etc., openly usurped the freedom of the Government, whilst in 1793 the outbreak of war with France and the Country stripped of regular soldiers though in a state of rebellion, brought about a reorganization of the Irish Militia to stop the tide of anarchy."

In 1809 under Act 49 Geo. III. 30,000 was to be the peace quota of Militia for Ireland with 15,000 more in times of war.

CHAPTER XVII.

ACTS, ETC, 1793 TO 1902.—AUGMENTATION BY VOLUNTEER COMPANIES.—LOCAL MILITIA.—FIRST VOLUNTEERING MILITIA TO LINE.—PRECEDENCE OF REGIMENTS.—TERRITORIAL SYSTEM OF 1881, ETC.

In 1793, by Act 33 and 35, Geo. III., we find London Train-Bands abolished and formed into six Militia Regiments.

1794.—Act 34, Geo. III., states: "It being necessary and highly expedient that the numbers of the Militia Force should be augmented "Lords Lieutenant were authorised to increase the Militia by raising Volunteer Companies or men for service with the Militia during the embodiment on the same conditions as to pay, bounty, clothing, etc., as the regular Militia.

1795.—Act 35, Geo. III., allowed ten per cent. of the Militia to join the Royal Navy or Royal Artillery on usual conditions to be replaced by recruits raised by beat of drum receiving ten guineas bounty, and half pay to be allowed Subaltern Officers on disembodiment.

There was also an Act to form Artillery Militia in Corps, though it will have been observed that besides the apparent existence of such-like bodies in much earlier times, the "spare men" drawn for the Militia were in 1698 used for the Field pieces (see p. 130).

1797.—Act 37, Geo. III., reorganized the Militia of Scotland, and an Act augmented the Militia of England and Wales by Supplementary Militia—a Proclamation being issued.

"Defence against Invasion" "the necessity of having on the shortest notice the numbers required, properly armed and clothed, as defence against invasion by France, to leave no doubt if any attempt should be made, of the contest being brought to a speedy and successful issue, and of the Country being delivered from all the Miseries and Horrors which would arise from the landing of the enemy," etc.

All persons enrolled in this Supplementary Militia were to be called out and exercised in the first instance within their own Counties for twenty-one days at a time, receiving one shilling per day and particular provision for their families while absent. No further service unless in the event of actual invasion, etc., etc.

The quota fixed and raised was 63878.

By War Office Circular (May) all Militiamen enlisted into the regular Army were to be given over to their Militia Regiments.

1798.—Act 38, Geo. III., empowered His Majesty to accept the services of the Militia in Ireland, limited to two years for any Regiment, and an Act was passed to allow ten thousand men of Supplementary Militia or one fifth of the number raised in any County to enlist into the regular Army for service during the War, not out of Europe, their places not to be filled by ballot, there was also an Act, giving the King power to embody one half of the Supplementary Militia selected by ballot, and such was the exigency state of the Country that two months later the remainder were embodied.

By Royal Warrant the Supplementary Militiamen were to be incorporated with the regular Militia.

By W. O. Circular, Grenadier and Light Infantry flank Companies of Militia Regiments were at this time formed into special Regiments and Brigades under Line Officers.

1799.—Act 39, Geo. III., was passed to reduce the Supplementary Militia by volunteering into the Regular Army—Bounty ten guineas for five years or during the War and six months beyond. Any County complete under the new establishment, to be allowed to enlist into the regular Army one fourth of its men, others being dismissed but held liable to serve again unless they had joined the regular Army.

An Act also reduced the quota of the Militia to 76566 by volunteering into the Line, limited to one fourth of the quota—Bounty ten guineas for European service—and an Act soon followed to enable the King to accept additional men under the same conditions, also to enlist Companies of eighty men complete, with Captain, Lieutenant, Ensign to receive Commissions, and be entitled to the half pay regulations.

In view of the system initiated at this period, of reinforcing the regular branch of the Army for important campaigns by obtaining trained men in large numbers from the Constitutional Force, it will be both interesting and instructive to mention what Grose says on the subject of the aid given in 1799.

"By these measures many of the marching Regiments which were mere skeletons were filled up and the Government enabled to send a large force to Holland which were subsequently reinforced by the same means."

It is recorded that out of 80626 Militia existing July 1, 1799, 15712 volunteered and served under Sir Ralph

Abercrombie in Holland, and that soon afterwards 10414 more were obtained.

1801.—Acts 41, Geo. III., authorised the King to assemble the Force for twenty-one days' training if he thought fit, and ordered that afterwards one third only should be drawn out annually, an Act being passed in December to reduce the Force when disembodied to 30776.

1802.—Act 42, Geo. III., Consolidated the Militia laws, and raised the quota to 40963, with power to increase the number by one half in case of war, as Supplementary men.

At this date the enlistment of Militiamen into the regular Army was forbidden, any such enlistments were to be null and void, and a fine of £20 to be imposed on any enlisting officer or person contravening the regulation.

1803.—Act 43, Geo. III., increased the period of training from twenty-one to twenty-eight days—and an Act in July authorised a " Levy en Masse " as necessary for the security of the Nation.

Recited " It is expedient to enable His Majesty more effectually and speedily to exercise his ancient and undoubted prerogative of requiring military service of all his liege subjects in case of invasion of the realm by the foreign enemy," etc.

Male inhabitants between 17 and 55 years of age were to be separated into four classes.

1. Those of 17 to 30 unmarried, having no child living under ten years.
2. Those of 35 to 50 and having no children.
3. Those of 17 to 30 who were or had been married and had more than two children living under age aforesaid.
4. All not included as above.

1804.—Act 44, Geo. III., provided for 9,000 men being raised annually as an " Army Reserve " to fill the places of those entering the regular Army, and we find at this date that Colonels of Militia were to fill future vacancies by the aid of money derived from penalties and amounts received from those not wanting to serve after being drawn in the ballot.

1805.—Act 45, Geo. III., was to allow men in excess of the Militia quota to volunteer into the regular Army—Bounty ten guineas, and one subaltern with every sixty men, one sergeant and one corporal with twenty men to be accepted, but not exceeding four-fifths of any Regiment to volunteer.

1806.—Act 46, Geo. III., suspended the ballot for two years owing to the numbers being still in excess of the quota.

1807.—Act 47, Geo. III., increased the Militia by three fourths of the original quota, or by 30720 men, and substitutes to be allowed in lieu of personal service, all Counties not raising their quota to be fined sixty pounds for each man deficient.

By a later Act, two fifths of the establishment serving were allowed to pass into the regular Army—Bounty fourteen guineas for unlimited and ten guineas for seven years' service.

The method adopted at this time for obtaining Volunteers from the embodied Militia was to appoint three days in every three months until the quota of a Regiment was completed.

Regimental records indicate, "that discipline was relaxed and much license prevailed."

The urgency for help in this crisis appears to have been of such import to the regular branch of the Army and Nation, that the following appeal was issued:

W. O. Circular dated Whitehall, 17th August, to Lords Lieutenant. "His Majesty entirely relying on your zeal and attachment to His Service, has commanded me to recommend the execution of this important law, and to explain his confident Persuasion that from the Spirit and Enterprise of His Militia Soldiers seconded by the encouraging countenance of the Officers of that important branch of the public Force, His Regular and disposable Army will receive an immediate Augmentation equal to the pressing Emergencies of the Public service," etc., and according to Parl. Papers, 19152 men volunteered.

1808.—Act 48, Geo. III., established a "Permanent Local Militia" to replace the regular Militia when embodied, and in place of Infantry Volunteer Companies, the Conditions being,

"No substitutes, age 18 to 30, service four years, Volunteers might transfer to the Local Militia receiving two guineas bounty, persons insuring against the payment of ballot fines and penalties, or paying volunteers beyond two guineas to transfer, to be fined £50. No ballot to be taken in any District if the quota between 18 and 35, height five feet two inches, and fit for service, not having more than two children under fourteen years of age enrol themselves."

The Local or New Militia were to be trained annually in the spring.

This Force was continued until the end of the War, June, 1815, and abolished by Act 55, Geo. III., which received the Royal assent four days after the Battle of Waterloo.

It is stated that by the above transfer of Volunteers, and the ballot, over 210,000 men were raised for the Local Militia.

1809.—Act 49 Geo. III. (March) allowed two-fifths of the Militia to enlist into the regular branch of the Army— Bounty fourteen guineas for life and ten guineas for seven years' service.

From Parl. Papers—15531 men volunteered under this Act.

By an Act in May, the Militia was to be increased one half the original quota or by 20481 men, raised by beat of drum, Bounty twelve guineas, and any deficiency in the numbers due from Counties to be made up by ballot under liability of £40 fine from Parishes for every man deficient.

Raikes records that between May 1809 and Oct. 1813— 43611 men and 2419 boys were obtained by beat of drum.

Lloyd-Verney gives the strength of the Militia at the end of May, 1809, as being

    Regular Militia   65,524
    Local   ,,   198,534

1811.—Act of April, 51 Geo. III., was passed to gradually reduce the Militia to its original quota of 40963, and supernumeraries 6856 to be raised yearly by ordinary enlistment to replace an equal number allowed to enter the regular Army receiving—Bounty ten guineas for limited service and fourteen guineas unlimited, afterwards reduced to six and ten guineas.

Act of July entitled the "Interchange Act," allowed the English Militia to Voluntarily serve in Ireland and the Irish in England limited to one fourth and one third respectively —Bounty for volunteering two guineas and no Regiment to serve out of its Country for longer than two years.

1812.—Act 52, Geo. III., increased the Local Militia and allowed one fourth to transfer their service to the embodied regular Militia — Bounty ten guineas besides two guineas to the recruiting party for expenses.

1813.—By W. O. Circular (May) the men of several Scotch Regiments were offered grants of land in North America to join the regular Army for service in that Country and to receive on their discharge Sergeants seventy-five acres, Corporals sixty and Privates fifty.

At this time Regiments were authorized to enlist recruits by beat of drum wherever quartered.

By Horseguards Circular July—the rank of Colour Sergeant was created.

By Circular (August) the Permanent Staff of the Local Militia were to recruit for the regular Militia. "Limit of age thirty-two, height 5 ft. 4 inches, and growing lads of 17 to 19 not under 5 ft. 2 inches—Bounty ten guineas and two guineas for expenses. We learn from the details of this latter charge on the public, the definite cost of recruiting men in 1813.

"The bringer received twenty-two shillings, Recruiter of the regular Militia six shillings, Local Militia Adjutant half a guinea, Medical examination two and sixpence and attesting one shilling." We also find an

Act repealing the "Interchange Act" and providing that the Militia be allowed to volunteer for service anywhere in the United Kingdom.

An Act in November asked for 30,000 Militia to volunteer for service in Europe as Militia. No Regiment to be reduced below three fourths of the men actually serving—Bounty eight guineas and volunteering under other Acts not to be affected. Three Field Officers were to be accepted with 900 men, Two with 600 and one with 300 (or three fourths of the number serving) and the usual proportion of Captains, Subalterns, etc. or Companies complete of one hundred men with three officers.

By Circular Whitehall of later date a Line Commission would be given to Captain with fifty men, Lieutenant with thirty and Ensign with twenty—Bounty of two guineas to each man in addition to the ordinary bounty.

1814.—Raikes records from "Commons' Journals," that the trained men received by the regular branch of the Army from the Militia between 1803 and 1813 numbered 99755, and in 1814, September to December, 11,177.

By Royal Warrant, under an Act passed to punish Mutiny and Desertion in the Army, the better payment of the Army was dealt with, etc.

"The officers of the Militia and Private Men shall during the time of their being embodied and drawn out, be subjected and made liable to all such Articles of War Rules and Regulations as shall then be by Act of Parliament in Force for the Discipline and good Government of any of His Majesty's Forces in Great Britain," etc.

1815.—Act. 55, Geo. III., discontinued volunteering from the Militia into the regular Army, and for all Statutes under which they had been obtained to be repealed.

We find that after this date until the next great War in 1852 the Force was kept in memory by few Acts or Orders which require to be recorded.

There were reductions of the Staff and returns to former strength influenced by the sensitive chances of Peace or War. At on time the Force was ordered to be completed by ballot, at another under Act 5, William IV., the Arms and Appurtenances were withdrawn, whilst in 1835 we find a quaint Order in Council again depleting the Staff, and allowing "the surplus to die off."

When the dream of perpetual peace had almost run its course, there appears to have been another re-organization of the Staff which discharged those unfit and filled the vacancies by picked pensioners from Chelsea Hospital. It should perhaps be mentioned, that in 1833 the precedence of Regiments received attention.

By W. O. Order Sept. 1759 "Militia Regiments were not to have any fixed rank or precedence but the first to arrive in any Camp or Garrison to have seniority and others as they arrive." By W. O. Order 1760 " precedence was to be drawn for by Regiments serving together." It appears that Regiments, as in earlier times, were until about the end of this century generally known by the name of their Commanding Officer, and it is stated that their social rank together with the uncertainty as to when Regiments were completed for service often caused jealousy and complications.

Between 1788 and 1803, Counties and Ridings drew lots yearly for seniority and all the Regiments of each area had only one number.

The Scotch Regiments were numbered on a separate list until 1803, and the Irish until about 1833.

In 1833 by an Order of King William IV. all Militia Regiments of the United Kingdom were to be numbered on one list, and separately, " to finally and permanently settle the precedence."

After a Banquet at St. James's Palace, July 28, at which all Lords Lieutenants and Colonels of Militia were commanded to attend, the Regiments were divided into three classes according to the dates when they were completed for service in 1756 and following years.

> First the 47 before the Peace of 1763.
> Second the 22 between 1763 and Peace of 1783.
> Third the 60 for Revolutionary War, the Ballot taking place in the presence of the King.

It is not important to give any list of the numbers drawn, as from time to time new Regiments have been raised and given numbers vacated by Units from various causes. It may be added that in August 1855 a Board of Militia Officers assembled at Aldershot to again settle the precedency, but by an Order afterwards issued, "County Titles were to be used in all Official Documents, the Regimental number being only a subsidiary Title not to be made use of alone."

In 1881 a Territorial system applied to both Line and Militia Infantry again changed the precedence of some Regiments. It is also worthy of note that "by W. O. Circular, 1848, November, attention was directed to the Contingent allowance of Regiments, from which we learn how large Regimental funds were accumulated.

It appears that the comparatively liberal allowance had gone on yearly during the many years when Regiments were not assembled for training between 1816 and the date of this Circular. In one known instance (and probably others) the amount of £1,181 16s. 8d. had been accumulated. A War Office Circular of January following whilst pointing out that in some cases the rules of the Pay and Clothing Acts had not been complied with, and in others that these funds had been applied to increase the incomes of Officers and N. C. Officers, ordered that in future the balance was to be a "Stock Purse Fund" for contingent expenses of Regiments, and the Colonel responsible for its proper use.

In 1852 History with almost mathematical precision repeated itself. The apparently ever recurring and uncontrollable cloud of coming trouble caused that rise in the Barometer of the Constitutional Force, which had in all ages brought this "Power of the Country" into evidence.

After the defeat of a Bill to revive the Local Militia of 1808, an Act was passed.

1852.—15 and 16 Vict. "to consolidate and amend the Laws relating to the Militia" under which the regular Militia Force was reorganized with a quota of 80,000 men to be raised by voluntary enlistment, bounty £6 for five years service age 18 to 35, height 5 feet 4 inches—50,000 to be raised in 1852, and 30,000 in 1853, the Queen having power to increase the Force to 120,000 after communicating with Parliament. The Training period was to be from 21 to 56 days under Order in Council, the quota to be furnished by each County being also fixed by Order in Council and the Ballot to be used if necessary. Bounty 10s. on enrolment and the like amount at the end of first training, afterwards at the rate of two shillings per month paid monthly, quarterly, or otherwise until the £6 was exhausted, this system of payment being at a later date changed to 10s. on enrolment and one guinea for each training, and balance on completion of engagement.

The Recruiting was to be carried out by the Staff of Regiments, under liberal allowances—subsequently five shillings being paid to any person bringing a recruit.

The Ballot Act has necessarily been so often referred to, that an epitome of its clauses should command interest, though the patriotic spirit of the Nation has made its use unnecessary in recent years.

"The Secretary of State to declare the numbers wanted.

Lords Lieutenants to assemble meetings to initiate the proceedings.

Householders to supply lists of all male persons between the ages of 18 and 30.

Parishes can supply Volunteers for the quota before Ballot.

Volunteers to count as balloted persons.

Any deficiency to be filled by Ballot.

Any person drawn can object, or claim exemption.

Deputy Lieutenants to settle questions of liability.

Those of necessary physique to be enrolled in turn according to the numbers drawn.

Another Ballot to take place if the numbers be insufficient.

Any Ballotted man may provide a substitute."

The rapid march of events and outbreak of the Crimean War brought in 1854 the War Office Circular of 20th November.

"The augmentation of the regular Army being at this moment of urgent importance it has become necessary to call upon all embodied as well as disembodied Militia Regiments to give Volunteers to the Guards, Line, and Royal Marines.

The Government is aware that the efficiency of Regiments will be impaired by the sudden loss of so large a proportion of highly trained men, etc. It is intended to limit the demand to twenty-five per cent. with priority to the recruiters of those Regiments having a County connection. Bounty £7 in all, but any larger number in the emergency will be accepted, and an Ensigncy without purchase given with each seventy-five men enlisting."

1855.—Produced the Act 18 Vict. to accept the services of the Militia out of the United Kingdom "for the vigorous prosecution of the War" limited to three-fourths of the establishment serving abroad and such men to be enrolled for five years, followed by a War Office Circular inviting officers, N. C. officers and men to volunteer, and to extend their service to Gibraltar, Malta and the Ionian Islands. A Bounty of £8 was paid, £2 on volunteering, £1 for extra necessaries, and £1 yearly or 5s. quarterly. Under this Act many Regiments offered their services, and ten were sent to Gibraltar and the Ionian Islands.

In 1855.—An Act known as the "Panmure Act of Grace" became Law consequent on some doubt having arisen whether men enlisted under former Acts prior to May 1854 could be embodied for more than fifty-six days in a year. This point reminding one of what wrecked the value of the Feudal Force in early days, whose obligation might expire after forty days, and which initiated daily pay to retain their services. It was met on the present occasion by an additional bounty of one pound for re-attestation and those objecting to be sent to their homes. Parliamentary Returns show that 11909 in England and Wales accepted the offer, and 16269 were disembodied. Scotland and Ireland were not affected.

1855.—By W. O. Circular March—all Militia correspondence was transferred from Home to War Office.

In 1858.—A Horse Guards Order was issued allowing seventeen per cent. of the effective rank and file of the Militia to volunteer into the rgular Army, Bounty £3 and one half of any embodied Militia service performed over 18 years of age to count for pension, an Ensign's Commission being given with every 75 men, afterwards increased to 100 men.

1859.—Act 22, 23 Vict. provided for men in future to be enlisted to serve in Great Britain and Ireland.

1860.—W. O. Circular February ordered that men re-enrolling after five years were to receive 10s. gratuity, whilst a W. O. Circular of the same year (June) must obviously in 1905 cause reflection.

"It is important for the Militia as a reserve Force upon which dependence can be placed in case of National danger that it should be raised from among men of settled habits and fixed residence within the County to which the Regiment belongs and who on leaving the Militia for the Line after receiving the Militia bounty disorganize the Militia while they enter the Army at an increased cost to the public. Stringent orders have been issued prohibiting any Line or other Recruiting party from attempting in the future in any way to induce Militiamen to leave their respective Regiments in order to enlist into Her Majesty's regular Forces or Marines, Militiamen having no more right to do so than men of one Line Regiment have to enlist in another without the consent of their Commanding Officer. Such a proceeding on their part amounts to desertion and will expose them to the penalties attached to that offence, a liability which every opportunity should be taken to make known," etc. "If the indulgence be granted men will require to refund 18s. 6d. to cover the bounty and other expenses of their enrolment also any balance of bounty they may have received in advance on account of their first engagement if re-attested for a second."

1862.—W. O. Circular, April, allowed Officers to proceed to the School of Musketry at Hythe and receive the pay of their rank with travelling expenses.

1865.—W. O. Order allowed soldiers of the regular Army to complete their period of service for pension by transfer to the Militia after eighteen years.

1869.—Act 32 Vict. (May) abolished the property qualification of officers, and conferred a step of Honorary rank on retirement, under a scale for each rank according to length of service.

Lodging allowance granted to officers during the training period if no public quarters available, and one half the amount for furniture if quarters provided—and a messing allowance of four shillings per day towards maintaining a Mess, not as a personal emolument.

The Force was at this time placed under the General Officers of Districts when assembled for Training.

1870.—By W. O. Circular of August, Schools of Instruction were established for Officers of all ranks and to receive pay and allowances when attending the course. The step of Honorary Rank previously referred to, to be conferred whilst serving, but without any right to higher command, and to increase the interest in the "Militia Reserve" we find that a Line Commission was to be given with every one hundred Militia reservists when called out for active service.

1871.—Act 34, 35 Vict. was a periodical "Regulation of the Forces Act," and under this one an Order in Council transferred the Command of the Militia from Lords Lieutenant to the Crown, and Officers to receive their Commissions direct from the Sovereign, Commanding Officers being authorized to extend the period of their recruits preliminary drill up to six months if required.

1872.—G. O. required Subaltern Recruit Officers to qualify in their duties within a fixed period and to serve three trainings before being eligible for promotion to the rank of Captain, and Officers of all ranks to pass before any promotion.

Honorary Colonels were at this time to be appointed to Regiments. A nomination for Commission in the regular Army to be given yearly to each Regiment of ten Companies, for Subalterns who had served two Trainings and were between the ages of 19 and 22.

The appointment of Adjutant was limited to five years only.

Good shooting badges were introduced into the Militia and to be worn as in the Line.

The system of quartering the Militia in billets or lodgings during their Training periods was superseded by Encampments when Barracks were not available, and at a later date grants appear to have been made by Parliament for the erection of suitable Barracks in some centres, to be successively used by several Units for their Trainings. After a time these became occupied by Regiments of the regular branch of the Army which were moved out for Field Training, etc., during the Militia Training Season, but under the exigencies of the service these Barracks seem to have been eventually altered by the construction of Canteen, Recreation accommodation, etc., to be suitable for the continuous occupation of Line Battalions.

1873.—By Royal Warrant the several Regiments of Militia, Yeomanry and Volunteer Corps were to be attached to and form part of respective Brigades of the Army.

By W. O. Circular the period of service for Militiamen and Militia Reserve was increased from five to six years, and no Candidate for a Militia Commission was to be eligible as Lieutenant above thirty years of age, or Captain over thirty-five, except those who had served three years in the regular Army who might be five years older provided they had held the rank or passed for promotion.

1874.—By Militia Regulations, Prizes for good shooting were now awarded.

Act 37, 38 Vict. was entitled "The Militia Law Amendment Act" its chief feature being to curtail the continual passing of Acts by giving "Power to the Sovereign to regulate the Militia by Warrants and Regulations."

1875.—Act 38, 39 Vict. was passed "to consolidate and amend certain Laws relating to the Militia of the United

Kingdom" cited as the "Militia Voluntary Enlistment Act." It dealt with the appointment and powers of Lords Lieutenant and Deputy Lieutenants of Counties, the fixing of quotas to be furnished by Counties, the uniting of Counties to form Regiments so long as the exigency existed, and of Counties in order to form Militia Artillery Units. Officers were to rank with those of regular forces, but as youngest of their rank, there was also the raising of men for six years' obligation service, and that the preliminary drill of recruits might be up to six months, and the Training period 21 to 28 days once or oftener in the year. The Militia was not to serve abroad without volunteering, and then liable to do so at Gibraltar, Malta and the Channel Islands.

Application of the Mutiny Act and Articles of War, Desertion, Trial and punishment of Deserters, etc., and the consequences of enlisting into the regular Forces or Royal Navy, exemption from Civil Offices, etc.

1877.—By W. O. Circular (May) Militia Officers were made subject to the Articles of War all the year round, and must report to their Commanding Officers before proceeding abroad, Commanding Officers to the Adjutant General.

1881.—Act 44, 45 Vict. was another "Regulation of the Forces Act" which included the right of investing persons to command who held superior rank, and applied the non-enlistment of men discharged with disgrace to the Militia, that desertion made a man liable to Court Martial, or if convicted by a Court of Summary Jurisdiction a fine of not less than forty shillings up to £25, and in default imprisonment with or without hard labour up to the maximum term allowed by law for the amount of fine.

To keep in memory the vast number of changes which have touched the Force of the People, it becomes necessary to include that in this year a kind of Territorialism was applied to the Infantry standing branch of the Army by association with the old Territorial County Force of the Country—Traditional designations of Royal, Light Infantry, etc., and of Scottish Clans enjoyed by the Constitutional Force were put aside for the common weal, and Territorial Regiments formed which were composed of both Line and Auxiliary Force Units as Battalions.

This change led up to the discontinuance of County and Militia Unit responsibility in the matter of recruiting for the emergency Force of the Country, and its time honoured system of Regimental recruit training. It might be controversial, and would not be History, to deal with the stated causes for this reorganization, but it can be placed upon record when now writing near a quarter of a century after the event, that 1881 has proved to have been a most gravely prejudicial year in the History of the "Constitutional Force." It is officially recorded, that in 1881 the strength of the Force was 127,863 and now under 90,000.

1882.—Act 45, 46 Vict. cited as a "Militia Act" sanctioned the enlistment of men into the regular Army and on so enlisting deemed to be discharged from the Militia. By an Order in Council the Training of 21 to 28 days might be increased to 56 days. There was also another Act the "Reserve Forces Act" to form an Army Reserve Force of Militiamen for Line service on occasions of actual war, the obligation being for six years or during the residue of their Militia engagement term, for which an extra yes ly bounty was paid.

By G. O. The Militia Regimental Preliminary Drill of Recruits was abolished, and in future Recruits were to be trained at the Depots on enlistment, and not under their own Officers.

1890.—By Order, Recruits after being trained at their Depots were this year to be assembled for fourteen days' recruit course of Musketry immediately before the Training period of their Battalions.

1899.—By W. O. Circular (Nov.) "Discharge by purchase from embodied Units was suspended except in cases when the indulgence may be specially granted by the General Officer Commanding, and all Sergeants of embodied Militia Units were appointed as unpaid recruiters to be entitled to the ordinary recruiting rewards. Militiamen of embodied Units not to join the regular Army without the consent of their Commanding Officer."

1901.—Act. Edw. VII. "To amend the law relating to Militia and Yeomanry" for application of Militia enactments to Yeomanry except as to Training periods, and for extending the Training of Mobile Artillery Militia up to eighty-four days.

1902.—Act 2 Edw. VII. cited as "The Militia and Yeomanry Act" found a place in the Statute Book for the purpose of forming reserve divisions of these two branches of the Army.

CHAPTER XVIII.

STRENGTH OF FORCE AT VARIOUS PERIODS.—TYPE OF THOSE WHO SERVED.—NUMBERS FURNISHED TO STANDING BRANCH OF THE ARMY, ETC.

Having now brought into focus the Commission of Array 1122, the Assize of Arms 1181, and some of the many Statutes and Orders which come into being after 1215, we should ponder over what must always appeal to the People and their Force.

There is a flood of light cast over the gradual development of this Power of the Country in respect of its use for the ever changing general military requirements of the State.

It is not difficult to trace in the character of enactments, and sometimes in the details, the semblance of customs and regulations existing in earlier ages.

We find on the ladder of progress many remarkable changes touching the duty of the people to defend their Country, its possessions and prestige.

There was first obligatory service by all classes of the people, then impressment for oversea expeditions, selection by ballot for the honourable duty of bearing arms, voluntary enlistment, augmentation of a standing branch of the army on emergency occasions, and employment of complete Units of the Constitutional Force in a great foreign campaign. Besides all this volume of matter reflecting the continuous patriotism of the people and importance of their Force, there is an insight into the strength and elasticity at certain periods, together with results for emulation which accrued to the State out of Royal Warrants issued during the Napoleonic times, the dark days of the Crimea, etc.

We learn from evidence before the Royal Commission on the late South African War what may well be kept within the memory of the People whose force stepped into the breach, that "it was necessary from almost the beginning to invite Militia Regts. to volunteer," and "we should have been at the end of our tether if we had not had extraneous aid." No searchlight has exposed to us the numbers that rendered service in the hundreds of years before the Reign of King Henry VIII., but the State is in possession of the original County returns made to the Sovereign by Lords Lieutenant in 1539, from which we find that the Constitutional Force as the only Army of the Country then numbered 145,276 men, most of them Archers and Billmen.

There was again a general muster in 1574 of all the Military Forces in England and Wales. Some writers speak of the "established strength" as being 182,929 men, of whom 172,674 were present. It is interesting though regrettable to observe that desertion even existed in those times, and was not unknown in the Anglo-Saxon Fyrd.

Although there is preserved in the Record Office the numbers (132,689) excluding the great force of London Trained Bands, assembled in 1588 to resist invasion by the Spanish Armada, and the Harleian MSS. exist stating "the numbers of everie sorte," it is difficult to follow the figures adopted by many Historians—nor can any reliable figures be traced of the total military strength of England at this important period of her History. There were several Counties not represented at this assembly.

According to the returns of Sir John Hawkins, quoted by Lloyd-Verney, the numbers raised and trained by counties were 123,268, of whom 82,001 were armed and 45,283 trained, the latter presumably meaning ready for service when drawn out, as in the times of Queen Elizabeth we know that the "Milecia" was exercised twice yearly.

Scott, in his History of the British Army, gives the disposition of the armies as being 24,000 at Tilbury to cover the capital, 36,319 for defence of the Queen's person, and 34,350 spread along the South Coast to resist landing.

We have no information as to the position of the remainder, and besides these there would be the force of Trained Bands from the City of London said to have numbered 20,000, which probably formed a distinct army, and the "Constitutional Force" of several counties in reserve.

At the muster in 1603 by Order of King James I., the county forces would appear to have been considerably reduced. A military MSS. referred to by Raikes tells us that England and Wales at that time had 17,280 pyoners and demi-launces, besides a supposed 20,000 men which should be supplied by Noblemen, Bishops, etc.

Thurloe, in his "State Papers of 1650," says, "The Militia under the common conduct of General Cromwell have taken upon themselves the direction of all the affairs, and are in the pay of England, Scotland and Ireland, 80,000 men both horse and foot, who receive great pay all of them."

It is recorded that in 1651 10,000 Militia were impressed for service in Ireland.

Hume states in his History of England that in 1660 the Militia numbered about 160,000 when at this time a standing branch of the Army was formed.

In 1672 the Militia strength was 130,000 men.

By Egerton MSS. Militia Returns, 1697, we have particulars of 108 regiments only, composed of 78,822 foot and 6,856 horse.

In 1712 it was estimated that the Force numbered 84,391 foot and 7,450 horse, but coming to more modern times we find that when the Act of 1756 was passed the numbers proposed by the House of Commons of 60,000 were reduced by the House of Lords to 32,040 for England and Wales, no horse being included.

To replace the Militia Horse a force of Yeomanry was raised in 1794, the Militia of Ireland and Scotland being dealt with at later dates in the century.

The following concentration of figures will keep on record the variations of strength at important periods since 1756, and some interesting details are included of the numbers of trained Constitutional Force soldiers furnished to the regular branch of the Army on emergency occasions.

	Strength.	Received by Regular Army.
1757—Quota for England and Wales, Act 30, Geo. II.	32,040	......
1779—Increased by Volunteer Companies 30,740, Total by Clode's Military Forces to Crown	62,780	......
1795—Ten per cent. allowed to join Royal Navy or Royal Artillery ...	......	6,270
1796—Increased by Supplementary Militia to 63,878. Total	120,388	......
1797—To be reduced by joining regular Army to	80,626	......
Numbers obtained	......	15,712
1798—One-fifth to join regular Army— Numbers obtained	......	10,414
1799—By Adjutant Generals Return Oct.	76,379	......
1801—To be reduced to	30,776	......
1802—Quota fixed at	40,963	......
Half additional in case of war and to be raised 9,000 in excess to make good those to Line ...	20,481	......
1804—To be reduced by volunteering to the Line to	40,963	......
Obtained	......	15,595

THE CONSTITUTIONAL FORCE.

	Strength.	Received by Regular Army.
1805—All the above quota allowed to join the regular Army. It is recorded that between 1805-1813, 110,000 were obtained.	......	......
1807—To be increased by 30,720; recorded strength	77,012	......
2/5ths allowed to enlist into regular Army—obtained	......	15,531
1811—To be reduced by joining regular Army to	40,963	......
By Home Office Records there were thus obtained—1811 to 1813	......	30,218
The strength of Militia at this time is recorded as:— Regular Militia—77,424 Local ,, —213,609 Total	291,033	......
1813—The Militia called upon to give 30,000 for foreign service, and establishment to be increased by 20,481 Supernumeraries	61,444	?
One seventh of total allowed to join regular Army	......	......
1852—Quota fixed for England and Wales	80,000	?
and 40,000 additional in case of War	......	......
1855—25 per cent. of embodied establishments allowed to join regular Army	......	?
50 Regiments volunteered for Crimea and 10 sent to Mediterranean Stations	......	......
1857—17 per cent. allowed to volunteer into the regular Army	......	?
1867—30,000 Militiamen to form Reserve under obligation to join the regular Army in case of War	......	......
1889—By the estimates	129,572	......
1899—Militia reservists drafted to regular Army in S. Africa	......	13,598
To augment regular Army, Officers	......	1,981
,, ,, Men	......	40,000
1902—Militia Regiments in S. Africa Officers	......	1,691
N.C. Officers and Men	......	43,875
10 Regiments Mediterranean	......	?

Whilst it cannot be doubted that Militia Commanding Officers have often regretted, as expressed by W. O. Circular, Nov. 20, 1854, "the sudden loss of a large proportion of highly trained men" and deplored that the exigencies of the Country should have obliged putting aside the decision promugated by W. O. Circular, June 14, 1860, which laid down "stringent orders prohibiting any attempts to induce Militiamen to pass into the Line," it becomes necessary to keep in mind that this concentrated interest in the Foreign Wars of the Nation enabled the Constitutional Force to continue its connection with the Military History of England which had by the services of the People's Army been founded in earlier centuries.

In this connection of reinforcing the actively employed regular branch of the Army it will be interesting to note the ages and type of men obtained by the Militia in the early part of the last century, and a passing remark upon "Substitutes" then in vogue would not be out of place. We are apt to forget that these Substitutes were really free men who voluntarily took the place of those who had been scathed by the ballot, and though "bought with a price" aspired to the honour of bearing arms. The recorded fact that on several occasions, and in different districts, the sporting instinct of the British people asserted itself in the form of sale for service by weight in the Militia—the standard price being apparently about seven shillings and threepence per lb., gives some colour to the type of trained men who, volunteering in large numbers from the Militia to the Line, took part in fighting the battles of the country in stirring times.

The following figures extracted from the published records of a typical Country Regt., and there appear to have been many such, emphasise in a more general way the composition of Militia Regts. at that period. The Regt. which has been selected had in 1803 a strength of 1127 men. Composed of

  867 between 20 and 30 years of age.
  218 ,, 35 ,, 40   ,,
  42 ,, 40 ,, 50   ,,

  168 were over 5.10 in height.
  363 ,, 5.8 to 5.10.
  477 ,, 5.6 to 5.8.
  119 ,, 5.5.

This same Regt. in 1813—strength 697—had 618 "substitutes,"

 245 having over 10 years' service.
 236 ,, between 5 and 10 years' service.
 156 ,, ,, 1 ,, 4 ,,
 60 ,, under 1 year.

It is also recorded, that in 1798 there was a Country Militia Regiment, 1300 strong, "that occupied more space in line of Brigade when drawn up than almost any other Regt. of the same number," and the person who furnished the clothing "found that a greater quantity of cloth was necessary than for others."

In later times we find by the Reports of the Inspector General for Recruiting presented to Parliament between the years 1882 (when the strength of the Militia appears to have been 112,953) and 1904, that 850,420 of the people had under the Voluntary System of the Country responded to the call upon them to bear arms in the Constitutional Force, representing with the 112,953 already serving on the 1st January, 1882, a total of 953,373, and that during this same period the Force furnished to the regular branch of the Army 327,496 of its men towards the 924,951 required to maintain the establishment strength of the Standing Army.

These figures present themselves to our notice for record as a form of Tradition which may be of value to all branches of the Army in years to come.

CHAPTER XIX.

WARS AND CONFLICTS ENGAGED IN BY THE PEOPLE'S FORCE 56 B.C. TO 1906 A.D., ETC.

Before parting from this concentration of many methods for enabling the People to render service in the Defence Force of their Country, and those means applied throughout the ages for associating that Force under its varied names with the general military requirements of the Nation, we are impelled to take some notice of the practical results following such bearing of arms.

In dealing with the Annals of a Force at one time the only Army of the Country, at others an emergency strength, and drawn upon to supply the fighting branch of the Army abroad, we have it from eminent writers versed in the History of England, that in effect they are interwoven with the sequence of events forming the great History of a Country which during two thousand years has grown out of a combination of Tribes into a vast Empire.

Whilst no attempt can therefore be ventured to recite all the Battles fought and taken part in at home and abroad by the Force of Defence, arising out of Rebellion and Invasion —Wars of Defence, Conquest, and Prestige, besides those many conflicts appearing to be the heritage of a progressive Nation advancing on the path of freedom and justice, it will be looked for in a work of this character to touch upon some of those operations of actual war reflecting both the nature of such wars and the conditions under which the People's Army performed its obligations, and other calls made upon it to render service.

History embraces both success and failure; we cannot ignore that the first known effort of the combined Tribal Forces of early Britain resulted in the conquest of the Country by the Romans, whose training for war, and tactics are said to have been superior to the Army of Cassivelaunus, selected as being in their intestine wars the most powerful and best warrior among them to be their Generalissimo. The arms used by his Army have been already referred to. It is interesting in these days of strategy and tactics to observe what Historians tell us about that invasion; the Romans were allowed to land unopposed, the "scheme of defence" being to harass the hosts of Caesar on their march inland and then defeat them at the passage of some river. It is recorded that the Tribal soldiers of Kent, Sussex, and the coast parts of Hampshire, vigorously carried out their duty of harassing the Invaders.

Scarth's "Early Britain" gives a most concise description of what happened, "the Britains were first defeated at a river, probably the Stour, a position strong by nature and art. Cæsar fixed the locality as being twelve Roman miles from hs place of landing, then marching with his legions to the Thames to a place which Camden has decided was the Conway Stakes at Walton-on-Thames, an ancient and fortified ford made into a still stronger position, and the only part of the river that could be forded on foot, the Romans forced the passage in face of the combined Tribal Forces congregated there under Cassivelaunus. Cæsar then advanced by way of Hertfordshire into Essex, devastating the country through which he passed, and opposed only by a large force of chariots, eventually followed Cassivelaunus to his stronghold at St. Albans. Meanwhile the four kings of the Kentish Tribes had failed in an attack on the Naval Camp of the Romans, and Cæsar's Army at St. Albans attacking the "Oppidum" of the Britons at two points overcame all obstacles, and it was hastily evacuated, many Britons being taken prisoners and slain in the pursuit. Peace being then sued for and agreed, the country as far as Caesar had penetrated became subject to Roman power."

In this epitome of the disaster which befel early Britain near 2000 years ago, we have before us the initial cause which influenced reorganizations of the Constitutional Force in after centuries.

Following this partial conquest of Britain there was much fighting for a long period of years before the Romans brought the whole Country under their rule.

It is only necessary to keep in memory the effect of successful invasion, the Tribal people as soldiers are said to have fought desperately for their homes, and as each District was conquered, the people were according to Roman custom required to serve in the Army of their Conquerors.

When the Romans evacuated the Country after an occupation of about four centuries, and left behind them the evidences of their engineering skill for defence, the Roman Wall across Northern Britain, military roads, entrenched positions, and the people better trained to protect themselves, there was still no peace for the constituted Force of all the People, the Country drifted into a state of war by the inrush of Angles and Saxons, against whom they are said to have fought stubbornly for freedom. In 457 the Kingdom of Kent was formed, and in 584 the defeat of the border lands of Mercia together with parts of Scotland and Wales enabled the Angle-Saxons to complete their seven separate Kingdoms of the Heptarchy. The Kingdoms then fought against each other, and History records numerous Battles until 827, when Egbert the King of Wessex, having conquered all the other Kingdoms, became King of all England. We may refer to the Battles of Winceod Field in the Parish of Barwick-in Elmet, Yorkshire, 635 A.D., between Prenda, King of Mercia, and the King of Northumberland, for evidence of the sanguinary character of the hand to hand fighting with the weapons of those days engaged in by their Forces composed of the People as soldiers. The King of Mercia having defeated Edwin of Northumberland at Hatfield Moor near Doncaster in 633, Prenda·and nearly all his thirty " Generals " were slain at Winceod Field two years later.

Passing over the succession of internal troubles and fighting of the Saxons, the incursions of the Danes, and the brief period during which Danish Kings ruled the Country, we must take notice of the great Battle preceding the next conquest of Britain and briefly record the disaster of this momentous year in England's History, an active one for the Force of the People.

In 1066 the popular Chieftain Harold became King of England, and the Fyrd had to contend with two distinct invasions from different countries, one ending in a brilliant victory for the Military History of England, and the other disaster which for a time changed the character of the old National Force.

The Norwegian invaders having defeated Earls Edwin and Morcar at Water Fulford on the River Ouse, and York in possession of their Forces, King Harold was victorious at Stamford Bridge near York, he himself to be vanquished at the Battle of Hastings by the Normans.

Abbreviating what Historians have passed down to us, we find that Tostig, who had been deposed by the Northumbrians as Duke of that County, united his Forces on the Tyne with those of King Harold Hardrada of Norway, and sailing thence to the Humber ascended the Ouse, defeating the English at Water Fulford Sept. 20th, 1066, hurling them back on York, which City surrendered on the 24th, but King Harold of England hastening from the South, brought the Invaders to Battle at Stamford Bridge on the 25th, near which place they had occupied an old Roman post commanding the junction of the Derwent River.

The importance of this Battle in a History of the Constitutional Force, is to show that the tactics on both sides were the same in character as prevailed at the invasion of Britain by the Romans, the position of the combatants being reversed, and that those hand to hand encounters tending to develop individual courage and skill were features of the British success. It is recorded that in this great Battle both Harold Hardrada and Tostig were slain, and their army of sixty thousand completely routed. The objective appears to have been a wooden bridge and ford, situated above where the stone bridge now exists. It is stated that one Norwegian killed forty assailants before he was pierced by a spear from below the bridge, from which it would appear that the Britains were actively engaged in the attack and their opponents defeated in defence. After this battle the enemy left hostages and were allowed to sail away with their vessels. King Harold then proceeded quickly to the South, and reinforced by the Fyrd of Middlesex marched to meet his Norman Invaders under Duke William, and unsuccessfully fight the historic Battle of Hastings, Oct. 14, 1066. All writers agree that Britain was defeated by the superior strategy of the Normans. The Fyrd or Army of the Country fought in its usual formation for battle in a dense mass of wedge shape surrounding the Standard —the mounted troops, those who had horses and Thanes in the rear, with the heavy battle axe men in front. The arms were varied as centuries rolled on —but it will be found that much the same battle formation continued in favour beyond the middle of the twelfth century.

King Harold was among the slain at this battle, which ended the Saxon Dynasty, and no better language can be found to describe the services of those who fought with him than expressed by the late Colonel Davis in his History of a Surrey Regt. "He died surrounded by his faithful Militiamen with their faces to the foe, those of London being under his immediate command."

We have had before us the Feudal system or class levy for the general military purposes of the Kingdom, with its defects which brought into active service abroad many of those belonging to the constituted Reserve Force of the remainder of the People.

Before detailing some of these exploits necessarily interesting to the "Constitutional Force" in later ages, there were numerous conflicts at home arising out of disagreements between ruling sovereigns and their Barons in the 12th, 13th and 14th Centuries. These Feudal Lords had become dangerously powerful under the Military tenure law and frequently used their strength in the suppression of which the People's Army had to be employed. As an example of the position presumed upon by the Barons and one of the Battles which arose out of their disturbing power in the land may be mentioned that called the "Fair of Lincoln," May 20, 1217. "The Dauphin of France being invited over by the discontented Barons in the last year of King John's Reign, was acknowledged by them as King of England, but the nobility at Gloucester to crown Henry III. marched with a large force against Louis and the Barons, defeating them in a most sanguinary fight."

We must also refer to England's great Civil War between the Houses of York and Lancaster—Lancaster adopting the red rose as its emblem, and York the white rose, 1455-1485. Hayden has it that in these Wars of the Roses "twelve Princes of the blood perished besides 200 Nobles and 100,000 gentry and common people."

This succession of Wars and long struggle, embracing the devoted attachment of all classes of the people as soldiers on one side or the other, ended with the death of King Richard III. at the Battle of Bosworth, Aug. 22, 1485, and union of the Roses by a Royal marriage of King Henry VII. in 1486.

Reverting to the Reign of William the Conqueror as King of England, and the following centuries under his Feudal system, we find the country engaging in Foreign expeditions of more or less important character. We know that the limited service required under the Military Tenure system of the Feudal Law—the excuses made, and evasions from rendering service—caused the successful prosecution of such wars to be doubtful, and often dangerous to the State without the help of the Defence Force of the People, whilst by Royal Warrants and Acts of Parliament we have in evidence that during some centuries the Soldiers of this Force were obtained by impressment and otherwise to form and maintain the strength of these Foreign service Armies.

It would appear that foreign expeditions became part of the policy of the Country soon after the introduction of the Feudal System, and in 1087 they were the cause of King William's death—quoting from the pages of History it is recorded that having promised to help his eldest son in obtaining the Duchy of Normandy and withdrawing from this promise, the son made war on his Father, who besieged the Castle of Gerberoi, where his son had taken refuge, followed in the same year by King William's attack on the City of Montes, which he ordered to be burned, and in the conflagration met with an accident that caused his death.

In 1106 we find Robert of Normandy aggrieved by the rupture of a compact between himself and a previous King of England and an invasion of England ending in reconciliation, but war breaking out again, King Henry I. invaded Normandy and defeated Robert at Tinchebrai, taking Robert prisoner and sending him to England, where he died; then in 1119 there was another claim to Normandy by Louis King of France on behalf of Robert's son, which led to further war between England and France, the English defeating the French at the battle of Brenneville.

In 1194 England again crossed swords with France, King Richard I. leaving England in May to give battle to Philip II., King of France, who was besieging Verneuil, Richard's brother John having leagued himself with Philip to obtain possession of his brother's dominions, invade England, and seize the Crown; the result of this War was that King Richard first forced John to surrender, then relieved Verneuil, and defeated King Philip at Tritville, but the war being renewed in 1196 Philip laid siege to Albemarle and took it. The English were more successful in 1198. King Richard won a great victory over Philip at Gisors, where the French King and some Nobles were forced into the river and extracted with difficulty. In 1199 King Richard met his death while besieging the Castle of Chabuze.

In 1242 King Henry III. aspired to aid the Count de la Marche and landed at Royan with an Army. It is a coincidence that the Militia Brigade which proceeded to France in 1814 also landed at this place or one of the same name.

King Henry's Army fought a battle at Faillebourg on the 20th July without result, and the English hastily moved to Saintes where another indecisive engagement was fought against Louis XI. King of France. In 1346 we find Edward III. sending an Army to France. After first defeating the French at Auberoche and then having to evacuate the Towns taken, we come to the celebrated Battle of Cressy. The connection of those who represented the "Constitutional Force" with this Battle being referred to in the Historical records of some Regts., it will be interesting tradition to quote what Historians have described. "Edward III. came to the relief of his Forces accompanied by his son Edward the Black Prince and forty thousand men, the King of France having 100,000. The English army consisted chiefly of English bowmen, Irish and Welsh footmen. His Army was drawn up on a small slope with the main body at the base divided into two parts—the Black Prince commanding the right division and the Earl of Northampton the left. The English loss was small, that of the French being about 30,000, among whom were John the Blind, King of Bohemia, the King of Majorca, and the Duke of Lorraine, all sovereign Princes. The Black Prince won his spurs by taking the King of Bohemia's crest (three ostrich feathers with the motto "Ich dien") which emblem is familiar to many Militia Regiments of the present day. Then followed the siege and surrender of Calais to the English in 1347.

After four years' peace abroad—oversea fighting again commenced in 1351 and with France—the English defeating the French at Poictiers. In this great battle we have evidence of the deadly skill of the English with their cherished weapon. "A sudden attack by the English and the steady shooting of their Archers produced a panic among the French, some ten thousand of whom were killed and 2000 men and arms and nobles taken prisoners, the King of France himself being made prisoner, taken to London and lodged in the Palace of the Savoy."

In 1359 Edward once more invaded France to defend Calais. In 1360 a treaty of peace, and 1367 more war, the Black Prince defeating the French.

Passing on now to 1413 we find another of those romantic wars which so often characterised the early History of England. King Henry V. asserted his right to the French Throne and demanded Catherine, daughter of Charles VI. in marriage, the negotiations ending in war, 1415, with the siege and capture of Harfleur by the English; and it is recorded by Historians that during the siege the Dauphin of France refused a challenge by King Henry to meet in single combat. Then followed Oct. 25th, 1415, the historic Battle of Agincourt—also associated with the People's Force and requiring brief notice. "Henry V. of England with 14,000 men, gave battle to the French Army numbering

50,000 or more. The French were supposed to have many cannon but did not make use of them (writers say perhaps for lack of room). The King of England's Army being small he did his best to make up for this by various devices, pointed stakes with iron at both ends were driven into the ground to protect his front line. Henry himself was in chief command. The battle was fought with great fury for three hours and 10,000 Frenchmen are supposed to have fallen, amongst them being the Dukes of Alencon, Brabant, and Bar the Achbishop of Sens and many Nobles.

We find that the martial ardour of King Henry the Fifth caused him to be again on French soil in July, 1417.

The length of this war and the character of its operations indicate that his great army must obviously have been largely composed of Constitutional Defence Force soldiers. Castles and Towns surrendered to the King until he reached Rouen, which withstood a siege for six months before capitulating. This success was followed by the capture of other smaller places until the English Fleet being defeated off La Rochelle Apr. 9, 1420, peace ensued which lasted for a year, when this adventurous king was once more attracted to France, where after some successes he died in Aug. 1422, the English afterwards defeating the French and Scots at Crevant, Aug. 17, 1424; also at Verneuil.

There was more war with France in 1428; first a victory to the English and then defeat, an incident of this war being the relief of Orleans by Joan of Arc, which obliged the English to raise the siege.

In 1449 France again became the battle field, with the defeat of England's Forces under King Henry VI., leaving only Calais of all their conquests in France.

With the reign of Queen Mary I., 1553, came the renewal of an old feud of her husband with France, and war in 1557, resulting in an English Victory at St. Quentin on Augt. 10th, and then the retaking of Calais by the French under the Duke of Guise, Jan. 7, 1558. We next find an English Army at Flushing allied with the Dutch against the Spaniards. There is abundant evidence in State Papers Foreign and Domestic of this and following Reigns that the Constitutional Forces of Counties were largely drawn upon for the prosecution of oversea Wars.

In 1588 we have recorded by Historians and preserved in the Archives of the State, the greatest test of County Organization for the purposes of defence which the Country experienced until the end of the eighteenth Century. It is not necessary to repeat or enlarge upon the response made by the People, and Constitutional Force, to Queen Elizabeth's appeal and trust in "their great love and loyaltie." The details in connection with this bearing of arms to resist attack by the Spanish Armada are included elsewhere.

Whilst England was engaged in hostilities abroad she was not during many of the centuries dealt with, free from troubles at home, and to the Force of the People fell the honourable duty of suppressing rebellions and preserving the peace under their obligation to render service.

There was war with the Principality of Wales in 1282 initiated in those days when Norman Knights were granted fiefs in the Country to conquer the land, though guerilla warfare on the marches in earlier ages is said to have produced on each side "a race of fearless soldiers acquainted with the use of arms" and in later times, "many who were proficient with the bow." The annexation of Wales to the crown of England soon after 1282 brought with it the advantages of united interest and patriotic defence so evident in after ages.

In connection with the services of the National Army, History takes notice of the Perkin Warbeck landing in Ireland, 1492. Son of a Florentine Jew personating the brother of Edward V., and claiming the Crown of England. He afterwards attempted to land in Kent with a small Force of whom some 170 were taken prisoners and executed. Then in 1496 we find King James IV. of Scotland invading England in his favour, and recognising him as King Richard IV. of England, followed by the surrender at Bodmin in Cornwall, Sepr., 1497, of 3000 rebels who had joined him.

Passing over the troubles arising out of Lady Jane Grey's claim to the Throne in 1553, we come in 1642 to the great Civil War of the 17th Century as being closely identified with the Militia Force, and which launched into active service, its whole strength augmented by new Regiments raised in Counties and by persons deeply interested in the cause of one side or the other.

The country having drifted into the misery and devastation of a great Civil War, during which we find families divided, brothers under arms and regiments of a county fighting against each other, ending in the execution of King Charles I. on the scaffold at Whitehall, Jan. 30, 1649, it will not be a digression to notice the causes which brought about the series of battles fought by the Constitutional Force.

Whilst it is generally stated that the Militia caused this

war, a dispute having arisen between the Sovereign and Parliament over the control of the Force, it will have been realised by Students of History that beyond the question of control and "the appointment of its officers" there was an under current of difference upon points which have so often disturbed and excited the minds of men. Gardiner, in his History of the War, conveys to his readers much in few words. He says: "Differences had manifested themselves on the question of religion," and "that it was doubtful whether proposed compromise by King Charles was to save the Protestants or to encounrage the Papists."

It will be very interesting to the many Constitutional Force Regts. of Yorkshire that the outbreak of this Civil War took place at Hull, where King Charles was refused admission within its walls. Then in Oct., 1642, came the indecisive battle of Edgehill, followed by another of fruitless character at Brentford in Novr. In 1643 we find a state of war in many parts of the Country, a Cornish Army for the King conquering the West, and Yorkshire recovered by the Marquis of Newcastle, then the Earl of Essex for Parliament relieving Gloucester, and defeating at Newbury the King's attempt to reach London, with many other engagements of more or less importance until 1647, when the King was delivered by the Scots at Nottingham into the hands of the English Parliament, and eventually imprisoned at Carisbrooke Castle in the Isle of Wight, which place had played a conspicuous part in the early days of the Civil War, as it had done on invasions in many previous centuries.

After the Commonwealth was established, and the Constitutional Force is recorded by historians to have been under the military skill and discipline of Cromwell in a highly efficient state, we find this great soldier entering Scotland with an army in 1650. After the battle of Dunbar and capture of Edinburgh came the battle of Worcester, Sept. 3, 1651, between the Parliamentary Forces and Scotch during the unsuccessful expedition of Charles the Second to England. It is noteworthy that at this battle the Constitutional Force Army of Parliament was not wanting in engineering skill. Low's Dict. of English History says, "The Severn was bridged by boats, which enabled Cromwell's Army to attack in two divisions, driving the Royalists through the streets without any attempt to rally.

In 1660, after the Restoration, and King Charles II. became King of England, we enter a new era of the Constitutional Force.

Whilst there were many rebellions in the suppression of which its services were availed under its obligation of service, we now find it taking a secondary part in oversea expeditions and by Acts of Parliament, Royal Warrants, and Official Utterances, an absolutely necessary part in foreign wars on occasions of national peril. Early in 1665 England declared war against Holland, and here again we obtain from State Papers Foreign and Domestic the details of help given by the Force of the People to the Standing Army in the prosecution of this war. Although it is incumbent on us when taking a retrospective view of the services of the Constitutional Force of Defence since 1660, to embrace some of the many occasions on which it voluntarily shared with the regular Army the glory of success, no impression should be created tending to detract from the zeal and valuable services of that special branch of the Army whose obligation takes it into all parts of the world. We have to keep in memory "the National spirit to develop the esprit of all troops, and the Army as a complete machine, all branches working harmoniously together for one common end," though under different obligations of service.

"State Papers Domestic" tell us that in 1666 the Militia was drawn out by King Charles II. for the purpose of resisting a threatened French and Dutch invasion, whilst in the same year there was trouble with the Covenanters and battles in which it is known that some Militia regiments were engaged.

The intermittent calls upon the Constitutional Force of Defence to bear arms proclaimed throughout the country during upwards of a century, now obtrude on our notice.

The magnetic influence of causes favourable to rebellion and mob law to be found in countries still wanting educational development, which according to history have so often drawn out the People's Army, brought about in 1685 the Monmouth rebellion.

The Duke of Monmouth landing in Dorsetshire from Holland with a few adherents, and people joining his Standard, the rebellion was crushed by the Battle of Sedgemoor, July 5th, all Militia regiments of the South-West taking part in its suppression.

A graphic description of Monmouth's capture will be found under the head of "Services," 3rd Battn. The Somersetshire Light Infantry.

In 1689 there was a defeat of the Jacobites at Newtonbutler, and in 1690 trouble in Ireland, where James II. of

England (deposed in 1688) had landed and created a state of rebellion, the Militia of Ireland being conspicuous for their loyalty and services in the restoration of peace. (See "Services," Cork Royal Garrison Artillery.) Smith's History says "it is not to be expressed what service the Militia did during this campaign. It was hoped to ruin the Army by the rapperees, who by infesting the roads, intercepting carriages, and alarming the country in great numbers would oblige the General to divide his forces and to employ many of them on convoys, the mischief being obviated by arming the Militia and sending Governors into every County to organise and increase their forces, and supply arms, ammunition and bread." It is further stated "that they were never worsted in any equal encounter, besides they were a great relief to the Army by supplying convoys, guarding passes, and even in assisting in the taking of Sligo and other places."

See "Services," 3rd. King's Own Royal Lancaster Regt. in respect of the employment of an English Militia Brigade under the command of His Majesty King William III. at the siege of Carrickfergus Castle, the Battle of the Boyne, and taking of Athlone.

In 1715 England had to contend with a Jacobite rising, and invasion from Scotland by the Chevalier de St. George, who had there been proclaimed King of Scotland and England.

An abbreviated account of the desperate fighting at the siege and taking of Preston by the Royal forces on Nov. 12-13, 1715, is included in the "Services" of the 3rd Battn. Royal Lancaster Regt., from the Regimental History of Colonel Whalley, this Militia Regt. having been engaged on the occasion.

In 1743 England expected a French invasion in connection with a Jacobite rising in favour of the Stuarts, the country being aroused and frightened into activity. The Militia was called out, and a large assembly of troops took place on the south coast.

In 1744 fear of war with France continued, and in the following year the romantic Prince Charles Stuart landed in Scotland from the French frigate Deutelle on his desperate enterprise and death warrant of many of his compatriots, whose enthusiasm brought in wavering Highland clans to serve under his standard.

After defeating the army of King George II. at Preston-Pans he was proclaimed as King James VII. of Scotland, upon which his army under Lord. Geo. Murray suddenly invaded England, marching through Northumberland, Cumberland, and Lancashire, hoping, but without much success, to collect the many Jacobites of those counties.

His army, having reached Manchester, was seized with panic at the approach of the King's forces, and retreated by way of Penrith and Carlisle.

No better abridged account of the Battle at Clifton Moor Dec. 18, 1745, can be given than is included in the "Services" of the 3rd King's Own Royal Lancaster Regt., whilst those of the 3rd Battn. Border Regt., concisely explain the surrender of Carlisle Castle to the rebels.

Passing on to disturbances of a somewhat different character in 1780, the suppression of the Gordon riots in London, which employed several Militia regiments, it is only necessary to read what Major Adamson compiled for the Regimental History of the 5th Northumberland Fusiliers, and others that took part in this painful duty, for a general insight into the nature of the outbreak and means adopted for restoring peace and safety to the Metropolis.

In connection with the quelling of these riots which placed London at the mercy of an excited and fierce mob, including in their ranks many notorious and desperate criminals set free from the various prisons, it would appear important to observe the bravery and discipline of the Militia troops, and tact displayed by those in command, as evidence of the efficiency of the "Constitutional Force" at this period. It is recorded that near 500 persons were killed or wounded, besides others that died in the streets and many who lost their lives in the buildings destroyed.

Although at this time England was engaged in a great foreign war lasting for about five years, there is no evidence that the People's Force materially contributed to this campaign beyond that embodied service at home as an occasion of emergency, which released the regular branch of the Army for duty at the front—but in 1798 we find many English Militia regiments serving in Ireland during the rebellion, a notable feature in its suppression being the loyal help rendered by the Militia Force of Ireland, as in 1690.

It would be difficult to give any brief account of the battles which were fought at New Ross, Arklow, Vinegar Hill and of other engagements, the landing of the French at Killala to aid the insurgents, etc., without referring to incidents and atrocities which embittered the fighting on several occasions.

In these days of a United Kingdom it would be tradition

best not kept in memory, though some details will necessarily be found among the "Services" of regiments which took a distinguished part in the restoration of peace.

In this same year it will have been noticed by the reference made to a Statute of the Realm, 38, Geo. III., c. 17, that the exigency condition of the standing branch of the Army occasioned a reflex of what existed in centuries gone by.

We find re-established by Act of Parliament the connection of the People's Force with foreign expeditions.

Whatever methods may prevail in future years for raising, organizing, and training those of the population who must under some name be ready to bear arms—a safeguard against war and for war if need be—it will doubtless continue to be the national wish for some tradition of 1798 and following years to be kept in memory.

In those years, during a prolonged strain upon the regular Army and military resources of the State, we have it recorded by official documents that it never became needful to re-impose impressment for the prosecution of oversea war.

In 1798, as already indicated, the golden key of the public purse was united with volunteering from the trained ranks of the "Constitutional Force," and as a matter of history it will remain upon record that amidst the many complications in which England was embroiled, the din of war and threatened invasion, this Force under its county organization and capability of vast expansion, satisfied all demands made upon it for protection at home and augmentation of the fighting army abroad.

Initiated in 1795 by a modest levy of ten per cent. of the establishment for the purposes of the Royal Navy and Royal Artillery, we find by Parliamentary Returns that the appetite of war was fed by tens of thousands as time rolled on, and throughout a series of wars which lasted for near the fifth part of a century, on occasions complete company units and half-battalions with their officers being accepted for European service, whilst in 1814 a Militia Brigade of three provisional regiments, commanded and entirely composed of Militiamen, landed in the South of France to strengthen the army of Wellington for all eventualities.

See "Services," 3rd Battn., The Oxfordshire Light Infantry, 5th Worcestershire Regt., etc., that formed this brigade.

Without again referring to the numbers actually furnished by the Militia to the successes of war in the period under review, including the influential Battle of Waterloo, and leaving undisturbed the blissful quarter of a century or more of appreciated peace preceding England's next great war, we can in Crimean days once more take up the thread of special services rendered by the Force.

The Militia was speedily embodied for home defence, and military history passed through the usual form of repeating itself.

Proclamations, Royal Warrants, and General Orders appear to have followed each other in rapid succession, appealing to the ever-reliable patriotic spirit and zeal of the "Constitutional Force," to fill gaps which were being caused in the ranks of the regular branch of the Army at the front. It is also on record that a large percentage of Militia regiments volunteered as units to join the Army in the field, and several regiments were sent to Mediterranean garrisons.

Following soon after this exhausting campaign, a Royal Warrant of Sepr., 1857, explains in its opening paragraph the military condition of the country, and further rendering of service by its emergency force.

> "We considering that the Military operations in which we are engaged in India render it necessary to send a large part of our Regular Forces abroad, deem it proper to provide without delay additional means for the military service at home."

In December special volunteering from the trained ranks of the embodied Militia to the Regular Army became necessary, also at later dates during the continuance of the Mutiny.

In August of 1858 Parliament intervened with an Act 21-22 Vict., c. 85, for allowing the Militia to serve abroad as in 1854.

By Regimental Records we learn that many regiments offered for service in India or elsewhere should such a contingency become urgent.

After the material help afforded by the Force towards the restoration of peace in India and safety of this jewel of the Empire, there is little to record until 1899, when a few regiments were drawn out pending the result of diplomatic negotiations relating to Canada, except that 1881 revolutionized the method of recruiting for the Constitutional Force, and introduced a new system of training its recruits at Regimental Depôts as they enlisted. Under these changes we find, according to Official Returns, that the regular branch of the Army obtained an acquisition of strength whilst the parent Force decreased in numbers, and became an agent for attracting the ordinary class of Line recruits to first enter the Militia. With these Returns in evidence, and that those having fixed homes and employment to be found when wanted were not obviously entering the Militia, we are unable to recognise in this extended service of a different class that patriotism of the People's Army, which had on many occasions of emergency added to Regimental Histories and brought honour to the Constitutional Force.

With the outbreak of the South African War in 1899, its initial failure and ultimate success, it can be recognised and recorded that the Force secured for its history another of those opportunities of oversea active service which on this occasion would appear to have been absolutely necessary for the prosecution of the war and bringing it to a conclusion (see evidence given before the Royal Commission on the War). Almost immediately after the war had commenced we find that numerous battalions offered their services, and it became necessary at once to send a number of them to the seat of war, and others to Mediterranean stations, the entire Force being then drawn out for a period, some units remaining embodied, it being expedient at a later date to re-embody most of the remainder and dispatch many of them to South Africa. Besides this service of units, official returns contain the numbers that individually extended their services to branches of the regular Army, and there is also the great force of officers that strengthened the administrative and regimental work of the campaign, at home and abroad, in other capacities than with their own regiments or branch of the Army.

The doings of units that proceeded to South Africa on active service, and which practically form a brief history of the Militia in South Africa, will be found under the head of "Services" dealt with regimentally in this volume, where we have also included copies of many Orders issued by distinguished officers in South Africa, which placed upon record at the time their appreciation of services rendered.

CHAPTER XX.

SAYTHED CHARIOTS OF EARLY BRITAIN.—PEEL HOUSES OF ROMAN TIMES.
—ARMOURED TRAINS SOUTH AFRICA, ETC.

Having made our "progress" round and about the methods and means of many ages, and noticed the vicarious services rendered by the People's Force, it is interesting to remember that these calls began with the obligatory bearing of arms on and among the saythed chariots of early Britain in 56 B.C., and for the present have ended under voluntary service on and about the armoured trains in a far-off foreign campaign.

We also find the blockhouse duty in 1901-2 rivalling the experience of those ancestral soldiers of the people, who during the Roman occupation had often to defend the chain of Peel Houses across Northern Britain.

There now only remains to be dealt with some data in respect of those units of the "Constitutional Force" which at present have an existence.

In presenting this the first collective historical record of all that is known of the origin, periods of embodied service, and special services of Battalions and corps, there will be found information valuable to the State for purposes of reference, and tradition interesting and likely to be influential in the districts concerned.

As counties would appear to have been practically for centuries until quite recent times the responsible and organizing authority in connection with the Force, we have, associated with the older regiments, those particulars which have been preserved of the Forces that existed in their respective counties before and since the introduction of regiments as the unit of organization, and no attempt has been made to trace out in detail what happened to county units during those periods of "repose" which have occasionally interfered with the continuous history of the Force.

THE ORIGIN,

PERIODS OF EMBODIED SERVICE,

AND

SPECIAL SERVICES

OF

MILITIA UNITS,

OCTOBER 31, 1905.

INDEX.

ARTILLERY.

	PAGE.
Lancashire Royal Field Artillery (Militia)	193
Antrim Royal Garrison Artillery (Militia)	193
Cardigan ,,	195
Carmarthen ,,	196
Clare ,,	197
Cork ,,	197
Cornwall and Devon Miners ,,	200
Devon ,,	201
Donegal ,,	201
Dublin City ,,	203
Durham ,,	203
Edinburgh ,,	205
Fife ,,	207
Forfar and Kincardine ,,	207
Glamorgan ,,	208
Hampshire and Isle of Wight ,,	208
Kent ,,	209
Lancashire ,,	210
Limerick City ,,	210
Londonderry ,,	211
Mid-Ulster ,,	212
Norfolk ,,	212
Northumberland ,,	214
Pembroke ,,	214
Sligo ,,	215
South-East of Scotland ,,	217
Suffolk ,,	218
Sussex ,,	219
Tipperary ,,	219
Waterford ,,	220
West of Scotland ,,	221
Wicklow ,,	221
Yorkshire ,,	222

ENGINEERS.

	Page.
Anglesey Royal Engineers (Militia)	224
Monmouthshire ,,	226

SUBMARINE MINERS.

Portsmouth Division, Royal Engineers (Militia)	227
Needles ,,	228
Plymouth ,,	228
Thames ,,	228
Medway ,,	229
Harwich ,,	229
Milford Haven ,,	229
Western ,,	230
Humber ,,	230
Falmouth ,,	231

INFANTRY.

3rd Battn.	Lowthian Regiment		232
3rd ,,	Royal West Surrey Regiment		236
3rd ,,	East Kent	,,	239
3rd ,,	Royal Lancaster	,,	242
4th ,,	,,	,,	247
5th ,,	Northumberland Fusiliers Regiment		249
5th ,,	Royal Warwickshire	,,	251
6th ,,	,, ,,	,,	253
5th ,,	City of London	,,	256
6th ,,	,,	,,	258
7th ,,	,,	,,	261
3rd ,,	Liverpool	,,	262
4th ,,	,,	,,	263
3rd ,,	Norfolk	,,	264
4th ,,	,,	,,	266
3rd ,,	Lincolnshire	,,	267
4th ,,	,,	,,	269
3rd ,,	Devonshire	,,	269
4th ,,	,,	,,	271
3rd ,,	Suffolk	,,	272
4th ,,	,,	,,	273
3rd ,,	Somersetshire Light Infantry Regiment		275
4th ,,	,, ,, ,,	,,	277
3rd ,,	West Yorkshire	,,	279
4th ,,	,,	,,	280
3rd ,,	East Yorkshire	,,	284
3rd ,,	Bedfordshire	,,	285

				PAGE.
3rd	,,	Bedfordshire	,,	286
3rd	,,	Leicestershire	,,	289
3rd	,,	Royal Irish	,,	292
4th	,,	,,	,,	293
4th	,,	,,	,,	294
3rd	,,	Yorkshire	,,	295
4th	,,	,,	,,	297
5th	,,	Lancashire Fusiliers	,,	299
6th	,,	,, ,,	,,	300
3rd	,,	Royal Scots Fusiliers	,,	302
3rd	,,	Cheshire	,,	303
4th	,,	,,	,,	305
3rd	,,	Royal Welsh Fusiliers	,,	307
4th	,,	,, ,,	,,	308
3rd	,,	South Wales Borderers	,,	309
4th	,,	,, ,, ,,	,,	313
3rd	,,	Scottish Borderers	,,	314
3rd	,,	Scottish Rifles	,,	316
4th	,,	,, ,,	,,	318
3rd	,,	Royal Inniskilling Fusiliers Regiment		324
4th	,,	,,	,,	325
5th	,,	,,	,,	325
3rd	,,	Gloucestershire	,,	326
4th	,,	,,	,,	327
5th	,,	Worcestershire	,,	328
6th	,,	,,	,,	330
3rd	,,	East Lancashire	,,	331
3rd	,,	East Surrey	,,	334
4th	,,	,,	,,	337
3rd	,,	Cornwall Light Infantry	,,	338
3rd	,,	West Riding	,,	339
3rd	,,	Border	,,	341
4th	,,	,,	,,	343
3rd	,,	Royal Sussex	,,	344
3rd	,,	Hampshire	,,	345
3rd	,,	South Staffordshire	,,	348
4th	,,	,,	,,	351
3rd	,,	Dorsetshire	,,	353
3rd	,,	South Lancashire	,,	354
3rd	,,	Welsh	,,	357
3rd	,,	Royal Highlanders	,,	360
3rd	,,	Oxfordshire Light Infantry	,,	361
4th	,,	,, ,, ,,	,,	362

				PAGE.
3rd	,,	Essex	,,	364
4th	,,	,,	,,	366
3rd	,,	Nottinghamshire & Derbyshire	,,	366
4th	,,	,, ,,	,,	368
3rd	,,	North Lancashire	,,	371
3rd	,,	Northamptonshire	,,	372
3rd	,,	Royal Berkshire	,,	375
3rd	,,	Royal West Kent	,,	376
3rd	,,	Yorkshire Light Infantry	,,	378
3rd	,,	Shropshire Light Infantry	,,	380
4th	,,	,, ,,	,,	381
5th	,,	Middlesex	,,	382
6th	,,	,,	,,	384
5th	,,	Royal Rifle Corps	,,	387
7th	,,	,, ,,	,,	388
8th	,,	,, ,,	,,	389
9th	,,	,, ,,	,,	390
3rd	,,	Wiltshire	,,	394
5th	,,	Manchester	,,	395
6th	,,	,,	,,	396
3rd	,,	North Staffordshire	,,	397
4th	,,	,, ,,	,,	399
3rd	,,	York and Lancaster	,,	401
3rd	,,	Durham Light Infantry	,,	403
4th	,,	,, ,,	,,	405
3rd	,,	Highland Light Infantry	,,	406
4th	,,	,, ,,	,,	406
3rd	,,	Ross-shire Buffs, The Duke of Albany's Regiment		407
3rd	,,	Gordon Highlanders	,,	408
3rd	,,	Cameron Highlanders	,,	409
3rd	,,	Royal Irish Rifles	,,	410
4th	,,	,,	,,	410
5th	,,	,,	,,	411
6th	,,	,,	,,	414
3rd	,,	Royal Irish Fusiliers	,,	415
4th	,,	,, ,,	,,	415
5th	,,	,, ,,	,,	416
3rd	,,	Connaught Rangers	,,	417
4th	,,	,, ,,	,,	417
5th	,,	,, ,,	,,	418
3rd	,,	Argyll & Sutherland Highlanders	,,	419
4th	,,	,, ,,	,,	420

				PAGE.
3rd	,,	Leinster (Royal Canadians)	,,	423
4th	,,	,, ,,	,,	426
5th	,,	,, ,,	,,	427
3rd	,,	Royal Munster Fusiliers	,,	427
4th	,,	,,	,,	429
5th	,,	,,	,,	429
3rd	,,	Royal Dublin Fusiliers	,,	430
4th	,,	,, ,,	,,	431
5th	,,	,, ,,	,,	432
5th	,,	The Rifle Brigade (The Prince Consort's Own) Regiment		434
6th	,,	,, ,,	,,	438
7th	,,	,, ,,	,,	439
		The Channel Islands Militia	,,	440

ARTILLERY.

The Lancashire Royal Field Artillery (Militia).

Hon. Colonel:—
Lt.-Colonel:—Sidney, Bt. Col. Hon. A., R. Fd. Art.

Origin.

Formed May 6, 1901.

The Antrim Royal Garrison Artillery (Militia).

Hon. Colonel:—McCalmont, J.M.
Lt.-Colonel:—Kinsey, E. J., hon c. (I)

Origin.

Formed as Artillery 1854, and known as the Antrim Militia Artillery, became after some changes in organization and title The Antrim Royal Garrison Artillery (Militia).

Embodiments.

Occasion.	
Crimean War	1854, Dec. 27 to 1856, May 21.
Indian Mutiny	1859, Apr. 5, to 1861, Feb. 28.
South African War	1900, May 8, to 1900, Nov. 6.

Services.

Volunteered for foreign service during South African War, and a Service Company composed of five officers, 153 N.C.O.'s and gunners under command of Major G. E. Elmitt embarked for South Africa March 26, 1900. Colonel, E. T. Pottinger—Antrim R.G.A. proceeding in command of the Antrim and Donegal R.G.A., Service Companies as an Artillery Brigade.

On arrival at Table Bay, April 15, 1900, the Force was encamped at Maitland, suffering severely from the pestilential character of this spot, but was soon detailed to escort a large number of Boer prisoners, including many of Cronje's ill-fated commando, to St. Helena in the SS. Bavarian. On return to South Africa the two companies took over the Artillery defences of the Cape Peninsula, Colonel Pottinger being appointed C.R.A. In September proceeded to Orange

River Station. Colonel Pottinger Commandant of the District, Major Elmitt in command of Artillery, and Captain Crawford in charge of the Bridge—with detachment at Naauwpoort under Captn. Allpress, other portions of the Brigade being located at Kimberley, Barkley West, Christiana, Taungo, Fourteen Streams, Schweitzer Reineke and other centres threatened by the Boers.

While in the Orange River Colony, "Fort Antrim" was constructed by the Brigade, for which it received much commendation "most creditable to both Officers and Men."

G.O.C. Lines of Communication.

"The finest bit of fortification I've seen in South Africa." —Inspector of Fortifications.

"A permanent testimony to the industry of the Irish Brigade."—A.I.G. Lines of Communication.

June 6, 1901, the Brigade being considerably reduced in strength, was relieved by the Norfolk R.G.A. Colonel Lord Coke, and left Capetown for home June 14, 1901.

Casualties.

Killed and died of disease, etc.: 3 N.C.O.'s and Gunners.

Names Mentioned in Despatches—

Colonel E. T. Pottinger, Antrim R.G.A.
Major G. E. Elmitt, Antrim R.G.A.
Captn and Adjt. F. H. Crawford, Donegal R.G.A.
Sergt. Major C. S. M'Cabe, Antrim R.G.A.
Sergt. Major C. W. Holt, Donegal R.G.A.
Sergt. Major A. W. Vyse, Londonderry R.G.A.
Sergeant J. M'Ilwaine, Antrim R.G.A.
Sergeant J. Clarke, Donegal R.G.A.

Special Honours.

Colonel E. T. Pottinger, C.M.G.
Sergt. Major C. S. M'Cabe, D.C. Medal.
Sergt. A. W. Vyse, D.C. Medal.

Medals, etc., received by Service Company.

Queen's S.A. Medal with Clasps Cape Colony, Orange River, Transvaal and S.A. 1901.

The Cardigan Royal Garrison Artillery (Militia).

Lt.-Colonel :—Jones. G. S., Maj. ret. pay, hon. c.

Origin.

Converted into Artillery 1877 from the Royal Cardigan Rifles Militia, which regiment was raised in 1644 by Colonel John Jones of Nanleos, Cardiganshire, for King Charles I.

In 1684 "The Militia of Cardiganshire consisted of one Troop horse and three Companies foot" when inspected by Henry the 1st Duke of Beaufort.

By Militia Returns 1697, the Militia Regt. of the County had a strength of 142 foot and 60 horse, Col. Lord Lisburn.

In 1788, when the quota of Militia to be furnished by Cardiganshire was ordered to be completed and trained, the regiment was prepared for service as the Cardigan Militia, afterwards becoming a Royal regiment, confirmed in 1804 by the Commander-in-Chief, and in 1814 a Rifle Regt., until converted into Artillery 1877.

Embodiments.

    Occasion.

French War, Revolutionary War, etc., 1797 to July 11, 1814, for periods almost continuous.

South African War, May 2, 1900, to October, 1900.

Services.

Formed part of the force assembled to oppose the French expedition of 1500 men, which had landed from three frigates at Fishguard, Pembrokeshire, Feb. 22, 1797, who after plundering the district surrendered to a hastily collected body of Militia under Lord Camdor, of about half the strength of the enemy. Tradition says that the invaders were alarmed at the sight of a number of Welsh women assembled on the heights to witness the expected battle, who being clothed in red cloaks commonly worn by their class were mistaken for a body of regular troops advancing to surround them.

Volunteered for and stationed in Ireland 1811-13.

The Carmarthen Royal Garrison Artillery (Militia).

Hon. Colonel :—W.C., Hills-Johnes, Lt. Gen., Sir J., G.C.B.
Lt.-Colonel :—p.s., Williams-Drummond, Sir. J. H., Bt., hon. c.

Origin.

Converted into Artillery 1861.

At the muster of armed and able men, April, 30, Henry VIII., Kermerdynshire had 753 harnessed men and 184 nags.

In 1588 the county furnished 300 trained men reduced into bandes under captains at the assembly to resist the attack of Spanish Armada.

In 1684, at the Duke of Beaufort's inspection, "the Militia of Carmarden County consists of one Troop of Horse and one Regiment of foot commanded by Sir Rice Williams as Colonel."

By Militia Returns, 1697, the county had one regiment, 341 men and troop of horse 40, Col. Rowland Groyn Esqr. A regiment was prepared for service, and quota of Militia to be furnished by the county prior to the peace of 1763, as the Carmarthen Militia Regiment; at a later date it became Fusiliers, and in 1861 was converted into Artillery as the Royal Carmarthen, and in 1892, after various changes of title, The Carmarthen Royal Garrison Artillery (Militia).

Embodiments.

Occasion.	
Revolutionary War, etc.	1793 to 1802, Apr.
French War	1803, March, to 1816.
South African War ...	1900, May 3, to 1900 Oct. 6.

Services.

Volunteered for and served in Ireland, 1798-9.

The Carmarthen, Colonel Johnes, M.P., being one of the 13 Militia regiments immediately sent there on the passing of the Act of Parliament empowering the King to send the Militia to that country for a limited time.

Volunteered for and stationed in Ireland for a period during the 1803-16 embodiment.

The Clare Royal Garrison Artillery (Militia).

Hon. Colonel :—Inchiquin, L. W., Lord.
Lt.-Colonel :—p.s. O'Callaghan-Westropp, G., Col., A.D.C. (H) (T).

Origin.

Raised as a regiment of foot 1793, converted into Artillery 1882.

Embodiments.

Occasion.

Revolutionary War, etc.   1793 (period not recorded).
South African War ...   1900, Feb. 12, to 1900, Nov. 16.

Services.

Took part in the suppression of the Irish Rebellion and engaged in the Battle of Ross, Co. Wexford, June 5, 1798, the force being under command of Major-General Johnson.

The Cork Royal Garrison Artillery (Militia).

Hon. Colonel :—Bandon, J. F., Earl of, K.P.
Lt.-Colonel :—p.s. Lemon, J. R. S.

Origin.

According to Smith's History of the County and City of Cork, "The Militia of the City of Cork in 1584 consisted of 300 shot and 100 Billmen."

In Aug., 1666, the Duke of Ormond made a progress through the county and was escorted by the Horse Militia of each Barony.

In the year 1667 the Militia of the City of Cork consisted of 600 foot and 60 horse, ready for duty.

In 1681 they amounted to 500 foot and "two gallant troops of horse."

Anno 1691 Sir Richard Cox, as Governor, largely increased the Militia Force of the county.

At an Array of the Militia of Cork taken in 1746 the number consisted of 3,000 foot and 200 horse.—Smith, Vol. I., p. 421.

In 1760 there were two regiments of eight companies, not to exceed 60 men in each, total 960.

In 1793 the Militia of the County of the City of Cork was re-organized and completed for service, as the 27th Royal Cork City Regt., and in 1854 was converted into Artillery, as the Royal Cork City Artillery, subsequently 3rd. Bde. S.I. Div., R.A.

In 1890 the 2nd. Bde. S.I. Div., R.A. (which had previously been the West Cork Artillery Regt., commanded by Colonel T. A. Lunham) was amalgamated with the 3rd Bde. as one Regt. under Colonel T. A. Lunham, now C.B.

After various changes of title, the regiment was ultimately designated "The Cork Royal Garrison Artillery" (Militia).

Embodiments.

Occasion.

Revolutionary War, etc.	1793 to 1814 for periods almost continuous.
Crimean War	1854 to 1856.
Indian Mutiny ...	1857 to 1858.
South African War ...	1900, May 9, to 1900, Nov. 6.

Services.

It is recorded by Sir R. Cox (MSS., Trinity College, Dublin) that the Militia of the County and County of the City of Cork in 1601, numbering 6,000 horse and foot, defended a frontier of eighty miles against the enemy, made "irruptions" into their quarters, and brought off booty worth £30,000.

When the siege of Limerick was formed, 1,000 of them guarded the important pass of Killaloe, as appears from General Ginkel's letters of thanks to them, where their courage, fidelity and diligence are applauded.

This Force occupied many garrisons, and were so far from losing ground that on the contrary they gained considerably, killing near 3,000 of the enemy; nor were they worsted in any equal encounter, and assisted at the taking of Sligo and some other places.

When posted at Annaghbeg (Smith, Hist., Vol. 2, p. 219) they brought off one hundred Protestants who were prisoners on an island in the Shannon. Musgrave and Gordon's Histories of the Rebellion, 1798, and State Papers, relate that the Royal Cork City Militia took an active part in suppressing the Rebellion. On the night of the expected outbreak in Dublin, being "Notorious for its loyalty," it was, with its two battalion guns under Lt.-Colonel Longfield, with Lord Mayor Fleming at its head, stationed in St. Stephen's Green.

According to these histories, MSS. in the Record Office, Dublin, "Treasury Grant of £121, etc., to survivors of Officers and Privates for losses suffered at Prosperous," MSS. Brit. Museum, Griffith's letter to Pelham, etc., the Light Company of the Regt. was at Prosperous May 24th, when Captain Swayne, two Sergts., one Corporal and 23 Privates perished in the flames and by the pikes of the enemy. The remainder of the Company (under Lt. Corker) had been detached on special service a day or two before. (Musgrave, *ubi sup*. and Adjutant's Roll.)

"Some 5000 rebels led by the traitor Esmonde Lieut. in the Clane Yeomanry, armed chiefly with pikes, flung themselves on the barracks at 2 o'clock a.m. on the 24th May, forced an entrance and stabbed Swayne as he rose from his bed.

"Failing in their attack, the mob then barricaded the doors, etc., and threw fire into the cellars, and those who jumped from the upper windows were received on the pikes of the mob with loud yells." (Musgrave, p. 234.)

According to Musgrave's and Lecky's Histories of the Rebellion, the Regt. took chief part in the successful attack on Rathangan, May 28th, when 60 rebels were killed and numerous prisoners liberated; whilst Lieut. Pearce was successful in his skirmish at Sallins, where the enemy were defeated with loss. (Hib. Mag. 1799.)

The Regiment furnished large numbers of men for the regular Army at the front during the Crimean War and Indian Mutiny.

The Cornwall and Devon Miners' Royal Garrison Artillery (Militia).

Hon. Colonel:—Rashleigh, Sir., C. B., Bt., late Lt.-Col., hon. c.

Lt.-Colonel:—Hext, F. J., Hon. C. (I.).

Origin.

Converted into Artillery as the Royal Cornwall and Devon Miners' Artillery Militia in 1853, out of the Royal Cornwall and Devon Miners (Infantry) Regt. of Militia.

By "State Papers, Foreign and Domestic of the Reign of Henry VIII.," the "King's Grace's tenants and tinners of his manors" and of the Stanneries, etc., are referred to in the return made by Cornwall of those present at the great muster of armed men held by virtue of Royal Commission, 1539, 30 Henry VIII.

In 1798 the duty of the Miners of Cornwall and Devon to participate in the defence of the kingdom was revived by Act. 38, Geo. III., c 74, entitled "An Act for raising a body of Miners in the Counties of Cornwall and Devon for the Defence of the Kingdom during the present war" and an Infantry Regt. was organized which soon afterwards became a Royal Regt.

The obligation ending with the termination of the War and disembodiment of the Regt. Apr., 1802, the Regt. was resuscitated June 22, 1802, under Act 42, Geo. III., and it continued as an Infantry Regt. until converted in 1853, when after many changes of title it became The Cornwall and Devon Miners' Royal Garrison Artillery (Militia).

Embodiments.

Occasion.

Revolutionary War	1798, Oct.	to 1802, Apr.
French ,,	1803, Jan.	,, 1814, June 24
Crimean ,,	1855, Jan. 16	,, 1856, May 26
Crimean ,,	1900, May 1	,, 1900, Oct. 5

Services.

Volunteered for and stationed in Ireland 1811-12.

The Devon Royal Garrison Artillery (Militia).

Hon. Colonel :—
Lt.-Colonel :— White, O. W., hon. c.

Origin.

Formed 1853 out of the North Devon Militia Regt. disbanded, Colonel Buck with several Officers and 367 men, joining the new corps (see 3rd Battn. The Devonshire Regt. for the origin, etc., of North Devon Regt.).

Embodiments.
Occasion.

South African War 1900, May 1 to 1900, Oct. 17.

The Donegal (Prince of Wales's) Royal Garrison Artillery (Militia).

Hon. Colonel :—Lifford, J. W., Visct.
Lt.-Colonel :—Saunders-Knox-Gore, W. A. G., Maj., hon. c.

Origin.

In 1854 four Companies of the Donegal Infantry Militia Regt. composed of twelve Companies, were formed into Artillery as the Donegal Artillery Militia, which after some changes in Title assumed it's present designation.

Embodiments.
Occasion.

Crimean War   1855, period not recorded.
South African War 1900, May 2 to 1900, Nov. 6.

Services.

Volunteered for Foreign Service during the South African War, and a Service Company of five Officers, 144 N.C.O.'s and Gunners, Captain and Hon. Major W. B. Reed, Commdg., embarked for South Africa.

On arrival at Cape Town, March 26, 1900, the Company was united with the Service Company of the Antrim Royal Garrison Artillery, and together formed the Brigade Division Irish Militia Artillery, Lt.-Colonel and Hon. Colonel E. T. Pottinger (Antrim R.G.A.) commdg.

Apr. 25th, 1900, the Brigade re-embarked in charge of 1000 Boer prisoners for St. Helena, and on return in September the Donegals assisted in manning the Cape Town and Simons Town Defences. Sepr. 29th Captn. and Adjt. F. H. Crawford with 25 men of the Antrims and like number of the Donegals proceeded to Orange River Station and took over three seven pounder mountain guns, and two maxims. Oct. 18th Major Elmitt of the Antrims with 50 men left Cape Town for Orange River, and relieved Captn. Crawford, who had been appointed as O. C. Troops at the Bridge.

Nov. 10th, Major Reed and Lt. Fullerton, with remainder of the Donegals, moved from Cape Town to Kimberley, and the Company was broken up into detachments at posts wherever a gun was required, those remaining at Kimberley being employed as Field Artillery, and with a gun on one of the armoured trains running out of Kimberley.

Nov. 20th, Lt. Milligan with 28 Donegals formed part of the relief column for Sweitzer Reinecke, fighting all the way during the march of three days, and were eventually shut up there until relieved by Lord Methuen's column, which brought them back to Kimberley, Jan. 28, 1901.

Oct. 12th, 1900, Maj. Reed was specially promoted Lt.-Colonel to command the S.S. Company, and acted as O.C. Troops at various places, including "A" Section, Kimberley Defences, in Feb., 1901, and C.R.A. to Maj.-Gen. Pretyman, C.B., Apr. 2, 1901, until June 7, 1901, when the Company proceeded to Cape Town en route for home. While at Orange River Station the Troops of the Brigade Div. Irish Militia Artillery took part under Captn. F. H. Crawford as O.C. Troops Orange River Bridge, in mining 32 miles of railway to the North, twice mined Zoutpans Drift, and laid about 40 military land mines on the adjoining kopjes, besides R.E. work in the outlying districts.

Casualties—Killed and died of disease, etc.

Donegal R.G.A.
2nd Lieuts. Hill-Motum and Woodhouse.
Two N.C.O.'s and men.

Names mentioned in Despatches.

Donegal R.G.A.
Captn. and Adjt. F. H. Crawford.
Bgde. Sergt.-Major C. W. Holt.   Sergt. J. Clarke.

Special Honours.

Brigade Sergt.-Major C. W. Holt.   D.C. Medal.

Medals, etc., received by Service Company.

Queen's South African, 1901, with Clasps "Cape Colony." "Orange Free State," and S.A., 1901.

The Dublin City Royal Garrison Artillery (Militia).

Hon. Colonel :—Iveagh, E. C., Lord, K.P.
Lt.-Colonel :—p.s. Smythe, W. L., hon. c. (I).

Origin.

Raised 1854 as the Dublin City Artillery Regt. of Militia, and after some changes in designation became in 1901 The Dublin City Royal Garrison Artillery (Militia).

Embodiments.

Occasion.

Crimean War	1854, Dec.	to 1856, Aug. 11.
Indian Mutiny	1859, Apr. 2	,, 1860, Nov. 29.
South African War	1900, May 9	,, 1900, Nov. 6.

The Durham Royal Garrison Artillery (Militia).

Hon. Colonel :—
Lt.-Colonel :—p.s. Ditmas, H. P., hon. c. T. (I).

Origin.

In 1853 the quota of men to be found by the County being 2000, an Artillery Unit was formed as the Durham Regt. of Militia Artillery besides an additional Infantry Regiment.

Embodiments.

Occasion.

Indian Mutiny 1859, June, for about three years.
South African War 1900, May 1 to 1900, Oct. 11.

Services.

A special service R.G.A. Compy. of five Officers and 170 N.C.O.'s and Gunners volunteered for and embarked for

South Africa, Mch. 24, 1900. After disembarking at Durban they were joined by a similar company of the Edinburgh R.G.A., and the Division known as the " Durham and Edinburgh Division R.G.A." was placed under the command of Colonel H. P. Ditmas (Durham R.G.A.) taking over duties at the base. In July a contingent of the Durhams moved to Eshowe, Zululand, and at later date the remainder of the Division proceeded to Ladysmith and were employed on Outpost duty, their carbines being replaced by rifles. The Durhams on the Zululand Frontier were often engaged with the enemy in the prevention of frontier raids, the Boers at times being very active. Sep., 1901, Louis Botha's commando about 3000 strong was threatening Zululand, and the Durham Company was moved to Melmoth, two positions being occupied and put in a state of defence by the construction of trenches, sangars, etc., to check his advance, the troops available being the Durham Company R.G.A., and 30 of the 5th Mounted Infantry under Capt. Rowley, Dorset Regt. Sep. 24th it being reported by Kaffir scouts that the Boers were advancing, the Mounted Infantry were detailed by Captain Rowley to defend the Sandbag Redoubt, the trenches, sangars, etc., being allotted to the Durham Artillery under Lieut. Johnson. At 4.30 a.m. on the 26th, a severe attack was delivered by the Boers on the North and West of the position, the brunt of the attack falling on the Durham Artillery, the enemy succeeded in getting through the wire entanglements to within twenty yards of the sangers but with the aid of the maxim gun were repulsed, another attack made later on the rear of the Fort Prospect redoubt held by Capt. Rowley and his Mounted Infantry, was also defeated. At this time the Post was reinforced by Sergt. Gumbi and small party of Zululand Native Police, who, hearing the firing, had marched from their post about four miles away and broke through to render help. The camp and positions were entirely surrounded. No further attack was however attempted, but a heavy fire was kept up by the enemy until they drew off. The attack had been made by five to six hundred Boers of the Ermelo or Carolina Commandos, the prisoners taken owning to a loss of sixty killed and wounded, and thirty dead horses were found next day. The Durhams soon afterwards moved to Eshowe and from thence to Durban by march route from the Tugela River.

The remainder of the Durham and Edinburgh Division R.G.A., under Major Lee, were brought down at about this time from the Natal-Transvaal Frontier and proceeded to

Bombay with a large contingent of Boer prisoners. On arrival in India part of the force escorted the prisoners to their destination and remained as guard over them for some time, the remainder embarking for England Nov., 1901, the Company from Zululand arriving home from the Cape a few days before them.

Casualties.—Killed and died of disease, etc., Nil.

Mentioned in Despatches.—Colonel H. P. Ditmas; Captains H. S. Streatfield and E. H. Place; Sergt.-Major J. Reilly, R.A.; Staff-Sergt. A. E. Barrett, R.A.; Lt.-Colonel Clerke; Captain A. G. Mayson-Johnson; Sergt. F. Doyle; Bombardiers J. Marsden and G. Gilligan; Major J. Gowans; Compy.-Sergt. J. O'Neil, R.A.

Special Honours.—Major James Gowans. D.S.O.

Medals, etc., Received by the Service Company.

Queen's and King's S. A. Medals, with Clasps "Cape Colony," "Orange Free State," S.A. 1901-S.A. 1902.

The Duke of Edinburgh's Own Edinburgh Royal Garrison Artillery (Militia).

Hon. Colonel:—Colquhoun, A. J., C.B., hon. c. (Hon. Lt.-Col. in the Army, 7 Oct., 1900.)

Lt.-Colonel:—p.s. Mercer, A., Hon. C. (I).

Origin.

Raised 1854 as the Edinburgh Artillery Militia. In 1876 designated The Duke of Edinburgh's Own Edinburgh Artillery Militia, and at a later date known by its present title.

Embodiments.

Occasion.

Crimean War	1855, Feb. 2 to	1856, May 26.
Indian Mutiny	1859, Apr. 4 ,,	1860, June 14.
South African War	1900, May 7 ,,	1900, Oct. 6.

Services.

Volunteered for Foreign service during S. A. War, and a Service Company composed of five Officers, 154 N.C.O.'s and Gunners, Major J. L. Lee, commdg. Embarked for South Africa Mch. 23, 1900. On arrival at Durban May 1, 1900, the Company formed with the Durham R.G.A. Service Company an Artillery Brigade known as the Durham and Edinburgh under command of Lt.-Colonel H. P. Ditmas (Durham R.G.A.), and was encamped on Congella Flats about three miles from Durban, taking over the duties of a guard of two Officers and 100 men on the prison ship SS. "Catalonia," Town Guard and escort duties, etc.

Dec. 2, 1900, the Company proceeded to "Tin Town" Camp, Ladysmith, and found in conjunction with other troops the guard over Prisoners of War Camp, manned the surrounding outposts of Ladysmith defences, with detachments from time to time as required at Van Reenans, Blan Bank, Acton Homes, and Harrismith. The Brigade had two Howitzers and two Maxims, one Howitzer being mounted on Rifleman's Post under Major Lee and one on King's Post under Captain W. H. Thornhill, whose composite Company of Mounted Infantry for about two months found the guard for all Bridges and Blockhouses from Colenso to Sandy's River on the Natal Railway. Sep. 9, 1901, the Brigade proceeded to Kakkerstroom to take over 1000 prisoners of war, and escort them to Durban and thence to Bombay. Nov. 8, 1901, embarked at Bombay for England.

Casualties.—Killed and died of disease, etc.

3 N.C.O.'s and Gunners.

Names mentioned in Despatches.

Major J. L. Lee.
Captain W. H. Thornhill (twice).

Medals, etc., received by Company.

Queen's South African, with Clasps "Transvaal," and "Orange River Colony."

The Fife Royal Garrison Artillery (Militia).

Hon. Colonel :—Baird, W., hon. c.
Lt.-Colonel :—Moubray, A.

Origin.

Raised 1854 as the Fife Artillery Militia, became the 4th Brigade Scottish Division, R.A., in 1882, subsequently Fife Artillery, Southern Division R.A., and at a later date as now designated.

Embodiments.

Occasion.

Crimean War	1859, Apr. 25 ,,	1860, Aug. 31.
Indian Mutiny	1900, May 4 ,,	1900, Oct. 12.
South African War	1900, May 4 ,,	1900, Oct 12.

The Forfar and Kincardine Royal Garrison Artillery (Militia).

Hon. Colonel :—p.s. Ogilvy, Sir, R.H.A., Bat. Col., A.D.C.
Lt.-Colonel :—p.s. Southesk, c.n., Earl of, hon. c.

Origin.

Converted into an Artillery Regt. 1854 out of the Forfar and Kincardine Regt. of Infantry Militia, which was raised as the Forfarshire Regt. for the Revolutionary War of 1793, and called in 1802 the Forfarshire and Kincardine Militia, until it became converted into Artillery.

Embodiments.

Occasion.

Revolutionary War ...	...	Period unknown.
French ,,	1803 ...	to 1816, May.
Crimean ,,	1855 ...	,, 1856.
Indian Mutiny	1857 ...	,, 1860, June.
South African War	1900, May 7	,. 1900, Oct. 6.

Services.

Volunteered for and Stationed in Ireland, 1814-16.

When at Sheerness in 1860 the Regt. was selected as one of the two Militia Artillery Units for proposed conversion into Royal Artillery.

Note.—The old Records of this Regt. having been destroyed, the above are furnished from memory by Colonel Blair-Imrie, of Leenar Bay, Montrose.

The Glamorgan Royal Garrison Artillery (Militia).

Hon. Colonel:—Dunraven and Mountearl, Rt. Hon., W. T., Earl of, K.P., C.M.G. (Hon. Capt. in Army, 26 July, 1901.).

Lt.-Colonel:—p.s. Alford, F. L., Capt. ret. pay (Capt. Res. of Off.), (S).

Origin.

Raised as the Royal Glamorganshire Artillery Militia in 1854, by Mr Talbot, of Morgan Abbey, the Lord Lieutenant of the County, under the power possessed of raising a local Militia in proportion to the population, all Officers and recruits being resident in the County—and first commanded by Colonel Morgan, of St. Helens, Swansea. In 1882 designated the 2nd Brigade Welsh Division Royal Artillery—and on the abolition of Divisions in 1902 The Glamorgan Royal Garrison Artillery (Militia).

Embodiments.

Occasion.

South African War ... 1900, May 1, to 1900, Oct. 2.

The Duke of Connaught's Own Hampshire and Isle of Wight Royal Garrison Artillery.

Hon. Colonel:—Field Marshal H.R.H. Arthur W. P. A. Duke of Connaught and Strathearn, K.G., K.T., K.P., G.C.B., G.C.S.I., G.C.M.G., G.C.I.E., G.C.V.O., S. Gds., A.S. Corps, and Col. in Chief 6 Dns., High L.J., R. Dub. Fus., and Rif. Brig., Personal A.D.C. to the King, Insp.-Gen. of the Forces—Bailiff of Egle Order of St. John of Jerusalem.

Lt.-Colonel:—p.s. Gordon, W. H. G. (t).

Origin.

Formed 1853 as The Hampshire Artillery Southern Division Royal Artillery by transfer of three Officers and 396 men from the South Hants. Militia and one Officer from the North Hants. (See 3rd Battn. Hampshire Regt. for the origin of that Battn.).

In 1891 amalgamated with the Isle of Wight Artillery Militia as the Duke of Connaught's Hampshire and Isle of Wight Artillery (Southern Division Royal Artillery).

Embodiments.

Occasion.

Crimean War ...	1854, Dec.	to 1856, June.
Indian Mutiny ...	1858, Oct.	,, 1860, Oct.
Threatened War...	1885, May	,, 1885, Sept.
South African War	1900, May 1	,, 1900, Nov. 6.

Services.

See 3rd Battn. Hampshire Regt. for services of the North and South Hants. and Isle of Wight Regts. of Militia out of which this Corps was formed.

The Kent Royal Garrison Artillery (Militia).

Hon. Colonel :—Stirling, Sir W. G., Bt.
Lt.-Colonel :—Elliot, W., Maj., hon. c.

Origin.

Raised May, 1853.

Embodiments.

Occasion.

Crimean War ...	1855, Jan. 3 to	1856, June 10.
South African War	1900, May 3 ,,	1900, Oct. 10.

The Lancashire Royal Garrison Artillery (Militia).

Hon. Colonel:—Walker, W. H.
Lt.-Colonel:—Burrard, W. D., Maj. ret. pay (Res. of Off.), hon. c.

Origin.

Formed in 1853 under Command of Colonel Sir Duncan McDonald, late Commanding 93rd Highlanders.

Embodiments.

Occasion.

Crimean War	1855, Jan. 1 to 1856, May 30.
Indian Mutiny	1857, Oct. 5 ,, 1860, June 15.
South African War	1900, May 3 ,, 1900, Oct. 11.

The Limerick City Royal Garrison Artillery (Militia).

Hon. Colonel:—Barrington, Sir C. B., Bt.
Lt.-Colonel:—Henn, R. A. M., Maj. ret pay (Maj. res. of Off.), hon. c.

Origin.

In 1854 The City of Limerick Regiment of Militia which had been formed in the year 1793, was converted into an Artillery Corps as the Limerick City Artillery Militia. After various changes in designation it became The Limerick City Royal Garrison Artillery (Militia).

Embodiments.

Occasion.

Revolutionary War and European Disturbances, etc.	1793 to 1802, May. 1803, Mch. 25, to 1814.
French War	1815, July to 1816, Mch. 22.
Crimean War	1855, Feb. 3, to 1856, July 22.
South African War	1900, May, to 1900, Nov. 6.

Services.

In 1798, July 19, when stationed in the Province of Leinster it was employed in quelling the disturbances. On the invasion of Ireland by the French under General

Humbert, the Regt. moved to Sligo, and when the French after their victory at Castlebar attempted to invade Ulster, it took an active part under Colonel Vereker, supported by some Dragoons and Fencibles, in the action at Colooney, checking their advance with so much gallantry that they gave up the intention of entering Ulster, and marching to the South came in for the large Army under Lord Cornwallis, to whom they were compelled to surrender themselves. Lieut. Rumley was killed and four other Officers wounded. "Of this action for his gallantry Colonel Vereker was granted by his Majesty King Geo. III. the privilege of bearing supportes and other honourable augmentations to his arms, with the motto "Colooney."

The Corporation of Limerick Resolved, "That the steady, loyal, and gallant conduct of our fellow-citizens of the Limerick City Regt. of Militia, who on the 5th Sept. last under the command of Colonel Vereker so intrepidly engaged and successfully opposed the progress of the whole French Army at Colooney, merits, etc., etc., and that Fifty guineas be paid towards a fund to purchase a suitable piece of plate for the Officers, and medals for the N.C.O.'s and men of the Regt. engaged in the Action."

The Londonderry Royal Garrison Artillery (Militia).

Hon. Colonel :—Bruce, Sir H. H., Bt.
Lt.-Colonel :—p.s. Bruce, S. A. M., hon. c.

Origin.

Raised in 1793 as the Londonderry Militia Regiment, became Light Infantry in 1855, and converted into Artillery April, 1882, as the 9th Brigade North Irish Division Royal Artillery, changed to the Londonderry Artillery Southern Division Royal Artillery in 1889, and to The Londonderry Royal Garrison Artillery (Militia) in 1902.

Embodiments.

Occasion.

Revolutionary War	...	1793 to 1798.
French ,,	...	1814 to 1816.
Crimean ,,	...	1855, Jan., to 1856, Aug. 20.
South African ,,	...	1900, May 1, to 1900, Oct. 3.

Services.

Served through the Irish Rebellion 1798, Lieut. Rowley Miller, with a detachment of the regiment, capturing one of the chief rebels named Talent, for whose apprehension the Government had offered a reward of £200, besides a private reward offered of £1,000.

The Mid-Ulster Royal Garrison Artillery (Militia).

Hon. Colonel:—Saunders, R. J. P., C.B., hon. c.
Lt.-Colonel:—Irwin, J. S., hon. c.

Origin.

Raised in 1855 as the Tyrone Militia Artillery, and the title Royal authorised in that year by Warrant of King Geo. III., changed in 1882 to the Mid-Ulster Artillery Militia, 6th Brigade, North Irish Division, R.A. In 1889 became The Mid-Ulster, Southern Division, R.A., and in 1902 Mid-Ulster R.G.A. (Militia).

Embodiments.

    Occasion.

Crimean War	1855, Nov., to 1856, July 21.
South African War	1900, May 3, to 1900, Nov. 6.

The Prince of Wales's Own Norfolk Royal Garrison Artillery (Militia).

Hon. Colonel:—THE KING.
Lt.-Colonel:—Coke, T. W., Visct., C.V.O., C.M.G., Col. ret. pay, A.D.C.

Origin.

Formed in 1853 as the Norfolk Artillery, out of detachments from the 1st and 2nd Norfolk Regts. In 1715 an Artillery Regt. existed in the county, the City of Norwich furnishing a Company of 100 men.

Embodiments.

   Occasion.

   Crimean War   ...   1855, Jan. 25, to 1856, June 15.
        ,,   ...   1859, Apr. 5, to 1860, Aug. 18.
   South African War ...   1900, May 2, to 1900, Oct. 13.

ervices.

A special service Company volunteered for and proceeded to South Africa, under Colonel The Viscount Coke, M.V.O. Strength embarked: 5 officers, 134 N.C.O.'s and men. On arrival Cape Town May 27, 1901, proceeded to Kimberley, thence Bultfontein Camp, the Head Quarters and Company moving to Orange River, leaving a detachment of 35 N.C.O.'s and men under Captain C. H. Walter for garrison duty at Beaconsfield Camp, Kimberley, the detachment taking over the famous "Long Cecil" gun, and other guns, two N.C.O.'s and six men being detached for the two Q.F. guns on armoured trains "Wasp" and "Challenger." The Company at Orange River occupied "Fort Antrim," twenty N.C.O.'s and men under Captain and Adjt. F. A. Twiss taking up a position with Q.F. guns on the north side of the river. 8 N.C.O.'s and men detailed for duty on the armoured trains "Bulldog" and "Blackhatla." Forty N.C.O.'s and men being trained as Mounted Infantry, were engaged on several occasions in preventing the enemy from crossing the line. Twelve N.C.O.'s and men proceeded to Koffyfontein for duty with 15p. B.L. guns—Jan. 28 the Fort having been dismantled, Head Quarters moved to Kimberley—Jan 31. Twenty N.C.O.'s and men sent to Christiana for duty. February 13, a detachment of 25 N.C.O.'s and men under Lieut. Hon. B. F. Guidon took over two 15 pr. B.L. guns at Boshof, and Lieut. L. G. Buxton, with fifteen N.C.O.'s and men a 15 pr. Q.F. Elswick gun, which was employed escorting convoys to and from Boshof, and on one occasion it assisted in driving off Jacob's commando in an attack on convoy. They also acted as escort for the R.E. whilst engaged in building blockhouses on the line from Kimberley to Boshof.

Casualties.

   Killed and died of disease, etc., 1 N.C.O. and 1 man.

Mentioned in Despatches.

   Colonel the Viscount Coke, M.V.O.
   Co. Sergeant Major G. C. McWyinn.
   Bombr. E. A. Shearing.

Special Honours.

Colonel, the Viscount Coke, M.V.O.—C.M.G.
Co. Sgt.-Major G. C. McWyinn—D.C. Medal.

Medals and clasps.

Queen's South African with clasps Transvaal, Orange River, Cape Colony, S.A. 1901, S.A. 1902.

The Northumberland Royal Garrison Artillery (Militia).

Hon. Colonel:—Reed, Sir C. J., K.C.B., hon. c.
Lt.-Colonel:—p.s. Blake, F. D., hon. c.

Origin.

Raised in 1854.

Embodiments.

Occasion.

Indian Mutiny	...	1859, for about two years.
South African War	...	1900, May 7, to 1900, Oct. 11.

The Pembroke Royal Garrison Artillery (Militia).

Hon. Colonel:—Edwards, F. P., hon. c. (Hon. Lt.-Col. in Army 4 Oct., 1900).
Lt.-Colonel:—Cope, W. C., hon. c. (I).

Origin.

Formed into an Artillery Regiment 1853 out of the Royal Pembroke Rifles Militia, the earliest known records of which as a regiment date back to Aug. 11, 1684, when at an Inspection near Haverford West by His Grace the Duke of Beaufort it was composed of "one Troop of horse and one Regiment all of Firelocks." By Militia Returns, 1697, Pembrokeshire had one Regiment of 456 men, and Troop of horse 36, total 492. Col., Sir Thomas Stepney Bart. In 1759, under the order issued to the Lords Lieutenant of the several counties to complete and train their Militia, a Regiment was prepared for service, and the quota to be furnished by the county. In 1804 became a Royal Regiment, and 1812 a Rifle Corps. In 1853 formed into Artillery as the Royal Pembrokeshire Artillery, changed in 1882 to 4th Brigade, Western Div., R.A., in 1889 to the Pembroke Artillery Militia, R.A., and to its present title in 1902.

Embodiments.

Occasion.

Seven Years War	1759, Dec. 15 to 1762, Dec. 4.
American War, etc.	1771, March 3, to 1783, Feb. 2.
French War	1803 to 1814, June.
Crimean War	1855, March, to 1856, July.
South African War	1900, May 4, to 1900, Oct. 3.

Services.

The Gordon Riots in 1780, when the regiment was detailed to protect Lord Petrie's house and chapel in Essex.

Volunteered for service in Ireland during the Rebellion, 1798, and under Colonel Colby was one of the 13 regiments immediately sent there on the passing of the Act empowering the King to employ the English Militia in that Country for a limited period.

Volunteered for and stationed in Ireland 1811-12.

The Duke of Connaught's Own Sligo Royal Garrison Artillery (Militia).

Hon. Colonel:—Field Marshal H.R.H. Arthur W. P. A., Duke of Connaught and Strathearn, K.G., K.T., K.P., G.C.B., G.C.S.I., G.C.M.G., G.C.T.E., G.C.V.O., S. Guards, A.S. Corps, and Col-in-Chief 6 Dns., High L.I. & Dub. Fus, and Rif. Brig., Personal A.D.C. to the King, Insp.-Gen. of the Forces, Bailiff of Egle Order of St. John of Jerusalem.

Lt.-Colonel:—Roberts, J. D. A.

Origin.

Converted into Artillery 1877, out of the Sligo Rifles Militia, and descended from the organized forces of the county which existed from about the middle of the 17th century. It is recorded that in 1655 a regiment commanded by Col. Sir Chas. Coote was disembodied, the members receiving grants of land in Sligo. During the Rebellion, 1685, every male capable of bearing arms appears to have been engaged either in the ranks of the Enniskillens or supporting the cause of James II., but a regiment of local Militia was on duty in the years 1715, 1745, 1759 to 1763, and 1778 to 1783, and was re-organized and prepared for service as the Sligo Militia Regt., for the Revolutionary War; in 1793 became Light Infantry at one period, and a Rifle Corps in 1855, until converted into Artillery as the 8th Brigade (Duke of Connaught's Own) North Irish Division, R.A., changed to the Duke of Connaught's Own Sligo Artillery, Southern Division, R.A., in 1891, and in 1902 to its present designation.

Embodiments.

Occasion.

Seven Years War	{ 1715 and 1745 periods unknown.
	1759 to 1763
American ,,	1778 to 1783.
Revolutionary War, etc.	1792 to 1814 almost continu-
Crimean ,,	1855 to 1856 [ously
South African ,,	1900, May 10, to 1900, Oct. 10.

Services.

Took an active part in the suppression of the Irish Rebellion, 1798; formed a portion of the first line which carried the rebel position at Vinegar Hill at the point of the bayonet, having many men killed and wounded, including Colonel King and two other officers among the latter, the regiment being favourably mentioned in Despatches. While stationed in the South of Ireland the Light Company formed part of the Light Brigade.

Volunteered for and stationed for a period in England during the embodiment of 1792-1814.

The South East of Scotland Royal Garrison Artillery (Militia).

Hon. Colonel:—Houston-Boswell-Preston, T. A., hon. c. (Hon. Lt.-Col. in Army, 6 Oct., 1900).

Lt.-Colonel:—Menzies, C. T., hon. c.

Origin.

Formed into a Regiment out of the Militia raised by Scotland in compliance with a letter of King Charles II., dated Whitehall, 10th of June, 1661, to the Estates of Parliament, addressed to the Lord High Commissioner, the Earl of Middleton.

Nov. 23, 1663, the numbers being settled and the proportion from the shyre of Berwick fixed at 800 foot and 74 horse, the Berwickshire Regiment was formed.

In 1688, it is on record by a Proclamation dated 15 Apr. calling together the Militia "on this side of the Tay," that the Militia Regiment of the Shyre of Berwick was still composed of foot and "Troupe" of horse, confined by a Warrant granted by the Committee of Estates, dated 3d. of May, 1689, that "eighteen horses and one halfe were deficient of the number appoynted by the Act to be raised by the Shyre."

In 1802, under an Act of the British Parliament, the quotas of Militia to be furnished by the Counties of Berwick, Haddington, Linlithgow and Peebles, were united for one Regiment of 448 men, to be named the Berwickshire (or 1st Regt. of North British) Militia, increased in strength July 25, 1803 to 674 men, and to be raised by ballot. In 1854 the regiment became Artillery, and after several changes in designation the South East of Scotland Royal Garrison Artillery (Militia).

Embodiments.

Occasion.

Scottish Rebellion, etc.	1670 to 1685.
Revolution	1689, period unknown.
French War	1803 to 1814.
,, ,,	1815, nine months.
Crimean War	1856, sixteen months.
South African War	1900, May 15 to 1900, Oct. 5.

Services.

Scottish Rebellion until 1685, when "King James the VII. of Scotland, fearing that the Militia might declare for Argyll, discharged the ordinary levy for the Militia, and it was recommended to the secret council to dispose of the Militia arms in the respective shyres as should seem most expedient for His Majesties service during the Rebellion."

During the Revolution, 1689, and embodiment, 1803-14, it was stationed for a few years in England.

The Suffolk Royal Garrison Artillery (Militia).

Hon. Colonel :—Rendlesham, F. W. B., Lord.
Lt.-Colonel :—

Origin.

Converted into Artillery 1853 as The Suffolk Artillery Militia, out of the East Suffolk Light Infantry, which was prepared for service in 1759 as the East Suffolk Militia (for its early origin, see 3rd Battn., The Suffolk Regt.).

In 1902, after many changes of title, it became The Suffolk Royal Garrison Artillery (Militia).

Embodiments.

Occasion.	
Seven Years War, etc.	1759, period unknown.
Revolutionary War	Dates unknown.
French ,,	1812 to 1814.
Crimean ,,	1854 to 1856.
Indian Mutiny	1859, April, to 1860, Nov.
South African War	1900, May 1, to 1900, Nov. 6.

Services.

Volunteered for and served in Ireland, 1798-9, under Colonel Goate, and was one of the thirteen Militia regiments immediately sent to that country on the passing of the Act empowering the King to accept the services of the Militia for a limited period.

1813.—Furnished two officers and 70 men for the 2nd Provisional Militia Battn., Lt. Colonel, Edwd. Bayley (W. Middlesex Regt.) of the Militia Brigade, which under the Duke of Buckingham landed near Bordeaux in the South of France.

The Sussex Royal Garrison Artillery (Militia).

Hon. Colonel :—Sadler, Sir J. H. K.C.M.G.
Lt.-Colonel :—Adamson, R. W., hon. c.

Origin.

Formed 1853, by transfer of 206 Volunteers from the Royal Sussex Infantry Militia Regt. The official designation of the regiment until the end of Augt., 1899, was the 3rd Brigade, Cinque Ports Division, Royal Artillery Militia, when it was changed to The Sussex Artillery, Eastern Division, Royal Artillery, and subsequently became The Sussex Royal Garrison Artillery (Militia).

Embodiments.

Occasion.

Crimean War ... 1855, Feb. 1, to 1856, June 16.
South African War ... 1900, May 1, to 1900, Oct. 17.

The Tipperary Royal Garrison Artillery (Militia).

Hon. Colonel :—V.C. Gough, Gen. Sir C. J. S., G.C.B.
Lt.-Colonel :—Lecky, F. J. S., hon. c.

Origin.

Converted into Artillery 1854, out of the 1st or South Tipperary Regiment of Infantry, which was formed in 1793; designated in 1812 The Tipperary (or Duke of Clarence's Munster) Regt. of Militia; subsequently Fusiliers until 1854, when it became the Tipperary Artillery Militia; changed in 1882 to the 5th Brigade, South Irish Division, Royal Artillery; in 1889 to The Tipperary Artillery (Southern Division, R.A.); and in 1902 The Tipperary Royal Garrison Artillery (Militia).

Embodiments.

Occasion.

Revolutionary War, etc. 1793 to 1816, April 24, almost [continuously.
Crimean   „   ...1855, Jan 25, to 1856, July 28.
Indian Mutiny   ...1858, Oct. 28, to 1861, Mar. 21.
South African War   ...1900, May 2, to 1900, Oct. 10.

Services.

Volunteered for and stationed in England 1811-13. In 1860, when at Sheerness, the regiment offered to become part of the new 16th Brigade, Royal Artillery, which was being raised, and in recognition twelve officers of the regiment were given (without purchase) Commissions in the Line.

The Waterford Royal Garrison Artillery (Militia).

Hon. olonel:—V.C., Roberts, Field Marshal, Rt. Hon. F. S., Earl, K.G., K.P., G.C.B., O.M., G.C.S.I., G.C.I.E., Col. Commdg. R. Art., Col. I. Gds. (R)

Lt.-Colonel:—Carew, R. T., hon. c.

Origin.

Converted into Artillery 1854, out of the Waterford Light Infantry Regt. of Militia, which had been organized for service under the Act of the Irish Parliament, 33, Geo. III., 1793.

In 1584 the City of Waterford had an organized force of 300 shot and 300 billmen.

In 1882 the designation of the regiment was changed from the Waterford Artillery Militia to 6th Brigade, South Irish Division, R.A.; in 1889 to The Waterford Artillery (Southern Division, R.A.); and later to its present designation.

Embodiments.

Occasion.

Revolutionary War ..	Period not recorded.
Crimean ,, ...	1855, Jan. 14, to 1856, July 23.
Indian Mutiny ...	1857, Oct. 1, to 1860, April 30.
South African War ...	1900, May 7, to 1900, Oct. 13.

The West of Scotland Royal Garrison Artillery (Militia).

Hon. Colonel:—Younger, Col. J., Lt.-Col., ret. pay.
Lt.-Colonel:—p.s. Walker-Jones, F. A., hon. c.

Origin.

Formed, 1881, into Artillery for the Counties of Lanark and Renfrew, out of the Argyll and Bute Rifle Militia Regiment, which was raised 1796 by conversion of the 117th or Argyll Fencibles into a Militia Regt.

Embodiments.

Volunteered for and served for a long period in Ireland at the end of 1700 and early 1800, being also in Ireland for second term in 1812.

Occasion.

Crimean War ... 1855 to 1856.
South African War ... 1900, May 8, to 1900, Oct. 3.

The Wicklow Royal Garrison Artillery (Militia).

Hon. Colonel:—Tottenham, C. G., Lt.-Colonel.
Lt.-Colonel:—Kemmis, W. H. O., Maj. (Maj. Res. of Off.).

Origin.

In 1793, under Act 33, Geo. III., c 22, a Regt. of Militia was completed for service and the quota of men to be furnished by County Wicklow known as the 37th "Wicklow Infantry Militia"—and became a Rifle Corps in 1855. In 1877 the "Wicklow Rifles" Regiment was converted into Artillery as the Wicklow Artillery Militia, its designation being changed in 1882 to the 7th Brigade North Irish Division Royal Artillery, and after other changes in name became as above recorded.

Embodiments.

Occasion.

Revolutionary War and European Disturbances ...
- 1793, June 10, to 1802, May.
- 1803, Mch. 25, to 1814, Aug. 2.
- 1815, May 25, to 1816, Mch. 29.

Crimean War ... ... 1855, Jan. 27, to 1856, Aug. 11.
South African War ... 1900, May 11, to 1900, Oct. 9.

Services.

Took part in the expedition to Bantry in 1796 for the purpose of repelling threatened invasion by the French.

In 1798, by Musgrave's History, "The Light Company of the Wicklow Militia," under the command of Captain Richardson, was in May stationed at Dunlavin, and took part in the defence of the place on the 24th and 25th of that month. On the 23rd of June, 1798, the Regt. forming part of the garrison of Kilkenny marched under Sir Charles Asgill to the relief of the town of Castlecomer, which place they retook from the Rebels, and on the 26th of June took part in the action near Kilcomney Hill against four thousand rebels, when near one thousand were killed and fourteen pieces of cannon, a quantity of ammunition, about fifteen car loads of provisions, upwards of 150 horses, oxen, etc., were captured. The Regt. received public thanks through General Asgill for their conduct on both of these occasions.

The Yorkshire (Duke of York's Own) Royal Garrison Artillery (Militia).

Hon. Colonel :—
Lt.-Colonel :—Legard, J. D., C.B., hon. c.p.s.c.

Origin.

Raised 1860, and amalgamated with the East York Militia Artillery as the "East and North York Militia Artillery," became the Yorkshire Artillery Militia in 1873, 4th Brigade Northern Division Royal Artillery in 1882, Yorkshire Artillery Western Division Royal Artillery in 1890, and at later date The Yorkshire (Duke of York's Own) Royal Garrison Artillery (Militia).

Embodiments.
   Occasion.

South African War ... 1900, May 1, to 1900, Oct. 12.

Services.

Riots at Scarborough, Mch., 1900, on the occasion of a meeting regarding the Boer War attended by Cronwright Schreiner, brother-in-law of the Premier of Cape Colony. A body of the Yorkshire Artillery and Depot under Captain W. E. Fell, Yorks Artillery, after patrolling the streets succeeded in inducing the crowd to disperse quietly without causing further damage, a Resolution of the Corporation being placed upon record of their high appreciation of the tact and judgment displayed by Captain Fell, etc.

ENGINEERS.

Royal Anglesey Royal Engineers (Militia).

Hon. Colonel :—Hampton-Lewis, T. L.

Lt.-Colonel :—p.s. Mathews-Donaldson, C. G., Maj. ret. pay (Maj. Res. of Off.), (H) (T) p.v.c. (b).

Origin.

From "Letters and Papers of the Reign of Henry VIII.," the Company of Anglesey and Merioneth then united for military purposes, were represented at the great Muster of 1539—30 Henry VIII. (see copy of the Certificate).

By Harleian MSS., 1588—Spanish Armada assembly, Anglesey had 1108 able men present, but the numbers trayned, ffurnished with weapons, and soarted into bandes under Captaines are not stated in the return—besides the able men there were "Light-hors 17."

In 1641, Feb. 12, the Earl of Northumberland was appointed as a "fit person to be entrusted" with the organization of the Militia "Isle of Anglesey."

In 1684 from "The progress of His Grace Henry the First Duke of Beaufort Through Wales," the "Militia of Isle of Anglesey consist of one Troop Horse commanded by Bulkeley, Esqr., as Captain And four Companyes of Foot."

By Militia Returns 1697, Egerton MSS., Anglesey had one Company 250 Foot, and 26 Horse, Col. Arthur Owen, Esqr.

In 1778 the Force of the County was reorganized for the quota of men to be found, and in 1780 the Unit was increased in strength by four Companies raised in Ireland, which were disbanded in 1782, and the force of the County reorganized in 1792 as the Royal Anglesey Fusiliers, changed to Light Infantry in 1810, and converted into Engineers 1877. In 1900 a Field Company was added, and in 1902 the Regiment was reorganized into one Field Company, two Service Companies, and one Depot Company.

Embodiments.

Occasion.

Revolutionary War, etc.	1793, to 1802.
French War	1803, to 1814.
Crimean War	1855, to 1856, May 31.
South African War	1900, May 7, to 1900, Oct. 13.

Services.

Volunteered for and stationed in Ireland 1811-13.

Volunteered for Foreign service during the South African War, the special service section embarking for South Africa Mch. 6, 1900. Strength, Captain J. L. Hampton-Lewis, with 25 N.C.O.'s and men, followed by a Company under command of Captain and Hon. Major F. H. Rawlins, 3 Officers, 103 N.C.O.'s and men, June 6, 1900.

On arrival at South Africa the Section was attached to "A" Pontoon Troop, R.E., at Ladysmith, assisting subsequently in the repair of the railway between Ladysmith and Standerton, including the clearing of the Laings Nek Tunnel, afterwards taking part in the erection of Pontoon Bridges for the column under General French in the S.E. Transvaal, and on trek with columns under General Smith-Dorrien and Colonel Campbell, returning to England June, 1901.

The "A" Company on arrival at South Afrca were stationed at Kimberley, Naawport, and De Aar, etc.

Sergeant Wilson with eleven N.C.O.'s and Sappers were with Colonel Chamier in the siege of Schwizer Renecke from Aug. 19 to Nov. 25, 1900, the following commendation being received from the Officer commandg.

"The conduct of the detachment was most exemplary, all work they had to perform was done cheerfully, and well. If I can mention any in particular where all have carried out their duties so thoroughly, they are Sergt. Wilson, Sapper Morris, Corpl. Bryan and Sapper Riley."

The Company was afterwards employed on the railway in construction work, erection of blockhouses, etc., returning to England Oct. 16, 1901.

Casualties.

Killed and died of disease, etc., two Sappers.

Medals, etc.—Special Service Section.

South Africa, 1900-1 with Clasps "Cape Colony," "Transvaal," and "Laings Nek."

"A" Company, South Africa, 1900-1 with Clasps, "Cape Colony," "Transvaal," "Orange Free State," and 1901 Clasp.

Royal Monmouthshire Royal Engineers (Militia).

Hon. Colonel :—Tredegar, G. C., Lord.
Lieut.-Colonel :—p.s. Raglan, G. FitzR. H., Lord, hon. c. (H).

Origin.

Formed under Act of Parliament in 1660. When inspected by the Duke of Beaufort in 1684, it comprised a "Regiment of Foot and a Troop of Horse." By Militia Returns, 1697 (Egerton MS.) Monmouthshire had one Regiment of seven Companies, 490 men and one Troop 55 horse, total 545 commanded by Colonel Sir John Williams, Bart. In 1757 when completed for service, and quota of Militia for Monmouthshire, under order issued to the Lords Lieutenant of the several Counties of the Kingdom, it was the first Regiment raised by ballot and composed of foot only. Between 1793 and 1820 it was amalgamated with the Brecon quota of Militia which in 1760 had been completed for service as the Brecon Rifles. In 1877 the Monmouthshire Regiment of Infantry was converted into Engineers, still with eight Companies of 100 men each and reorganized 1902 into four service Companies with one Depot Company, a field Company being added in 1903. The Monmouthshire Regt. became a Royal Regiment before the Peace of Amiens, and Light Infantry in 1854.

Embodiments.

Occasion.

Seven Years' War	1757 to 1763.
American War	1778 to 1783.
Revolutionary War, etc.	1793 to 1802, Apl. 11.
,, ,,	1803 to 1816, Jan. 6.
Crimean War	1854, Apr. 25, to 1856, Jan. 22.
South African War	1900, May 1, to 1900, Oct. 31.

Services.

Volunteered for and stationed in Ireland 1811-15.

Volunteered for Foreign Service during South African War, two Companies and one special service section embarking for South Africa and remaining there from March, 1900, to the conclusion of the War. Strength embarked, 7 Officers, 231 N.C.O.'s and men, Major H. E. M. Lindsay, commanding. On arrival at the seat of war, the special service section was employed by the "B" Troop Bridging

Battalion in Cape Colony and Orange River Colony; the 1st Service Company on the Orange Free State and Transvaal Railway; the 2nd Service Company on the Transvaal Railway and in construction of blockhouses in the Transvaal.

Casualties.

Died of disease, 6 N.C.O.'s and men.

Mentioned in Despatches.

Major and Hon. Lieut.-Col. H. E. M. Lindsay.
Compy. Sergt.-Major J. Brown.
Sergeants A. Edwards and J. Johns.
2nd. Corpl. A. J. Sharp; Lance-Corpl. J. Stanton.

Special Honours.

Lance-Corporal J. Stanton. D.C. Medal.

Medals and Clasps.

Queen's South African Medal with Clasps "Cape Colony," "Orange Free State," and "Transvaal."

The Portsmouth Division Submarine Miners, Royal Engineers (Militia).

Major :—(P), Hawley, W.

Origin.

Formed in 1878, and with Hampshire in 1884 designated The Southern Submarine Mining Militia. In 1888 called the Portsmouth Division, and subsequently known by its present title.

Embodiments.

Occasion.

South African War ... 1900, Apr. 14, to 1900, Nov. 6.

The Needles Division Submarine Miners Royal Engineers (Militia).

Major :—(P), Somerset-Leeke, A. FitzR., W. H. hon. l.c. (H).

Origin.

Formed in 1894 as the Needles Division, etc., etc.

Embodiments.
    Occasion.

South African War   ...   1900, Apr. 14, to 1900, Oct. 13.

The Plymouth Division Submarine Miners Royal Engineers (Militia).

Major :—(P), James, E. D. L. (H).

Origin.

Raised 1885 as the Devon Company Southern Submarine Mining Militia.

Embodiments.
    Occasion.

South African War   ...   1900, Apr. 14, to 1900, Nov. 6.

The Thames Division R.E. (Militia) Submarine Miners.

Hon. Lt.-Colonel :—(P), Boyd, C.P., hon. l.c.
Major :—(P), Holland, C. G., hon. l.c. (H).

Origin.

Raised 1884 as the Kent Company Southern Submarine Mining Militia, the name being changed in 1888 to the Thames and Medway Division Engineer Militia (Submarine Miners) Royal Engineers, and at a later date to its present designation.

Embodiments.
    Occasion.

South African War   ...   1900, Apr. 23, to 1900, Nov. 6.

The Medway Division Royal Engineers (Militia) Submarine Miners.

Hon. Lt.-Colonel:—(P), Wellesley, R. C., hon. l.c.

Origin.

Formed April, 1902, out of the Thames and Medway Militia Division Royal Engineers.

Embodiments.
    Occasion.

South African War   ...   1900, Apr. 14, to 1900, Oct. 13.

The Harwich Division Royal Engineers (Militia) Submarine Miners.

Hon. Colonel:—p.s., Robbins, A. B., Maj. ret. pay, hon. l.c. (T) (H).

Major:—(P), Bartley, E. B. (Maj. Res. of Off), (H), hon. Lt.-Col.

Origin.

Formed October, 1888.

Embodiments.
    Occasion.

South African War   ...   1900, Ap. 14, to 1900, Nov. 6.

The Milford Haven Division Submarine Miners, Royal Engineers (Militia).

Major:—

Origin.

Formed July, 1888, as the Milford Haven Submarine Mining Militia and known in 1894 by its present designation.

Embodiments.
    Occasion.

South African War   ...   1900, May 1, to 1900, Oct. 10.

The Western Division Submarine Miners, Royal Engineers (Militia).

Major :—(P), Willis, A. R. (H) (T).

Origin.

Formed July, 1888, as the Severn Division Submarine Mining Militia, designated in 1889 the South Wales and Severn Division, which title was changed in 1894 to the Western Division, etc.

Embodiments.
    Occasion.
    South African War ... 1900, Apr. 14, to 1900, Oct. 13.

The Humber Division, R.E. (Militia), Submarine Miners.

Hon. Lt.-Colonel :—Rollit, Sir A. K., Knt., M.P., Knt. of Grace Order of St. John of Jerusalem.

Major :—

Origin.

Raised as Militia in 1891 as the R.E. Militia Submarine Miners by Sir Albert Rollit afterwards Lt.-Colonel Commandant, and Mr. W. H. Wellsted afterwards Major, by convertion of a Volunteer Corps of the City of Hull formed in 1886, the first Commission in which was issued to Sir Albert Rollit, M.P., then Mayor of Hull.

Embodiments.
    Occasion.
    South African War ... 1900, May 1, to 1900, Oct. 31.

The Falmouth Division Submarine Miners Royal Engineers (Militia).

Hon. Lt.-Colonel :—Tremayne, A., Lt.-Colonel.
Major :—(P), Baskerville, C. H. L., Lt.-Col. ret. pay, hon. Lt.-Col. (H) (S) (T) (Lt.-Col. Res. of Off.).

Origin.

Formed Nov., 1892, out of the Falmouth Division Royal Engineers (Volunteers) Submarine Miners.

Embodiments.
    Occasion.

South African War ... 1900, Apl. 14, to 1900, Nov. 6.

INFANTRY.

3rd Battalion The Royal Scots (Lowthian Regiment).

"South Africa, 1900-02."
Hon. Colonel :—Gordon, G. G., C.V.O., C.B., hon. c.
Lt.-Colonel :—Grant, E. J., C.B., hon. c. (H).

Origin.

In 1881 the Edinburgh or Queen's Regiment Light Infantry Militia became the 3rd Battn. The Royal Scots (Lowthian Regiment) under Territorial Organization of the Forces.

By the Records of the Battn. and Local Historical Works, Edinburgh had a Militia Force in 1588 which was in the habit of being mustered on the Borough Moor for exercise, and in that year was drawn upon by the King for his active army.

In 1663 by the Acts of the Scottish Parliament the quota of Militia to be furnished by the Shyre of Edinburgh, resulting from the action taken by King Charles II., June 10, 1661, to organize the Militia in Scotland, was fixed at 800 foot and 74 horse.

Under Act 37, Geo. III., Edinburgh County found 320 men, and City 83 men, for the 10th North British Regt. of Militia 684 strong, which was disbanded Apr. 26, 1802, and under Act 42, Geo. III., June 26 of the same year a complete Regt. was formed for the County and City of Edinburgh— 333 men as the quota for the County and 310 for the City— called the 51st or Edinburgh Regt. of Militia, many of the Officers in the old Regt. receiving Commissions in the new one. In 1855 the name was changed to the "Queen's Regiment of Edinburgh County Militia," and again in 1856 to the Queen's Regiment of Light Infantry Militia until 1881, when its designation became as already recorded.

Embodiments.

Occasion.

European Disturbances	1803, Apr. 11, to 1815, Apr. 3.
Crimean War	1855, Feb. 12, to 1856, May 28.
South African War ...	1899, Dec. 6, to 1902, May 28.

Services.

Volunteered for and stationed in Ireland 1813-14.

Volunteered for Foreign service during the South African War, and embarked for that country, strength 21 Officers, 570 N.C.O.'s and men. Colonel E. J. Grant commdg. After arrival at East London Mch. 21, 1900, the Battn. proceeded on the 30th to Queenstown, in Cape Colony, and thence to Bethulie Bridge and Bloemfontein, where not being expected it was sent back to Bethulie, Orange River Colony. Having fortified this place the Battn. proceeded by march route to Kaffer River Bridge and was employed in putting the Bridge in a state of defence under Col. W. G. Knox, C.B. July 13, 1900, moved to Kroonstad, and whilst at this Station was suddenly ordered to Honing Spruit to reinforce that command, and form part of a Force to operate against a commando that had broken the railway and destroyed a train at Serfontein a few miles away. The Battn. covered the repair of railway by the Pioneer Corps, and the Commando under De Wet having kept off was attacked and driven West during the day by Colonels Ridley and Little's Mounted Infantry. July 24, Battn. returned to Kroonstad. Aug. 1st marched from Kroonstad, as part of a Force composed of the 17th Battery R.F.A., 1st Oxfordshire Light Infantry, 3rd Battn. Royal Scots with 100 Mounted Infantry and one Pompom, under General Charles Knox, the objective being Rhenoster Kop where De Wet was supposed to be in force. The Brigade did a great deal of marching, but De Wet was not to be caught by an Infantry Force. Aug. 1st the Battn. came under fire, losing Sergt. Hill killed. Aug. 7th the Brigade was again in touch, the M.I. having four casualties. Aug. 9th it reached Venterstroon and took part in the action of that name under Lord Methuen. Aug. 17th the 3rd Cavalry Brigade sent out to make a reconnaissance, got engaged with the enemy, and the 3rd Scots forming the advanced guard of Gen. Knox's Force appearing on the scene, engaged the Boers, and the Artillery coming up they were soon forced back in the opposite direction to that they intended going, the Battn. witnessing the gallantry of Sergt. Lawrence, 17th Lancers, for which he was afterwards awarded the Victoria Cross. Oct. 21st the Battn. left Heilbron under Sir C. Knox to relieve Maj.-Gen. Barter's Brigade besieged at Frederickstad by De Wet.

Oct. 28th General Sir Charles Knox handed over his Force to Colonel Grant, 3rd Royal Scots, the Oxford L.I. being left to garrison Heilbron, and it was chiefly used to convoy the accumulated baggage of the Colonial Division, etc.

Nov. 7th. The Force followed De Wet and Kritzinger into Cape Colony, and was afterwards broken up. Between Aug. 1st and Nov. 7th the Battn. covered a distance of about 672 miles, and at one period was on quarter rations for a considerable time. The following was received by Col. Grant from Maj.-Gen. Sir C. Knox, K.C.B., on leaving Dewetsdorp:

"I wish to express to yourself, your Officers, N.C. Officers and Men my appreciation of the way they have carried out their duties since they have been under my command, etc. The esprit de corps and the admirable system which prevails in the Battn. leaves nothing to be desired and might well serve as an example to many Line Battns. I could name."

Nov. 10th the Battn. proceeded south of Kroonstad to take over a number of Posts on the railway, and whilst in this section the Regimental M.I. under Captn. C. P. Wood were out with Major Pine-Coffin's Column and many times engaged. In July, 1901, Detachments under Captn. E. L. Strutt and Lieut. C. E. Lambert took part in the first organized "drive" to the Modder River, and afterwards in the big Eastern movement under Lieut.-Gen. Sir W. Eliot from Winburg. While engaged in these operations the Detachments of the Battn. were for three successive nights encamped at an altitude of over 9000 feet, and were subsequently present at the night attack on Commandant Marais' Laager, which resulted in his capture with 76 Boers.

Jan. 12th, 1901. The following appeared in "L. of C. Orders":

Kroonstad—"*Gallantry in the Field*," May 29, 1901.

"Corporal Cummings, 3rd Royal Scots, when in charge of a standing picquet successfully maintained his position against a party of Boers said to number fifty who attempted to operate on the railway track. The G.O.C. Northern Section O.R.C. wishes to notify to his command his appreciation of the conduct of this N.C.O. and Men of the 3rd Royal Scots mentioned below.

Corporal Cummings and Private Flint.

"Kroonstad, 25 June."—"*Gallantry in the Field.*"

"Lce.-Corpl. McKinnan and six men were occupying a small post near Holfontein siding and being attacked and surrounded by nearly 100 Boers, the engagement lasting about twenty minutes, the enemy were driven off, leaving behind them a waggon laden with salt, and from the traces left had suffered considerable loss. The names of the men being Ptes. Binnie, Clark, Donelly, Finlay, Colasgow and Moore, all of "D" Company, 3rd Royal Scots."

After this date the Battn. occupied the Blockhouse line for about forty miles between Kroonstad and Klip Drift, etc., and embarked at Cape Town for home, May 7th, 1902.

Casualties.

Killed and died of disease, etc.
Major The Earl of Munster.
Captain D. H. Forbes.
2nd Lieut. R. J. Gibson-Craig.
31 N.C.O.'s and Men.

Mentioned in Despatches.

Colonel E. J. Grant.
Majors R. Dundas and The Earl of Munster.
Captn. and Adjt. W. H. Davidson.
Captains C. P. B. Wood and E. L. Strutt.
Lieut. A. Douglas Pennant.
Sergt.-Major Johnston.
Cr.-Sergt. W. Edden.
Cr.-Sergt. C. Fox.
Sergt. R. Mansen.
Cr.-Sergt. H. Bradford.
Cr.-Sergt. W. Chalmers.
Cr.-Sergt. S. Kelly.
Pte. S. Purvis.

Special Honours.

Colonel E. J. Grant, C.B.
Major The Earl of Munster, D.S.O.
Captn. and Adjt. W. H. Davidson, D.S.O.
Captn. C. P. B. Wood, D.S.O.
Sergt.-Major Johnston, D.C. Medal.
Cr.-Sergt. Bradford, D.C. Medal.
Cr.-Sergt. Kelly, D.C. Medal.

Medals, etc., received by Battalion.

Queen's S.A. Medal with Clasps "Transvaal," "Orange River Colony," "Cape Colony."

King's S.A. Medal with Clasps "S.A., 1901," and "S.A., 1902."

3rd Battalion, The Queen's (Royal West Surrey Regiment).

"South Africa, 1900-02."

Hon. Colonel :—

Lt.-Colonel :—p.s. Fairtlough, F. H., C.M.G., hon. c. (H) (T).

Origin.

Formed as the 2nd or Western Regiment of Surrey Militia in 1761, by division of the Surrey Regt. into two units, which were again united in 1763.

In 1797 this Battalion was the 1st of three supplementary Militia Regiments raised for Surrey under Acts 37, Geo. III., and designated the 2nd Surrey in 1798.

When Supplementary Militia Regiments were abolished, the 2nd Surrey was retained on the establishment in 1799 as a regular Militia Regiment to replace the unit which had been absorbed in 1763; became a Royal Regiment 1804, and under territorial organization of 1881 the 3rd Battalion, "The Queen's Royal West Surrey Regiment" (see 3rd Battn., The East Surrey Regt., for the origin prior to 1761, and services, etc., of the Constitutional Force of Surrey).

Embodiments.

Occasion.

Seven Years War	...	1761, July 3, to 1762, Dec.
Revolutionary War, etc.		1798, Feb. 20, to 1802, Apr. 25.
French War	...	1803, Mar. 11, to 1814, June 24.
Crimean War	...	1855, Feb. 1, to 1856, June 12.
South African War	...	1899, Dec. 4, to 1902, Apr. 1.

Services.

Volunteered for and stationed in Ireland 1811-13.

In 1814 furnished four officers—Captn. Bacchus, Lieut. Martin, Ensigns Sadler and Usher—120 N.C.O.'s and men for the 1st Provisional Battn. of the Militia Brigade under Colonel the Marquis of Buckingham (Bucks. Militia), which landed near Paulliac and was for some time quartered at Bordeaux. The Brigade afterwards marched to Soisson, Chateau Margaux, Cantenac, etc., but arrived at Toulouse too late to take part in the last battle of the campaign, Wellington having crossed the Garonne and defeated the French in their entrenched camp on the heights above the City, this resulted in the abdication of Napoleon.

Volunteered for foreign service during the South African War, and embarked for the seat of war Feb. 20, 1900; strength —24 officers, one M.O. (Civil), one W.O., 515 N.C.O.'s and men; Colonel F. H. Fairtlough commanding.

On arrival at Cape Town, March 27th, the Battalion proceeded to De Aar and occupied various outposts of the garrison and district, but was soon moved to Springfontein for points on the lines of communication at Deelfontein, Richmond Road, Victoria West Road, Kroom River, Fraserburg Road, and Kettering Siding, with Head Quarters at Beaufort West, covering a distance of about 350 miles. Major W. D. Shelton appointed Commandant of Victoria West Section, and Captain H. F. Wilkinson of Beaufort West Section. Aug. 2nd, two officers with 200 N.C.O.'s and men under Major F. G. Parsons proceeded to De Aar, and on the 16th the machine gun detachment, Lieut. Birchan, moved to Vryburg for duty on the armoured train running between Kimberley and Mafeking. In Oct. the Battn. was ordered down to Green Point Camp, Cape Town, to act as guard over Boer prisoners. Jan., 1901, Maj. and Hon. Lt.-Col. Shelton became Commandant of Namaqualand, and Major Parsons at De Aar. At this time, owing to the invasion of Cape Colony by the Boers, local town guards were formed, ten thousand being enrolled and equipped at Cape Town, and No. 1 Battn., about 1,800 of all ranks, was placed under command of Colonel F. H. Fairtlough, who about the middle of March took over command of the Simonstown District.

In July the 3rd Royal West Surrey Regt. furnished detachments, three officers and 100 other ranks for Namaqualand District, six officers and 160 other ranks for Touws River. Head Quarters under Colonel Fairtlough moving to Beaufort West. On arrival at this place, owing to the immediate presence of Boer commandoes, the Head Quarter Companies were ordered to push on to De Aar for reinforcing the blockhouse line and protection of convoys through the district. During the next few months the whole Battalion was continuously employed in turning Boer columns when driven in by mounted forces. An idea of the magnitude of this work can be gained when it is considered that the various detachments of the Battalion were scattered over about 20,000 square miles, often at isolated posts, and sometimes hard pressed by the Boers. In September, Commandant Scheepers threatened to wreck the Touws River Station, and the place was put into a state to resist any attack. At this time Colonel Fairtlough was invalided to

Cape Town, Lt.-Col. Shelton assuming command. In November three officers with 115 other ranks moved to Worcester, other detachments joining Head Quarters at De Aar to strengthen the Garrison, and in December four officers and 124 other ranks escorted a convoy of 160 waggons to Prieska, a distance of 120 miles, each waggon having an average team of 12 animals.

In April, 1902, Colonel Shelton was in charge of the defence of Ookiep, which contained 6,000 men, women and children. The place was closely invested by General Smuts for nineteen days with eleven commandoes, the enemy using dynamite freely in their attacks, but without success. On the 12th a desperate attempt to take the place was made. After a heavy rifle fire from daybreak until 9 a.m. a general attack followed, but the garrison successfully kept the besiegers at bay. All attacks failed, the town was relieved and the Boers driven off.

Feb. 9, 1902, the Head Quarter Companies at De Aar were ordered to occupy the blockhouse section between Victoria West and Beaufort West. The Namaqualand detachment was at this time operating with Colonel White's column against the united efforts of three Boer commandoes to seize the copper-mines in the neighbourhood of Ookiep.

March 4, 1902, the Head Quarter Companies and blockhouse parties proceeded to Cape Town, en route for home, the Prieska Companies under Major Parsons, then on half rations and cut off without immediate prospect of relief, following later in the transport "Britannic."

Casualties

Killed and died of disease, etc., 12 N.C.O.'s and men.

Mentioned in Despatches.

Major and Hon. Lt.-Col. W. D. Shelton
Captain A. G. Shaw.
Captain and Adjt. R. B. Swinton. } twice.
Captain and Qr.-Mr. J. Dyke.
Sergt. I. of M. G. Fane.
Cr.-Sergt. A. J. Stevens.
Sergt. J. Palmer.
Ptes. J. Beale and H. Border.

Special Honours.

Lt.-Colonel and Hon. Col. F. H. Fairtlough, C.M.G.
Major and Hon. Lt.-Col. W. D. Shelton, D.S.O.
Major F. G. Parsons, D.S.O.

Sergt. Major J. Woulds, D.C. Medal.
Cr.-Sergt. A. Norris, D.C. Medal.
Cr.-Sergt. A. J. Stevens, D.C. Medal.
Captain and Qr.-Mr. J. Dyke, granted next higher pay for services S.A.

Medals, etc., received by Battalion.
Queen's S.A. Medal with Clasp "Cape Colony."
King's S.A. Medal with Clasps "1901 and 1902."

3rd Battalion, The Buffs (East Kent Regiment).

"Mediterranean."
"South Africa, 1900-02."

Hon. Colonel:—Rundle, Lt.-Gen. Sir H. M. L., K.C.B., K.C.M.G., D.S.O., R. Art., s.
Lt.-Colonel:—Brinckman, Sir T. F., Bt., C.B., hon. c.

Origin.

Raised 1778 as a second Militia Regiment for the county of Kent, and designated the East Kent Regt. In 1881, under the territorial organization of the Forces, the regiment became the 3rd Battn. of "The Buffs (East Kent Regiment)."

Embodiments.

Occasion.

Crimean War	...	1855 to 1856.
Threatened War	...	1885, March 9, to 1885, Sept. 30.
South African War	...	1900, Jan 18, to 1902, July 17.

Services.

Volunteered for foreign service at the time of the Crimean War, and stationed at Malta.

Volunteered for foreign service during the South African War, and embarked March 9, 1900. Strength: 20 officers, 530 other ranks; Colonel T. F. Brinckman commanding. On arrival at Cape Town, 28-3-00, the Battalion proceeded on the 2nd April to join the 3rd Division under General Gatacre at Bethany, the Division marching on the following day under General Chermside to re-occupy Rendersburg, and eventually to Dewetsdorp, reaching this place April 29th. On June 9th the Battalion moved with all haste to strengthen the Garrison at Kroonstad, and June 23rd to Lindley, forming part of a column about 2,000 strong with six guns, to escort reinforcements and supplies for Gen. Paget. The column met with considerable opposition in the engagement at Lindley, June 26th, but the object was successfully achieved, and Lindley entered on the evening of the latter day. General Kelly-Kenny, in his despatch to Lord Roberts, said "he was pleased to observe that a Militia Battn. (the 3rd Buffs) distinguished itself on this occasion"; leaving 1,500 men and four guns at Lindley, the Battalion returned to Kroonstad with a large sick convoy.

Sept. 25th, the 3rd Buffs left for Wolverhoek and Vredeford Road, going on to Heilbron as escort of the construction train repairing the branch line between Wolverhoek and Heilbron, and, returning on Oct. 3rd, took part in the operations between Heilbron and Wolverhoek.

Oct. 10th, the Battalion joined the column under Genl. Sir A. Hunter for the Bothaville district, and the district having been cleared and town destroyed, returned on the 26th, two companies of the 3rd Buffs joining the column of Sir A. Hunter and Genl. Bruce Hamilton for Ventersburg.

The Despatch of Lord Roberts to the Secretary of State for War, dated Oct. 31, 1900, says, "Hunter mentions that in the attack on Ventersburg a company of the 3rd Buffs got hotly engaged and behaved with conspicuous steadiness."

After this date, until Dec. 15th, the Battalion was employed in guarding the railway, when at Genl. Hunter's request it formed part of the force sent into Cape Colony to oppose the threatened invasion, and took an active part in the operations at Bethulie Bridge, Olive Siding, and Colesburg, returning to Kroonstad on Dec. 30th. Convoys and blockhouse duties then occupied the Battalion during the remainder of its stay in South Africa.

On Aug. 1, 1901, a blockhouse at Hontneck garrisoned by Sergt. Pincott and six men was attacked by some 300 Boers, and the construction being defective Sergt. Pincott was soon killed, but the six men held out until five of their number were wounded and the Boers forced an entrance. The blockhouse fighting was constant until the departure of the Battalion, Jan. 21, 1902. Genl. Sir W. G. Knox issued the following order: Jan. 21, 1902.—The Genl. Officer Commanding, Kroonstad, desires to place on record his appreciation of the services rendered by the 3rd Battalion.' "All ranks have fully maintained the reputation bequeathed to them as part of the old 'Constitutional Force' of England."

He also addressed the Regiment before entraining: "You have acquitted yourselves nobly, and I cannot recall a single instance in which you have failed me. Whenever I expected an attack and knew the 3rd Buffs were there, I always felt perfectly safe and never had a moment's anxiety."

Jan. 21, 1902, the Battalion embarked for St. Helena, remaining there as guard over Boer prisoners of war for about six months.

Casualties.

Killed and died of disease, etc., 29 N.C.O.'s and men.

Mentioned in Despatches.

Colonel T. F. Brinckman.
Majors A. H. Tylden-Pattenson and M. J. R. Dundas.
Major and Adjt. R. Bayard.
Captains C. Vipan, W. F. Tufnell, L. E. L. Triscott, H. R. Hirst.
Captain and Qr.-Mr. H. C. Cumber.
2nd Lieut. J. H. Thomson.
Sergt.-Major T. Cheal, Q.M.-Sergt. G. Johnson.
Cr.-Sergts. A. J. Hall (twice) and F. Wright.
Sergt. Dr. J. Kennedy, Sergt. J. Lacey.
Lce. Sergt. J. Mockford, Pte. W. J. Thomason.

Special Honours.

Colonel T. F. Brinckman, C.B.
Major A. H. Tylden-Pattenson, D.S.O.
Major and Adjt. R. Bayard, D.S.O.
Captain C. Vipan, D.S.O.
Sergt. Major T. Cheal, D.C. Medal.
Qr. Mr.-Sergt. G. Johnson, D.C. Medal.
Pte. W. J. Thomason, promoted Corporal.

Medals, etc., received by Battalion.

Queen's Medal with Clasps "Cape Colony" and "Orange Free State."

King's Medal with Clasps "S.A. 1901" and "S.A. 1902."

Two Companies received, in addition, the Transvaal Clasp.

3rd Battalion, The King's Own (Royal Lancaster Regiment).

"Mediterranean."
"South Africa, 1900-02."

Hon. Colonel :—Derby, Rt. Hon., F.A., Earl of, K.G., G.C.B., G.C.V.O., Col., A.D.C.

Lt.-Colonel Commandant :—North, B.N., C.B., M.V.O. (t) hon. c., Kt. of Grace of the Order St. John of Jerusalem.

Origin.

In 1588, by Harleian MSS., the county assembled 1170 ffurnished men reduced into bandes under captaines besides Horsemen, Launces 20, lighthorse 50, for the Armies formed to resist invasion by the Spanish Armada.

1641, Feb. 12, Lord Wharton appointed as "a person fit to be entrusted" with the organization of the Militia of "Lancaster."

In 1689 the Lancashire Regiment of Militia was completed for service by William George Reid, 9th Earl of Derby, as Colonel, under an Order in Council directing the Lord Lieutenants of Counties to call out and train the Militia Forces of the Kingdom under powers of certain Acts of Parliament of the reign of King Charles II.

1697, by Militia Returns, Egerton MSS., the "Militia in Co. Palatine of Lancashire" comprised three regiments of 22 companies and 1601 men, with three troops of horse 150. Cols., Earl of "Maclesfell," Roger Kirkby, Sir Ralph Ashton.

In the re-organization of the Militia under Act 30, Geo. II., 1757, the regiment was completed for service in 1760 and made a Royal regiment in 1761, designated His Majesty's Royal Regt. of Lancashire Militia, and by Command of His Majesty the Colonel's Company to be called "The King's Company," changed in 1799 to 1st Royal Lancashire Militia, and in 1831 to 1st Royal Lancashire Militia (The Duke of Lancaster's Own). Formed into two Battalions 1877, and as the 1st of these became in 1881 under the territorial arrangement the 3rd Battalion of the King's Own (Royal Lancashire Regiment).

Embodiments.

Occasion.

Irish Rebellion	... 1689 to 1691.
Jacobite Rising	... 1715, July, to 1716, Jan.
Scottish Rebellion	... 1745, Sept., to 1746, Jan.

Seven Years War	...	1760, Dec., to 1762, Dec.
American War	...	1778, April, to 1783, March.
French War, etc.	...	1793, Jan., to 1799, Dec.
,, ,,	...	1801, Aug., to 1802, April.
,, ,,	...	1803, April, to 1816, April.
Crimean War	...	1854, May, to 1856, July.
South African War	...	1900, Jan. 23, to 1902, Feb. 8.

Services.

1666, by State Papers, Dom. Chas. II., a Levy of Militia was made by the King on the County for the threatened French and Dutch invasion.

Volunteered for and embarked June 11, 1690, with His Majesty King William III., and the expedition to put down Rebellion and re-conquer those parts of Ireland which had been subjugated by King James, who landed at Kinsale 1689, supported by Louis XIV. of France with an expedition of 14 ships of the line, 6 frigates, and transports conveying twelve hundred disciplined soldiers, and 100 French officers to organize the 40,000 men then under arms in Ireland. The Royal Forces landed at Carrickfergus June 14th, and the Brigade of Lancashire Militia (2 regiments of foot with 3 troops of horse) was present at the siege of Carrickfergus Castle, the memorable Battle of the Boyne, the siege and taking of Athlone, and other engagements during the campaign in Ireland.

In 1715 the regiment took part in the suppression of the Jacobite rising, when the Northern Counties of England were thrown into a state of great disturbance by advance of the rebels from Scotland and Northumberland in support of the Pretender, the "Chevalier de St. George," who had been proclaimed King of Scotland and England, and for whose capture a reward of £100,000 was offered. The regiment was first detailed to protect the town and Castle of Lancaster, then partially a fortress, afterwards being actively engaged at the siege and capture of Preston, Nov. 12, 1715.

(From Colonel Whalley's History): "The entrenchments, Barricades and loopholed houses for the defence could not have been improved by any military engineer. The attack was carried out by a diversion at the East Cliff by the Lancashire Regiment of Militia under Colonel Hoghton with three troops of dismounted Dragoons, who were eventually to attack the Fishergate Barricade, while the 26th Cameronians formed in quarter distance column led by Lord Forrester were to storm the churchyard defences, wherein after desperate resistance had been overcome, a most bloody encounter took place against musket, Highland claymore, and Lochaber axe, the slaughter on both sides being terrible. The left wing of the Lancashire Militia under Major Bland with one troop of dismounted Dragoons were then detached to attack the Friargate Barricade, the right wing led by Colonel Hoghton along with two remaining troops of dismounted Dragoons, storming the Fishergate Barricade without success and suffering heavily by the continuous fire from the houses, but darkness coming on Colonel Hoghton reformed his men without being seen by the rebels, and carried the Barricade with a rush before any resistance could be offered, the rebels escaping in the utmost confusion to the houses, which were soon set on fire and in flames. It was midnight before the fighting ceased, the rebels fighting with a halter round their necks, and the Militia giving no quarter in consequence of the great loss they had suffered in officers and men. About this time the town, barricades, and rebels' position were in the entire possession of the Royal troops. The return of the day's casualties was very heavy in the regiment. It lost one captain, one lieutenant, and two ensigns killed; one field officer (Major Bland), two captains, four subalterns, with 105 N.C. officers and privates killed and wounded. The rebels laid down their arms on the 15th—the Lancashire Regiment escorting the prisoners to the several gaols of the county. Previous to leaving, Generals Wells and Carpenter publicly thanked Colonel Hoghton for the gallant and brave conduct of his regiment in storming the barricades, and the good discipline and endurance of the men, and expressed their sympathy with him for the loss of officers and men experienced in this short but highly creditable campaign.

The Scottish Rebellion, 1745. Prince Charles Edward having landed from France at Moidart, Inverness-shire, and with the aid of Highland Clans who had joined his cause, obtained a victory, Sept. 21st., over the troops of His Majesty King George II. at Preston-pans, and been proclaimed at the Town Cross of Edinburgh as King James the VII of Scotland, his Force under General Lord George Murray invaded England and reached Manchester, but failing to evoke the support expected, and threatened by the Royal Forces, a retreat was determined by way of Penrith and Carlisle. Captain Bradshaw's Company of the Regiment (attached as the Right Company of the "Liverpool Regiment of Blues") took an active part in the engagement with the rebels at Shap Fells Village on Dec. the 18th, and battle at Clifton Moor Bridge, near Penrith. (From Captain Bradshaw's letter in Colonel Whalley's History): "Ye clouds over ye moor disappeared and revealed to us ye desperate attack made by ye Highlanders on ye dismounted troopers, and ye whole rebel Artillery and Waggon Train in movement attempting to get over ye Bridge. Ye sharpshooters on ye right flank and ye Liverpool Regt. powered into them volley after volley as each Company got into line, ye squadron of Dragoons charged from ye reverse flank prevented them passing over ye bridge, ye enemy's Baggage Guard was immediately doubled up, traces cut, and those who did not surrender had but a short shrift of it." On the evacuation of ye City of Carlisle, Decr. 19th, by ye Prince Charles Edward with his Rebel Army of Scotch Insurgents, the Lancaster Company of Militia under command of Captain Bradshaw was ordered to escort the prisoners left at Penrith to Lancaster Castle.

Volunteered for and stationed in Ireland Sep. 11, 1798, to Oct. 9, 1799.

Volunteered for foreign service during Crimean War, and stationed at the Ionian Islands where the Regiment lost by Asiatic Cholera in a fortnight, one Officer, 2 N.C.O.'s and nearly 300 men.

Volunteered for foreign service in 1900, and proceeded to South Africa—strength embarked 25 Officers, 686 N.C.O.'s and men, Colonel B. N. North Commanding. On arrival at Cape Town March 1, 1900, employed on the lines of communication in the Orange River Colony, three Companies and Head Quarters holding Zand River Bridge, an important post commanding the railway bridge, and a very large Depot of supplies. March 14th attacked by the enemy whose attack lasted all day. The enemy had one 12 pounder gun, 2 pompoms and 1 maxim. The garrison had no artillery. The Boers were driven off leaving many killed, wounded and prisoners. Captain R. N. de le Bere distinguished himself by leading a most successful charge, and Lieut. and Qr. Master Batchelor with some picked shots put a maxim out of action. Captain G. D. Timmis discovered the enemy who tried to surprise the post. Lord Kitchener issued orders thanking the Regt. for their "gallant conduct."

The Mounted Infantry of the Battn. under command of Lieut. A. G. M. F. Howard took part in the engagement of Ventersburg with the columns under command of Colonel B. N. North of the Battn., and Colonel W. L. White, R.A., Colonel North, Captains Timmis and Chaloner commanded

Armour Trains, and the M.I. Company with a few Yeomanry under Colonel North obliged the enemy to retire from their position at Zeegatacht near Brandfort, capturing their laager. Jan. 16 and 28, 1901, the M.I. and Armoured Train, all under Colonel North, drove the enemy from their position at Huten Beck. The Regt. at this time held the Blockhouse line and railway from Kroonstad to Bloemfontein, repulsing several attacks. Oct., 1901, the Regt. was split up into several detachments and engaged with Theron's Commando about Ceres. It reassembled Jan. 10, 1902, for embarkation for England.

Casualties.

Killed and died of disease, etc., 51 N.C.O.'s and men.

Mentioned in Despatches.

Colonel B. N. North.
Lt.-Colonel F. E. Fitzherbert.
Captain R. N. de la Bere.
Captain J. Challoner.
Captain G. O. Timmis.
Captain and Adjt. C. J. Daniel.
Lieut. and Qr.-Mr. T. B. Batchelor.

Special Honours.

Colonel B. N. North, C.B.
Lt.-Colonel F. E. Fitzherbert, D.S.O.
Major and Adjt. C. J. Daniel, D.S.O.
Captain R. N. de la Bere, D.S.O.
Sergt.-Major Disley, D.C.M.
Qr.-Mr.-Sergt. Hardman, D.C.M.
Sgt.-Inst. Musketry Alcock, D.C.M.

Medals and Clasps Received in Battalion.

Queen's South African Medal with Clasps "Cape Colony" and "Orange Free State." King's South African Medal with Clasps "South Africa, 1901" and "South Africa, 1902."

4th Battalion, The King's Own (Royal Lancaster Regiment).

"Mediterranean."
"South Africa, 1900-01."

Hon. Colonel :—Derby, Rt. Hon., F. A., Earl of, K.G., G.C.B., G.C.V.O., Col., A.D.C.

Lt.-Colonel :—Kemmis, W., C.M.G., M.V.O., hon. c.

Origin.

Formed 1877, by division of the 1st Royal Lancashire Militia (The Duke of Lancashire's Own) into two Battalions (for origin and services prior to that date see 3rd Battalion Colonel Whalley's History). In 1881 became the 4th Battalion of the Territorial King's Own (Royal Lancaster Regiment).

Embodiments since 1877.

Occasion.

Egyptian Complications 1882, July, to 1882, Sep.
South African War ... 1899, Dec. 13, to 1901, Aug. 3.

Services since 1877.

Volunteered for and embarked for South Africa strength 25 Officers, 660 N.C.O.'s and men under command of Lt.-Colonel W. Kemmis. On arrival at Cape Town Feb. 1, 1900, proceeded to Naauwpoort at that time the advanced base of the Colesburg operations, and employed on the lines of communication, having detachments at various times assisting to guard the towns, bridges and culverts on the line between Norvals Pont and Port Elizabeth, also at Graaffreinet and Hanover Road. Aug. 1900, a column consisting of 200 of the Battn. and 40 of Nesbitt's Horse, demonstrated through the disaffected district of Hanover, where it was feared that the farmers were about to rise. Dec. 30, 1900, the Boers attacked and burnt a train at the "Gates of Hell," about 16 miles from Naauwpoort, Captain Evans with two Companies being sent to clear the line, but arriving in time only for a few flying shots at the enemy as they retired. Dec. 1900, Colonel Kemmis appointed Commandant of Naauwpoort. Feb. 23, 1901, Sec. Lieut. Hunt with 30 men guarding Fish River Bridge and Station, successfully held the position for four hours against an attack made by Kritzinger and about 250 Boers, until the armoured train came to their assistance and the enemy driven off. Lord Kitchener telegraphed his congratulations for gallantly maintaining the defence and continually refusing to surrender. March 7, 1901, Captain Worsley Taylor with 40 N.C.O.'s and men Royal Lancaster Regt., and about 60 Mounted Infantry, when repairing the Colesburg Phillippolis telegraph line were attacked by a superior force. A position was taken up on a kopje which they held successfully for about 24 hours until a relief column arrived from Colesburg. May 29, 1901, Head Quarters moved to Norvals Pont, the Battn. occupying the northern bank of the Orange River, and on July 5 concentrated at De Aar preparatory to proceeding home.

Casualties.

Killed and died of disease, etc.
Lieut. Walton and 21 N.C.O.'s and men.

Mentioned in Despatches.

Lt.-Colonel W. Kemmis.
Major F. H. F. Evans.
Lieut. E. F. Hunt.
Sergt.-Major H. Bacon.
Cr.-Sergt. T. Tite.
Sergt. J. Lowe.
Sergt. J. Searson.
Private J. Smith.
Major and Adjt. Hibbert.
Captain T. Worsley Taylor.
Lieut. and Qr.-Mr. B. Daly.
Qr.-Mr.-Sergt. J. Moore.
Sergt. J. T. Bratherton.
Corporal J. Durant.
Lce.-Corporal J. Connelly.

Honours Received in Battalion.

Lieut.-Colonel W. Kemmis, C.M.G.
Major and Adjt. Hibbert, D.S.O.
Major F. H. F. Evans, D.S.O.
Lieut. E. F. Hunt, D.S.O.
Sergt.-Major H. Bacon, D.C.M.
Cr.-Sergt. T. Tite, D.C.M.
Sergt. J. Lowe, D.C.M.
Sergt. J. Searson, D.C.M.

Medals and Clasps Received in Battalion.

Queen's South African Medal with Clasps for "Cape Colony," "Orange River Colony," and 1901.

5th Battalion, The Northumberland Fusiliers.

"Mediterranean, 1900-01."

Hon. Colonel:—Northumberland, H. G., Duke of, K.G., Col., A.D.C.

Lt.-Colonel:—Percy, Lord A. M. A., Col., A.D.C. (H).

Origin.

See certificate of the Force of the County, 27 Mar., 1539, at the muster held by virtue of a Royal Commission issued March 1, 30, Henry VIII., from "Letters and Papers of the Reign of 30, Henry VIII."

In 1641, Feb. 12, the Earl of Northumberland was appointed as "a person fit to be entrusted" with the organization of the Militia of the County.

By MS. at Alnwick Castle, a Northumberland Militia Regiment was in existence 1662. After the Restoration in 1660 an Act of Parliament was passed—13th., Charles II.—regulating the Militia and ordering out the Forces of the several Counties. The Regiment was composed at that time of horse and foot soldiers. The Light Horse were furnished by Peers and called the Lords' Horse, and by Gentlemen charged according to their estates. It is recorded that in 1696 the effective strength of the Regiment was 91 Horse, 296 Foot. Total 387. When reorganized, completed for service, and embodied in 1759, the full quota of the County, 560 foot, had been raised—Sir Edward Blackett, Bart., Colonel, it became a Light Infantry Regiment at later date, and 3rd Battalion of the Territorial Northumberland Fusiliers Regiment in 1881, changed to 5th Battalion when the Regiment was augmented by two additional Line Battalions.

Embodiments.

   Occasion.

—	1662, period unknown.
Seven Years War	1760, Feb. 25, to 1762, Dec.
American War	1778, Apr. 13, to 1782, Dec.
Revolutionary War, etc.	1793, Jan., to 1802, Apr.
French War	1803, Apr., to 1814, June 24.
Crimean War	1855, Jan 9, to 1856, June 20.
South African War	1899, Dec. 12, to 1901, July 8.

Services.

Took part in the suppression of the Gordon Riots in 1780 and quartered in Lincolns Inn.

From the London Papers, June, 1780, and "Scott's Magazine," "The Northumberland Militia, a great part of which had marched near 40 miles, commanded by Lord Algernon Percy and Colonel Holroyd, marched into Lincolns Inn, the old six Clerks' Office being converted into a Barrack, from thence patrols were immediately sent out and a large detachment to the great scenes of riot and destruction at Mr. Langdale's, Barnard's Inn, Holborn Bridge, where the fires were so great there was no expectation of stopping them even when the soldiers had escorted and defended the firemen. As soon as the soldiers appeared before the bonfire in front of Mr. Langdale's house, the Insurgents attacked them, and the detachment fired their pieces, but as they were only loaded with powder no harm was done. The Insurgents continued their attack and, one of the officers being badly hurt, it was found absolutely necessary to fire with ball; yet the fire was very prudently conducted, for the soldiers were not permitted to fire along the street, their officers drew them up on the north side of Holborn, fronting the bonfire and the house on fire, so that no person could be hurt but those who were rioting round the fire, burning the furniture and casks, and those who were still in the house plundering it. By the second volley two or three were killed; this had the proper effect and drove off the Insurgents, but many rioters and plunderers were still within the house, when they appeared at the door and windows the soldiers on the flank of the party came up in Indian file, firing singly and each falling off as he fired."

"The Northumberland Militia under Lord Algernon Percy occasioned a most effective check to the violence of the rioters at the burning of the Fleet Prison, though it is a known fact that after firing, the Corps twice presented and recovered their arms without a single man discharging his piece, although the mob were using every means to irritate and provoke them. This instance of discipline ought to be recorded for the honour of that Regiment to whose efforts and example the City of London in a great measure owes its preservation.

"The inhabitants of Took's Court, Castle Yard, and Cursitor Street, present their thanks to Lord Algernon Percy, Colonel of the Northumberland Militia, and the Officers, for the timely assistance received in the protection of their lives and properties from wicked and lawless rioters, and in consideration of the great hardship and expense the soldiers must necessarily suffer, they beg leave to present the amount of a subscription £50 19s."—From "London Advertiser," 19th June, 1780.

"The great fears and apprehensions which the inhabitants suffered was owing to the office of the Sheriff of Middlesex being situate in Took's Court, which office was violently threatened by the rioters; yet it is wonderful that neither the Sheriff, Under Sheriff, or his Deputy subscribed a single shilling for the benefit of the poor soldiers who after a very harrassing and fatiguing march, were immediately employed to protect this office and the neighbouring inhabitants from danger."

Volunteered for and served two years in Ireland, 1811-13.

Volunteered for Foreign Service during South African War and stationed at Malta.

5th Battalion, The Royal Warwickshire Regiment.

"South Africa, 1902."

Hon. Colonel :—Leigh, Rt. Hon. W. H., Lord.
Lt.-Colonel :—Earl, Maj. F. A., ret. pay.

Origin.

According to Rushworth's "Historical Collections," Lord Brook was appointed Feb. 12, 1641, as "a fit person to be entrusted with" the organizing of the Militia of Warwick and the County and City of Coventry.

By Militia Returns 1697, Egerton MSS., the County had one Regt. of seven Companies 625 foot, and 4 Troops of horse 181, including from Coventry one Company 40 foot and one Troop 7 horse, Col. Sir Charles Shuckbury.

In 1759 a Regiment was completed for service and the quota of men to be furnished by the County and known as the Warwick Militia.

In 1853 the quota of men having been increased, the Force of the County was divided into two Units as the 1st and 2nd Warwickshire Regiments, this Battn. being the former, and in 1881 under the Territorial Regimental Organization of the Forces, became the 3rd Battn. of The Royal Warwickshire Regiment.

In 1898 the Regiment being augmented by two additional Line Battns. numbered as the 3rd and 4th, the two Militia Battns. became the 5th and 6th.

Embodiments.

    Occasion.

Crimean War	1854, Dec., to 1856, June 24.
South African War ...	1900, Jan. 23, to 1900, Oct. 18.
South African War ...	1901, Dec. 2, to 1902, Sept. 29.

Services.

In 1797, consequent on the Mutiny at the Nore, the Regiment furnished 94 Officers and other ranks for duty as Marines on board the Man-of-War "Standard." In 1798 volunteered for service in Ireland during the Rebellion, and under Colonel the Marquis of Hertford was one of the thirteen Regts. immediately sent to that country on the passing of the Act which empowered the King to employ the English Militia in Ireland for a limited period.

Formed part of the Army under Lord Cornwallis, which with the co-operation of General Lord Lake's Force compelled the surrender of the French, etc., at Ballinamach on Sept. 8th, 1798.

Musgrave says, 1500 rebels accompanied the Force of Gen. Humbert at the time of this surrender, and that the French troops taken prisoners numbered 96 Officers and 748 privates of the 1036 landed at Killala.

Volunteered for Foreign service during the South African War, and embarked Dec. 16th, 1901, for South Africa, strength 23 Officers, 743 other ranks, Colonel Barklie McCalmont, commdg. On arrival the Battn. furnished detachments at several places in Cape Colony with Head Quarters at Worcester.

Feb. 10th, 1902, proceeded to Beaufort West and took over the Blockhouse line between that place and Victoria Road.

Apr. 14th marched to Carnarvon for duty on the Blockhouse line from this place to Kaffirs Kraal.

A detachment of the Battn. was present at the siege of Ookiep, Captain H. Lutwyche being dangerously wounded.

On May 19th the Blockhouses about Carnarvon were attacked, and the Boers driven off. June 19th Col. McCalmont proceeded to England, the command devolving on Major J. F. Cheyne.

June 25th Punaar's Commando surrendered at Carnarvon, the Battn. furnishing the guard over them.

June 27th the Battn. concentrated at Victoria Road, and on Sept. 10th left Cape Town for England.

Casualties.

Killed and died of disease, etc., Major and Hon. Lt.-Col. A. E. Thursby, 2nd Liut. R. H. Tremearne, and 8 N.C.O.'s and men.

Mentioned in Despatches.
Sergt.-Major Stevens.
Qr.-Sergt. Geare.

Special Honours.
Colonel Barklie McCalmont, C.B.

Medals, *etc.*, received by Battalion.
Queen's Medal with Clasps "Cape Colony" and "South Africa, 1902."

6th Battalion, The Royal Warwickshire Regiment.

"South Africa, 1900-01."
Hon. Colonel :—Perkins, G. D. S.
Lt.-Colonel :—Dawes, E. W., Capt. ret. pay (H).

Origin.

Formed 1853, under the Act of 1852 increasing the quotas of Militia for each County, and by division of the Royal Warwickshire Militia Regt. into two Regts., this Battn. being the 2nd, and in 1881 became the 4th Battn. of the Territorial Royal Warwickshire Regiment, changed in 1898 to the 6th Battn. on augmentation of the Regt. by two Line Battalions. For origin and special services prior to 1853 see 5th Battn. of the Regiment.

Embodiments.

Occasion.

Crimean War ...	1854, Dec. 15, to 1856, June 30.
Indian Mutiny...	1857, Oct. 14, to 1860, Apr. 30.
South African War ...	1899, Dec. 14, to 1901, June 3.

Services.

Volunteered for Foreign service during the South African War, and embarked for the seat of War. Strength 26 Officers, 1 W.O., 682 N.C.O.'s and men, Colonel H. L. B. McCalmont, M.P., comdg. On arrival at Cape Town, Jan 29th, 1900, the Battn. proceeded to Green Point Camp as guard over Boer prisoners, and for the many duties of the Station. Mch. 2nd, 1900, the Battn. furnished a guard of 100 men under Major Kelso to receive the Boer General Cronje as prisoner, and Captain J. B. Ludford-Astley with 2 Officers and 100 of other ranks embarked with him for St. Helena.

The duties at Simons Town were very heavy, some of the forts being nearly four miles apart, and owing to the hot weather most irksome.

May 25th, moved to Hopetown, and June 10th to Bloemfontein, where the Battn. was chiefly employed on outpost duty until Mch. 30th, 1901, and in frequent contact with the enemy. The outposts furnished were situated in a semi-circle from Bloemspruit past Sussex Hill over the railway near St. Andrews Hill, and so on to St. George's Hill which was in sight and touch of the outpost from Spitzkop, the Head Quarters being at Warwick Hill. The enemy were very active and daring, and in the habit of approaching the outposts at night to snipe them. Feb. 27th, 1901, took part in a small skirmish about four miles out, when some kopjes held by 140 Boers were shelled and captured. The Mounted Infantry worked round the flanks, and when the enemy was charged they turned and ran, but as the top was reached several Boer saddles were emptied. Strong patrols were at this time being constantly sent out to clear the district, and were frequently in contact with the enemy. At the end of March, 1901, the Battn. moved to Sanna's Post, 25 miles due East of Bloemfontein with posts along the Bloemfontein and Thabanchu Road. Major and Hon. Lt.-Colonel Campbell being appointed Commandant of the Station, extending from Boesman's Kop to Israel's Poort, the Post was defended by five redoubts to protect the Waterworks for supply of Bloemfontein. While at Sanna's Post, escorts for various Convoys were furnished, the Mounted Infantry of Battn. under Captain Williams being constantly employed in scouting and patrolling. On Apr. 10th a number of loose horses were rounded up, and about 50 or 60 Boers appearing, a strong position was taken up, but the line of retreat being threatened a retirement became necessary under heavy fire into a better position from which the Boers eventually withdrew, and the horses were brought into camp at Sanna's Post. Escorted Convoy to Israel's Poort and on return cleared out a farm near Vlakraal, the women and children being sent to Refuge Camp. Apr. 17th Patrol being fired on North of the Camp, the Farm at Mamena was cleared and 20 women and children brought in, part of V Battery R.H.A.

equipment lost in the action at Koornspruit being found in the Farmhouse. The Patrols were frequently exchanging shots with the Boers but at long ranges and no casualties on British side. Apr. 24th to 27th many Boers being reported by the Patrols, a party of M.I. was sent out to reconnoitre, who having seen a force of quite 100 Boers forced them to retire after exchange of shots at long ranges, their camp fires and forage being found and the latter burnt.

May 6th, 1901, Battn., having concentrated at Bloemfontein proceeded to Cape Town for return to England.

Casualties.

Killed and died of disease, etc., 26 N.C.O.'s and men.

Mentioned in Despatches.

Colonel H. L. B. McCalmont, M.P.
Lt.-Colonel J. E. R. Campbell.
Major Adjt. F. G. F. Browne.
Major A. Kelso.
Captain C. H. L. Beatty (twice).
Sergt.-Major 918 W. Parker.
Qr.-Mr.-Sergt. 1801 T. Powell.
Cr.-Sergt. 3956 W. Bell.
Sergt. 5156 W. Allen.
Sergt. 7121 W. T. Howes.
Corpl. 5484 J. Hoare.

Special Honours.

Lieut.-Colonel and Hon. Colonel H. L. B. McCalmont, C.B.
Major and Hon. Lt.-Colonel J. E. R. Campbell, D.S.O.
Captain C. H. L. Beatty, D.S.O.
Sergt.-Major W. Parker, D.C.M.
Qr.-Mr.-Sergt. T. Powell, D.C.M.

Medals and Clasps Received in Battalion.

Queen's South Africa Medal with Clasps "Cape Colony," "Orange Free State," and "South Africa, 1901."

5th Battalion, The Royal Fusiliers (City of London Regiment).

"Mediterranean."
"South Africa, 1901-02."

Hon. Colonel :—Cadogan, Rt. Hon. G. H., Earl, K.G.
Hon. Colonel :—Weatherall, H. B., C.B., hon. c. (H).

Origin.

In 1641, Feb. 12th, the Earl of Holland was appointed as a "fit person to be entrusted" with the organizing of the Militia of Middlesex.

In 1646, Dec. 2nd, the City of Westminster is included in the Ordinance "for setling the Militia in the severall Counties," etc.

According to Militia Returns 1697, Middlesex had three Regts., the "Westminster Troop of Horse" being referred to—see Egerton MSS. Brit. Mus.

In 1797 a Regt was completed for service as the 3rd Middlesex or Westminster.

By W.O. Letter 23rd April, 1804, the "Middlesex Westminster Regt." appears on the list of those "Regiments of Militia which have received his Majesty's gracious permission to bear the appellation of Royal Regiments."

In 1881, under the Territorial organization of the Forces, the Royal Westminster Militia Regt. became the 3rd Battn. of The Royal Fusiliers (City of London Regt.).

When the Territorial Regt. was augmented by two additional Line Battns. numbered as the 3rd and 4th, this Battn. became numbered as the 5th.

Embodiments.

Occasion.

Crimean War	...	1855, Feb. 6, to 1856, July 18.
Threatened War	...	1885, Mch. 9, to 1885, Sept. 30.
South African War	...	1899, Dec. 18, to 1900, Oct. 16.
South African War	...	1901, May 6, to 1902, July 26.

Services.

Volunteered for Foreign service during the Crimean War, embarked for Corfu and was stationed at the Citadel, and at Vido, Oct., 1855, to June, 1856.

Volunteered for Foreign service during the South African War, and embarked for the front June, 1901, Strength 24 Officers, one W.O., 594 other ranks, Colonel B. Weatherall Commdg.

On arrival at South Africa 27th June, 1901, the Battalion was quartered at West Hill, near Kroonstad, Orange River Colony, detachments garrisoning the Blockhouses on the railway line North of Kroonstad for about eight miles, and some of the local defences. On Aug. 21st the Battn. was moved to Ventersburg Road Station about thirty miles South of Kroonstad, and took over all Blockhouses from Bloomspruit Bridge to one mile South of Ventersburg Road, with Head Quarters at Ventersburg Road Station, relieving the 3rd Royal Scots. Jan. 7th, 1902, a detachment of two Officers, 61 N.C.O.'s and men commanded by Captain C. M. Hastings proceeded to Eengevonden for duty at that Station, and on the 18th Feb., two Officers with 108 other ranks under Capt. V. J. Forbes Smith occupied the Blockhouses near the Vet River Station. June 19th, 1902, Head Quarters entrained for Cape Town, picking up detachments at Eengevonden and Vet River on the way. On arrival at Cape Town the Battn. was quartered in the Boer Laager Camp at Green Point until embarkation for England July 4th, 1902.

Casualties.

Killed and died of disease, etc., Major A. Lund, Lieut. F. C. D. Brenes killed in action Mch. 29th, 1902, 24 N.C.O.'s and men.

Mentioned in Despatches.
  Captain H. Compton.
  Lt. and Qr.-Mr. F. Sutton.
  Sergt.-Major W. Old.
  Cr.-Sergt. T. Knight.
  Sergt. C. Hirons.

Special Honours.
  Colonel H. B. Weatherall, C.B.

Medals, etc., received by Battalion.

Queen's South African Medal with Clasps "Cape Colony," "Orange Free State," "Transvaal," "South Africa, 1901" and "1902."

6th Battalion, The Royal Fusiliers (City of London Regiment).

Hon. Colonel :—Dundas, L. G., C.B., Col.
Colonel :—p.s. Helpman, R. H. R. (T).

Origin.

By Regimental and other records, this Battn. is directly descended from the old Trained-Bands of the City of London, established in the Reign of Queen Elizabeth about 1559 as a new form of those Forces which the City of London had possessed for the defence of the Country from early times, the first indication of a regulated system of Military service being met with about the 5th century.

In 1559 Queen Elizabeth issued regulations for mustering, etc., of a regular City Militia.

The Encyclopaedic Dictionary describes the Trained-Bands as being "A band or company of a force partaking of the nature of both Militia and Volunteers" and "that after the Train-Bands instituted throughout the Country by James I. were dissolved by Charles II. (except London), the term was applied to the London Militia."

In the "Militia Returns," 1697, Egerton MSS., the Force is referred to both as Militia and Train'd Bands.

"Militia in the City of London."

The Orange, White, Green, Yalow, Red, and Blew Regts.—48 Companies, 6770 men, Cols. Sr. Robert Clayton, Sr. Wm. Ashurst, Sr. Wm. Hedges, Sr. Thos. Stamp, Sr. Thomas Lane, Sr. Owen Buckingham, with the footnote :—

"We humbly represent That all the Six Regts. of Train'd Bands of this City are very well compleated, and of great affection to his Maty and the Government."

In 1794 by Special Act 34, Geo. III., c. 81, the Train-Bands of London were abolished, and became two Regts. of Militia under the Commissioners of Lieutenancy. By Act 1795, 35 Geo. III., c. 27, the two Regts. were united and distinguished as the East and West Regts., one to be serving within the City or its Liberties, and the other to march where required not exceeding twelve miles beyond. It was enacted that they shall possess and enjoy all rights and privileges possessed and enjoyed by the Ancient Trained Bands of the City. In 1820 the two Regts. were united and designated the Royal London Militia. In 1881 under the Territorial Regimental system, the Regt. became the 4th Battn. of The Royal Fusiliers (City of London Regiment).

In 1898 when the Regt. was augmented by two Line Battns. numbered as the 3rd and 4th, this Battn. became known as the 6th Battn. Royal Fusiliers, still retaining its right and privilege as the old and original Trained Bands of London, of marching through the City with Colours flying, Bands playing, and Bayonets fixed.

Embodiments.

  Occasion.
  Crimean War ... ... 1855, Feb. 20, to 1856, June 12.
  South African War ... 1900, May 1, to 1900, Oct. 18.

Services.

The importance of London and its geographical position have connected its constitutional Forces in all ages with so many of the events in the Military History of England, that an epitome of some which have been disclosed by the researches of Colonel Helpman can only be here recorded together with a few interesting details obtained from other sources. In 886 the troops of the City of London defeated the Danes, and in 936 King Athelstan by the bravery of Londoners gained a complete victory over Constantine, King of Scotland.

We find in 1321, the Forces of London employed in the wars against the Barons when they held the suburbs of London, and that they also took part in the siege of Leeds Castle in Kent after a night's lodging had been denied to the Queen of Edward II., while journeying from Canterbury.

In the Wat Tyler rebellion, the rebels 30,000 strong were so panic-stricken on the approach of the City army numbering about one thousand, that the rebels laid down their arms.

In 1355 by Hollingshed's Chro. the City sent 500 Archers and 25 men at Arms for the Army going to France, whilst in 1436 the troops furnished by London were of great use in raising the siege of Calais. In 1539 the contingency of German and French interference caused a general muster throughout England and Wales, London assembling 5000 armed men who were reviewed by the King and Queen in great state.

In 1545 the City at its own expense furnished 1000 men in two units to reinforce the Army in France, and in 1548 sent 300 Light horsemen to the King's Army in Scotland.

In 1553, 500 men from London marched to Rochester to help the Duke of Norfolk's force in dislodging Wyat, but when advancing to attack the bridge they mutinied, compelling the Duke to retire in confusion.

In 1559 London sent twelve Companies, 1400 men to Queen Elizabeth's assembly of her Forces at Greenwich.

The City of London furnished for the Army formed to resist invasion by the Spanish Armada in 1588, 10,000 men fully equipped—some Historians put the number at about 20,000—and it is likely that the great emergency caused augmentation of the regular City Force, which in 1587 appears to have been 6,000 enrolled "under Captaines and Ensignes, the soaldiers with their several armour and weapons appoynted to them."

By S. P. Dom., 1591, London sent 350 men under Captains Goring and Baskerwyl as part of 4,000 levied from certain Counties. Stowe's Chron: says "In the month of Julie Robert Earle of Essex was by her highnesse appointed to have the charge and conduction as her M. Lieutenant Generall of 4,000 foot, etc., sent into Fraunce for the assistance of the French Kinge against the Confederates of the League."

In 1596, by S. P. Dom., London sent its quota of the 6,000 men that joined the French King in relieving Calais besieged, and in 1598 its proportion of 2,000 men for the Rebellion in Ireland.

In 1599 the City supplied 6,000 men completely armed for the service of the Queen, apprehensive of danger from the intrigues of Essex, who formed the Bodyguard for Her own Person at the public expense.

In 1602 the City of London sent 500 men for service in Ireland.

In 1614, at a general muster by King James I., London paraded 6,000 armed men.

In 1624, 2,000 "Trained Bands" were sent as the share of London to the assistance of the Elector Palatine the King's Son-in-law.

By "Remembrancia," 3,000 of the Trained-Bands proceeded for service against the Scots in 1638, and by Clarendon's Hist., at a later date, 4,000 more independently of the Trained Bands, for the same purpose.

In 1640, May 15th, by a Warrant from the King, 1,000 men of the Trained-Bands were to suppress tumultuous assemblies in Southwark, Blackheath, etc.

In Oct., 1642, the six City Regiments formed part of the Earl of Essex's Parliamentary Army assembled near St. Alban's. At the Battle of Edgehill the defeat of the Royal Army is stated by History to have been mainly due to the London Militia.

In 1643, The City of Gloucester besieged by the King, was relieved by a force from the City of London under command of the Earl of Essex, and it may be generally stated that the "Constitutional Force" of London took part in most of the chief engagements during the Civil War, including the second Battle of Newbury, when four of its regiments distinguished themselves, aided by the Tower Hamlets, Westminster and Southwark Regiments. It is stated that the City, and the City Militia, were most instrumental in bringing about the Restoration of King Charles II.

In 1689, the City Militia had to suppress a riot of the Weavers, and in 1745 we find the City Militia guarding all the approaches against any surprise of the Pretender's Forces. In 1780 the "Trained-Bands" of London took an active part in the suppression of the Gordon Riots in London, whilst in more recent times the London Militia or ancient Trained Bands of London, has borne its share of duty on all emergency occasions.

7th Battalion, The Royal Fusiliers (City of London Regiment).

Hon. Colonel :—Edgcumbe, Hon. C. E.
Lt.-Colonel :—Heseltine, C.

Origin.

In 1881 the Royal South Middlesex Regt. of Militia which had been raised in 1853, and affiliated with the 2nd and 4th Battns. of the King's Royal Rifle Corps 1873, became under Territorial Regimental Organization of the Forces the 5th Battn. Royal Fusiliers (City of London Regt.) subsequently changed to 6th and then 7th Battn. on augmentation of the Regt. by additional Line Battns.

Embodiments.

Occasion.

Crimean War	1854, July, to 1856, July 21.
Indian Mutiny... ...	1857, Oct. 1, to 1858, June 4.
South African War ...	1900, May 14, to 1900, Oct. 15.

3rd Battalion, The King's (Liverpool Regiment).

"South Africa, 1902."

Hon. Colonel :—Hesketh, Sir T. G. F., Bt.
Lt.-Colonel :—p.s. Weston, E. C., hon. c. (Q) (H).

Origin.

Raised 1797 as the 1st Royal Lancashire Supplementary Regt. of Militia, its Title being changed in 1798 to the 2nd Royal Lancashire Militia, and retained on the establishment of regular Militia Regiments; became a Rifle Regt. in 1854, and under Territorial Regimental organization of the Forces in 1881 formed the 3rd and 4th Battns. of The King's (Liverpool Regiment).

Embodiments.
   Occasion.

Revolutionary War, etc.	1798, Mch. 10, to 1802, Apr. 29.
European Disturbances	1803, Mch. 14, to 1816, Mch. 3.
South African War ...	1900, Jan. 23, to 1900, Oct. 16.
South African War ...	1901, Dec. 2, to 1902, Sep. 15.

Services.

Volunteered for and stationed in Ireland 1814 to 1816.

Volunteered for Foreign service on the occasion of the South African War, and embarked for South Africa Dec. 16th, 1901, strength 23 Officers, 561 N.C.O.'s and men, Colonel J. Mount Batten Commdg. On arrival at Durban, The Battn. sent detachments to Durban Road, Phillipstown, Hopetown, and Steynsburg, and took over the Blockhouses near Modder River, all in Cape Colony.

Mch. 21st, 1902, the Battn. furnished the escort for a Convoy from De Aar to Prieska, a march of about 150 miles, which safely reached its destination though often harassed by the Boers.

Head Quarters and the different detachments took part in several night alarms.

The Battn. left South Africa Aug. 27th, 1902, for England.

Casualties.

Killed and died of disease, etc., Nil.

Mentioned in Despatches.
   Captain S. D. Norris.
   Sergt. N. Hayes.

Special Honours.
   Colonel J. Mount Batten, C.B.

Medals, etc., received by Battalion.

Queen's South African with Clasps "Cape Colony" and "South Africa, 1902."

4th Battalion, The King's (Liverpool Regiment).

"South Africa, 1902."
Hon. Colonel:—Hesketh, Sir T. G. F., Bt.
Lt.-Colonel:—Gosset, E. F., Maj. ret. pay (Res. of Off.) p.s.c.

Origin.

See 3rd Battn. The King's (Liverpool Regt.)

Embodiments.

Occasion.—Since 1881.

South African War	...	1900, May 3, to 1900, Nov. 1.
South African War	...	1902, Jan. 6, to 1902, Sept. 15.

Services.

Volunteered for Foreign Service during the South African War, and embarked Strength 23 Officers, one W.O., 677 N.C.O.'s and men, Lt.-Colonel W. H. Hand, commdg. On arrival at Port Elizabeth Feb. 15, 1902, the Battn. proceeded to Mafeking and was employed until the 6th July on Blockhouse duty, the Mafeking defences, Lichtenberg, Palfontein, Maritzana, Maribogo, etc. The Battn. also furnished detachments at Labatzi and Vryburg. The Blockhouse line was vacated on July 6th and Battn. moved to Vryburg. Aug. 6th proceeded by march route to Tygerskloof until Aug. 24th when it entrained for Capetown and embarked Aug. 27th for England.

Casualties.

Killed and died of disease, etc., 2nd Lieut. Chapman, 5 N.C.O.'s and men.

Mentioned in Despatches.

Captain Sheen (attached) and Lieut. A. Lindemere.
Sergt.-Maj. Burnett and Sergt. Haynes.

Medals etc., received by Battalion.

The Queen's South African Medal with Clasps "Cape Colony." "Transvaal," "South Africa, 1902."

3rd Battalion, The Norfolk Regiment.

"South Africa, 1900-02."

Hon. Colonel:—Custance, F. H., C.B., hon. c. (Hon. Lt.-Col. in Army, 12 Apr., 1902).

Lt.-Colonel:—Kemp, Sir K. H., Bt.

Origin.

Completed for service 1759 as the 1st or Western Norfolk Militia Regiment and one of two for the quota of men to be found by the County.

At the muster 1539, 30 Henry VIII., by "Letters and Papers" of this Reign the County Force numbered by the Certificate 163 archers and 246 billmen "sufficiently harnessed."

By Harleian MSS. Norfolk assembled for the Armies formed to resist the Spanish Armada invasion 2200 trained men besides Horsemen Launces 80, Lighthorse 321, Petronells 324, and Petronells of the Justices 53.

In 1641, Feb. 12, the Earl of Warwick was appointed a "fit person" to organize the Militia of the County and Co. and City of Norwich.

In 1644, July 29, by "Calendar of State Papers Domestic," Norfolk thanked by the "Committee of both Kingdoms" for forwardness in furnishing their proportion of forces upon the new ordinance of 12 July.

By Militia Returns, Egerton MSS., 1697, the County had six Regiments, 38 Companies, 4382 Foot with six Troops of Horse and Lyme-Regis two Companies 250 Foot.

The Blew Regt. Col. Sir Jacob Ashley, Knt.
The Yellow Regt. Col. Robert Walpole, Esqr.
The Purple Regt. Col. Sr. Richard Berney.
The Yarmouth Regt. Capt. John Robbins.
The Norwich Regt. Col. Duke of Norfolk.

In 1881 the 1st Norfolk Regt. of Militia became the 3rd Battn. of the Territorial Norfolk Regiment.

Embodiments,

Occasion.

Seven Years' War ...	1759, June 24 to 1762, Dec. 15.
American War, etc. ...	1778 to 1783, and 1792 to 1802, 1803 to 1814.
French War	1815, June, to 1816, Mch.
Crimean War	1854, Dec. 27, to 1856, July 24.

Indian Mutiny ... ... 1857, Nov. to
South African War ... 1900, Jan. 25, to 1902, Apr. 11.

Services.

By Calendar of S. Papers, 1644, the Force of Norfolk served against the King.

In 1666 by S. P. Dom. Chas. II a levy was made by the King on the Militia of Norfolk for the threatened French and Dutch invasion.

Volunteered for and stationed in Ireland 1815-16.

1816, June, took part in the suppression of serious riots, etc., in the City of Norwich, the Regiment receiving the thanks of the Civil authorities for " assistance rendered and conduct highly meritorious and praiseworthy."

Volunteered for Foreign service during South African War, and embarked Feb. 25, 1900, strength 22 Officers, 503 other ranks, Colonel F. H. Custance, commdg. On arrival at Cape Town proceeded to, and disembarked at, East London, Mch. 21, 1900. Apr. 4, Battn. concentrated at Bethulie Bridge, afterwards proceeding to Springfontein and Edenburg, dropping small detachments at various bridges and culverts on the way. July 13, Battn. moved to Kaffir River between Edenburg and Bloemfontein, Head Quarters remaining there for twelve months when the Blockhouse system was established. Col. Custance appointed Commandant of the section about fifty miles. The Blockhouses were frequently attacked, the Kaffir River being a favourite place for their despatch riders to cross. July 13, 1901, the Battn. proceeded to Norvals Pont where the main line crosses the Orange River, and occupied the Blockhouses extending twelve miles south and eighteen miles north—often subjected to attack—but the barbed wire, trenches parallel to the railway line and telephonic communication between the posts, rendered the railway an almost impassable barrier to the Boers. Proceeded 1902 to Port of embarkation for England.

Casualties.

Killed and died of disease, etc., 11 N.C.O.'s and men.
Lieut. Hylton Joliffe of the Battn. attached to 2nd Battn. The Norfolk Regt. being killed at Paardeburg Drift.

Mentioned in Despatches.

Colonel F. H. Custance.
Major and Adjt. A. H. Y. Beale.
Capt. and Hon. Maj. H. Forbes Eden.

Captains S. L. Barrett, Rd. Bagge, E. R. Harbord (3rd Cheshire Regt.)
Lieut. D. R. Hunt.
Sergt.-Major Turnell.
Qr.-Mr.-Sergt. Quantrell.
O.R.-Sergt. Hendry.
Cr.-Sergt. Frost.
Sergt. Culvers.
Lce.-Corp. Coates.

Special Honours.

Colonel F. H. Custance, C.B.
Captain R. L. Bagge, D.S.O.
Captain E. R. Harbord, D.S.O.
Maj. and Adjt. A. H. Y. Beale, D.S.O.
Sergt.-Major Turnell, D.C. Medal.
Qr.-Mr.-Sergt. J. Quantrell, D.C. Medal.
Sergt. C. Vincent, D.C. Medal.

Medals etc., received by Battalion.

Queen's South African with Clasps "Cape Colony" and "Orange Free State." King's South African with Clasps 1901 and 1902.

4th Battalion, The Norfolk Regiment.

Hon. Colonel:—Albemarle, A. A. C., Earl of, C.B., M.V.O., A.D.C. (Hon. Lt.-Col. in Army 1st Dec., 1900).
Lt.-Colonel:—Danby, W. E., Maj. (H).

Origin.

In 1881 under Territorial organization, the 2nd Norfolk Militia which had completed for service in 1759 under Act 30, Geo. II., as the 2nd or Eastern Regiment, afterwards called the East Regt., became the 4th Battalion of "The Norfolk Regiment." (For particulars of the Constitutional Force of Norfolk prior to 1759 see 3rd Battn. Norfolk Regt.).

Embodiments.

Occasion.

Seven Years War ... 1759, June 24, to 1762, Dec. 15.
American War ... 1778, Apr., to 1783, Mch.

Revolutionary War etc.	1792, Dec. 19, to 1802, Apr. 30.
European Disturbances	1803, Mch. 26, to 1814, June 24.
Crimean War	1854, Dec. 27, to 1856, June.
South African War ...	1900, May 1, to 1901, July 17.

Services.

In 1800 the Regt. was moved to Newcastle-under-Lyne and Lichfield District, to suppress riot and disturbances. Volunteered for and stationed in Ireland 1811-13.

3rd Battalion, The Lincolnshire Regiment.

"South Africa, 1902."

Hon. Colonel :—Yarborough, C. A. W., Earl of
Lt.-Colonel :—Swan, C. A., C.M.G., hon. c. (H).

Origin.

See copy of County Muster, 30, Henry VIII., 1539, from "Letters and Papers of the Reign of Henry VIII."

1588 by Harleian MSS. Lincolne assembled to resist invasion by the Spanish Armada 2958 Trained men reduced into bandes under Captaines, besides horsemen Launces 60, Lighthorse 80, Petronell 80, Argolets 300.

1641, Feb. 12, The Earl of Lincoln appointed as "a fit person" to be entrusted with the organization of the Militia of the "Parts of Kesteven and Holland and the City of the County of Lincoln." Lord Willoughby of Parham being at the same time appointed for the "Parts of Lindsay in the Co. of Holland."

1697, by Militia Returns Egerton MSS. the County had three Regiments, fifteen Companies, 1494 men, with four Troops of Horse 333, Col. E. of Lindsey; for Part of Kesterton Major Reuben Parke; in Lindsey Coast Col. Charles Dymocke (Champion of England). When the Militia was reorganised under the Act 30, Geo. II., 1757—two Regiments were completed for service in 1759, and the quota of men to be found by the County, this Battalion being designated the North Lincolnshire Regt. of Militia, became a Royal Regiment in 1760, and 3rd Battalion of the Territorial Lincolnshire Regiment under the Organization of 1881.

Embodiments.

Occasion.

Seven Years War	1759, Oct. 27, to 1763.
American War	1778, to not recorded.
Revolutionary War, etc.	1792, to 1802.
French War	1803, to 1814.
Crimean War	1854, Dec. 27, to 1856, June 1.
Indian Mutiny	1857, Oct. 7, to 1860, July 21.
South African War	1900, May 9, to 1901, July 5.
South African War	1902, Feb. 17, to 1902, Oct. 6.

Services.

In 1666 by "State Papers Dom" Charles II. the County Militia was drawn out by the King to serve during the threatened French and Dutch invasion.

1760, Mch., Forced march to Liverpool to resist feared attack by Thurot's French Squadron from Ireland. Volunteered for and stationed in Ireland 1814. Volunteered for Foreign Service during the South African War, and embarked strength 20 Officers, 1 W. O., 580 N.C.O.'s and men, Colonel C. A. Swan Commdg. On arrival at Cape Town, Apr. 10, 1902, proceeded to garrison Blockhouses between Grootfontein and De Aar, extending over two hundred and sixty miles with Head Quarters at Beaufort West—Captain Fane with three other Officers and one hundred men being trained as Mounted Infantry at De Aar, and employed for escort duty and patrolling to Bretstown, Prieska, etc., along with Captain Massingberd's "B" Company. After peace was signed Golding's rebel Commando 206 strong came in and surrendered June 26 at Beaufort West, and guards formed over them. July 8 all detachments were brought in and Colonel Swan appointed Commandant of the Station, the Battn. furnishing the escort for the surrendered rebels to Frazurburg. Embarked at Cape Town for England Sep. 11—eighteen men taking their discharge to settle in the Country.

Casualties.

Killed and died of disease, etc., one drummer.

Special Honours.

Colonel C. A. Swan, C.M.G.

Medals etc., received by Battalion.

South Africa with Clasps "South Africa, 1902" and "Cape Colony."

4th Battalion, The Lincolnshire Regiment.

Hon. Colonel:—Brownlow, Rt. Hon. A. W. B., Earl A.D.C.

Lt.-Colonel:—Joicey-Cecil, Lord J. P., Lt. ret. pay, hon. c.

Origin.

For particulars of the Forces of Lincolnshire prior to 1757—see 3rd Battalion of the Regiment. In 1757 two Regiments were completed for service, this Battalion being designated the South Lincolnshire Regiment. It subsequently became a Royal Regiment, and in 1881 the 4th Battn. of The Lincolnshire Regt. under the Territorial Regimental organization of that year.

Embodiments.

Occasion.

Seven Years War	...	1759, to 1762, Mch. 5.
American War	...	1778, to not recorded.
Revolutionary War, etc		1792, to 1802.
French War	...	1803, to 1816, Feb. 24.
Crimean War	...	1854, July 11, to 1856, July 7.
South African War	...	1900, Jan. 29, to 1900, Oct. 17.

Services.

Forced march to Liverpool in 1760 to resist the feared attack by Thurot's French Squadron from Ireland.

In 1798 volunteered for service in Ireland during the Rebellion, and stationed at Dublin. Volunteered for and stationed in Ireland 1813-14.

3rd Battalion, The Devonshire Regiment.

Hon. Colonel:—Mountsteven, F. H., C.M.G., hon. c. (Hon. Lt.-Col. in Army 21st Oct. 1900), (H).

Lt.-Colonel:—Moore-Stevens, R.A., hon. c.

Origin.

In 1881, under Territorial organization of the Forces of the kingdom, the 2nd Devon Militia Regt. became the 3rd Battn. of "The Devonshire Regiment."

At the great muster of armed men of Counties in England and Wales, 1539, by virtue of Royal Commission, March 1, 30, Henry VIII., Devonshire was represented, see certificate from "State Papers Foreign and Domestic of the Reign Henry VIII."

By Harleian MSS., " abstract of the certificates returned by ye Lieuftenants of the able trayned and furneshed men in the severall counties reduced into bandes under Captaines and how they were soarted wt. weapones " for resisting invasion by the Spanish Armada, 1588, Devonshire ffurnished 3661 Trained men, besides Horsemen, Launces " they find non but instead 200 muskets," Lighthorse 150, Petroneles 50. 1641, Feb. 12, The Earl of Bedford appointed as a " fit person to be entrusted" with the organizing of the Militia of Devon and County and City of Exon.

By Militia Returns, 1697, Egerton MSS., Devon had 41 companies in six regiments, 4920 men with three troops of horse 236. Colonels, Earl of Stamford, Sr. Francis Drake, Bart., Sr. Wm. Davy, Sr. Walter Yonge, Bart., Saml. Roll, Esqr., Arscot, besides a Dartmouth Independent Company, 60 Horse, Capt. John Whitson; an Exeter Regiment of eight companies 480 men, Col. Earl of Stamford, and a Plymouth Regiment of five companies 467 men, Major Mayor.

In 1759, under Act 30, Geo. II., two regiments were completed for service, and the quota of men to be found by the county, which under the Consolidation Act of 1763 were reorganized into three regiments as the North, East and South.

In 1853 the N. Devon Regiment was converted into Artillery, Colonel Buck with several officers and 367 men joining the new Corps, the East and South Regiments then becoming the 1st and 2nd Regiments of Devon Militia, the latter or original South Regiment of 1759 being made the 3rd Battalion of the new Territorial Regiment in 1881.

Embodiments.

   Occasion.

Seven Years War	...	1759, June 21, to 1762, Dec.
American War	...	1778, Mar. 26, to 1783, Mar. 3.
Revolutionary War, etc.		1792, Dec., to 1802, April 24.
French War	...	1803, March 31, to 1814, Aug. 9.
,, ,,	...	1815, July 17, to 1816, Feb. 8.
Crimean War	...	1854, May 31, to 1856, June 10.
Indian Mutiny	...	1857, Nov. 9, to 1858, May 14.
South African War	...	1899, Dec. 4 to 1900, Oct. 20.

Services.

By "State Papers Domestic, Chas. II." a levy on the Militia of the County was made by the King, 1666, for the threatened French and Dutch invasion.

Volunteered and served in Ireland at the time of the Rebellion—1798 to 1799.

In 1812 the regiment was part of the force employed in the suppression of the Luddite Riots, and operated in the neighbourhood of Nottingham, Major General Hawker thanking it officially for its conduct and zeal during the arduous duty which it was required to perform.

4th Battalion, The Devonshire Regiment.

Hon. Colonel :—
Lt.-Colonel :—Palk, Hon. E. A., hon. c.

Origin.

See 3rd Battalion of the Regiment for details of the Forces of the County prior to 1763, when the men to be furnished by the county were organized into three regiments, this battalion being the East one, or 1st Devon Militia, which under the territoral organization of the Forces in 1881 became the 4th Battalion of "The Devonshire Regiment."

Embodiments.

   Occasion.

Seven Years War	1759 to 1762.
American ,,	1778 to 1783.
Revolutionary War, etc.	1792 to 1799.
French War	1803 to 1805.
Crimean War	1852 to 1856.
South African War	1900, May 11, to 1901, July 16.

Services.

Stationed in the Channel Islands, 1900-01.

3rd Battalion, The Suffolk Regiment.

Hon. Colonel :—Bristol, F. W. J., Marquis of.
Lt.-Colonel :—Scudamore, F. W., Maj., ret pay (Maj. Res. of Off.), hon. c., (H) (S) (Q).

Origin.

Prepared for service in 1759 as the West Suffolk Militia, and as one of two regiments (the East and West Suffolk) for the quota of Militia to be furnished by the county, the East Suffolk being converted into Artillery 1853.

At a muster, 9th and 11th Apr., 30, Henry VIII., of armed men of the county and view of their arms, the Hundreds of Suffolk appear by the certificates to have produced 219 archers and 358 billmen.

At the assembly to meet the Spanish Armada, 1588, the numbers of "trayned and ffurnished" men and horses are not given, only that 3,892 trained and untrained men were present out of the 4,239 able men in the county.

1641, Feb. 12, the Earl of Suffolk recommended by the House of Commons as "a person fit to be entrusted" with the organization of the Militia of the County.

By Militia Returns 1697 (taken in 1692 when last called together) the county then had 4 regiments—the Red, White, Blew, and Yellow—besides two Ipswich companies, 31 companies 2,467 foot, with four troops of horse 208. Total of both 2675. Colonels, Anthony Crofts, Sir Phillip Parker, late Col. Sir Phillip Skipton, Sir Thomas Bernardiston—Lord Cornwallis (Horse).

In 1881 the regiment became the 3rd Battalion of the Territorial Suffolk Regiment.

Embodiments.

Occasion.

Seven Years War ...	1759 to 1762, Dec. 24.
American ,, ...	1778 to 1783.
French War, etc. ...	1793 to 1814, Oct.
Crimean War ...	1854, Dec., to 1856, June.
South African War ...	1899, Dec. 4, to 1901, July 3.
,, ,, ...	1902, Feb. 24, to 1902, Sep. 27.

Services.

Volunteered for and served in Ireland 1798-9, also in 1813.

Stationed in the disturbed districts of Yorkshire during the Luddite Riots, 1812, with orders to cover the country to the West and North of Halifax, including the whole of Bradford Vale, patrols being sent out night and day to prevent meetings of the disaffected and give confidence to the inhabitants. In a letter dated April 8, 1813, from the Secretary of State (Lord Sidmouth) to the Lord Lieutenant of the County of Suffolk, Lieutenants Cooper and Young, of the West Suffolk Militia, were specially mentioned for their "zeal and discretion" while lately employed under the orders of Major-General Maitland "on a service of peculiar difficulty," the latter expressing the deep sense he felt "of the eminent propriety and zeal manifested by all the officers and men of the Militia regiments under his orders."

Stationed in the Channel Islands, Jan. 5, 1900 to April 29, 1901, during South African War.

4th Battalion, The Suffolk Regiment.

Lt.-Colonel :—
Lt.-Colonel :—Bacchus, R. S.

Origin.

In 1881, under the territorial regimental organization of the forces, the Cambridgeshire Militia Regiment became the 4th Battn. of The Suffolk Regiment.

By Harleian MSS., "Cambridgscire" assembled in Aprille ano dom 1588 to resist invasion by the Spanish Armada, 500 traynedand furneshed men reduced into bandes under Captaines, besides Horsemen, Launces 60, Lighthorse 40, and Petronelles 80.

In 1641, Feb. 12, when "fit persons to be entrusted" with organizing the Militia of the kingdom were appointed, Lord North acted for the I. of Ely.

By Militia Returns, 1697—Egerton MSS.—the County of Cambridge and Isle of Ely had five Companies for Cambridge, East Division, West Division, Wisbech, and Ely— 677 foot with three troops of horse for East Div., West Div., and Isle of Ely, 151 men each company and troop commanded by a captain, there being no regimental organization or Colonel.

In 1760, under Act 30, Geo. II., a regiment was completed for service and the quota of men to be furnished by the county, as the Cambridgeshire Militia, which in 1881 became a Battalion of the Suffolk Regiment.

Embodiments.

Occasion.

American War ... 1778 to 1783
Revolutionary War, etc. 1793 to 1802.
European Disturbances 1803 to 1816.
Crimean War ... 1854 to 1856.
South African War ... 1900, Jan. 23 to 1900, Oct. 15.

Services.

In 1666, by State Papers Domestic, Chas. II., a levy on the Militia of Cambridge was made by the King for the threatened French and Dutch invasion.

In 1780 the Cambridge Regiment of Militia, when on march to St. Albans, en route for Tiptree Heath, was stopped at Hampstead for the suppression of the Lord George Gordon No Popery Riots then raging in London.

In 1798 the regiment, under Col. the Earl of Hardwicke, volunteered for service in Ireland, and was one of the thirteen regiments sent there immediately upon the passing of an Act which empowered the King to employ the English Militia in that country owing to rebellion.

In 1810 the regiment was brought to Hampstead and Highgate owing to apprehended disturbances and riot in London.

In 1814 the Cambridgeshire Militia furnished five officers (Captain Robertson, Lieuts. Black, Lyster, Hepburne, and Ensign Burks) with 160 N.C.O.'s and men for the 1st Provisional Battn. of the Militia Brigade under Col. the Marquis of Buckingham, which landed in France near Bordeaux to serve under the Duke of Wellington.

3rd Battalion, The Prince Albert's (Somersetshire Light Infantry).

Hon. Colonel :—Henley, H. C., hon. c.
Lt.-Colonel :—Hicks, H. E., (H).

Origin.

By "State Papers Foreign and Domestic" of the reign, 30, Henry VIII., 1539, the certificate for Somersetshire is incomplete in respect of the numbers present at the muster of the Force of the County who were armed.

In the history of "Somerset and the Armada" by Emanuel Green it is stated : "The following will therefore be the first complete list of names, as existing in Sepr., 1559, of the Cappetaynes and pety Cappetaynes with their livelodes, appoynted to lead one thousand footmen in Somerset the first known complete Regiment of Somerset Militia."

The details are given as being probably typical of what existed in other counties.

"Richard Mychell	in land £40	} 100 men
Richard Sydenham	,, livelyhood £40	
Thomas Benfylde	,, land £20	} 100 men
Thomas Isham	,, lyvelode	
George Harnyge	,, lands 20 mares	} 100 men
Peter Grene	,, lands £10	
Wyllyam Crouche	,, land £40	} 100 men
John Sturggis	,, land £6. 13. 4	
William Leversedge	,, land £30	} 100 men
John Champnes	,, land £5	
Humfrey Worthe	,, land £20	} 100 men
Bartholomew Lyte	,, lyvelode £10	
Hughe Smithe	,, lands £40	} 100 men
Tristram Dillyngton	,, lyvelode £6. 13. 4.	
John Ayshe	,, lands £20	} 100 men
Thomas Walle	,, lyvelode £5	
Harry Clarke	,, lands £20	} 100 men
James Persyvalle	,, lands £10	
Thomas Payne	,, lands £40	} 100 men
George Ken	,, lyvelode £5	

By "The Abstract of the Certificate from ye Lieuftenant" 1588, Harleian MSS., the county assembled for service against the Spanish Armada invasion—1588—4,000 Trained and ffurnished men, besides Horsemen Launces 50, Lighthorse 250, and Petroneles 60.

In 1641, Feb. 12, the Marquis of Hertford was appointed as "a fit person to be entrusted" with the organization of the Militia of Somersetshire.

By Militia Returns, 1697 —Egerton MSS.—the county had for its 42 hundreds, five regiments of 3,434 men in forty companies, with five troops of horse 259; total of both 3,703.

Bridgewater Regt., Col. Sr. John Trevillian.
Wells Regt., Col. Edward Berkeley.
Bathe Regt., Col. ———
Crewpthorne Regt., Col. Harry Henly.
Taunton Regt., Col. Sr. Fr. Warr.

With foot note—That all are charged to the Militia, etc., "ffor they do not believe the parishes out of which the men comes will hardly sufferr their neighbours to escape scot free and they to bear the Burthen."

When the Militia of Counties was reorganized under Act 30, Geo. II., two regiments were completed in 1759 for service, and the quota of men to be found by Somersetshire, this Battalion being the 1st Somersetshire Militia, it became Light Infantry at later date, and in 1881 under territorial organization the 3rd Battn. of The Prince Albert's (Somersetshire Light Infantry) Regiment.

Embodiments.

Occasion.	
Monmouth Rebellion	1685, period unknown.
French War, etc., ...	1792 to 1816, for periods almost [continuous
Crimean War ...	1854 to 1856.
South African War ...	1900, May 15, to 1900, Dec. 4.

Services.

In 1685 "The Somersetshire Militia (Yellow Regiment) under the command of Sir William Portman, Bart., K.B., of Orchard Portman, was in arms to suppress the Monmouth Rebellion, and after the Battle of Sedgmoor formed a chain of posts from the sea to the northern extremity of Dorset. 'In a healthy country on the boundaries of Dorset and Hants, hidden in a ditch, a body of the Somerset Militia discovered James Scott, Duke of Monmouth, in the dress of a shepherd, for whose apprehension a reward of £5,000 had been offered. In his pockets were found some raw peas, a watch, a purse of gold, and the St. George with which many years before King Charles II. decorated this his illegitimate son, but the Colonel (Sir William Portman) forbade all violence, and he was conveyed under a strong guard to Ringwood, in Hampshire, thence under escort of a large body of Militia to London, where he was brought within the walls of the Palace, and delivered by Sir William Portman to King James II." The regiment was afterwards allowed to wear the Duke of Monmouth's crest as a badge.

In 1793 took part in the suppression of the tinners' riots at Falmouth.

4th Battalion, The Prince Albert's (Somersetshire Light Infantry).

"South Africa, 1900-02."

Hon. Colonel:—p.s. Long, W., C.M.C., hon. c. (Hon. Lt.-Col. in Army 15 May, 1902).

Lt.-Colonel:—p.s. Woodhouse, S. H. (t) (Hon. Maj. in the Army).

Origin.

See 3rd Battn. of the Regiment for early records of the Constitutional Force of Somersetshire.

In 1759, when two Regiments were completed for service and the quota of men to be found by the county under Act 30, Geo. II., this Battalion was the 2nd Regt. of the Somersetshire Militia, became Light Infantry in 1876, and in 1881 4th Battalion, The Prince Albert's (Somersetshire Light Infantry) Regiment, under territorial organization of the forces.

Embodiments.

Occasion.

Peninsula War	...	Dates not recorded.
Crimean ,,	...	1854, Sep. 25, to 1856.
South African War	...	1899, Dec. 4, to 1902, May 14.

Services.

Volunteered for foreign service 1899, and embarked for South Africa, strength 27 officers, 361 N.C.O.'s and men, Colonel W. Long commanding. On arrival East London, April 2, 1900, furnished details for guarding from East London to Queenstown, with Maxim gun and detachment at Burghersdorp. Dec., 1900, four officers and 200 men proceeded to Stormburg Garrison, E Company to Queenstown and Bowkers Park. March, 1901, formed Garrison for Cathcart, threatened by the Boers. May, 1901, B. Company to Wonderboom and Bamboo Siding, D Company to Bushman's Hoell. Oct., 1901, J Company employed on blockhouse line, Sterkstroom section, B Company Baileytown, etc. Captains John Mildmay and Swaffield being employed on remount duty, Lt.-Col. Llewellyn commanding at Queenstown, Lt.-Col. West Staff Officer, East London, and Captains Hinde and Woodhouse acting as Press Censors.

Casualties.

Killed and died of disease, etc., Lieut. E. L. Reeves, 21 N.C.O.'s and men.

Mentioned in Despatches.

Colonel W. Long.
Captain M. Foster.
Captain S. H. Woodhouse.
Captain S. Owen Swaffield.
Captain R. Manley.
Sergt.-Major Tobias.
Qr.-Mr.-Segrt. Kemp.
Cr.-Sergts. Hackett and Stevens.
Sergts. Hillier and Hill.

Special Honours.

Colonel W. Long, C.M.G.
Captain M. A. Foster, D.S.O.
Lieut. and Qr.-Mr. H. Powis, The hon. rank of Captain.
Sergt.-Major Tobias, D.C. Medal.
Qr.-Mr.-Sergt. Kemp, D.C. Medal.
Cr.-Sergt. Bastable, D.C. Medal.

Medals etc., received by Battalion.

Queen's South African Medal with Clasp "Cape Colony." King's South African Medal with Clasps "1901-1902."

3rd Battalion, The Prince of Wales's Own (West Yorkshire Regiment).

"Mediterranean."
"Mediterranean, 1901-02."

Hon. Colonel :—Gen. H.R.H. George F. E. A., Prince of Wales and Duke of Cornwall and York, K.G., K.T., K.P., G.C.M.G., G.C.V.O., I.S.O., Col. in Chief R. Fus., R.W. Fus., R. Mar., K.R. Rif. C., and Cam'n. Highrs., Personal A.D.C. to the King, Grand Prior of the Order St. John of Jerusalem, etc.

Lt.-Colonel :—Hine-Haycock, R. W., hon. c. (H).

Origin.

See 3rd Battn. The King's Own Yorkshire Light Infantry prior to the changes in 1763. In 1854 the Regiment became the 2nd West York Light Infantry until 1881, when it formed the 3rd Battn. of the Territorial Prince of Wales's Own West Yorkshire Regiment.

Embodiments.

Occasion.

Seven Years' War ...	1759, Sep. 6, to 1763.
American War ...	1778, Apr., to 1783.
Revolutionary War, etc.	1793, to 1802.
French War	1803 to 1816, Mch.
Crimean War	1854 to 1856.
Indian Mutiny	1857 to 1858.
South African War ...	1899, May 4, to 1902, Oct. 1.

Services.

See 3rd Battn. The King's Own Yorkshire Light Infantry, for services of the Constitutional Force of The West Yorks. District between 633 and middle of the Fifteenth century.

In 1780 the 2nd West York Regiment took part in the suppression of the Gordon Riots in London, and was encamped in the British Museum Gardens (a Painting and Engraving of the camp being in the collection of His Majesty at Windsor Castle).

In 1797 when in Garrison at Sheerness, furnished the boarding party to arrest Parker, the ringleader of the mutiny at the Nore, on board H.M.S. "Sandwich," when the place was threatened with bombardment by the insurgents of the

Fleet, a duty which is chronicled as being fraught with danger, the Regiment being also detailed to provide for his safe escort to Maidstone Gaol, and to be present at his execution.

Volunteered for service in Ireland during the 1798 rebellion, and under Colonel Viscount Downe was one of the thirteen Regts. immediately sent there on the passing of the Act giving power to employ the Militia in that Country.

In 1814 volunteered for Foreign service, and nine Officers (Major Yarburgh, Captns. Lees and Dodsworth, Lieuts. Lockhurst, Nash, Sharp, Ensigns Webster, Singlehurst, and Taylor, A.-Surgeon Lawrence), with 300 N.C.O.'s and men embarked at Portsmouth, March 10, 1814, as part of the 3rd Provisional Battalion under Colonel Sir Watkin Williams Wynne, Bart. (Denbigh Militia), of the Militia Brigade which landed in France near Bordeaux for service under the Duke of Wellington.

Volunteered for and stationed in Ireland, 1814 to 1816.

Volunteered for Foreign service during the Crimean War, and formed part of the Garrison at Gibraltar.

Volunteered for Foreign service during the South African War, and stationed at Malta, 1901-2.

4th Battalion, The Prince of Wales's Own (West Yorkshire Regiment).

"South Africa, 1900-02."
Hon. Colonel :—THE KING.
Lt.-Colonel :—Mahon, Sir W. H., Bt., D.S.O., hon. c.

Origin.
Raised 1853.

Embodiments.
    Occasion.
Crimean War ... ... 1855, Jan. 24, to 1855, May 27.
South African War ... 1899, Dec. 11, to 1902, Mch. 25.

Services.
Volunteered for South Africa, 1899, and embarked Strength 20 Officers, 1 W.O., 479 N.C.O.'s and men (the

Militia reservists having been previously withdrawn to augment the Line Battns. of the Regiment), Lt.-Colonel A. J. Price, C.M.G., commanding.

On arrival at Cape Town stationed at Green Point as guard over 2000 Boer prisoners. May 11, 1900, the Battn. moved to Simonstown for guard duty over prisoners at Belle Vue Camp, sending detachments to Wynburg, Tunnel Siding, De Doorn's, etc. July 4, Head Quarters moved to Worcester in relief of the 3rd West Riding Regt., with detachment at Tulbagh Road. The duty of guarding the Bridges and Posts at Tunnel Siding was most onorous and important, as destruction by the Boers would have stopped all communication by this route if they had held Hex River Pass as originally intended. At this time 201 Line recruits were posted to the Battn. as being too young and unfit to take their places at the front. Aug. 15, Head Quarters suddenly ordered to Vryburg, an attack being expected. On arrival at this Station the Battn. was employed in forming entrenchments and the construction of three Forts called "Cork," "Leeds" and "York," and in furnishing a complete chain of Outposts with Patrols round the Town. The defence comprised an outer and inner line, divided into sections. The alarms were frequent, the men regularly standing to their arms before dawn. A considerable force of Boers under Van Zyl was in the neighbourhood, attracted by the large accumulation of stores. Nov. 15, Head Quarters moved by rail to Warrenton, with Machine Gun loaded ready for action, a probable attack having been officially notified; on arrival at Warrenton the place was made safe by entrenchments and barbed wire entanglements, Commandants Maritz and De Beers were known to be in the neighbourhood on the line of the River. Jan. 26, 1901, in response to urgent appeal from Windsorton Road Station threatened by five hundred Boers, one Company with Machine Gun under Captain and Adjt. Richie proceeded thither. When the Boer laager had been located by Mounted Infantry a mobile column from Kimberley dispersed them. The A.A.G. at Kimberley placed upon record "the good and hard work done by the 4th West Yorks at Windsorton Road and thanked them for the same." Feb. 8, Head Quarters and two Companies moved to Kimberley, the other Companies being out on detachment at various places. Apr. 30, Head Quarter strength moved to De Aar to strengthen that portion of the railway line. May 22, Head Quarters with four Companies concentrated at

Worcester to furnish detachments at Piquetburg Road, Wellington, Tulburgh Village, Waterfall and Brede Bridges. Worcester was surrounded by small Forts and others towards the Bridge over the River. Jan. 6, Worcester was visited by H.E. the Governor of Cape Colony, the Battn. furnishing Guard of Honour. July 23, the Boers were collecting in large numbers in the Piquetburg District, and threatening Worcester, Ceres, and Hex Mountain Pass. Lt.-Colonel Bennett of the Battn. was at this time O.C. Troops, Worcester. The men slept with their arms and ammunition by their sides, and stood to their arms before dawn. Aug. 31, Major Sir W. Mahon, Bt., with 98 men proceeded to Swellendam to check a movement of the Boers South. Sep. 13, Major Sir W. Mahon's command was attacked at Heidleburg by a portion of Theron's Commando, who were obliged to draw off after three hours' fighting. The defences of this Town had not been completed and at about 3 p.m. eighty or more Boers swooped down on the Bridge, their attempt being defeated by a heavy cross fire forcing them back on the railway cutting, from which position they kept up a continuous fire, and made great efforts to get round the flank, about thirty who had got into the side streets of the Town were unable to stand the fire from some hastily constructed sangers containing half a dozen men each. Sep. 14, Corporal Lumby on escort duty with nine men defeated an attack of 26 Boers and captured the noted rebel Geldenhuys (see report Colonel Helme, C.B., 6th Middlesex Regt.). Jan. 4, 1902, the Battn. took over the Blockhouses around Worcester and Wellington, with two Companies at Beaufort West. Feb. 5, one hundred men 4th W. Yorks. with fifty District troops on Convoy duty under Major Crofton, 3rd E. Surrey Regt., were defeated and captured by Boers under Malan with Commandants Hugo, J. J. Smidt, Marias and Pypers, after a severe fight lasting from midnight until dawn, the hastily constructed sangers being captured in detail. Major Crofton was killed, five men dangerously and thirteen others slightly wounded. Boer losses unknown. One kopje was attacked by Smidt with 200 men, and the others by Hugo with like number, Malan, van Rennan, and Pypers attacking on the flanks.

The Boers had allowed Colonel Crabbe's Column in advance to pass, and then closed on Major Crofton's Convoy, engaging the advanced Column simultaneously.

Casualties.

Killed and died of disease, South Africa.
17 N.C. Officers and men.

Mentioned in Despatches.

Lt.-Colonel A. J. Price, C.M.G.
Captain and Adjt. A. B. Richie (twice).
Captain and Qr.-Mr. T. Wilson.
Cr.-Sergt. W. Chapman.
Sergt. H. Tempest.
No. 4631 Pte. B. Halstead.
Major Sir W. H. Mahon, Bt.
Captain H. C. Bulkley.
Sergt.-Major J. Henry.
Cr.-Sergt. E. J. Harrison.
No. 4415 Pte. J. Haley.
Major A. C. Bennett.
Captain A. W. Speyer.
Captain B. Metcalfe-Smith.
No. 4491 Corpl. A. Lumby.
Cr.-Sergt. C. Woodcock.
Cr.-Sergt. W. Barker.

Special Honours.

Major Sir W. H. Mahon, Bt., D.S.O.
Captain and Hon. Major H. C. Bulkley, D.S.O.
Major and Hon. Lt.-Col. A. C. Bennett, D.S.O.
Sergt.-Major J. Henry, D.C. Medal.
Cr.-Sergt. W. Chapman, D.C. Medal.
Corpl. A. Lumby, D.C. Medal.

Medals etc., received by Battalion.

South African with "Cape Colony" Clasp. The King's Medal with two Clasps, "South Africa, 1901," "South Africa, 1902."

3rd Battalion, The East Yorkshire Regiment.

"South Africa, 1902."

Hon. Colonel:—Duncombe, G. A.

Lt.-Colonel:—Walker, H., Lt.-Col. ret. pay (Lt.-Col. res. of Off.).

Origin.

In 1539 by "Letters and Papers of the Reign of Henry VIII.," under a Royal Commission issued March 1, 30, Henry VIII., Yorkshire, East Riding, was represented at the muster of able persons and others with sufficient horse and harness to serve the King—but "in some Wapentakes the numbers having abiliments of war" had not been separated. 1641, Feb. 12, The Earl of Essex was appointed as "a person fit to be entrusted" with the organization of the Militia of Yorkshire and Co. of the Town of Kingston-upon-Hull.

By Militia Returns Egerton MSS., 1697, the East Riding of York had one Regiment of eight Companies 679 foot and two Troops of horse 128, Col. The Marquis of Carmarthen. A footnote says it had been mustered in 1696 "and appeared in very good order."

In 1760 the Regt. was completed for service and quota of men to be found by the East Riding, as the East Yorkshire Militia, afterwards known locally as the "Beverley Buffs," and in 1881 became the 3rd Battn. of the Territorial East Yorkshire Regiment.

Embodiments.

Occasion.

Revolutionary War, etc. 1797, period not Regimentally recorded.
Crimean War ... ... 1855, Feb. 4, to 1856, June.
South African War ... 1900, May 4, to 1900, Dec. 4.
South African War ... 1902, Feb. 17, to 1902, Oct. 10.

Services.

1797 Formed part of the Force stationed at Sheerness at the time of the Mutiny at the Nore, and while there Sergt. Sutherland of the Regt. received an Ensign's Commission in recognition of his conduct in having, with a small detachment, repressed a party of mutinous seamen and marines who attempted to land at Minster in the Island of Sheppey, H.R.H. The Duke of York as Commander-in-Chief referring to the incident in general orders.

In 1810 the Regt. was brought to London for suppression of apprehended riots, and located at the Mint, Tower Hill.

Volunteered for Foreign service during South African War, and embarked in 1902 for the seat of war, strength 20 Officers, 564 N.C.O.'s and men (192 men of the Militia Reserve being already at the Front with Line Battns.), Lt.-Colonel H. Walker, Commdg. On arrival it was chiefly employed in guarding the Bridges over the Orange River near Bethulie and a section of the railway line.

Casualties.

Killed and died of disease, Nil.

Medals, *etc.*, received by Battalion.

Queen's South African with Clasps "Cape Colony," "Orange Free State," and "South Africa, 1902."

3rd Battalion, The Bedfordshire Regiment.

Hon. Colonel:—Burgoyne, Sir J. M., Bt., hon. c.

Lt.-Colonel:—Bedford, H. A., Duke of, K.G., hon. c. (H).

Origin.

By "Letters and Papers Foreign and Domestic of the Reign Henry VIII.," Bedfordshire had 219 Archers and 528 Billmen present on April 8, 1539, at the great Muster of armed men throughout England and Wales by virtue of a Royal Commission issued March 1, 30 Henry VIII.

In 1641, Feb. 12, The Earl of Builingbrook was appointed as a "a fit person to be entrusted" with the organizing of the Militia of the County.

By Militia Returns, 1697, Egerton MSS., Bedfordshire had one Regt. of five Companies 420 foot with two Troops of horse 119, Coll. Edw. Lord Russell, Lieut.-Col. Sir John Burgoyne, Bart.

In 1760 under Act 30, Geo. II., a Regt. was completed for service and the quota of men to be found by the County, as the Bedfordshire Regt. of Militia, which in 1854 became Light Infantry, and in 1881 under Territorial organization the 3rd Battn. of The Bedfordshire Regiment.

Embodiments.

 Occasion.

Seven Years' War	...	1760 to 1761.
American War	...	1778 to 1783, Mch. 14.
French War, etc.	...	1793, Feb. 4, to 1801, Dec.
European Disturbances		1803, Mch. 25, to 1815, Feb. 1.
Crimean War	...	1854, Dec. 27, to 1856, June.
Indian Mutiny	...	1857, Nov. 2, to 1861, Feb. 14.
South African War	...	1900, May 8, to 1900, Dec. 4.

Services.

"By State Papers Dom. Chas. II.," the Bedfordshire Militia was drawn out by the King for the threatened Dutch and French invasion.

In 1798 the Bedford Militia under Colonel Moore, was one of the thirteen Regts. immediately sent to Ireland for service during the Rebellion on the passing of the Act which empowered the King to employ the Militia in that country.

4th Battalion, The Bedfordshire Regiment.

"South Africa, 1900-02."

Hon. Colonel :—

Lt.-Colonel :—Salisbury, J. E. H., Marq. of, C.B., Col. A.D.C. (H).

Origin.

The "Hartfordshire" Militia Regiment completed for service and the quota of the County in 1758, became the 4th Battn. of The Bedfordshire Regiment in the Territorial organization of 1881.

The earliest records of the Constitutional Force in Hertfordshire appear in the Muster by Order 30, Henry VIII., when on Friday before Palm Sunday the Hundreds of the County assembled those "in the harness lists."

At the Spanish Armada assembly 1588, the County of "Hartfordshire" (Harleian MSS.) assembled trained men 1500, reduced into bandes under Captaines.

By State Papers Dom. Elizabeth 1591, Hertfordshire furnished a Levy of 150 men under Captain Grymston for the Netherlands expedition under Lord Essex.

1641 The Earl of Salisbury was appointed as "a fit person to be entrusted" with the organization of Hartfordshire.

1666 by State Papers Dom. Charles II., the King made a levy on the Militia of Hertford for service against the French and Dutch Invasion, also for the Great Fire of London. "On Sept. 6th, 1666, by Letter, Ld. Arlington to Ld.-Lieut. of Hertfordshire, on the 4th warned to draw the Militia troops together for service of the City," "the raging fire is now abated but all hands being wearied with working, 200 foot soldiers are to be marched thither with food for 48 hours and carts laden with pickaxes, ropes, buckets, etc., to prevent further spreading of fire, etc."

By Militia Returns (Egerton MSS.), 1697, Herts. had one Regt. of ten Companies 1025 foot with three Troops of horse 183, Colonel the Earl of Essex.

Embodiments.

Occasion.

Seven Years War	1759, Oct., to 1762.
American War	1778 to 1783, Oct.
Revolutionary War, etc.	1793, Feb., to 1802, Apr.
European Disturbances	1803, May, to 1814, July 30.
Crimean War	1854, Dec. 27, to 1856, June.
South African War	1900, Jan. 16, to 1902, June 11.

Special Services.

Encamped in Hyde Park and took part in the suppression of the Gordon Riots, 1780.

Volunteered for and stationed two years in Ireland, 1811-13.

Volunteered for Foreign service and served in South Africa, 1900-02. Embarked strength 25 Officers, 451 N.C.O.'s and men, Lt.-Colonel Viscount Cranborne Commanding. On arrival at Cape Town Mch. 24, 1900, proceeded to Dronfield and formed part of the 9th Brigade under General Hutton, occupying the South bank of the River Vaal between Warrenton and the Railway Bridge, General du Troit's Commando being on the opposite bank. Apr. 4, occupied the Stations between Modder River and Orange River until ordered to Fourteen Streams on May 19th, remaining there until June 26th; proceeded to Mafeking on Aug. 1st and formed a Mounted Infantry Company which during the greater part of 1901 was attached to Lord Methuen's column, taking part in many engagements.

Before leaving South Africa the following was received from the General Officer commanding Western District: Vryburg,

1st May, 1903."

"I cannot let the 4th Bedfordshire Regt. and South Wales Borderers leave the Command without expressing admiration at their good conduct and gallantry in the field during the time they have served under my command; the 4th Bedfordshire Regt., helped by the South Wales Borderers, supplied a Company of Mounted Infantry which, for gallantry in the field and endurance of continuous hardships, was second to nothing in the Division, the high state of efficiency reached by these two Battalions being due to the high tone and knowledge of their duties which exist amongst the Officers and N.C. Officers, the men having perfect confidence in their leaders.

By Order—C. B. Vyvyard,
Lt.-Col. A.A.G.,
C.S.O. Western District.

and from Col. S. B. von Dunop, Commdg. Column Slypotein, Ap. 26, 1902, "The Detachment 4th Bedfordshire having left my command I have the honour to convey my high appreciation of the services rendered by those Officers, N.C.O.'s and men of the Mounted Infantry who served in the Columns commanded by Lord Methuen and myself; their excellent work in the field was only equalled by their quiet and orderly behaviour in camp. The following are brought forward as deserving of special mention: Captain Norman, Lieuts. Sladen, Talbot, Henry and Wray, Cr.-Sergt. Coote, Sergts. Baker and Butcher, Ptes. Day and Prior (these two showed conspicuous bravery on several occasions), O'Brien, Hare and Hutchins."

Casualties.

Killed and died of disease, etc.
32 N.C.O.'s and men.

Mentioned in Despatches.

Lt.-Colonel The Viscount Cranborne.
Captain and Adjt. H. W. U. Coates.
Captain M. C. Norman.
2nd Lieut. F. H. Barton.
Lieut. and Qr.-Mr. J. Richardson.
Sergt.-Major W. Bond.
Sergt. I. of M. D. Clark.
Sergts. W. Baker and A. Decks.

Pte. Blackwell.
Lieut. G. C. Sladen.
Captains C. P. Boulton and R. P. Croft.
Cr.-Sergts. F. Shambrook and W. Stocker.
Sergt. H. Verrinder.
Corpls. A. Reynolds and S. Chapman.
Ptes. W. H. Maylin and H. Maylin.

Special Honours.

Lt.-Colonel The Viscount Cranborne, C.B.
Captain and Adjt. H. W. U. Coates, D.S.O.
Captain M. C. Norman, D.S.O.
Captain C. P. Boulton, D.S.O.
Sergt.-Major W. Bond, D.C. Medal.
Sergt. I. of M. D. Clark, D.C. Medal.
Cr.-Sergt. F. Shambrook, D.C. Medal.
1056 Pte. W. Maylin, D.C. Medal.
3597 Pte. H. Maylin, D.C. Medal.

Medals, etc., received by Battalion.

Queen's South African Medal with Clasps "Cape Colony," "Orange Free State," "Transvaal," several earning the "Wittebergen" bar. King's Medal with Clasps "South Africa, 1901"—"South Africa, 1902."

3rd Battalion, The Leicestershire Regiment.

"South Africa, 1902."

Hon. Colonel:—Rutland, Rt. Hon., J. J. R., Duke of, K.G., G.C.B.

Lt.-Colonel:—Humphrey, B.B., Maj. ret. pay (T) (H) (Maj. Res. of Off.), hon. c.

Origin.

In 1881 The Leicestershire Militia Regt. became under the Territorial Regimental Organization of the Forces the 3rd Battn. of "The Leicestershire Regiment."

1539 See Copy of the Certificate, "Letters and Papers of the Reign of Henry VIII.," for the Force of the County Mch. 17th on the occasion of the great muster of the Forces of the Kingdom held by virtue of Royal Commission, 30, Henry VIII.

In 1641, Feb. 12, the Earl of Stamford was appointed as a "fit person to be entrusted" with the organizing of the Militia of the County.

By Militia Returns, 1697, Egerton MSS., Leicestershire had 3 Troops horse 175, Col. John Ld. Ross, 6 Companies foot 609, Col. Richard Lister. Total of both, 784.

In 1760 a Regiment was completed for service and the quota of men to be found by the County as the "Leicestershire Militia" which in 1881 became as already recorded.

Embodiments.

Occasion.

No record of dates prior to 1854.

Crimean War	1854, Dec. 14, to 1856, June 12.
Indian Mutiny	1857, Nov. 3, to 1858, May 18.
South African War ...	1900, Feb. 20, to 1900, Dec. 5.
South African War ...	1902, Feb. 24, to 1902, Oct. 4.

Services.

In 1666 by State Papers Dom. Chas. II., June 27, the Militia of Leicestershire was "drawn out" by the King for the threatened French and Dutch invasion. In 1814 the Regt. having volunteered for Foreign service, 14 Officers (Lt.-Col. Hulse; Captains Phelp, Fell, Jarvis; Lieuts. Holt, Bass, Cooper, Singleton, Langdon, Freer, Salkeld; Ensigns Crotty, Fosbroke, Bryne), with 420 N.C.O.'s and men formed part of the 2nd Provisional Militia Battn. under Lt.-Col. E. Bayly (W. Middlesex Mil.) of the Militia Brigade commanded by Colonel the Marquis of Buckingham which landed in France near Bordeaux for service under the Duke of Wellington.

In 1856, Feb. 13, a detachment of 14 Officers and 324 other ranks proceeded from Cork to Limerick to aid the Civil Power.

Volunteered for Foreign service during the South African War, and embarked Mch. 26, 1902. Strength 25 Officers, 580 N.C.O.'s and men, Colonel Lord Braye Commdg. On arrival at Cape Town April 13th, the Battn. was broken up into detachments for various stations, "F" and "G" Companies left by train at 6 p.m. on the 14th and Head Quarters with "A," "B," "C," "D," "E," and "H" Companies under Command of Major and Hon. Lt.-Col. B. G. Humfrey (Colonel Lord Braye being left in Hospital at Cape Town and invalided home), following at 10 p.m. across the vast and desolate Karoo, through Matjesfontein, Victoria West, De Aar, Naauwpoort, Steynsberg and Stormberg to Burghersdorp, two men in each truck being on sentry duty day and night, as the whole Colony was full of roving bands of rebels and attack possible at any moment. On the next day "B" and "D" Companies were sent on to Aliwal North and Lemoenfontein, whilst "A," "C," "E," "H," with Head Quarters proceeded to occupy a portion of the Blockhouse line between Burghersdorp and Bethulie Bridge, the train dropping detachments at each Blockhouse about half a mile apart, and relieving those of the 3rd Battalion Yorkshire Regt. in occupation. Head Quarters being at the wayside station of Knapdaar. The extent occupied was from twenty-five to thirty miles, the Head Quarter Station comprised two small sand-bag Redoubts with a long galvanized iron building surrounded on three sides by rough stone walls loopholed with sand-bags, there being another small triangular sangar on the other side of the line to the west of the station, and two Blockhouses on a hill to the S.W. called "Observation Hill," each Blockhouse was surrounded by a barbed wire "Crinoline" fence and a similar fence ran along the line between the Blockhouses, with spring guns at intervals which were set at night, fired automatically should the wire be cut or broken, the Head Quarters being in telephonic connection with Burghersdorp and Bethulie. May 15 the Blockhouse line was ordered to be depleted, leaving two men in each, and all available strength to proceed to Rosmead where it was found that "F" Company had arrived to rejoin Head Quarters, General French being about to draw a cordon round the Boers in the district and endeavour to sweep them up. Commandants Malan and Fouche were to be the special objects of attention. May 19 moved to Graaf Reinet to form part of a moveable column but the Boers having rapidly dispersed during the night to the Eastwards, the Battn. proceeded to Steynsberg and occupied an extent of Blockhouse line, the defences of which required completion and had to be carried out. Head Quarters were at Steynsberg as Fouche and other Commandoes were moving Northwards and an attack daily expected, firing being heard nightly. June 5 Battn. returned to Knapdaar. June 20 marched across country to Aliwal North, and captured the three brothers Vanstein who had got separated from Fouche's Commando. The snow was very deep at Knapdaar and progress of the Transport ox waggons dreadfully slow and difficult, whilst the crossing of the swollen Stormberg Spruit afforded no little amusement, though attended with some risk of safety. Arrived at Aliwal on the 23rd, and encamped just outside the Orange River Colony, with the large concentration camp of some 5000 Boer men, women and children on the opposite side of the river, about two miles higher up, and below away to the left the battle-field where the Colonial Troops under Col. Dalgetty, C.M.R., defeated the Boers, and saved the Bridge from destruction. July 14, the Lemoenfontein Detachment rejoined Head Quarters, the others from Plantation Post and Moltens coming in on Aug. 7th. Aug. 9, took part in the Parade of Troops to celebrate the Coronation of His Majesty King Edward VII. Sep. 2, proceeded by rail to East London, picking up the remaining ("G") Company on the way, and embarked on Sep. 8th for England.

Casualties.

Killed and died of disease, etc., 10 N.C.O.'s and men.

Medals, etc., received by Battalion.

Queen's South African Medal, with Clasps "South Africa, 1902" and "Cape Colony." A small number also receiving the "Orange River" bar.

3rd Battalion, The Royal Irish Regiment.

Hon. Colonel :—Templemore, H. S., Lord.
Lt.-Colonel :—Stopford, J. W. M., Visct., hon. c.

Origin.

In 1881, the Wexford Regt. of Militia became under Territorial organization the 3rd Battn. of The Royal Irish Regiment. Tradition in Wexford says that the Regt. dates back to Queen Elizabeth's time when there were organized Forces in the County. The History of Wexford by Captain Hore refers to County Troops about the middle of the seventeenth century which were in character Militia.

When the Forces of Ireland were reorganized, a Regiment was completed for service in 1794, and the quota of men to be found by the County, as the Wexford Regiment.

Embodiments.

    Occasion.

Revolutionary War, European Disturbances, etc. ...	1794, to 1816, Mch. 25.
Crimean War ...	1855, Jan. 1, to 1856, Mch. 31.
Indian Mutiny...	1857, Oct. 26, to 1859, Mch. 31.
Threatened War	1885, Mch. 9, to 1885, Sep. 17.
South African War ...	1900, Jan. 11, to 1900, Oct. 17.

Services.

When stationed at Weymouth during the Indian Mutiny embodiment, a Company of the Regiment under Captain Pigott at Portland was called upon to suppress a serious outbreak among the convicts, H.R.H. the Commander-in-Chief, and the Secretary of State for War, communicating their satisfaction with the prompt action and efficient services rendered by the detachment on the occasion.

4th Battalion, The Royal Irish Regiment.

Hon. Colonel :—Donalley, H. O'C., Lord
Lt.-Colonel :— Cane, C. R. J., hon. c.

Origin.

In 1881 the North Tipperary Light Infantry Militia Regt., raised and completed for service in 1855, became under the Territorial Regimental Organization of the Forces, the 4th Battalion of The Royal Irish Regiment.

Embodiments.

    Occasion.

Crimean War ...	1855, Mar. 6, to 1856, Sep. 2.
South African War ...	1900, May 2, to 1901, July 5.

5th Battalion, The Royal Irish Regiment.

Hon. Colonel:—Ormonde, Rt. Hon. J. E. W. T., Marquis of, K.P.,

Lt.-Colonel:—Keatinge, M.D., Capt., hon. c. (H).

Origin.

Formed in 1793 as the Kilkenny Regiment of Militia, Lord Viscount Thurles (afterwards 1st Marquis of Ormonde), Lieut-Colonel Commanding, a ballot being held Aug. 8, 1793, in the Trinity Chambers, Dublin, for settling the precedence of the several Militia Regiments then being organized in Ireland. In 1881 became the 5th Battn. of The Royal Irish Regt. under Regimental Territorial Organization of the Forces.

Embodiments.

Occasion.

Revolutionary War, etc.	1793, Aug. 10, to 1802.
European Disturbances	1803 to 1814, Oct. 14.
,, ,,	1815 to 1816, Apr. 2.
Crimean War ...	1855 to 1856, Aug.
South African War ...	1900, May 14, to 1901, July 6.

Services.

In 1798, during the Irish Rebellion, the Light Company under Captain Nicholas Loftus was brigaded with the Light Companies of other Militia Regiments and took part in the battles of New Ross and Vinegar Hill, the whole Regiment being engaged against the French under General Humbert at Castlebar, when Major Alcock was seriously wounded and taken prisoner, and there were many casualties. Volunteered for and stationed in England 1813-14, and took part June 23, 1814, in the great Naval and Military display at Dover on the landing of the allied Sovereigns, the Emperor Alexander of Russia and the King of Prussia.

3rd Battalion, Alexandra, Princess of Wales's Own (Yorkshire Regiment).

"South Africa, 1900-02."

Hon. Colonel :—

Lt.-Colonel :—Hoole, J., C.M.G., hon. c. (H) (T).

Origin.

Raised as the 5th West York Militia 1853, and under the Territorial Organization of 1881 became the 3rd Battn. of the Yorkshire Regiment.

Embodiments.

Occasion.

South African War ... 1899, Dec. 14, to 1902, May 14.

Services.

Volunteered for foreign service and embarked for South Africa. Strength, 25 officers, 588 N.C.O.'s and men, Colonel J. Hoole commanding. On arrival at Port Elizabeth March 23, 1900, the Battalion formed part of the garrison at that place, sending detachments of two companies to Craddock and one company to Barkley Bridge. Sep. 3, 1900, moved to Bloemfontein, the greater part of that garrison having been removed for the relief of Ladybrand besieged by the Boers. The Battalion took over No. 1 Section of the Outposts. Oct. 16, moved to Rhenoster Bridge for duty on the line of communications. From Garrison Orders, Bloemfontein, 27-12-00, "The O.C. Troops cannot allow the 3rd Yorks. Regt. to leave his command without placing on record his high appreciation of the excellent services rendered by the Regiment. The conduct of the men on outpost duty has been excellent, although at times very heavy. It has constantly been observed by him how thoroughly and cheerfully the officers performed their duties, an example which the N.C.O.'s and men followed." Signed. C. J. Long, Colonel, O.C. Troops.

Three Companies of the Battalion formed part of a column sent out under Lt.-Col. Hickie to destroy Uitick and disperse the enemy, which having been accomplished, returned to camp with the loss of one man killed, one officer and five men wounded. The marching and steadiness under fire of the three companies, which enabled him to anticipate the enemy in occupying a position of security for retirement with so few casualties, being communicated to the Battalion. Between March 8, 1901 and April 10, 1901, several attempts by the enemy to cross the line in force were frustrated. June 11, a determined attempt was made at Roodival Spruit and beaten off with a loss to the enemy of two killed and two wounded left behind, after which the Battalion moved to Honing Spruit, taking over the blockhouses from thence to Kroonstadt.

Oct. 31, an attack on Honing Spruit was repulsed. Nov. 25, the Battalion, reinforced by the Royal Scots, protected the line during "a drive" from the East, and in an attack Jan. 20, 1902, Sergt. I. of M. May was wounded. Jan. 21, Battalion moved to Aliwal North. On leaving, the following order was issued by Maj. General Sir W. G. Knox, K.C.B., commanding N. Sec. L. of C. —O.R. Colony, Kroonstadt, Jan. 19-02.

"On departure of the 3rd Battn. Yorks. Regt., the G.O.C. wishes to testify to all ranks his appreciation of the work done on the line of communication through a trying time, and the efficiency of the defensive works constructed, etc.

"By Order, Signed, Arthur H. S. Hart, Capt. C.S.O."

On arrival at Aliwal North took over the blockhouses between there and Knapton.

Feb. 1, took part in "drive" eastwards of Homberg, a party with No. 6 armour train, being engaged near Burghersdorp, one man severely wounded; after the action, the train shunted back and coming into collision with another train sent to assist, one man of the Battalion was killed and twenty-two others were injured.

Apr. 19, 1902, embarked at Capetown for England.

Casualties.

Killed and died of disease, etc., Lieut. G. L. Dorman and 39 N.C.O.'s and men.

Mentioned in Despatches.

Colonel J. Hoole,
Captain H. A. C. King (twice),
Captain the Hon. A. G. Lascelles,
Captain Rd. Aspinall,
Captain G. W. L. Hoole, Lowsley-Williams,
Captain and Qr.-Mr. G. Croft,
Captain R. B. N. Gunter,
Captain M. Sykes,
Sergt.-Major G. J. Smith.
Qr.-Mr. Sergt. J. Lowther,
Cr.-Sergt. P. Hall,

Sergt. S. Rushton,
Sergt. J. Conroy,
Sergt. C. Reisdale.

Special Honours.

Colonel J. Hoole, C.M.G.
Major R. L. Aspinall, D.S.O.
Captain and Adjt. Cacking, Bevet Majority.
Captain and Qr.-Mr. G. Croft,   ,,
Sergt. Major G. J. Smith, D.C. Medal
Sergt. J. Conroy   ,,
Qr.-Mr. Sergt. J. Lowther   ,,

Medals, etc., received by Battalion.

Queen's S. African Medal with Clasps "Cape Colony," "Orange Free State."

King's S. African Medal with Clasps "South Africa 1901," "South Africa 1902."

4th Battalion, Alexandra, Princess of Wales's Own (Yorkshire Regiment).

" South Africa, 1902."

Hon. Colonel :—Hopkinson, R. G., hon. c.
Lt.-Colonel :—Rivis, J. C. (H).

Origin.

In 1881, the North York Rifles Militia Regt. became the 4th Battn. of the Territorial Yorkshire Regiment, Alexandra, Princess of Wales's Own.

See copy of Certificate from "Letters and Papers Foreign and Domestic of the Reign Henry VIII.," of the muster of armed and able men in Yorkshire North Riding, 20 March, 1539, by virtue of Royal Commission issued 1 March, 30, Henry VIII.

In 1641, Feb. 12, the Earl of Essex was appointed to organize the Militia Forces of the entire county of York.

By Militia Returns 1697, Egerton MSS., the N. Riding, Co. York, had a Richmondshr. Regt. of seven Companies 326 men, Col. Sr. Chr. Wandesford.

Cleveland Regt. of six Companies 308 men, Col. Sr. Thos. Pennyman.

Bulmer Regt. of five Companies 276 men, late Col. Sr. Bar. Boucher, besides one Troop each of horse 172.

In 1759, July 2, under Act 30, Geo II., a Richmondshire Regt. of Militia was completed for service, and a Regt. for Cleveland with Bulmer, to complete the quota of men to be found by the N. Riding of York.

In 1778 the two Regiments were amalgamated as the North York Regt.

In 1795 the Regiment was uniformed in green jackets.

In 1853 officially recognised as a Rifle Regt., and in 1881 formed the 4th Battalion of its present Territorial Regt.

Embodiments.

Occasion.

Seven Years War	1759, July 14, to 1762, Dec. 3.
American War	1778, April 21, to 1783, Mar. 12.
Revolutionary War, etc.	1792, Dec. 20, to 1802, Apr. 23.
French War	1803, Mar. 11, to 1816, June.
Crimean War	1854, Dec. 12, to 1856, June 17.
South African War	1900, May 5, to 1901, July 1.
,, ,, ,,	1902, Feb. 17, to 1902, Sept. 28.

Services.

1761, the suppression of riots at Hexham, in Northumberland.

1810, when stationed at the Tower of London, furnished, April 10 to 25, the Force necessary for protection of the Mint, Tower Hill, during apprehended disturbances in and about London.

Volunteered for and stationed in Ireland 1813-15.

Volunteered for foreign service during the South African War, and embarked for seat of war. Strength, 29 officers, 564 N.C.O.'s and men, Lt.-Col. B. G. Harrison commanding. On arrival April 1, 1902, the Battalion proceeded to Vryburg to garrison the blockhouse line between that place and Maribogo on the Vryburg-Mafeking railway. On the declaration of peace the Battalion moved to Devondale siding on the railway, and Sept. 1, 1902, arrived at Cape Town and embarked on the sixth for England.

Casualties.

Killed and died of disease, etc., 6 N.C.O.'s and men.

Medals, *etc.*, received by Battalion.

Queen's S. African Medal with Clasps "Cape Colony" and " S. Africa 1902."

5th Battalion, The Lancashire Fusiliers.

"South Africa, 1901-2."

Hon. Colonel:—Kitchener of Khartoum, Gen. H. H., Visct. G.C.B., O.M., G.C.M.G., R.Eng., C.-in-C., E. Indies.

Lt.-Colonel:—p.s. Lockhart-Ross, H. S., (H).

Origin.

Raised in 1855 as the 7th Royal Lancashire Militia Regt.

In 1881 it became, under the Territorial Regimental Organization of the Forces, the 3rd Battn. of the Lancashire Fusiliers Regiment.

In 1891 the Battalion was formed into two separate units as the 3rd and 4th Battalions, which upon the augmentation of the Territorial Regiment by two additional Line Battalions numbered as 3rd and 4th, became the 5th and 6th Battalions of the Regiment.

Embodiments.

Occasion.

South African War ... 1900, Feb. 19, to 1900, Oct. 17.
 ,,   ,,   ,, ... 1901, May 6, to 1902, July 25.

Services.

Volunteered for foreign service and embarked for South Africa June 4, 1901. Strength, 903 of all ranks (the Militia Reserve of about 300 men having been previously withdrawn for service in South Africa), Lt.-Colonel F. F. Mackenzie commanding.

On arrival Cape Town June 23rd the Battalion proceeded in two wings to Springfontein, and was soon split up into small detached posts at various places, Head Quarters moving to Naauwpoort, where two companies remained until December 28th. At this date Head Quarters were ordered to Colesburg and employed on blockhouse duty from Norval's Pont to Rensburg, Steynsburg to Stormburg, De Aar to Britstown, while two companies were sent to garrison Port Elizabeth, and one company to Cradock, several complimentary letters being received from General Officers commanding various districts on the way in which the Battalion had acquitted itself under somewhat trying conditions.

No. 13 armoured train was manned by detachments of the

Battalion under Major H. A. Schank, and took part in the operations against the commandoes of Smuts, Scheepers, Lotter, Maritz, Theron, and Wessels.

Casualties.

Killed and died of disease, etc., 15 N.C.O.'s and men.

Mentioned in Despatches.

Colonel F. F. Mackenzie.
Major H. S. Lockhart-Ross.
Major and Adjt. H. C. E. Westropp.
Sergt.-Major Kingston.
Qr.-Mr. Sergt. Bowyer.

Special Honours.

Colonel F. F. Mackenzie, C.B.

Medals, etc., received by Battalion.

Queen's South Africa Medal with Clasps "Orange Free State," "Cape Colony," "South Africa 1901 and 1902."

6th Battalion, The Lancashire Fusiliers.

"South Africa, 1900-01."

Hon. Colonel:—Argyll, J. D. S., Duke of K.T., G.C.M.G., G.C.V.O.

Lt.-Colonel:—p.s. Romer, F. C., C.M.G., hon. c., (Q) (H) (S) s

Origin.

Formed 1891. See 5th Battalion of the Regiment.

Embodiments.

Occasion.

South African War ... 1899, Dec. 13, to 1901, Oct. 14.

Services.

Volunteered for foreign service, and embarked for South Africa. Strength 25 officers and 659 N.C.O.'s and men, Colonel F. C. Romer commanding. On arrival Cape Town March 7, 1900, orders for Kimberley were countermanded, and Battalion proceeded to the Orange River Colony in consequence of the threatening attitude of rebels in the

Preska and Kenhardt districts, Head Quarters being at Orange River, with detachments at the important Orange River Bridge on the direct line to Kimberley and Rhodesia; Zoutspandrift, a frontier station, and one of the earliest British posts established in the enemy's country, Hopetown the frontier depot for the trade of Griqualand West, Fourteen Streams and Christiana, these detachments being employed on a duty occasioning frequent skirmishes with the enemy, and necessitating constant patrolling, escorting of convoys, etc., large quantities of Boer stock were secured, while many prisoners, and on one occasion a whole Boer picket were captured. The Christiana detachment remained there for over a year, performing arduous duty frequently for weeks, not a day passing without shots being exchanged with the Boer pickets, while no fewer than nineteen minor engagements were recorded. Nov. 25, 1900, the Battalion received welcome orders to join General Settle's Column to operate against a commando led by the notorious Judge Hertzog, and the Battalion had the good fortune to take a prominent part in a stubborn fight on the 28th near Luckoff, the enemy under the immediate command of Hertzog occupied a commanding position on a precipitous range of kopjes, which completely barred the progress of the column, and extended some nine miles in a semi-circle. The Boers held on tenaciously for nearly five hours against a heavy artillery and rifle fire, and they had eventually to be cleared out at the point of the bayonet, this duty being entrusted to the 6th Lancashire Fusiliers, and was carried out in a manner which earned the highest praise from the General Officer commanding, who placed the following in Orders: "The final assault which contributed to the rout of the Boers was highly creditable to the Battalion." If fell to the lot of few Militia units to take part in an engagement of this character, and the cool intelligent manner in which the Battalion carried out the attack showed what Militiamen can do when given the opportunity. Jan. 7, 1901, the Battalion took over charge of the Carnarvon district, where it was actively employed in patrolling, escorting guns and convoys and in operating against the Boer Commandant Maritz.

July 26, 1901, the Battalion proceeded to Victoria Road, and later to Beaufort West, detachments being employed in fortifying posts in the district and building forts for the defence of Worcester. Sept. 19, 1901, entrained for Cape Town to embark for home.

Casualties.

Killed and died of disease, etc., 18 N.C.O.'s and men.

Mentioned in Despatches.
Colonel F. C. Romer.
Major F. Lee Sanders.
Capt. and Adjt. A. F. Owen-Lewis.
Capt. R. V. K. Applin.
Capt. D. F. Robinson.
Lieut. and Qr.-Mr. A. W. Smith.
Sergt.-Major A. McGarry.
Qr.-Mr. Sergt. W. Thompson.
Cr.-Sergt. F. Crowcroft.
Cr.-Sergt. P. McKenna.
Sergt. J. Barret.
Sergt. A. Geraghty.

Special Honours.
Colonel F. C. Romer, C.M.G.
Capt. and Adjt. A. F. Owen-Lewis, D.S.O.
Capt. R. V. K. Applin, D.S.O.
Sergt. Major A. McGarry, D.C. Medal.

Medals and Clasps Received in Battalion.

South African Medal with Clasps for Cape Colony, Orange Free State, and Transvaal.

3rd Battalion, The Royal Scots Fusiliers.

Hon. Colonel:—Campbell, W. H., hon. c. (Hon. Lt.-Col. in the Army).

Lt.-Colonel:—p.s. Twisleton-Wykeham-Fiennes, Hon. G.C., Capt. ret. pay (H).

Origin.

Formed 1802 as the Ayrshire Regt. of Militia, out of the "disembodied" Non-Commissioned Officers and Drummers of the Ayr and Renfrew (7th North British) Militia, and quota by ballot of 436 men under the Act.

In 1813 became The Prince Regent's Royal Regiment of Ayrshire Militia, the Title being changed in 1854 to The Prince Regent's Royal Regiment of Ayrshire Rifles.

In 1860 the Wigtownshire quota of Galloway Rifles was amalgamated with the Regt., which then became designated as The Royal Ayrshire Regt. of Militia Rifles.

In 1866 the Title was changed to The Prince Regent's Royal Regt. of Ayr and Wigtown Militia, and in 1881 under the Territorial Regimental Organization it became the 3rd Battn. of "The Royal Scots Fusiliers."

Embodiments.

Occasion.

European Disturbances 1803, Apr. 6, to 1816, Mch. 23.
Crimean War ... ... 1855, May 1, to 1856, July 10.
South African War ... 1899, Dec. 8, to 1900, Dec. 4.

Services.

Furnished a Detachment for Dumbarton Castle in 1812 to guard General Simon and other French prisoners of war.

Volunteered for and stationed in Ireland from Aug., 1813, to Mch. 2, 1815, the duties consisting mostly in the prevention of smuggling and assisting to keep the peace. Received the thanks of the Lord Lieutenant and approbation of the Commander-in-Chief for their uniform zeal and good conduct consequent on its disclaiming any knowledge of, or participation in certain proceedings which had caused abhorrence in 1813. During the embodiment eleven Officers and 694 men joined the Line as Volunteers.

3rd Battalion, The Cheshire Regiment.

"South Africa, 1902."

Hon. Colonel :—France-Hayhurst, C. H., hon. c.
Lt.-Colonel :—p.s. Lees, C. P., hon. c.

Origin.

By Harleian MSS. Cheshire was represented at the Spanish Armada Assembly of Forces, 1588, but no numbers are given in the certificate, of the " trayned men reduced into bandes under Captaines."

In 1641, Fb. 12, Lord Strange was appointed as "a person fit to be entrusted" with the organization of the Militia of the County and Co. of the City of Chester.

By Militia Returns 1697, Egerton MSS., the County nad one Regiment of seven Companies 929 foot with two troops of horse 104, besides Chester one Company of 120 foot, total 1153, "Coll Earle of Rivers."

In 1759 under the Act 30, Geo. II., a Regt. was completed for service and the quota of men to be furnished by Cheshire, as the Cheshire Regt. of Militia; became a Royal Regt. at later date, and Light Infantry in 1853. When a second Battn. was formed it became known as the 1st Royal Cheshire, and in 1881 under Territorial organization formed the 3rd Battn. of "The Cheshire Regiment."

Embodiments.

Occasion.

Seven Years War, etc.	1759, jeriod not recorded.
French War	1803, Apr. 4, to 1816, Feb. 24.
Crimean War	1855, Jan. 18, to 1856, May 27.
South African War	1900, May 4, to 1900, Dec. 4.
South African War	1902, Jan. 23, to 1902, Oct. 4.

Services.

1666 by "State Papers Dom." Charles II., the County Militia was drawn out by the King for the threatened French and Dutch invasion.

Volunteered for Foreign service during South African War, and embarked—Strength 28 Officers, 1 W.O., 575 N.C.O.'s and men, Colonel Arthur Hill, commdg. On arrival at Cape Town, Feb. 11, 1902, the Battn. proceeded via Port Elizabeth to Smaldeel, Orange River Colony, and found detachments for the posts at Doorn River, Virginia and Riet Spruit. Apr. 15, Battn. moved to Winburg for Blockhouse duty on part of the Winburg-Smaldeel Railway, with detached posts on the kopjes overlooking the Town, viz.: Yeomans Kop, Station Kop, Wooded Kop, Kaffir Kop, and Detached Kop, Headquarters being at the Western Trenches. The Battn. remained at Winburg until the conclusion of peace. Aug. 31, 9 Sergts., 6 Corpls., and 70 men received a free discharge to settle in the Country, and remainder of Battn. proceeded to Port Elizabeth and embarked for England.

Casualties.

Killed and died of disease, etc., 8 N.C.O.'s and men.

Mentioned in Despatches.

Captain E. T. Logan.
Captain C. W. Anderson.

Special Honours.

Captain E. T. Logan, D.S.O.
Captain E. R. Harbord, D.S.O.
Captain C. W. Anderson, D.S.O., and to be Hon. Lt.-Col. in the Army.

Medals, etc., received by Battalion.

Queen's Medal with Clasps "South Africa, 1902," "Orange Free State" and "Cape Colony."

4th Battalion, The Cheshire Regiment.

"South Africa, 1900-02."

Hon. Colonel:—Beck, C. H., C.B., hon. c. (Hon. Lt.-Col. in Army, 11th May, 1902).

Lt.-Colonel:—Nicholls, H. M., hon. c.

Origin.

Raised 1853 as the 2nd Royal Cheshire Militia and in 1881 became the 4th Battalion of the Territorial Cheshire Regiment.

Embodiments.

Occasion.

Crimean War ...	1855, Jan. 18, to 1856, July 24.
Indian Mutiny...	1857, Nov. 10, to 1860, Oct. 12.
South African War ...	1900, Jan. 22, to 1902, May 9.

Services.

Volunteered for Foreign Service and embarked for South Africa Feb. 25, 1900. Strength 26 Officers, 606 N.C.O.'s and men. Colonel C. H. Beck, Commdg. The Battn. was employed during the whole time of its service in South Africa at Bethulie and four Bethulie Bridges for the protection of the very important railway bridge over the Orange River, with two Companies as part of the Garrison of Burghersdorp, in Cape Colony.

Casualties.

Killed and died of disease, 33 N.C.O.'s and men.

Mentioned in Despatches.

Colonel C. H. Beck.
Major W. Woodward.
Captain F. C. Turner.
Captain R. M. Cadell.
Lieut. L. H. T. Friederichs.
2nd Lieut. E. B. Flanagan.
Sergt.-Major J. C. Willis.
Cr.-Sergt. R. Bull.
Sergt. M. Havakin.
Sergt. G. Branson.
Sergt. I. of M., E. Davies.
Sergt. S. Young.
Sergt. J. McDonald.
Corpl. A. Heaton.
Corpl. W. Shaw.
Lce.-Corpl. J. Dobson.
Pte. J. Harding.

Special Honours.

Colonel C. H. Beck, C.B.
Captain F. C. Turner, D.S.O.
2nd Lieut. E. B. Flanagan, D.S.O.
Sergt.-Major J. G. Willis, D.C. Medal.
Sergt. I. of M., E. Davies, D.C. Medal.
Sergt. S. Young, D.C. Medal.
Corpl. W. Shaw, D.C. Medal.

Medals, etc., received by Battalion.

Queen's South African Medal with Clasps "Cape Colony," and "Orange Free State." King's South African Medal with Clasps "South Africa, 1901" and "South Africa, 1902."

3rd Battalion, The Royal Welsh Fusiliers.

Hon. Colonel:—Mostyn, L. N. V., Lord.
Lt.-Colonel:—Godfrey, R. F.

Origin.

In 1881 the Royal Denbigh and Flint Regiments of Militia both of which had become Rifles in 1808, were united to form the 3rd Battn. of "The Royal Welsh Fusiliers" under the Territorial organization of the Forces in that year.

In 1539, by "Letters and Papers of the Reign of Henry VIII., the "harnessed men" of Denbigh and "able men" of Flint, were present at the muster ordered 30 Henry VIII.

By Harleian MSS. 1588, Spanish Armada Assembly, Denbighe ffurnished 400 trained men besides Horsemen 30 Lighthorse, 30 Petroneles, Flintshire 200 trained men besides Horsemen 30 Lighthorse.

In 1641, Feb. 12, Lord Fielding was appointed as "A fit person to be entrusted" with the organization of the Militia of Denbigh and Flintshire.

In 1684 at the inspection of His Grace the first Duke of Beaufort in his progress through Wales, "The Militia of Denbighshire consisteth of five Companies of foot and one Troop of horse commanded by Sir Richard Middleton Captain." "The Militia of Flintshire consisteth of five Companies of foot Sir Roger Mostyn, Bart, Captain."

The Militia Returns, 1697, Egerton MSS., include Denbigh "one Company 500 men, with horse 62, Col. E. of Macclesfield."

Flint "one Company 250 men, with horse 25, Col. Sir Roger Puleston."

In the reorganization under Act 30, Geo. II., each County had a Regiment completed for service in 1759 and their quotas of men to be furnished.

Embodiments.
    Occasion.

DENBIGH.

Peninsular War	... Period unknown.
Crimean War ...	... Period unknown.
Indian Mutiny...	... Period unknown.

Embodiments.
    Occasion.

FLINT.

Crimean War ...	... Period unknown.

AS 3RD BATTALION, THE ROYAL WELSH FUSILIERS.
South African War ... 1899, Dec. 8, to 1901, July 5.

Services.

The Denbigh Regt. volunteered for and was one of the thirteen Regts. immediately sent to Ireland, under Col. Sir Watkins Wynne, M.P., in 1798, after the passing of the Act empowering the King to employ the Militia in Ireland owing to the Rebellion in that Country.

In 1814 the Denbigh Militia furnished six Officers (Captains Lloyd and Rowland, Lieuts. Lovett and Wynn, Ensigns Nicholls and Jones), and 200 men for the 3rd Provisional Battn., under Lt.-Col. Sir Watkins Williams Wynne, Bt., Denbigh Militia), of the Militia Brigade commanded by Col. the Marquis of Buckingham, which embarked for France and landed near Bordeaux for service under the Duke of Wellington.

4th Battalion, The Royal Welsh Fusiliers.

Hon. Colonel :—Penrhyn, G. S. G., Lord.
Lt.-Colonel :—Lloyd-Mostyn, Hon. R. H. H., hon. c.

Origin.

By the Certificate of Commissioners 30 Henry VIII., the hundreds of Merioneth furnished 420 men at the muster, weaponed with bills, spears, elm bows, arrows, clubs and staffs; Carnarvonshire 729, with weapons. In 1641, Feb. 12, The Earl of Pembroke was recommended by the House of Commons to His Majesty " as a person fit to be entrusted with the Militia of Carnarvon and Merioneth."

In 1684, The Militia of Caernarvonshire "consisteth of three Companies of Foot and one Troop of Horse." The Militia of Merionethshire "consists of one small Troop of Horse and two Companies Foot." By Militia Returns 1697, the Militia of the two Counties formed one Regt. of 530 foot and 48 horse "Colonel Hugh Nanny, Esquire." In 1778 when the Militia of Counties was prepared for service, two separate Regiments were organized as the Carnarvonshire and Merionethshire, both afterwards becoming Rifles; the Carnarvonshire a Royal Regt., and Lt. Infantry in 1804. In 1881 the two Regts. were again united as the 3rd Battn. Royal Welsh Fusiliers under the Territorial system.

Embodiments.
Occasion.
American War... ... 1778, period unknown.
French War ... ... 1804 to 1814.
South African War ... 1900, May 11, to 1900, Oct. 17.

Services.

In 1798 the Merioneth Rifles, Colonel Vaughan, having volunteered for service in Ireland during the Rebellion, was one of the 13 Regts. immedately sent there on the passing of the Act. The Carnarvonshire Rifles volunteered for and were stationed in Ireland, 1811-13.

3rd Battalion, The South Wales Borderers.

"South Africa, 1900-02."

Hon. Colonel:—Ormathwaite, A., Lord.
Lt.-Colonel:—Bailey, Hon. J. H. R., D.S.O., Maj. (Maj. Res. of Off.).

Origin.

In 1881 the Royal South Wales Borderers (Rifles) Militia Regt. became under Territorial Regimental organization of the Forces the 3rd Battn. of "The South Wales Borderers" Regiment. See certif. 1539 (State Papers Foreign and Domestic of the Reign Henry VIII.) of the Muster of the Forces of the Lordship of Brecknock 30 Mch., 30 Henry VIII., and of the Town and lordship of Radnor (Radnor Foren and Radnor Bridge).

By Harleian MSS., Radnorshire assembled Aprille anno dom. 1588 to resist invasion by the Spanish Armada, 200 traynd men reduced into bandes under Captaines and soarted wt. weapones.

In 1641, Feb. 12, Lord Philip Herbert was appointed for Brecknock, and Lord Littleton (Lord Keeper of the Gt. Seal of England), for Radnor, as "fit persons to be entrusted" with the organizing of the Militia.

1684, "Wednesday, August 6, His Grace the Duke of Beaufort accompanied by the Earl of Worcester Sir John Talbot and other persons of quality, took a view of the Militia of County Brecknock in a meadow near the Town, and made several close and laudable Fireings. It consists of one Troop commanded by a Captain, Lieutenant, Cornet, and Quartermaster; and four Companies of Foot by a Colonel, Captains, Lieutenants and Ensigns."

By Militia Returns Egerton MSS., 1697, Brecknock and Radnor had one Regt. of 505 men, Col. Edward Price, Esqr., and one Company of 48, Captain Sir Edw. Williams, also 224 Horse.

In 1760 under the Act 30, Geo. II., a Unit was completed for service and the quota of men to be found by Brecon—which subsequently became Rifles and a Royal Corps. In 1763 Radnor had a Unit for its quota of men. Between 1793 and 1820 Brecon and Monmouth found one Regt. The Brecon as a separate Corps subsequently becoming Rifles and a Royal Corps. In 1876 the Royal Brecknock Rifles and Royal Radnor Rifles were amalgamated under command of Lt.-Colonel W. J. Thomas as Senior Officer of the two Corps, respectively composed of four and two Companies, and under the designation of The Royal South Wales Borderers (Rifles) which in 1881 became as already recorded.

Embodiments since 1876.

Occasion.

South African War ... 1900, Jan. 23, to 1902, Mch. 25.

Services.

During the Crimean War the Royal Radnor, Brecon, and Cardigan Rifles served together as one Regt.

The 3rd Battn. South Wales Borderers Regt. having volunteered for Foreign service during South African War, it embarked strength 26 Officers, 709 N.C.O.'s and men. Lt.-Colonel C. Healey, Commdg.

On arrival at Cape Town Mch. 8, 1900, the Battn. proceeded to Newton Camp, Kimberley, Head Quarters with Left Half Battn. subsequently moving to Boshof, and Right Half Battn. under Major Jones to Windsorton Road, Dronfield and Content Siding. April 4, the Battn. was united at Boshof and the Left Half Battn. occupied Frankfort Pass, whilst the other half was moved to Lieuwfontein guarding Kimberley and Boshof Road. May 12, the Battn. again concentrated at Boshof, and 300 men under Major Jones trekked with the 1st Division under Lord Methuen to Hoopstad, where they remained until April, 1901, the Mounted Infantry formed under Captn. Gunter occupying Bloemhof, captured 20,000 rounds of ammunition and 100 shells, etc. June 1, Commandants Wessels and Pretorius surrendered to Major Jones and were sent to Bloemfontein. Aug. 5, Reinforcements arrived, and on Sep. 5 the Town having been attacked, a demand by the Boers to surrender was refused. Oct. 5, Town again attacked without success. Oct. 17, General Settle's Column arrived, but without supplies, the garrison being then on three-quarter rations which had to be reduced to half rations, though 12,000 head of cattle were left for the Garrison to look after. At the end of October the Garrison was put on quarter rations of Kaffir corn and mealies, no convoy having come through. Oct. 2 the M.I. were sent with empty waggons to Brandfort for supplies, which on their return journey were stopped at Bulfontein, Hoopstad being invested by De Villiers, Potgieter, etc., with about one thousand men.

The Garrison remained with scarcity of supplies until Dec. 29th, when it was relieved by General Bruce Hamilton.

Jan. 4, 1901, the waggons and escort sent out Oct. 2nd returned, but the supplies had been consumed while waiting at Bulfontein.

Feb. 1, a Cossack Post was rushed by the Boers and the M.I. pursued but had to retire. At this time the population had to be fed on biscuits, which further diminished the supplies, and Joubert's Farm about four miles out was occupied in order to protect the mealie gathering parties.

Mch. 22, Lord Methuen tried to cross the Vaal to Hoopstad without success.

April 1, Lord Erroll arrived with a column and food.

April 2, Fortifications destroyed and Hoopstad evacuated, the garrison proceeding to Warrenton.

Between May, 1900, and Mch., 1901, the Left Half Battn. (under Major Morgan after Colonel Healey was invalided home Nov. 25) remained at Fourteen Streams and Warrenton, moving Mch. 7, 1901, to Taungo as guard over a large Stock Farm of captured stock.

Apr. 9, the Right Half Battn. on arrival at Warrenton, moved to Vryburg, many men being in rags and without boots. Apr. 20, proceeded to Mafeking and performed escort duty to various convoys until June.

The Left Half Battn. detached Captn. Shaw with 100 men to Christiana, where they remained until joining Head Quarters at Mafeking in October. Towards the end of 1901 the Battn. was united at Mafeking and remained there until Feb., 1902, chiefly employed on escort duty, except that a Detachment was provided for Maritzain in Novr. and Captain Phillips with 114 men including M.I. Section, trecked with 1st Div. under Lord Methuen to Klerksdorp. Feb. 14, 140 men were sent to strengthen the garrison at Vryburg, Feb. 22, 1902, the Battn. having concentrated, proceeded to Cape Town, and embarked Mch. 1 for England.

Casualties.

Killed and died of disease, etc., 3 Officers (Lieuts. W. H. Amedroz, J. S. B. Gething, H. Harboard), and 34 N.C.O.'s and men.

Mentioned in Despatches.
Major T. W. Jones.
Captain H. H. Bromfield.
Captain G. Maxwell-Heron.
Captain H. J. V. Phillips.
Captain Darley.
Captain J. M. Gibson-Watt.

Special Honours.
Colonel C. Healey, C.M.G.
Captain H. J. V. Phillips, D.S.O.
Captain H. H. Bromfield, D.S.O.
Captain Darley, D.S.O.
Sergt.-Major Busby, D.C. Medal.
Q.M.-Sergt. Griffith, D.C. Medal.
Sergt. Phelps, D.C. Medal.

Medals, etc., received by Battalion.

Queen's South African Medal with Clasps "Cape Colony" and "Orange River Colony." King's Medal with Clasps "1901" and "1902."

4th Battalion, The South Wales Borderers.

Hon. Colonel :—Powis, G. O., Earl of.
Lt.-Colonel :—Sladen, E. S. St. B.

Origin.

In 1881 The Royal Montgomery Rifle Regt. of Militia under Territorial Regimental organization of the Forces became the 4th Battn. of the Shropshire (King's Light Infantry) Regiment, soon afterwards changed to the 4th Battn. of The South Wales Borderers.

The earliest record of the Constitutional Force of Montgomery appears in Harleian MSS. Spanish Armada Assembly of Queen Elizabeth's Forces, 1588. "The certificate returned from ye Lieuftenant of traynd and furneshed men reduced into Bandes under Captaines and how they were soarted in Aprille ano dom 1588 record 300 Trained besides Horsemen Launces one, Lighthorse 19, Petroneles 30.

In 1641, Feb. 12, the Earl of Essex was appointed as a "fit person to be entrusted" with organizing the Militia of the County.

By Militia Returns 1697, Egerton MSS., Montgomery had one Company of 364 men and Horse 64, Col. Sr. John Price, Bart.

When the Militia of England and Wales was reorganized in the 18th century a Regt. was completed for service in 1763, and for the quota of men to be furnished by the shire as the Montgomery Regt. of Militia. It became a Royal Regt. in 1804, Light Infantry 1810, and a Rifle Corps in 1853 officially known as The Royal Montgomery Rifle Regt., which in 1881 became as already recorded.

Embodiments.

Occasion.

American War... ... 1779 to 1783.
Revolutionary War, etc. 1793, Feb. 2, to 1814, June 24.
Crimean War ... ... 1854, Dec. 12, to 1856, June 19.
South-African War ... 1900, May 3, to 1900, Dec. 5.

Services.

In 1798 the Regt. volunteered for, and under command of Colonel Browne was one of the thirteen Regts. immediately sent to Ireland upon the passing of the Act which empowered the Sovereign to employ the Militia in that Country during the Rebellion.

Volunteered for and stationed in Ireland 1811 to 1813.

3rd Battalion, The King's Own Scottish Borderers.

"South Africa, 1900-02."
Hon. Colonel:—p.s. Hume, A., hon. c. (H) (T).
Lt.-Colonel:—p.s. Laurie, C. V. E., D.S.O. (H) (T).

Origin.

In Mch., 1798, a Regiment commonly known as the Dumfries Militia was completed for service out of the quotas of men to be found by the Counties of Dumfries, Peebles, Selkirk, Roxburgh, Kirkcudbright and Wigtown, the Earl of Dalkeith being appointed Colonel.

The numbers fixed by Order in Council were obtained by ballot out of those liable to serve, and substitutes allowed. The obligation to serve ended with the Peace of Amiens, Mch., 1802.

In 1802 the Scotch Militia being placed on a more permanent footing under Act 42, Geo. III., c. 98, a Regt. was formed out of the quotas of men to be furnished by the Counties of Dumfries, Roxburgh, and Selkirk, the Earl of Dalkeith being Colonel and most of the former Officers re-appointed besides many of the N.C. Officers and Drummers.

In 1860 on disbandment of the Galloway Rifles Regiment, the two Kirkcudbright Companies were added to the Dumfries Militia Regt., and in 1864 the Regt. was designated the "Scottish Borderers" until 1881, when under the Territorial Regimental Organization of the Forces it became the 3rd Battn. of The Royal Scots Fusiliers, and subsequently in 1886 the 3rd Battn. of "The King's Own Scottish Borderers."

Embodiments.

Occasion.

Revolutionary War, etc.	1798, June, to 1802, Apr.
French War	1803, Apr. 5, to 1814, Aug. 15.
Crimean War	1855, Feb. 12, to 1856, May 27.
Indian Mutiny	1857, Oct. 1, to 1858, Apr. 29.
South African War	1900, Jan. 25, to 1902, June 18.

Services.

In 1810 the Regt. volunteered for service anywhere in the United Kingdom, and in July embarked at Leith for the South of England.

In 1811, under the Interchange Act, volunteered for and was stationed in Ireland, Sepr., 1811, to Sepr., 1813.

Volunteered for Foreign Service during the South African War, and embarked for South Africa Mch. 9, 1900, strength 30 Officers, 425 other ranks (not including a Gun detachment of one Officer and 7 N.C.O.'s and men which afterwards joined from Hythe), Colonel J. K. M. Witham, Commdg.

On arrival at Cape Town Mch. 29th, the Battn. was sent up to Kimberley and there divided, Half Battn. to Modder River, the other to Dronfield, except for a few weeks at Modder River and when on column under General Settle. The Battn. was not united again until May, 1902, at Cape Town, having had detachments in many places, including Modder River, Dronfield, Riverton Road, Warrenton, Vryburg, Christiana, Schweizer Reneke, Koffyfontein, Jacobsdal, Bulawayo, Goromonzi, Crocodile River, Manzingama, etc.

Extract from Kimberley District Orders, 19th Apr., 1902:

"On the departure of the Detachment of the 3rd Bn. King's Own Scottish Borderers from Kimberley the Officer commanding the District desires to thank them for the excellent service rendered by them during so many long, weary, and at times critical months at Koffyfontein and later at Jacobsdal.

The Battn. as a whole has been more or less intimately connected with the Kimberley District from an early stage in the War and its services are by no means forgotten or unappreciated.

It is doubtful if any Militia Battn. leaves South Africa to enjoy its well earned rest at home with a higher reputation than the 3rd Battn. King's Own Sco. Borderers.

Sd. P. Holland-Pryor, Major,
C.S.O. Kimberley District.

19. 5. 1902.

Kimberley."

The Battn. re-embarked for home May 29, 1902.

Casualties.

Killed and died of disease, etc.
Captain A. D. R. Pott.
Lieut. G. G. Moir (serving with 1st Battn.).
10 N.C. Officers and men.

Mentioned in Despatches.

Lt.-Colonel J. K. M. Witham.
Majors C. V. E. Laurie and J. McKie.
Captn. and Adjt. F. J. Carruthers (twice).
Captain Sir A. D. Grierson, Bart.
Sergt.-Major W. Smith.
Qr.-Mr.-Sergt. W. H. Soper.
Cr.-Sergts. J. Anderson, J. B. Saunderson.
Cr.-Sergts. J. Hughes, and G. Robson (twice).
Sergts. W. McLean and W. Howe.
Corporal W. Rennie.

Special Honours.

Lt.-Colonel J. K. M. Witham, C.M.G.
Major C. V. E. Laurie, D.S.O.
Major J. McKie, D.S.O.
Captain and Adjt. F. J. Carruthers, Brevet Majority.
Sergt.-Major W. Smith, D.C. Medal.
Qr.-Mr.-Sergt. W. H. Soper, D.C. Medal.
Cr.-Sergt. J. Anderson, D.C. Medal.

Medals, etc., received by Battalion.

Queen's South African Medal with Clasps "Cape Colony," "Orange Free State" and "Transvaal." King's South African Medal with Clasps "South Africa, 1901" and "South Africa, 1902."

3rd Battalion, The Cameronians (Scottish Rifles).

"South Africa, 1901-02."

Hon. Colonel:—Home, Col. Rt. Hon. C. A., Earl of, K.T.

Lt.-Colonel:—Douglas, W. C., D.S.O.

Origin.

In 1854 a second Militia Regt. was raised by Sir D. Carrick-Buchannan for the County as the 2nd Royal Lanarkshire, which in 1877 was divided into two Battns. In 1881 the 1st Battn. became the 3rd Battn. of the Cameronians (Scottish Rifles) as the Territorial Regt. under the organization of that year.

Embodiments.

Occasion.

As 2nd Lanarkshire Regiment.

Crimean War ... ... 1855, Feb. 5, to 1856, June 30.
Indian Mutiny, etc. ... 1857, Oct. 21, to 1860, June 12.

As 3rd Battalion Cameronians.

South African War ... 1900, May 5, to 1902, July 15.

Services.

Volunteered for Foreign service and proceeded to South Africa. Strength embarked 26 Officers, 738 N.C.O.'s and men, Colonel Farie Commanding. On arrival May, 1901, after six days at Modder River, and participating en route from Kimberley in a brush with the enemy near Lieufontein, the Battn. relieved the 4th Battn. Scottish Rifles at Boshof, a Town in the Orange River Colony held as a large depot for supplies for Hoopstadt, and for the safe defence of Kimberley, the latter town being much dependent upon it for help and support. In conjunction with a section of R.F.A. (subsequently relieved by a detachment of the Royal Norfolk Artillery Militia) and a few men of the A.S. Corps, the Battn. formed the garrison of this Station for fifteen months, during three of which it was without communication from outside and bereft of supplies—until the end of the War and the town was evacuated June 6, 1902. On the Battalion's arrival at the station it was found necessary to reduce the perimeter of defence, there not being sufficient men to occupy the trenches which had done duty with a much stronger garrison; thus a full share of hard work filling in trenches, forming rough blockhouses, etc., with what materials could be obtained at hand, fell to the lot of the young partially trained boys who so largely composed the Battn. consequent on the withdrawal of the Militia reservists for Line Service prior to their Militia Battn. proceeding to South Africa. Although threatened day and night with a concentrated attack by Commandoes in the District under Erasmus, Jacobs, and Badenhorst, and being subjected to much sniping, only two abortive attempts were made on the town. The Battn. formed its own Mounted Infantry for cattle guard duties which as time went on, were very onerous owing to the daily decreasing pasture available, and increased distance from the base. The Battn. was strengthened by a detachment to assist in manning the Blockhouses when established at Windsorton Road. It co-operated when required with passing or incoming columns and with the gunners provided a strong force at frequent intervals for the necessary duty of obtaining wood for fuel in face of possible attack by the Boers at any moment, the cattle guard duties and wood cutting expeditions coming as a relief to both Officers and men from the tedious and wearisome monotony of garrisoning the Station. During the last six weeks or two months of the War, on completion of the Blockhouse line between Kimberley and Boshof, the greater portion of which was manned by the Battn., the cattle guard and wood cutting duties became comparatively safe and Officers were at last enabled to venture beyond the precincts of the town without an escort.

Casualties.

Killed and died of disease, 13 N.C.O.'s and men.

Mentioned in Despatches.

Major W. C. Douglas.
Lieut. and Qr.-Mr. F. Brightman.
Sergt.-Major P. W. Carroll.
Cr.-Sergt. S. C. Simm.
Pte. D. Walker.

Special Honours.

Major W. C. Douglas, D.S.O.
Sergt.-Major P. W. Carroll, D.C. Medal.

Medals and Clasps Received by Battalion.

South African Medal with Clasps "Cape Colony," "Orange Free State," and "1901"—2 date Clasps.

4th Battalion, The Cameronians (Scottish Rifles).

"South Africa, 1900-01."

Hon. Colonel:—Home, Col. Rt. Hon. C. A., Earl of, K.T.

Lt.-Colonel Commandant:—Courtenay, A. H. C.B., hon. c.

Origin.

In 1854 the quota of men to be furnished by Lanarkshire having been increased, a Regiment was raised by Col. Sir D. Carrick-Buchanan as the 2nd Royal Lanarkshire Militia, which in 1877 was divided into two Battns. under a Colonel Commandant. In 1881 the 2nd Battn. became the 4th Battn. of the Cameronians (Scottish Rifles) as the Territorial Regiment under the organization of that year.

Embodiments.

Occasion.

As 2nd Royal Lanarkshire Regiment.

    Crimean War ...   ...   1855, Feb. 5, to 1856, June 30.
    Indian Mutiny, etc. ...   1857, Oct. 21, to 1860, June 12.

As 4th Battalion Cameronians.

    South African War ...   1899, Dec. 12, to 1901, June 27.

Services.

Volunteered for Foreign Service during the South African War, and embarked for South Africa Feb. 19, 1900. Strength 28 Officers, 543 N.C.O.'s and men, Colonel A. H. Courtenay, Commdg. Arrived at Cape Town Mch. 26, 1900. Formed part of the Garrison of Kimberley April-May, often taking part in the many skirmishes with the enemy. May to Augt. four Companies under Major and Hon. Lt.-Colonel M. Johnstone served with the 20th Brigade 1st Div. in all the operations in which the Brigade was employed, including the two attacks by the Boers on Lindley and three days' fighting between that place and Bethlehem, also Prinsloo's surrender at Slabbert's Nek, and escort of 2252 prisoners of war to Winburg. Three Companies under Captains Mellish, Blake, and Littledale serving with the Kimberley Flying Column Dec., 1900, to May, 1901, took part in the action at Wachteen-Beetje when the detachment carried at the point of the bayonet a kopje in possession of the enemy.

Among the many incidents arising out of this active service of the Battn. it is detailed in " With the 4th Battn. Cameronians (Scottish Rifles) in South Africa " by Col. Courtenay, that forming part of the 9th Brigade it arrived at Boshof the day before the action in which Villebois de Marueil was killed and his whole force taken prisoners, his plan of attack for retaking Boshof found in his pocket being handed to Colonel Courtenay, with orders to prepare the defence of the place accordingly, as Commandant of Boshof when the 1st Division under Lt.-General Lord Methuen left on the 7th. Apr. 9th Frankfort Pass, which commanded the Kimberley Boshof Road, was occupied and placed in a state of defence, by two Companies of the Battn. under Captain T. K. Gardner. Apr. 10, a renewed attack being feared at Kimberley, the Battn. was ordered back to that place, and garrisoned five redoubts. On May 1st 82 N.C.O.'s and men under Captains Blaikie-Hislop, Mellish, and Burne-Macdonald forming part of an escort of seven Traction Engines with stores for Frankfort arrived safely, though threatened by the Boers. May 10th the Battn. brigaded with 4th Battn. S. Staffordshire, Colonel Courtenay commdg., marched to Boshof and joined the 20th Brigade. May 14, four Companies of the 4th Scottish Rifles under Major and Hon. Lt.-Col. Johnstone proceeded with the 20th Brigade, Colonel Courtenay being again appointed Commandant of Boshof, Major Chavasse assuming command of the Battn. The mixed force for defence of the place comprised 48 Officers and 1370 of other ranks. It was known that when the Division left an attack was contemplated. On May 19th Commandant Du Plessis and three Field Cornets came in and surrendered, and up to 3rd June, 564 of their men did so with upwards of 406 horses, 5 mules, 123 oxen, 25 other cattle and 571 sheep; 4 waggons, 6000 lbs. of corn, 3400 lbs. of maize, etc. On June 3rd the detachment under Lt.-Colonel Montague Johnstone with 20th Brigade came under fire en route to Lindley. After this date to July 3rd, the 20th Brigade was shut up at Lindley and subjected to daily shelling, etc., also two heavy attacks by the two De Wets with six guns. June 26th the detachment Scottish Rifles occupied a Hill named " Lanark Hill," east of Lindley, and on this day alone, 200 shells fell or burst over them with the small loss of two men killed and one wounded, chiefly due to the manner in which they had entrenched themselves. July 3, when acting as escort to "C.I.V." Guns 20th Brigade on march to Bethlehem, heavy fighting was encountered at Lieuwkop. July 5, the Scottish Rifles held a ridge shelled at long range until relieved, and again on the 7th the 2nd Yorks. L.I. with 42 men of the 4th

Scottish Rifles maintained their position on a ridge until the Boer guns were silenced by Lyddite shells. July 16th, when acting as right flank guard, the column came in touch with C. de Wet's force having five guns, which attacked the right flank, but were held in check 400 yards off by the 4th Scottish until the column had passed.

The detachment, 4th Scottish Rifles, assisted in holding Slabhert's Nek to prevent escape of the enemy on the important occasion of Prinsloo's surrender, and on Aug. 4th, with the 20th Brigade, escorted 2,250 prisoners of war to Winburg. In common with the rest of the troops engaged in these operations, the 4th Scottish Rifles suffered great hardships, especially in the very cold weather, for want of warm clothing and boots, the detachment arriving at Winburg practically in rags. Major-General Paget, in his report on the detachment, commented on their steadiness and pluck under "a heavy shell fire enough to shake the nerves of any but the best troops." Aug. 15, 1900, the detachment rejoined Head Quarters at Boshof, Lt.-Colonel Johnstone taking over the duties of Commandant, Sept. 6th until 25th, during Colonel Courtenay's absence on sick leave, and Major Chavasse those of O.C. 4th Scottish Rifles. At this time the district continued to be in a very disturbed state, patrols often in contact with the enemy. In October it became necessary for the Battalion to be encamped in rear of their trenches, with two companies in strongly entrenched positions at the Green and West Kopjes. On Nov. 1st, a steam convoy was in danger of capture at Lieuwfontein, and a force of Scottish Rifles was sent out under Captain J. Campbell Gardner, reinforced next day with a mixed force, including 100 men of the Battalion under Captain Henning, and the convoy was safely brought in. During November frequent skirmishes took place between the Boshof mounted troops and the enemy. After Nov. 22nd, Boshof became practically invested, and on the 29th heavily attacked, the enemy being driven off and never getting nearer than 500 yards, the depth of trenches and head cover causing the casualties of the garrison to be small. From Nov. 25th the place became closely invested, no letters received for weeks, despatch riders captured, telegraph wires destroyed, etc. Dec. 15th, a convoy got through under Colonel Parke, a party of the 4th Scottish Rifles with M.I. under Colonel Courtenay meeting it at Lieuwfontein and taking part in an engagement at the Farm of Viljoens Hoef, which was captured and burnt as the enemy continued to fire after hoisting a white flag.

Dec. 16th, the convoy returned, taking with it 100 N.C.O.'s and men of the 4th Scottish Rifles under Captain Mellish and Lieut. Seagrim, which remained with the Kimberley Flying Column throughout its operations until the Battalion left South Africa.

The duties of maintaining the defence, foraging parties, wood cutting, etc., were now carried out at increased distances from Boshof, often bringing the parties into contact with the enemy. On Dec. 27th a foraging party under Captain Henning composed of two guns, all available mounted troops and 100 N.C.O.'s and men, 4th Scottish Rifles, Captains Clifford and Lynch, visited the Farms of Pretorious and Van Wijk, taking prisoner the latter, and brought in 100 cattle, 34 horses, 500 sheep, and 1,700 lbs. of forage. Expeditions of this character were frequent.

On Jan. 5th, 1901, the scouts on Boschrand Ridge were fired on, and the enemy had to be driven off by two guns R.F.A. and 100 4th Scottish Rifles, all under the Commandant. On the 7th an ambulance under the Red Cross was captured by the Boers, and skirmishes of minor importance took place daily until Jan. 17th, when a convoy under Colonel Milne, Kimberley Column, for Boshof, required support, and the Commandant with S.O. and all available troops occupied Boschrand and neighbouring kopjes just in time to prevent the enemy doing so, enabling the Column to reach its destination, the steam transports being left at Lieuwfontein for the night commanded from four kopjes by 125 of the 4th Scottish Rifles under Captain Campbell-Gardner. It was on this occasion that Capt. Mellish and Lieut. Seagrim with 100 men of the 4th Scottish Rifles attached to the Kimberley Column distinguished themselves by taking a strongly occupied kopje at the point of the bayonet. "The detachment advanced against it for some 2,000 yards across the open, and at about 800 yards came under a heavy fire, some cover being obtained by lying down in the long grass by half companies while the others 'rushed.' When the foot of the kopje was reached the whole charged, and on gaining the summit the Boers were seen galloping away on their horses." Feb. 6th, a reconnaisance in force was made to ascertain the whereabouts of Badenhorst's and other commandoes, and thoroughly scout Merriesfontein Ridge. During these operations about 1,500 cattle and sheep were rounded up by the M.I. under Lieuts. Viner-Johnson and Brudenell-Murphy, the Boers opening fire on them, and attacking later in large numbers until the infantry and guns were met and brought into action as they were retiring from Eickenboom Farm, which had been visited. While at this Farm, the ridge commanding it was held by Lieut. Hazlerigg and forty men. A large force of the enemy attempting to get between the guns and the ridge, much fighting ensued, the mounted troops which had joined the party keeping up a brisk rearguard engagement. The forces engaged, including guns, etc., brought up, numbered about 130 against near 400 of the enemy, and the fighting lasted over five hours. Lieut. Brudenell-Murphy and five men wounded, two taken prisoners, and seventeen horses killed or wounded. Apr. 9th, a wood-cutting party under Colonel Johnstone with two guns, M.I., and 100 Scottish Rifles was heavily attacked, and held the enemy in check until the Commandant arrived with a strong reinforcement, and shelled the Boers at short range with shrapnel, forcing them back in confusion. May 6th, the inhabitants were on "starvation rations." May 10th, Christian de Wet was reported moving towards Boshof, and the enemy's patrols were shelled at long range. May 13th, the Commandant co-operated with an incoming convoy, 100 of the 4th Scottish Rifles being under Captain Clifford. The enemy on "Swart Kop" were first shelled and then charged off the position. Maj.-General T. Pretyman, R.A., G.O.C. Kimberley, was with the Column and inspected the the garrison on the 14th, congratulating them "on the excellent work done and upon having successfully held a corner of the Empire for so long a period." The blockhouse system was then being established, and on May 22nd Lieut-Col. Johnstone took over the command from Colonel Courtenay, who proceeded to Cape Town pending embarkation of the Battalion. At this date the Kimberley Column for Boshof required assistance, and Colonel Johnstone took out two guns R.F.A. with 100 4th Scottish Rifles under Captain Lynch to Lieuwfontein and occupied all the ridges and kopjes in the neighbourhood until the convoy passed. May 26th, 1901, the Battalion left Boshof, was stopped at Worcester, and proceeded on the 31st to Cape Town, and embarked on the following day for England.

Casualties.
Killed and died of disease, etc., 15 N.C.O.'s and men.

Mentioned in Despatches.
Colonel A. H. Courtenay.
Major and Lt.-Colonel M. Johnstone.
Captain and Adjt. C. M. S. Henning.

Captain A. F. Townshend (twice).
Lieuts. Murphy (twice) and Boyd-Rochfort.
Cr.-Sergts. J. Campbell, E. Rowe, A. E. Slade.
Sergts. T. Morris, T. McLeod, and J. Wilson.
Corpls. J. Dailly and J. Higgins.

Special Honours.

Colonel A. H. Courtenay, C.B.
Lt.-Colonel M. Johnstone, D.S.O.
Cr. Sergt. J. Campbell, D.C. Medal.
Sergt. T. Morris, D.C. Medal.

Medals, etc., received by Battalion.

South African with Clasps "Orange River Colony," "South Africa 1901," and "Cape Colony," the Half Battn. with 20th Brigade, 1st Div., obtaining the Wittebergen Clasp in place of the Orange River Colony Clasp.

3rd Battalion, The Royal Inniskilling Fusiliers.

Hon. Colonel:—Enniskillen, L. E., Earl of, K.P.
Lt.-Colonel:—Stewart, Sir H. H., Bt., hon. c. (Maj. Res. of Off.).

Origin.

Completed for service as the Fermanagh Militia Regt. for the Revolutionary War, and became in 1881 under the Territorial Organization of the Forces the 3rd Battn. of its present Regiment.

Embodiments.
 Occasion.

South African War ... 1899, Dec. 5, to 1900, Oct. 16.
Note.—The Regimental Records of this Unit have been lost or destroyed.

4th Battalion, The Royal Inniskilling Fusiliers.

Hon. Colonel:—Charlemont, J. A., Visct., C.B.
Lt.-Colonel:—Irvine, H., hon. c.

Origin.

Raised for the Revolutionary War, 1793, as the Tyrone Regiment of Militia, which shortly afterwards became a Royal Regiment, and at later date Fusiliers. In 1881 became the 4th Battn. of the Territorial Royal Inniskilling Fusiliers.

Embodiments.

   Occasion.

Revolutionary War, etc. 1793, Aug., to 1802, May.
French War ... 1803, May, to 1816, Mar.
Crimean War ... 1855, Jan., to 1856, Aug.
Indian Mutiny ... 1857, Nov., to 1858, May.
South African War ... 1900, May 2, to 1900, Oct. 18.

Services.

Took part in the suppression of the Irish Rebellion, 1798, including the battles of Arklow, June 9th, Gorey, Vinegar Hill, and other engagements.

Stationed in England during Crimean War embodiment.

5th Battalion, The Royal Inniskilling Fusiliers.

Hon. Colonel:—Hamilton, Lord C. J., Col., A.D.C., Kt. of Grace Order of St. John of Jerusalem.
Lt.-Colonel:—Barton, B. J., Col., A.D.C.

Origin.

Raised April, 1793, and known as the Prince of Wales's Own Donegal Militia. In 1881 became the 5th Battn. Royal Inniskilling Fusiliers under the Territorial organization.

Embodiments.

   Occasion.

Revolutionary War, etc. 1793, April, to 1802, May 12.
French War ... 1803, Mar. 15, to 1816, April.
Crimean War ... 1855, Jan. 6, to 1856, Aug. 4.
Indian Mutiny ... 1857, Nov. 5, to 1860, Aug. 31.
South African War ... 1900, May 9, to 1901, July 3.

Services.

Served through the Irish Rebellion, 1798, taking part under General Johnston in the engagements at Vinegar Hill, Wexford and New Ross, the Light Company being also engaged with the Rebels at Enniscorthy, and the Regiment at Rock Wexford in May, 1798, and New Ross on June 15th, and again at Vinegar Hill. Previous to the Battle of Ross, Sergt. Finch and 12 Privates were surrounded by rebels at Borrisodine, Sergt. Finch for his distinguished conduct being given an Ensigncy in the Line, and Sergt. Hamilton for his bravery at New Ross an Ensigncy in the 1st Royals.

3rd Battalion, The Gloucestershire Regiment.

Hon. Colonel:—p.s. Guise, Sir W. F. G., Bt.
Lt.-Colonel:—p.s. Guise, C. D., hon. c. (T) (H).

Origin.

In 1881 the Royal South Gloucester Light Infantry Militia Regiment became, under the Territorial Organization of the Forces the 3rd Battn. of "The Gloucestershire Regiment." See copy of the certificate 1539 (incomplete), "State Papers Foreign and Domestic of the Rign, Henry VIII.," for details of the armed Force of the County at the great muster held throughout the kingdom, by virtue of Royal Commission, 30, Henry VIII. By Harleian MSS. anno. dom. 1588, Gloucestershire assembled 3,000 "Trayned men reduced into bandes under Captaines and soarted wt weaponones," besides horsemen, 20 Launces, 180 Lighthorse, 35 Petronelles.

In 1641, Feb. 12, Lord Shandois was appointed a "fit person to be entrusted" with organizing the Militia of Gloucester and County of the City of Gloucester.

By Militia Returns 1697, Egerton MSS., the County had four Regiments, thirty-six Companies, 2,199 foot, and six Troops of horse 243. The White Regt., Col. Sir John Guise; Green Regt., Col. Sir Ralph Dutton, Bart.; Blew Regt., Col. Sir Tho. Stephens; Red Regt., Col. Maynard Colchester, and Col. Ld. Dursley commanding the Horse.

In 1759, under Act. 30, Geo. II., this Battalion was completed for service as the South Battalion of the Gloucester Regt. of Militia, and part of the quota of men to be furnished by the county. In 1763 the Battalion became a separate Regiment. It became a Royal Regiment in 1795, Light Infantry in 1854, and in 1881 as already recorded.

Embodiments.

Occasion.

Seven Years War	1760 to 1763.
American War	1778 to 1782.
Revolutionary War and European Disturbances...	1792 to 1802. 1803 to 1814.
Crimean War	1854 to 1856.
South African War	1900, May 15, to 1901, July 13.

Services.

1666, by "State Papers Foreign and Domestic, Chas. II.," the Militia of Gloucester was "drawn out by the King" for the threatened French and Dutch invasion. In 1901, during the South African War, furnished to the 4th Battn. 124 N.C.O.'s and men, who volunteered for foreign service and were stationed at St. Helena as guard over Boer prisoners of war.

4th Battalion, The Gloucestershire Regiment.

"St. Helena, 1900-01."

Hon. Colonel:—Kingscote, Sir R. N. F., G.C.V.O., K.C.B., Eq.

Lt.-Colonel:—Bathurst, S. H., Earl, C.M.G., hon. c.

Origin.

See 3rd Battn. of the Regiment for particulars of the County Forces prior to 1759.

In 1759 two Battalions were completed for service as the North and South of the Gloucester Militia and quota of men to be provided by the County, this Battalion being the former.

It was a Battalion of Fusiliers in 1761.

1763, Apr. 20, the two Battns. became separate Regiments, this Battn. being the North Regt., a Royal Regt. in 1795, and Light Infantry 1854.

In 1881, under the Territorial organization of the Forces, it formed the 4th Battn. of "The Gloucestershire Regiment."

Embodiments.

Occasion.

Seven Years War	1761, Apr. 4, to 1763, Feb.
American War	1778, Mch., to 1782, Mch.
Revolutionary War	1792, to 1802, Apr. 23.
and European Disturbances	1803, Mch., to 1814, Sepr. 4.
Crimean War	1854, Dec. 26, to 1856, June 12.
Indian Mutiny	1857, Nov. 3, to 1858, May 18.
South African War	1900, Jan. 11, to 1901, July 27.

Services.

Volunteered for service in Ireland during the Rebellion, and in that Country from Sepr. 5, 1798, to Apr., 1799.

Volunteered for and stationed in Ireland 1813-14.

Volunteered for Foreign service during the South African War, and embarked under Colonel the Earl Bathurst for St. Helena, Apr. 2, 1900, to furnish the Guards over Boer prisoners of war at Deadwood Camp, two Companies under the command of Captain the Hon. A. B. Bathurst being at Broad Bottom Camp. The Battn. furnished the guard of N.C.O.'s at Kent Cottage over General Cronje and his family.

Casualties.

Died of disease, etc., 3 N.C.O.'s and men.

Special Honours.

Colonel The Earl Bathurst, C.M.G.

Medals, etc.

Queen's South African Medal.

5th Battalion, The Worcestershire Regiment.

Hon. Colonel:—Coventry, G. W., Earl of.

Lt.-Colonel:—Stephenson, S.A. (Hon. Maj. in the Army.

Origin.

In 1881 the Worcestershire Militia which in 1874 had been divided into two Battns. became under Territorial organization of the Forces the 3rd and 4th Battns. of " The

Worcestershire Regiment," this Battn. being the 3rd. In 1890 the two Militia Battns. became respectively the 5th and 6th on augmentation of the Territorial Regt. by two additional Line Units, numbered as the 3rd and 4th Battalions. For strength of the armed Force of Worcestershire in 1539, see copy of certificate of muster held 30 Henry VIII., from State Papers Foreign and Domestic of the Reign Henry VIII., giving details of the "Archers Billmen and those with the harness any of them possess."

In 1641, Mch. 12, Lord Edward Howard was appointed as a "fit person to be entrusted" with the organizing of the Militia of "Wighorn and of the County of the City of Worcester."

By Militia Returns 1697, Egerton MSS., the County and City of Worcester had one Regt. of seven Companies 786 men with two Troops of horse 120, total of both 906, Col. D. of Shrewsbury.

With Note—"that at the last muster they appeared full and in good order."

In 1778 a Regt. was completed for service and the quota of men to be found by the County under Act 30, Geo. II., which in 1874 was divided into two Battalions.

Embodiments.

Occasion.

American War	1778 to 1783.
French War	1793 to 1797.
Irish Rebellion, etc.	1798 to 1802.
French War	1803 to 1814, Aug. 5.
French War	1815, July 13, to 1816, May 15.
Crimean War	1854, Dec. 14, to 1856, July 14.
Indian Mutiny	1857, Nov. 12, to 1858, May 11.
South African War	1900, May 7, to 1900, Oct. 15.

Services.

Volunteered for and served in Ireland at the time of the Rebellion 1798-9.

Volunteered for Foreign service in 1814 and furnished three Officers (Lieuts. Rudge, Atcherley, Beale) with 90 N.C.O.'s and Men for the 1st Provisional Battn. of the Militia Brigade under command of Colonel the Marquis of Buckingham, which landed at Paulliac and marched through Bordeaux to Toulouse, to reinforce Lt.-General the Earl of Dalhouse's Division of Wellington's Army.

Volunteered for and stationed in Ireland 1815 to 1816.

6th Battalion, The Worcestershire Regiment.

"South Africa, 1902."

Hon. Colonel :—Coventry, G. W., Earl of.

Lt.-Colonel :—Everard, H. E. E. (Hon. Maj. in the Army).

Origin.

In 1881 the 2nd Battn. of the Worcestershire Regt. of Militia became the 4th Battn. of the "Worcestershire Regiment," and in 1890 the 6th Battalion (see 5th Battalion of the Regiment for origin, and services, etc., prior to 1874).

Embodiments since 1874.

Occasion.

South African War ... 1900, May 8, to 1900, Oct. 19.
South African War ... 1901, Dec. 9, to 1902, Oct. 10.

Services.

Volunteered for Foreign service, and embarked for South Africa in 1902, Strength 15 Officers, 1 W.O., 535 N.C.O.'s and men, Colonel E. H. Bearcroft Commdg. On arrival the Battn. was chiefly employed in holding the Blockhouse line from Bethulie on the Orange River to Stormberg, Garrison of Stormberg, etc., also taking part in the operations and drives in the North Eastern and North Central parts of the Colony. After Peace was declared it concentrated at Burghersdorp and from thence proceeded to East London where it embarked Sep. 12, 1902, for England.

Casualties.

Killed and died of disease, etc., 20 N.C.O.'s and men. Captain Stanley Clarke, serving with Yeomanry, being killed in action at Lindley.

Mentioned in Despatches.

Lt.-Colonel Everard.
Capt. and Adjt. Westmacott.
Sergt.-Major Lubberley.
Cr.-Sergt. Ray.

Special Honours.

Colonel E. H. Bearcroft, C.B.

Pte. Banks attd. 2nd Battn. awarded D.C. Medal for bringing in a comrade under heavy fire at the action of Boschfontein, Sepr., 1900.

Medals, etc., received by Battalion.

Queen's South African Medal with Clasps "Cape Colony" and "South Africa, 1902."

3rd Battalion, The East Lancashire Regiment.

"South Africa, 1900-02."

Hon. Colonel:—

Lt.-Colonel:—p.s. Parker, J. W. R., Maj. ret. pay, hon. c. (H).

Origin.

Raised 1853 as the 5th Royal Lancashire Regiment, and in 1881 under Territorial organization of the Forces became the 3rd Battn. of the East Lancashire Regiment.

Embodiments.

Occasion.

Crimean War ... ... 1854, Mch. 6, to 1855, Jan. 1.
South African War ... 1900, Jan. 24, to 1902, Mch. 25.

Services.

Volunteered for Foreign service and embarked for South Africa Feb. 16, 1900. Strength 26 Officers, 674 other ranks, Major R. H. Milne-Redhead Commdg.

On arrival at Cape Town Mch. 13th, 1900, the Battn. was stationed at De Aar and six weeks later moved to Norvals Pont. Apr. 2nd, Maj. and Hon. Lt.-Col. J. W. Parker took over the command. Apr. 27th the Battn. was ordered to Edenburg and out-stations, all heavy baggage being returned to the base for want of transport—while on the march from Springfontein the destination was changed to Glen, Orange Free State. After moving North of Bloemfontein the Battn. was in advance of the main body of the Army. Apr. 30th, two Companies forming the escort for guns proceeded to Karree, the most advanced point then held. May 16th Head Quarters were ordered to Brandfort (which place had been captured on the 3rd May) two Companies under Captn. Broad being left to garrison Glen, and two others under Captn. Allen at Karree. The duties of commandant at Brandfort were taken over by Colonel Parker, Captains Broad and Allen being appointed respectively Commandants at Glen and Karree.

The insanitary state of the encampment ground occupied at De Aar was now telling on the Battn., six Officers and many men being down with enteric. During June much annoyance and some casualties were caused by the sniping of the Boers. In July there were several Company changes of Station and in Aug. a draft from England of one hundred Line recruits considered too young to proceed direct to their

Battn. was attached to the Battn. until Jan., 1902. Aug. 5th, Lt.-Col. Milne Redhead rejoined from England and resumed command, the Battn. being soon afterwards ordered to furnish the garrison at Eensgevonden, and reinforce that at Vet River, Captn. Ashford with a Company proceeding to the former place and Captn. Roberts with 200 men to Vet River. Aug. 22nd Col. Milne Redhead took over the duties of Commandant at Brandfort. On Sept. 11th 1500 Boers under Kotbe and Haasbrook were located at Pietersburg in view of crossing the Line, and the 3rd East Lancashire was detailed to furnish strong posts at intervals between Brandfort and Allemans Siding where a force under General Allen (including a detachment of the 3rd East Lancashire under Major Jupp) was waiting for them. The Boers, however, warned by spies, turned North and eventually crossed the Smaldeel-Winburg Line near Winburg, where General Macdonald captured most of their transport.

Sep. 30th the Battn. was distributed along the railway between Smaldeel and Glen, a distance of forty-eight miles.

Jan. 11th, 1901, Lt.-Col. Parker was appointed Commandant at Vet River, and several Company changes of station occurred about this time. In Feb. sections of mounted Infantry were formed and trained at Vet River, Smaldeel, and Karree which were usefully employed in scouting and clearing the farms of disaffected Boers, the M.I. Section at Vet River under 2nd Lieut. Preston being successful in large captures of horses, sheep, and cattle. At Smaldeel a Krupp gun being available, a gun detachment was trained by Captn. Ringer. On the night of Feb. 20th the post at Houtenbeck was attacked and the Boers driven off by small detachment under Lieut. Conant.

Apr. 21st at night a party of eighty Boers attacked a post on the Winburg Railway garrisoned by Lce.-Sergt. T. Wilson and eight men, the engagement lasting from 9 p.m. to 2 a.m., when the enemy withdrew, Colonel Napier commdg. centre sec. L. of C., O.R.C., on visiting the post expressed his satisfaction with the conduct of the garrison.

In June the whole Battn. with Head Quarters at Virginia occupied Blockhouses which had been constructed between Smaldeel and Riet Spruit—and the men were continuously engaged in repelling the attempts of small parties of Boers to cross or injure the line.

Aug. 16th, Lt.-Col. Milne Redhead returned to England and was succeeded in the command by Lt.-Col. T. W. R. Parker.

Jan. 28th, 1902, Head Quarters moved to Smaldeel, and on Feb. 20th the Battn. entrained for Cape Town en route for England, embarking Mch. 1, 1902.

Casualties.

Killed and died of disease, etc.,
50 N.C.O.'s and men.

Mentioned in Despatches.

Lt.-Colonel R. H. Milne-Redhead.
Lt.-Colonel J. W. R. Parker.
Major C. W. T. T. Goff.
Captain R. L. Broad.
Lieut. Mackenzie.
2nd Lieut. E. N. Buchan.
2nd Lieut. H. C. Conans.
Cr.-Sergt. W. H. Willis.
Q.-M. Sergt. C. H. Harroll.
Sergt. J. McLoughlin.
Sergt. W. Miller.
Sergt. W. Harvey.
Sergt. J. Carney.

Special Honours.

Lieut.-Colonel R. N. Milne-Redhead, C.M.G.
Major C. W. T. T. Goff, D.S.O.
2nd Lieut. E. N. Buchan, D.S.O.
Cr.-Sergt. W. H. Willis, D.C. Medal.
Sergt. W. Miller, D.C. Medal.
Sergt. J. McLoughlin, D.C. Medal.

Medals, etc., received by Battalion.

Queen's South African Medal with Clasps "Cape Colony" and "Orange Free State." King's South African Medal with Clasps "South Africa, 1901" and "South Africa, 1902."

3rd Battalion, The East Surrey Regiment.

"South Africa, 1901-02."
Hon. Colonel:—Lemmon, T. W., C.B., hon. c.
Lt.-Colonel:—Worthington, J. C., hon. c. (H).

Origin.

In 1881, the 1st Royal Surrey Militia became under Territorial organization of the Forces, the 3rd Battn. of The East Surrey Regiment.

The exhaustive researches of the late Colonel John Davis, A.D.C., have placed the constitutional Force of the County in possession of many particulars relating to the military Force of Surrey in early times.

The Tribal Force of Surrey united with Sussex and parts of Hampshire, is referred to in connection with Caesar's second invasion of Britain.

By "Letters and Papers of the Reign of Henry VIII." Surrey was represented at the great Muster 27 Mch., 30 Henry VIII., by 334 Archers, 1129 Billmen, "411 harness."

In August, 1587, the strength of the County Force was "400 shotmen strongest to have muskets the others harquebuses, 600 bowmen, 600 billmen, and 400 pikemen with corslets."

In 1588 by Harleian MSS., Queen Elizabeth's assembly of her forces to resist the Spanish Armada, Surrey had present 1522 "trayned and furneshed men reduced into bandes under Captaines" also Horsemen 8 Launces, 98 Lighthorse, 29 Petroneles.

In 1641, Feb. 12, the Earl of Nottingham was the "fit person to be entrusted" with the organization of the Militia of Surrey.

By Militia Returns, 1697 (Egerton MSS.), the County had one Regiment of nine Companies "1209 foot with two Troops of horse 132—and a Southwark Regt. of six Companies 910 foot, both commanded by Col. D. of Norfolk."

In 1759 under the Act 30, Geo. II., a Regiment was completed for service and the quota of men to be found by the County, which was soon afterwards divided into two Units as the 1st and 2nd Surrey. In 1763 the two Regiments were amalgamated. In 1797 the second Regiment was again organized, and both became Royal Regiments known as the 1st and 2nd Royal Surrey, the former becoming in 1881 the senior Militia Battn. of the Territorial East Surrey Regiment.

Embodiments.

Occasion.

Seven Years War	1759, July 3, to 1762, Dec.
American War	1778, Mch. 26, to 1783, Feb. 28.
Revolutionary War, etc.	1792, Dec. 1, to 1814, for periods almost continuous.
French War	1815, to 1816, Apr. 30.
Crimean War	1854, Dec. 28, to 1856, June 10.
Indian Mutiny	1857, Nov. 5, to 1858, Jan. 22.
Threatened War	1885, Mch. 9, to 1885, Sep. 30.
South African War	1900, May 9, to 1900, Oct. 15.
South African War	1901, May 6, to 1902, July 26.

Services.

In 1587 attended the muster and training at St. George's Fields in view of Spanish invasion.

1588—Assembly to resist Spanish Armada, see certif. Harleian MSS.

1591, by S.P. Dom. Elizabeth, Surrey furnished its quota under Captain Yaxley, of the 3000 men for the Netherlands expedition under Lord Essex. 1596, by S. P. Dom. its proportion of the 6000 men for relief of Calais besieged.

1596, by Stowe's Chronicle, the force of Surrey 1047 Launces, Lighthorse, and Footmen, formed part of the Camp at Tilbury under the Earl of Leicester to oppose an expected attack by the Spaniards. 1597 by S. P. Dom. Surrey furnished 150 men for the Force brought together for the coming of the Cardinal of Austria.

1598 by S. P. Dom. the County sent its quota of the 2000 men required for the Rebellion in Ireland. 1603, by S. P. Dom. "The Militia of Surrey was brought to London to guard the person of James I. at his coronation." 1642, took part in the Civil War, Surrey being at an early period a battle field between King Chas. I. and his rebels.

1666, by S. P. Dom. Chas. II. Surrey furnished a contingent of Officers and men for duty during the great fire of London, and a levy on its Militia for the Force which was assembled consequent on threatened French and Dutch invasion. 1780, the Gordon Riots in London, it being chronicled that the Surrey Militia "cleared with the bayonet the City and Bridges and rolling back the flood of Anarchy and Rebellion, saved the Metropolis of the Empire from Pillage and Fire."

In 1814 furnished one Officer (Capt. Whitby) and 30 men for the Militia Bde. which landed in France.

1901, volunteered for Foreign service and embarked for South Africa. Strength 23 Officers, 617 N.C.O.'s and men. Colonel Sir G. D. Clerk, Bart., Commdg.

On arrival at Port Elizabeth July 1, 1901, the Battn. proceeded to Colesberg as Head Quarters and occupied posts at several places in that district along the line of communication from Port Elizabeth to the Orange River Bridge at Norvals Pont, Colonel Inigo Jones, C.B., Brigadier, and in General Sir J. D. P. French's command. Dec. 29, 1901, Battn. proceeded to Naauwpoort thence to De Aar, and took over the Blockhouse line from Victoria West to Beaufort West, which was occupied and defended by the Battn. until Feb., 1902, when two Companies ("D" and "C") proceeded on trek to Clanwilliam and Williston to assist in the building and defence of the new Blockhouse line, "H" Compy. joining this party later. Mch. 9, 1902, seven Companies moved to Simonstown for guard over 1700 Boer prisoners. June 28, 1902, the Battn. concentrated at Green Point for embarkation for England.

Casualties.

Killed and died of disease, etc.
Major H. W. G. Crofton killed in action at Witspanfontein, Feb. 2, 1902.
2nd Lieut. H. Lyons died of wounds recd. in action at Klakfontein Nov. 28, 1901.
Sergt.-Major Robertson and 8 N.C.O.'s and men.

Mentioned in Despatches.

Major J. C. Worthington.
Capt. and Adjt. H. D. Lawrence.
Lt. and Qr.-Mr. W. Coleman.
Sergt.-Major J. G. Wisher.
Sergt. J. Boyden.

Medals, etc., received by Battalion.

Queen's Medal with Clasps "Cape Colony," "Orange Free State," "South Africa, 1901," "South Africa, 1902."

4th Battalion, The East Surrey Regiment.

"South Africa, 1902."

Hon. Colonel:—Daniell, J. le G., hon. c.

Lt.-Colonel:—Sulivan, E. F. (Maj. Res. of Off.) (H) (S).

Origin.

Raised as 3rd Royal Surrey Militia 1798, disbanded 1799, revived 1852, and became 4th Battn. of "The East Surrey Regt.," in the Territorial organization of 1881.

Embodiments.

South African War ... 1899, Dec. 4, to 1901, July 12.
South African War ... 1902, Feb. 24, to 1902, Sep. 25.

Services.

Volunteered for Foreign service and embarked for South Africa. Strength 21 Officers, 637 N.C.O.'s and men. Colonel E. F. Sulivan Commdg.

On arrival South Africa Ap. 10, 1902, half Battn. proceeded to the Sterkstroom District for Blockhouse duty, Head Quarters and remainder landed at Port Nolloth for service with the Namaqualand Field Force in relief of Ookiep, a forced march being made along with Company of Cape Volunteers to secure the safety of the important railway viaducts towards Klipfontein, the advance being through a district held by the enemy, who were gradually pushed back and Klipfontein reached April 20, 1902. The mounted troops having now come up, Colonel H. Cooper, C.M.G., commanding the column moved out on 28th to attack the Boer position at Steinkop. They were found to be strongly posted on high rugged kopjes and occupying a front of at least two and a half miles. The engagement began about 8 a.m. and lasted until 5 p.m., the total strength of regiment engaged being 380, and losses 4 killed, 4 wounded, 8 prisoners. The Boer numbers were estimated at 800 to 1,000, their known losses being 7 killed, 12 wounded.

The enemy withdrew on the following day, and on May 1st a portion of the force moved into Steinkop. May 13th, Colonel Cooper paraded the half-battalion and expressed his appreciation of the good work done by all ranks, and of its excellent behaviour in action.

May 13th, Head Quarters moved to Ookeip, the Boers having raised the siege of that place after the fight at Steinkop. May 31, Peace proclaimed. June 16, the Namaqualand Field Force was broken up and Head Quarters with half-battalion moved to Cape Town to guard prisoners at Green Point, afterwards proceeding to Simons Town for like purpose.

Casualties in South Africa.

Killed and died from disease, etc., 22 N.C.O.'s and men.

Medals, etc., received by Battalion.

Queen's South African Medal with Clasps "Cape Colony"' and "South Africa 1902."

3rd Battalion, The Duke of Cornwall's Light Infantry.

Hon. Colonel:—THE KING.
Lt.-Colonel:—Valletort, P. A. H., Visct. (Hon. Captn. in the Army).

Origin.

Raised 1759. A Royal Regiment in 1799. Royal Cornwall Light Infantry in 1810. Duke of Cornwall's Rangers (Rifles) in 1831. Royal resumed by W.O. authority June, 1874, and became, in 1881, the 3rd Battn. of the Territorial "Duke of Cornwall's Light Infantry."

Embodiments.

Occasion.

French War ... 1803 to 1814, Aug.
South African War ... 1899, Dec. 5, to 1900, Dec. 4.

Services.

One of the four Militia Regiments brought to London April, 1810, and located in Kentish Town for the suppression of apprehended riots in London and vicinity.

Volunteered for and stationed in Ireland 1811-13.

3rd Battalion, The Duke of Wellington's (West Riding Regiment).

"South Africa, 1900-02."

Hon. Colonel :—Wemyss, F. C., hon. c.
Lt.-Colonel :—Johnston, H. J., D.S.O. (H).

Origin.

Raised as the 6th Regiment of West York Militia in 1853 under Act 15, 16, Vict.

Formed into a double Battalion (of six companies each) in 1879, which became, under Territorial Organization of 1881, the 3rd and 4th Battns. of the Duke of Wellington's (West Riding Regiment).

In 1890 the two Battalions were amalgamated as the 3rd Battalion, two Companies being absorbed.

Embodiments.

   Occasion.

South African War ...   1900, Jan. 17, to 1902, May 10.

Services.

Volunteered for Foreign Service at the time of the South African War, and embarked for South Africa, strength 27 officers, one W.O., 487 N.C.O.'s and men, Colonel A. K. Wyllie commanding.

On arrival Table Bay, March 20, 1900, the Battn. proceeded to Worcester on the 23rd, and was there split up into several detachments—C Company, Major Bruce, going to Wellington, A Company reinforcing it soon afterwards; G and H, under Captain Goldie, to Tunnel Siding; I Company, Captain Mayor, to Touwns River; K Company, Captain Digby, to De Doornes, and on May 23rd a detachment under Captain Wayman moved from Wellington to Tulbagh Road. On July 2nd Head Quarters and all Companies on detachment were ordered to Simons Town, to take over the charge of prisoners of war, the numbers varying from 1,300 to 2,000, a detachment under Lieut. Greenwood proceeding to Wynberg. While the Battalion was on this duty at Simons Town the Boer prisoners gave much trouble by attempts to escape. The following remarks made by Lieut.-General Sir T. W. E. Forestier Walker, commanding lines of communication, upon the measures taken to frustrate an attempt July 12th, appeared in Orders.

"Colonel Wyllie acted with promptitude, and his resolute proceedings will have a good effect, his arrangements were good, and appear to have been well carried out."

Lord Roberts, when at Cape Town returning to England, communicated through the Base Commandant "that he had been pleased to receive such satisfactory reports of the Battalion."

Jan. 7, 1901—The prisoners of war having been all placed on transports, Head Quarters of the Battalion, with five companies, proceeded to Durban Road by march route, and two companies to Stellenbosch, H Company from Wynberg coming in on the 11th, two companies under Captain Wayman moving on the 14th to Malmsburg, where "F" became Mounted Infantry. Jan. 17th, 1901, Head Quarters with five companies were sent to Rondebosch, and on 22nd Head Quarters with three companies marched to Wynberg, another company on the same day under Major Johnston proceeding to Muizenburg, and two other companies under Major Bruce to the Prince of Wales Bastion, near Woodstock. After several other moves of companies in relief, etc., between this date and March 12th, Head Quarters with three Companies proceeded by march route to Green Point Camp, Table Bay, four companies, G, D, K, and B, rejoining Head Quarters from Durbanville, Muizenburg, Wellington and Paarl during the month.

The duties at Green Point were very heavy, upwards of 200 officers, N.C.O.'s and men being required almost daily for prisoners' war guard, inlying picquet, brigade fire picquet or garrison guard.

April 10, Head Quarters with five companies ordered to Beaufort West, D Company, Lieut. Davis, being dropped at Frazerburg Road, the two companies left at Green Point rejoining the Battalion on 25th. Major H. J. Johnston appointed Assistant Staff Officer, Western District.

Jan. 4, 1902, Major F. A. Haydon assumed command, vice-Colonel Wyllie invalided to Wynberg, and three officers with 150 N.C.O.'s and men ordered in haste to occupy the intermediate trenches between Three Sisters and Victoria Road, remaining there until Jan. 28th. Lieut. Thompson took over the duties of Adjutant on March the 8th.

April 13th, 1902, Head Quarters with six companies proceeded to Green Point for return to England, and embarked on the 21st at Cape Town, the remaining four companies from Frazerburg Village. etc., embarking about three weeks later.

Casualties.

Killed and died of disease, etc., 10 N.C.O.'s and men.

Mentioned in Despatches.

Lt. Colonel and Hon. Colonel A. K. Wyllie.
Major E. L. Cordes.
Major H. J. Johnston (twice).
Captain H. H. Wayman.
Lieut. A. C. Adams.
2nd. Lieut. C. C. Dangan.
Hon. Lieut. and Qr.-Mr. C. Hyde.
1065 Q.M.-Sergt. Yeoman.
Sergt.-Major L. Bellew.
4499 Sergt. F. Briggs.
240 Sergt. C. Bryne.
1717 Cr.-Sergt. J. Churchman.
647 Cr.-Sergt. Hobson.
3774 L.-Corp. P. Quinn.
6066 Pte. J. Kelly.
132 Pte. F. Coulon.

Special Honours.

Lt.-Colonel and Hon. Col. A. K. Wyllie, C.B.
Major F. A. Hayden, D.S.O.
Major H. J. Johnston, D.S.O.
Sergt.-Major L. Bellew, D.C. Medal.
Cr.-Sergt. J. Churchman, D.C. Medal.
Cr.-Sergt. W. B. Hobson, D.C. Medal.

Medals, etc., received by Battalion.

Queen's South Africa Medal with Clasp "Cape Colony."
King's South Africa Medal with Clasps "South Africa 1901," "South Africa 1902."

3rd Battalion, The Border Regiment.

Hon. Colonel :—Lonsdale, H. C., Earl of.
Lt.-Colonel :—Le Fleming, G. F. A. H.

Origin.

In 1881, under Territorial Organization, the Royal Cumberland Regt. became the 3rd Battn. of The Border Regiment.

By "State Papers Foreign and Domestic of the Reign Henry VIII.," the Counties of Cumberland and Westmoreland were united in the Certificate of Muster ordered 30, Henry VIII., 1539, of armed men throughout England and Wales, but the return is incomplete for these two shires. (See copy of certificate.)

In 1641, Feb. 12, Lord Gray of Wark was appointed as a "person fit to be entrusted" with the Organization of the Militia of Cumberland. By Militia Returns 1697, Egerton MSS., the Counties of Cumberland and Westmoreland united had one Regiment of Foot in seven Companies, 537 men, with one Troop of horse 70, Coll. Sir George Fletcher, Bart., and Sir Daniel Fleming, Kt., Lt. Coll.

In 1760, under Act. 30, Geo. II., a Regiment was organized for Cumberland, and the quota of men to be found by the County.

Note.—The records from this date were destroyed in the fire at Carlisle Castle in 1890.

Embodiments.

   Occasion.

(See Note above.)

South African War ... 1899, Dec. 18, to 1900, Nov. 1.

Services.

1666, by "State Papers Domestic, Chas. II.," the Militia of the County was drawn out by the King, for the threatened French and Dutch Invasion.

By an ancient history of Cumberland, "the Militia of Cumberland and Westmoreland were called out in 1715 by the Earl of Lonsdale and Bishop Nicholson, to quell the insurrection of Lord Derwentwater and Foster."

In 1745, "consequent upon the rising in the Highlands under Prince Charles Stewart, and his near approach to Carlisle, the Militia, Col. Sir John Pennington, Bart., were called up at Penrith, one Cumberland and one Westmoreland Company being sent to assist in the defence of Carlisle Castle, the rest were posted at Whitehaven, Cockermouth, Workington, Penrith, Appleby and Kendal. On Oct. 6th Colonel Durand arrived to take command of the garrison at Carlisle, which consisted of about eighty men who were old, infirm, or invalids, besides two companies of Militia about one hundred and fifty men, and one troop of Militia horse about seventy men.

On Saturday, Nov. 9th, the rebels arrived before the Castle, which after six days' and six nights' defence in expectation of relief, surrendered to Prince Charles."

By Marchant's History of the Rebellion, a number of the prisoners after the battle of Clifton Moor, near Penrith, were escorted "to York under a strong guard of Gentlemen and Westmoreland Militia."

(Records between 1760-1890 destroyed, see previous note.)

4th Battalion, The Border Regiment.

Hon. Colonel:—Salkeld, L. C.
Lt.-Colonel:—p.s. Anderson, W. C., D.S.O., Capt. ret. pay. (Hon. Lt.-Col. in Army, 9 Oct. 1902).

Origin.

In 1881, the Royal Westmoreland Light Infantry Militia Regt. became the 4th Battn. of "The Border Regt." under Territorial Organization of the Forces.

In 1539 and 1697, Cumberland and Westmoreland were united for military purposes, (see origin, 3rd Battn, The Border Regt.).

Feb. 12, 1641, The Earl of Cumberland was appointed as the "fit person to be entrusted" with the organization of the Militia in Westmoreland, there being another appointment for Cumberland. When the Militia of Counties was re-organized under Act 30, Geo. II., a Regiment was completed for service, and the quota of men to be found by Westmoreland in 1759, which became a Royal Regiment and Light Infantry until the changes in 1881.

Embodiments.
   Occasion.

Note.—Records destroyed in the fire at Carlisle Castle, 1890.
South African War ... 1900, May 4, to 1901, July 16.
For Services, 1715-1745, see 3rd Battn. Border Regt.

Services.

In 1810 the Westmoreland Regt. was brought to London owing to apprehended disturbances and located at Hackney.

In 1814 volunteered for Foreign Service, eight officers (Captains Bell, Richardson, Yeates, Lieuts. Watson, Wilbraham, Richardson, Ensigns Mawbey and Moses) and 300 N.C.O.'S and men forming part of the 3rd Provisional Battn., Lt.-Colonel Sir Watkin Williams Wynne, Bt., of the Militia Brigade, which embarked for France under Col. the Marquis of Buckingham and landed to serve under the Duke of Wellington.

3rd Battalion, The Royal Sussex Regiment.

"South Africa, 1901-02."

Hon. Colonel :—

Lt.-Colonel Commandant : Richmond and Gordon, C. H., Duke of, G.C.V.O., C.B., Col., A.D.C.

Origin.

For details of the Force of the County, April 8, 1539, 30, Henry VIII., see copy of State Papers Domestic of this reign.

1588, April, see copy of Harleian MSS.

1641, Feb. 12, The Earl of Northumberland was appointed as a "person fit to be entrusted" with the organization of the Militia of Sussex.

1697.—By Militia Returns, Egerton MSS., Sussex had for the Eastern and Western parts, two Regiments of 19 Companies, and one independent Company for Chichester, total 1,733 foot, with two Troops of horse 105. Colonels Sir W. Thomas and Sir John Fagg, Bart.

In June, 1778, a Regiment was completed for service, and the quota of men to be furnished by the County, under Colonel the Duke of Richmond, K.G., at later date becoming a Royal Regiment, and subsequently Light Infantry. In 1881, under Territorial Organization of the Forces it became the 3rd Battalion of The Royal Sussex Regiment.

Embodiments.

Occasion.

American War	...	1778, June 6, to 1783, March.
French War, etc.	...	1792, Mar. 11, to 1802, Apr.
,, ,,	...	1803, May 5, to 1816, Jan.
Crimean War	...	1854, Dec., to 1856, June.
Indian Mutiny	...	1857, Nov. 12, to 1861, Feb.
South African War	...	1899, Dec. 11, to 1902, Sep. 11.

Services.

In 56 B.C. the Tribal Forces of Sussex with Surrey and coast parts of Hampshire, opposed Cæsar's second invasion.

In April, 1588, the County assembled its Force to resist the Spanish Armada, 2004 "trayned and furneshed men reduced into bandes under Captaines," besides horsemen Launces 200, Light horse 204, Petronels 30.

In 1591 (S.P. Dom.) Sussex sent 2 Companies, 300 men, under Captains St. John and Poer for the Netherlands expedition of Lord Essex. In 1596, by letter from Queen Elizabeth to the Earl of Essex, the County was one of the five with the City of London to send its quota cf the 6,000 men required to join the forces of the French King for succouring the besieged citadel of Calais. In 1814 the Sussex Militia Regiment contributed 3 officers (Captain Evans, Lieut. Rogers, Ensign Dimond) and 100 men to the 2nd Provisional Battn. (commanded by Colonel Ed. Bayly, Middlesex Regt.) of the Militia Brigade under the Duke of Buckingham, which landed near Bordeaux to serve under the Duke of Wellington. March, 1901, volunteered for Foreign Service and proceeded to South Africa. Strength embarked (the Militia reservists of Battn. having been previously withdrawn) 23 officers, one W.O., 476 N.C.O.'s and men, Colonel The Earl of March commanding. On arrival at the seat of war, the Battalion was employed in guarding lines of communication, outposts, and guards to Boer prisoners, the Mounted Infantry party formed of 5 officers and 225 N.C.O.'s and men, being employed on patrol duties, escorts to convoys, etc. The Regiment took part in the driving operations around Volkrust and Ingogo districts.

Casualties.

Killed and died from disease, etc., 24 N.C.O.'s and men.

Honours.

Colonel the Earl of March, C.B.
Sergt.-Major C. Amos, D.C. Medal.

Medals, etc., received by Battalion.

Queen's South African Medal with Clasps "Cape Colony," "Orange Free State," "Transvaal," and "South Africa 1901," "South Africa 1902."

3rd Battalion, The Hampshire Regiment.

Hon. Colonel :—p.s. Selborne, Rt. Hon. W.W., Eearl of G.C.M.G., hon. c. (T) (Hon. Lt.-Col. in Army, 5 Dec., 1900).
Lt.-Colonel :—Nicholson, W. W., hon. c.

Origin.

According to Lloyd-Verney's History, in 1377 the "Trained bands" of the County of Southampton were assembled by Lord Arundel.

At the assembly of the "Milecia" in 1588 to resist the Spanish Armada invasion, Hants was represented by 806 trained foot men, and other able men who were "ffurnished."

In 1641 The Earl of Pembroke was appointed "as a fit person to be entrusted" with the organization of the Militia of the County of "Hamps."

In 1666, by State Papers Dom., Chas. II., the Militia of Hampshire was drawn out for the threatened French and Dutch invasion. By Militia Returns (Egerton MSS.) 1697, the Militia of the County of Southampton comprised 34 Companies, 2,459 foot, in six Regiments, with two Troops of horse 120, besides Southampton independent Company 200, and Winchester 150, Colonels, Duke of Bolton, Marqs. of Winchester, Henry Compton, George Rodney Bridges, Henry Dawley, and Winchester Capt. Ld. Wm. Paulet, Southampton Capt. John Smith, Esqr.

The earliest record of the Isle of Wight Forces is met with in 1341, when nine troops of Militia, 100 men each, were organized and a series of quaint regulations issued for defence of the Island. In 1560 all able bodied men were enrolled in the Militia of the Island, and mustered twice a year for training, it being recorded that the cannon for each Parish were kept in the churches. In 1625, May 12, by Sir John Oglander's MS. "Noate of Strength" the Force was composed of twelve bands 2,020 men, which were "new-modelled" into sixteen companies, and in 1628 referred to as two Divisions under the two Lieutenants of the Island. In 1697 the Force formed sixteen companies of 1482 men in two Regiments, with 174 "sparemen," besides Cowes independent Company of 96 men.

In 1757 the quota of men to be found by the County of Southampton and including the Isle of Wight completed two Regiments of foot as the North and South Hants Militia, there being a Cowes Company dealt with independently for some years.

In 1811 the South Regiment became Light Infantry.

In 1852 the two Regiments were amalgamated as the Hampshire Regt. of Militia, three officers and 396 men of the South Regiment and one officer of the North Regiment being transferred in the formation of the Hampshire Regiment of Artillery Militia.

In 1881, under the Territorial Organization of the Forces, the Hampshire Regiment of Militia (Infantry) became the 3rd Battn. of "The Hampshire Regiment."

Embodiments.

Occasion.

	I. of Wight.	N. Hants.	S. Hants.
French Invasion ...	1341		
French Invasion ...	1377		
French Invasion ...	1545		
Spanish Armada ...	1588	1588 as one Corps.	
Civil War ...	1642	1642 as one Corps.	
Threatened Invasion	1651		
Seven Years War ...		1759 to 1762	1760 to 1762
American War ...		1778 to 1783	1778 to 1783
Revolutionary War, etc.		1792 to 1802	1792 to 1802
French War ...		1803 to 1814	1803 to 1816
French War ...		1815 to 1816	1815 to 1816

AS THE HAMPSHIRE REGIMENT OF MILITIA.

Crimean War ... ... 1854, May, to 1856, June.
South African War ... 1900, Jan., to 1900, Dec.

Services.

In 56 B.C. the Tribal Forces of the coast parts of Hampshire forming part of what Ptolemy called the "Regni" tribe are referred to by Davis as being actively engaged in opposing Cæsar's invasion of Britain.

In 1377, according to Lloyd-Verney's History, the Constitutional Force of the County of Southampton under Lord Arundel forced the French to evacuate Southampton, and in 1415 proceeded to France with King Henry V., taking part in the battle of Agincourt.

In 1588 (Harleian MSS.) it formed part of the Force assembled by Queen Elizabeth to resist invasion by the Spanish Armada.

In 1642, when "blockading" Portoridge for Parliament, it defeated an attack by Cavaliers and others of the King's party, of whom fifteen were killed and nine mortally wounded. The Country Force was for some time entrenched at Orams Arbour adjoining the Old Training Ground at Winchester and engaged in the defence of the Castle.

By S.P. Dom. Chas. II., 1666, the Militia of Hampshire drawn out by the King for threatened French and Dutch Invasion.

North Hants.—The Gordon Riots in London 1780, and encamped near the Marble Arch, afterwards at Blackheath.

Volunteered for and stationed in Ireland 1811-13.

South Hants.—Gordon Riots, 1780.

Luddite Riots in Yorkshire, June, 1812.

Isle of Wight Forces.—Defence of Carisbrooke Castle against the French in 1377. Invasion of the French 1545, on both occasions being engaged and many slain. The Spanish Armada Assembly 1588. The attack on Carisbrooke Castle, 1642, against the King's Forces. Watch of the Island, 1651, etc.

3rd Battalion, The South Staffordshire Regiment.

"Mediterranean."
"South Africa, 1901-02."

Hon. Colonel:—Broun, M. A. W., hon. c. (Hon. Lt.-Col. in Army).

Lt.-Colonel:—p.s. Pearse, E. V. D. (t) (H) (b).

Origin.

1539, see Muster of armed men of the County, 27 Apr., 30 Henry VIII. (Letters and Papers of the Reign of Henry VIII.), arranged by Gardiner.

In 1588, by Harleian MSS., Staffordshire furnished 400 able trayned men reduced into bandes under Captaines at the great assembly of Forces to resist attack by the Spanish Armada, besides Horsemen Launces 28, Light Horse 50, Petroneles 26.

In 1641, Feb. 12th, the Earl of Essex was appointed as "a fit person to be entrusted" with the organizing of the Militia of the County.

In 1648, by Regimental Records, a County Regt. of Stafford Militia existed, which consisted of Foot and two Troops of Horse under the command of Colonel John Bowyer of Knypersley.

By Militia Returns 1697, Egerton MSS., the County had one Regt. of five Companies 500 foot and two Troops 120 horse, total of both 620, with the footnote—

"They know of none but what are either Finders, Maintainers or Contributers to Horse or Foot."

In 1776, during the War between Great Britain and her American dependencies, a Regt. was completed for service and the quota of men to be provided by the County.

According to R.O. June 30, 1797, Negroes were employed in the Band for beating the cymbals and triangles. The big drummer being also a negro "Musick in jackets, the Blacks in their best turbans."

In 1805, by command of His Majesty King George III., the Staffordshire Militia became "The King's Own Staffordshire Militia."

In 1874 the Regt. was divided into two Battalions under a Colonel Commandant, and in 1881 under the Territorial organization of the Forces, the two Battalions became respectively the 3rd and 4th Battns. of "The South Staffordshire Regiment."

Embodiments.

 Occasion.

Civil War, Charles I....	Period unknown.
American War... ...	1776 to 1783.
Revolutionary War, etc.	1793 to 1801, Apr. 26.
French War and European Disturbances ...	1803, Mch. 30, to 1814. 1815, to 1816, Apr.
Crimean War	1854, May, to 1856, Oct.
Indian Mutiny... ...	1857, Nov. 3, to 1860, Nov. 30.
South African War ...	1900, May 3, to 1900, Dec. 4.
South African War ...	1901, May 6, to 1902, July 19.

Services.

In 1648, the Regiment composed of both horse and foot formed the garrison of Leek.

According to the "History of the House of Stuart" the Regt. was employed in the seizure of Major-General Harrison. "Colonel Bowyer, without any order, took a party of the Staffordshire Militia, and by his own authority seized Major-General Harrison with his horses and arms.

"The Major-General had notice that Bowyer would do so if he did not fly from it, which he absolutely refused, looking upon it as flying from the Cause, tho' in truth the Cause fled from him. But there was as much enthusiasm in his political as in his religious principles."

In 1797, by special command of H.M. King Geo. III., the Regt. took over the Royal duties at Windsor, and again in 1800, His Majesty receiving the Regt. also on its arrival at Weymouth in 1801, and accompanied it for about two miles on departure. When re-embodied in 1803 the Regt. resumed its duties at Windsor, and moved to Weymouth in 1804, returning to Windsor in the Autumn.

In 1813 the Regt. was sent from Colchester to London with 60 rounds of ball ammunition to relieve the Foot Guards at St. James's and Kew Palaces.

During the Crimean War embodiment 1854 to 1856, the Regt. gave 1200 men to the Line.

In 1855 it volunteered for Foreign service, and embarked for Corfu with detachment at Ithaca, and subsequently proceeded to Argostoli in Cephalonia with detachments at Luxuri and Fort George. While at these Stations it suffered severely from the fever of the country, and there were many deaths; when at Argostoli in 1856 no less than one third of the Regt. was in hospital at one time.

Volunteered for Foreign service during the South African War, and embarked for the Seat of War 20 Officers, 561 other ranks, Colonel M. A. Swinfen-Broun, commdg.

On arrival at Cape Town July 10, 1901, the Battn. was at first placed in charge of Boer prisoners at Simons Town with two Companies on detachment at Stellenbosch and Lowrey's Pass. In Sepr. Head Quarters moved for a short time to Stellenbosch.

At the end of Decr. the Battn. took over a new line of Blockhouses extending over one hundred miles from the coast at Lambats Bay via Calvinia to Victoria West, with Head Quarters at Clanwilliam, Cape Colony.

Re-embarked for England July 2, 1902.

Casualties.

Killed and died of disease, etc., 27 N.C.O.'s and men.

Mentioned in Despatches.

Colonel M. A. Swinfen-Broun.
Captain and Adjt. C. S. Davidson.
Sergt.-Major A. Cooper.
Pte. C. Bell.

Special Honours.

Captain and Adjt. C. S. Davidson, Brevet Majority.
Sergt.-Major A. Cooper, D.C. Medal.
Pte. C. Bell, Promoted Corporal for gallant conduct in the field.
2nd Lieut. A. de Trafford, attached to 1st Battn. South Staffordshire Regt., D.S.O.

Medals, etc., received by Battalion.

Queen's South African Medal with Clasps "Cape Colony," "South Africa, 1901," "South Africa, 1902."

4th Battalion, The South Staffordshire Regiment.

"Mediterranean."
"South Africa, 1900-01."

Hon. Colonel :—Aylesford, C. W., Earl of.
Lt.-Colonel :—Charrington, F., C.M.G., hon. c.

Origin.

See 3rd Battn. of the Regt. for origin, embodiments and services prior to 1874, the two Battns. forming one Regt. until that year, and in 1881 became under the Territorial Regimental organization the 3rd and 4th Battns. of "The South Staffordshire Regt."

Embodiments since 1874.
   Occasion.

South African War ... 1899, Dec. 5, to 1901, Aug. 12.

Services since 1874.

Volunteered for Foreign service during South African War, and embarked for the Seat of War, Strength 22 Officers, 615 N.C.O.'s and men, Colonel F. Charrington, commanding. On arrival at Cape Town Mch. 8, 1900, the Battn. proceeded to Kimberley and Modder River, joining the 20th Bde. under General A. Paget in April, and took part in forcing the passage of the Vaal River in May at Fourteen Streams. Proceeded with the 1st Division from Boshof to Kroonstad and Lindley; remained in Lindley with the 20th Bde. till July, 1900; engaged in the attack 26th June; attack and capture of Bethlehem 6th and 7th July; attack on de Wet's rearguard near Stabbarts Nek on 16th July; escort of 2500 Boer prisoners who were captured with Prinsloo, to Winburg, and then to Cape Town, without the loss of one of them. Returned to Winburg for garrison duty Aug., 1900; attack on Winburg Aug. 26th, and operations in that District between Aug., 1900, and July, 1901. Then held the Blockhouse line along Smaldeel-Winburg Railway.

Copy of Letter from General Lord Methuen (Commdg. 1st Division) to Colonel Charrington—

"I knew from the manoeuvres at Aldershot how well your men would march, and they did not belie their reputation. In discipline and in conduct on the 'trek' from Boshof to Lindley you had a fine opportunity of showing what you were all made of, and I felt perfect confidence in your men and Officers alike. I always say 'show me the Officers and I will tell you the value of the Battn.' This remark applies in a favourable degree to your Battn."

Copy of Letter from General Arthur Paget Commdg. 20th Brigade to Colonel Charrington—

"It will always be a source of regret to me that I was not able to say a few parting words to you, your Officers, N.C.O.'s and men on the field for the gallant way in which they supported me during a very trying period of the Campaign. I hope you will place on record my hearty appreciation of the gallant service rendered to 20th Bde. by the 4th South Staffordshire, notably at Lindley, and the subsequent operations at Bethlehem, ending in the capture of 4000 of the enemy, of which your Battn. escorted 2500 to Winburg, and I believe subsequently to Cape Town without the loss of one prisoner; my best thanks are due to you for the cordial support you invariably gave me; and the excellent example set your men by the Officers and N.C.O.'s no doubt contributed largely to the efficiency, good behaviour and excellent marching of your Battalion whilst with me in South Africa."

Casualties.

Killed and died of disease, etc., 41 N.C.O.'s and men.

Mentioned in Despatches.

Colonel F. Charrington.
Major B. T. Seckham.
Captain and Adjt. E. A. Bulmer (twice).
Captain Stewart.
Lieut. and Qr.-Mr. J. Penketh (twice).
Sergt.-Major Brown.
Qr.-Mr.-Sergt. Payne.
Sergt. Medlicott.
Sergt. Beddowes.
Cr.-Sergt. Hickey.
Sgt.-Insr. Musky. Craddock.
Sergt. Bates.
Lce.-Sergt. Mannison.
Private Donovan.

Special Honours.

Colonel F. Charrington, C.M.G.
Major Seckham, D.S.O.
Sergt.-Major Brown, D.C. Medal.
Cr.-Sergt. Payne, D.C. Medal.
Sergt.-Insr. Musky. Craddock, D.C. Medal.

Medals and Clasps Received by Battalion.

Queen's South African Medal with Clasps "Cape Colony," "Wittebergen," and "South Africa, 1901."

3rd Battalion, The Dorsetshire Regiment.

Hon. Colonel:—Digby, E. H. T., Lord Col.
Lt.-Colonel:—Batten, H. C. G., hon. c.

Origin.

In 1539, the County of Dorset was represented at the great Muster held by virtue of Royal Commission issued 30 Henry VIII. (see copy of certificate dated 10 and 11 Apr. "Letters and Papers of the Reign of Henry VIII.").

By Harleian MSS., Spanish Armada Assembly 1588, Dorsetshire mustered 1500 "trayned men reduced into bandes under Captaines," and Horsemen 120 Launces, 90 Lighthorse, 40 Petroneles.

In 1641, Feb. 12, the Earl of Salisbury was appointed as a "person fit to be entrusted" with the organization of the Militia of Dorset and Co. of the Town of Poole.

In 1759, under Act 30, Geo. II., for reorganizing the Militia of the kingdom, a Regt. was completed for service, and the quota of men to be found by the County, as the Dorsetshire Regt. of Militia, which in 1881 became the 3rd Battn. of the Territorial Dorsetshire Regt.

Embodiments.

Occasion.

Seven Years War	1759, June, to 1763.
American War	1778, Apr. 20, to 1783.
Revolutionary War, etc.	1792, Dec. 17, to 1802, Apr. 24.
French War	1803, Mch. 28, to 1815, Feb. 4.
Crimean War	1854, Dec. 7, to 1856, June.
South African War	1899, Dec. 14, to 1901, July 13.

Services.

Volunteered for and served in Ireland 1798. It is recorded, that a Picquet of the Regt. having succeeded in tracing to a wood near Carrick two notorious murderers, Welsh and Aldridge, who had taken an active part in the rebellion, and for whom a reward was offered, the Picquet supported by the Light Company and some Carrick volunteers, followed them up, and failing capture alive, they were shot, the Dorset Company receiving the reward of £100 in Irish currency.

Volunteered for and stationed in Ireland 1813-14.

3rd Battalion, The Prince of Wales's Volunteers.
(South Lancashire Regiment.)

"South Africa, 1900-01."

Hon. Colonel:—Blackburne, R. I., C.B., hon. c. (Hon. Lt.-Col. in Army, 4 Aug. 1901).

Lt.-Colonel:—Hall, M. H., D.S.O. (T).

Origin.

Raised 1853 under Act 15 and 16 Vict., c. 50, as the 4th Duke of Lancaster's Own Light Infantry Regt. of Royal Lancashire Militia, and became in 1881 under Territorial organization the 3rd Battn. The Prince of Wales's Volunteers (South Lancashire Regiment).

Embodiments.

Occasion.

Crimean War ...	1854, Dec. 8, to 1856, June 24.
Indian Mutiny...	1857, Sep. 22, to 1859, Apr. 1.
South African War	1899, Dec. 13, to 1901, Aug. 3.

Services.

Volunteered for Foreign service and embarked for South Africa Jan. 16, 1900. Strength 24 Officers, 763 N.C.O.'s and men, Colonel R. I. Blackburne, Commdg.

Arrived at Cape Town Feb. 13, 1900, Head Quarters and the left half Battn. proceeded to Naauwpoort, the right half following on the next day was stopped at Hanover Road Feb. 17th to meet an expected attack of the enemy, the Head Quarters and remainder returning to support them the object of the G.O.C. being to prevent the Boers from getting round the left flank of his operations and cutting the Railway between De Aar and Naauwpoort, the effect of which would have disturbed the line of communication between Cape Town and Lord Roberts, who was then on his way to Paardeburg.

Major Tarbet with A.D.C. Companies were posted at the Diamond Mine kopje to check any advance from the East. On Feb. 18th, the Force at Hanover Road stood to arms at daybreak, the enemy 1500 strong with six guns being reported near, and being reinforced by 50 engineers and 100 mounted troops during the day, entrenchments were formed for defence of the place and Bridge over the river.

Feb. 21, the Victorian and Tasmanian Mounted Rifles were sent out in the direction of Arundel in view of effecting a junction with General Clements' Cavalry, the Battn. being ordered to cover their retreat if necessary.

Mch. 4, the Boers having retired from Arundel to the North of Colesberg, Head Quarters with left half Battn. moved to Rensburg, and the right half to Arundel. From this time the two half Battns. operated separately.

Mch. 20, Head Quarters and left half Battn. advanced to Colesberg Junction, and the right half to Colesberg.

Apr. 21, the two half Battns. joined hands again at Norvals Pont for 36 hours, when the right half was sent to the north bank of the river, the Head Quarters and left half remaining on the South side and furnished strong outposts for defence of the kopjes near the Orange River, the work being heavy owing to the many fatigue parties also required daily to assist the Railway Pioneer Regt. in repairing the Railway Bridge, three spans of which had been destroyed by the Boers on the 6th of March. Apr. 25, Col. Blackburne was invalided, the command devolving upon Major Hall until the return of Col. Blackburne to the Battn., Nov. 23.

May 27, Head Quarters moved to the North side of the River, Major Tarbet taking command on South Bank. At this time "Lancashire Fort" and other defences had been formed on the North bank. Aug. 1, part of the Battn. proceeded to Springfontein, Head Quarters and remainder following. Oct. 5, there were indications of the Boers moving South. Oct. 6, all Huts on the Railway North and South were ordered to be protected by small parties at night. Oct. 9, a mounted patrol was fired on, and at night the trenches on West side were subjected to firing, and next day a section of the 87th Battery, R.A., with some Mounted Infantry, and 100 men of the Battn. under Major Tarbet with Captain Vaughan and Lieut. Clarkson were taken out by Col. Wortham, Commandant of Springfontein, in a N.E. direction to Pretorius' Farm about nine miles off, which was destroyed.

From this time the Head Quarters of the Battn. remained at Springfontein until July, 1901, the place being frequently threatened by the enemy. Oct. 13, the M.I. at Jagersfontein Road sent two patrols to search the district and meet at a farm house known to be frequented by Boers, one patrol was ambushed by the enemy with a loss of one man killed, and one Officer and man captured, while the other patrol escaped with the loss of its Officer, Lieut. E. M. Hanbury, killed. On the death of this Officer, Lieut. A. H. Spooner succeeded to the command at Jagersfontein Road, and was called upon by Commandant Pretorius to surrender, but instead of any reply being given reinforcements were obtained under

Major A. F. Tarbet, who remained in command of the post.

One half of the M.I. Company of the Battn. took part in the defence of Fauresmith and Jagersfontein, with reference to which the G.O.C. of the District issued the following Order: "Lieut.-General Kelly-Kenny is pleased to place upon record the successful defence of Fauresmith and Jagersfontein, which determined in such a satisfactory manner, and reflect the greatest credit on all those concerned."

During Oct. there were nightly attacks to destroy the railway line, repairs being carried out under covering parties of the Battn. Between Oct. 13 and Nov. 6, the trenches were nightly occupied; on the 25th Oct. there was some firing and an attempt to approach the Knilfontein Bridge, which was defeated after a short struggle, Sergt. Chapman of the 1st Battn. being mortally wounded. Nov. 11, "D" Company under Lieut. Clarkson at Krugers Siding was called upon by letter from Commandant Scheeper to surrender, and the post subjected to warm attention until the enemy were driven off with the help of two Companies of the 3rd Grenadier Guards and an armoured train. Dec. 12, Major Hall was appointed Press Censor, and soon afterwards, for five months, Commandant at Springfontein during the absence of Colonel Wortham on sick leave. Feb. 6, 1901, an outpost of the Battn. captured Barend Enslin, a noted scout of De Wet's Force which crossed the railway line between Springfontein and Jagersfontein Road that night. Feb. 9, the M.I. of the Battn. from Jagersfontein, and an armoured train, engaged the enemy who were attempting to cross the line some six miles North of Springfontein, killing three of the Boers. At this time the Blockhouse system was introduced on the section of about forty-five miles held by the 3rd S. L. Battn., no post being ever captured by the enemy.

Embarked at Cape Town for England, July 3, 1901.

Casualties.

Killed and died of disease, etc., 3 Officers (Capt. and Hon. Major E. K. Heath, Lieut. E. M. Hanbury, Lieut. C. H. Parker), and 31 N.C.O.'s and men.

Mentioned in Despatches.

Colonel R. I. Blackburne.
Major M. H. Hall (twice).
Major A. F. Tarbet.
Captain R. A. Greg.
Lieut. H. G. Clarkson.

Qr.-Mr. and Hon. Lieut. J. Morrell.
Sergt.-Major J. A. Altmann.
Qr.-Mr.-Sergt. S. T. Boast.
Sergt.-I. of M. J. H. Kirk.
Sergt. H. Lynes.
Sergt. J. Matthews.
Sergt. J. J. Richardson.
Lce.-Sergt. Sunners.
Lce.-Sergt. Holden.
Lce.-Sergt. Noonan.

Special Honours.

Colonel R. I. Blackburne, C.B.
Major M. H. Hall, D.S.O.
Major A. F. Tarbet, D.S.O.
Sergt.-Major J. A. Altmann, D.C. Medal.
Qr.-Mr.-Sergt. S. T. Boast, D.C. Medal

Medals, etc., received by Battalion.

Queen's South African Medal with Clasps "Cape Colony," "Orange Free State," and "South Africa, 1901."

3rd Battalion, The Welsh Regiment.

"South Africa, 1900-02."

Hon. Colonel:—Windsor, Rt. Hon. R. G., Lord, C.B. Kt. of Grace Order of St. John of Jerusalem.

Lt.-Colonel:—p.s. Watts, W., C.B. (Capt. Res. of Off.). (H) (Q) (S) (a) (b) Kt. of Grace Order of St. John of Jerusalem.

Origin.

Formerly the Royal Glamorganshire Light Infantry. At a muster throughout the kingdom in 1539, under Royal Commission 30 Henry VIII., the certificates record 1000 able men in Glamorganshire besides 29 harnessed, and seven horsemen.

In the list of Persons nominated by the House of Commons Feb. 12, 1641, to His Majesty as being "fit to be entrusted" with the Militia, Lord Philip Herbert appears for Glamorganshire.

In 1684 "The Militia of Glamorganshire maketh one Regiment of foot and one Troop of horse" when inspected by His Grace Henry the First Duke of Beaufort in his progress through Wales.

By Militia Returns 1697, the Glamorganshire Regiment was composed of 9 Companies 483 foot with one Troop horse 40, Sir Edward Mansell, Bart., Colonel.

In 1761 under the order issued to Lords Lieutenant of the several Counties to complete and train their Militia the Glamorganshire Regiment was prepared for service, the Rt. Hon. Lord Talbot being Colonel. At later dates it became a Royal Regiment and Light Infantry, and in 1881 the 3rd Battn. of the Territorial Welsh Regiment.

Embodiments.

   Occasion.

Revolutionary War, etc.	1793 to 1814, June 25, for periods almost continuous.
,, ,,	1815, July 16, to 1816, May 17.
Crimean War ...	1855, Jan. 4, to 1856, May 27.
South African War ...	1899, Dec. 4, to 1902, Mch. 8.

Services.

Volunteered for service in Ireland and stationed there in 1799.

Volunteered for Foreign service and embarked for South Africa Feb. 12, 1900. Strength 31 Officers, 580 N.C.O.'s and men (186 Militia Reservists of the Battn. having been previously withdrawn for Line service in South Africa). Lt.-Colonel A. T. Perkins Commanding. On arrival Mch. 1, 1900, the Battalion proceeded to De Aar, and on Mch. 15th formed part of the Flying Column under General Lord Kitchener which was operating between De Aar and Prieska, the Rebels evading the Column by crossing the Orange River. Apr. 3, 1900, Convoy duty to Prieska, twelve Officers and 240 rank and file under Colonel Perkins. Apr. 20, 1900, Reconnaissance in force composed of Prieska mounted troops, 2 guns 44th R.F.A., and 3rd Welsh Regt., across the Orange River. Battle of Kies near Kenhardt, Aug. 16, 1900, Battn. moved to Vryburg. Nov. 22, 1900, Convoy duty, two Officers and 200 rank and file under Colonel Milne, D.S.O., to Schweitzer Reneke, repulsing a determined attack made on the Convoy at Du Toits Kopje; several casualties in the Mounted Troops; also another heavy attack by 500 Boers on the return to Vryburg. Jan. 2, 1901,

Convoy duty, four Officers, 200 rank and file under Colonel Perkins to Kuruman, returning via Swatfontein, distance about 280 miles. Apr. 13, 1901, Convoy duty at Kuruman, four Officers, 150 rank and file leaving Lieut. Linton and 40 rank and file to strengthen the Garrison. Convoy duty to Kuruman Colonel Perkins, six Officers, 200 rank and file; while passing a house flying a "White Flag" the Convoy was fired on; the house burnt and three Boers captured (two brothers named Poetgeter and one Botha) who were subsequently tried at Vryburg. Sep. 28, 1901, the Battn. Head Quarters moved by march route to Kimberley for duty in the Blockhouses south of that Station, and Column duty under Lord Methuen. The Battn. entrained for Cape Town Feb. 8, 1902, en route for England.

Copy of Order issued by Lieut.-General Lord Methuen Commanding 1st Division Western Transvaal—

"Vryburg, 15. 2. 1902.

"The G.O.C. Western Transvaal wishes to record his appreciation of the work performed by the 3d Welsh Regt. during the time the Head Quarters of that Battn. served at Vryburg. The Town was in the centre of a rebellious district and the Battn. had to find the escort of two large Convoys to Kuruman 80 miles distant, a duty which was carried out successfully on both occasions. No doubt the safety of Vryburg was secured to a great extent by the careful manner in which the duty was carried out by this Battalion.

By Order—sd. C. B. Vyvyan, Lt.-Col., A.A.G.,
C.S.O., W.D.,
South Africa."

Casualties.

Killed and died of disease, etc., Captain H. W. Masterman, Sergt.-Major Murphy, and 33 N.C.O.'s and men.

Mentioned in Despatches.

Lt.-Colonel A. T. Perkins.
Major and Hon. Lt.-Col. W. Watts.
Major W. Forrest.
Captain and Adjt. R. W. Taylor.
Captain A. T. Perkins.
Sergt.-Major A. J. Bryant.
Cr.-Sergt. R. Foster.
Cr.-Sergt. J. Fidler.

Special Honours.

Major and Hon. Lt.-Col. W. Watts, C.B.
Major W. Forrest, D.S.O.
Captain and Hon. Major A. T. Perkins, D.S.O.
Sergt.-Major A. J. Bryant, D.C. Medal.
Cr.-Sergt. R. Foster, D.C. Medal.
Cr.-Sergt. J. Fidler, D.C. Medal.

Medals and Clasps Received by Battalion.

Queen's Medal, "Cape Colony," "Orange Free State," "Transvaal" and date Clasps. King's Medal and two date Clasps.

3rd Battalion, The Black Watch (Royal Highlanders).

Hon. Colonel:—Atholl, J. J. H., Duke of, K.T.
Lt.-Colonel:—p.s. Rollo, Hon. W. C. W. (Master of Rollo), hon. c.

Origin.

The County Force was completed for service during the French Revolutionary War as the Perthshire Militia Regt. and the quota of men to be furnished by the County. It became a Royal Regt. at later date, and Rifles in 1855, under the designation of the Royal Perthshire Rifles. In 1881 it formed the 3rd Battn. of the Territorial Regt. The Black Watch (Royal Highlanders).

Embodiments.

Occasion.

French War	1803, Apr. 27, to 1814, Oct. 21.
French War	1815, July 25, to 1816, Feb. 28.
Crimean War	1855, Feb. 20, to 1856, June 17.
South African War ...	1899, Dec. 14, to 1900, Dec. 4.

Services.

Stationed in the South of England 1805 to 1810, and at Dartmoor in 1813.

3rd Battalion, The Oxfordshire Light Infantry.

Hon. Colonel:—Lee, E. D., hon. c.
Lt.-Colonel:—Terry, W., hon. c.

Origin.

The County of Buckingham assembled 600 Trained foot men, with horsemen 18 Lances, 83 Light-horse, 20 Petroneles, to be reduced into bandes under Captaines for meeting invasion by the Spanish Armada, 1588. (Harleian MSS.).

1641, Lord Paget was appointed as "a person fit to be entrusted" with the organization of the County Militia. In 1642 the Force of the County was formed into a Regiment by G. H. Bulstrode, Esquire, as Colonel, and designated the Buckinghamshire Militia. By the Militia Returns (Egerton MSS.) 1697, the County had one Regiment of ten Companies 820 foot, and three Troops of horse 177, William Cheyne, Esquire, Colonel, a note upon the return stating "that all the arms were good at the last muster in 1695."

In 1760 a Regiment was completed for service as the Buckinghamshire Militia and quota to be furnished by the County, which afterwards became a Royal Regiment until 1881, when under Territorial reorganization it formed the 3rd Battalion of The Oxfordshire Light Infantry.

Embodiments.

Occasion.

Civil War	1612, period unknown.
Civil War	1642, period unknown.
American War	1778 to 1783.
Revolutionary War, etc.	1793 to 1802.
French War	1803 to 1814.
Crimean War	1854 to 1856.
South African War	1900, Jan. 17, to 1900, Nov. 1.

Services.

Civil War, 1612, taking part in the battle at Holmans Bridge where many were killed and buried in a field adjoining. In 1818 the remains were discovered and the skeletons of 247 persons removed to Hardwicke Church Yard. A Tablet was erected by the late Lord Nugent: "Within are deposited the remains of those Officers and men concluded to have perished in an engagement fought A.D. 1612 between the troops of King Charles I. under command of Prince Rupert and the garrison who held Aylesbury for the Parliament," etc.

Served through the Civil War, 1642, taking a prominent part in the battle of Edgehill under Colonel Bulstrode.

In 1666 by State Papers Dom. Chas. II., the Militia of the County was drawn out by the King to resist threatened French and Dutch invasion.

Formed the personal Guard to King George III. at Weymouth in 1794. Volunteered for and served under Col. The Marquis of Buckingham in Ireland 1798, being one of the thirteen English Regiments sent there immediately upon the passing of the Act which allowed the King to employ the English Militia in Ireland consequent on the Rebellion.

In 1814, volunteered for service in the Militia Brigade to be formed and employed in France, embarked March 10th at Portsmouth 21 Officers (Lt.-Col. W. L. Young, Majors Forster and Dean, Captains McDermott, Vasser, Beatty, Cape and Fellows, Lieuts. Dardis, Keane, Brown, Mason, Carrington, Harland, Grove, Shillingford and Spier, Ensigns Donolan and Bridger, Adjt. J. T. Brown, Qr.-Mr. J. Masters, Surgeon T. Ledbrooke), 560 N.C. Officers and men, as part of the 1st Provisional Battalion, and Brigade under command of The Marquis of Buckingham, Lieut.-Colonel Commandant Royal Bucks Militia. On landing in France near Bordeaux the Brigade was placed in the Division of the Earl of Dalhousie for service under the Duke of Wellington. On leaving France the Officers of the Royal Bucks were decorated by King Louis XVIII. with the Fleur de Lys.

4th Battalion, The Oxfordshire Light Infantry.

"Mediterranean."

Hon. Colonel:—p.s. Annesley, Hon. A. S. A., hon c.
Lt.-Colonel:—Willan, F., hon. c. (T) (H).

Origin.

1539. See Certificate of Muster Armed men of the County, dated Apr. 25, 30 Henry VIII. (incomplete).

1588, according to Harleian MSS. Spanish Armada Assembly of Militia, "Oxenford furnished 1144 able trayned men reduced into bandes under Captaines and Horsemen Launces 23, Lighthorse 103, Petroneles 32."

In 1641, Feb. 12, Lord Viscount Say and Seal was nominated to the King as "a person fit to be entrusted" with the organization of the Militia of Oxfordshire.

1697 Militia Returns, Egerton MSS., Oxfordshire had one Regt of 8 Companies 742 "effective private men," and one Troop horse 130. Col. Lord Norreys. With foot-note, "The Militia within this Lieutenancy are in as good a condition as the Militia is capable off and may in a little time be made very fitt for service, whenever his Maty. hath occasion. And I doe not know of any estates in the County that ought to be contributing to the Militia which are not charged either to Horse or Foot."

In 1778 a Regiment was completed for service and quota of Militia to be furnished by the County, known as the Oxfordshire Militia Regiment. In 1881 it became the 4th Battalion of the Territorial "Oxfordshire Light Infantry."

Embodiments.

Occasion.

Monmouth Rebellion...	1685, Period unknown.
American War ...	1778, Mch. to 1783, Mch.
Revolutionary War, etc.	1792, Dec., to 1800.
French War	1803, Mch., to 1816, Feb.
Crimean War	1854, Dec., to 1856, July.
Indian Mutiny... ...	1857, Sep., to 1860, Feb.
South African War ...	1900, May 1, to 1901, July 3.

Services.

Monmouth Rebellion, 1685.

Volunteered for and actively engaged in the suppression of the Irish Rebellion, 1798, being under Colonel Lord Charles Spencer, M.P., one of the 13 Regts. immediately sent to that country on the passing of the Act which empowered the King to employ the English Militia in Ireland for a limited time.

Volunteered for and stationed in Ireland 1813-15.

Volunteered for Foreign service during Crimean War and stationed at the Ionian Islands.

3rd Battalion, The Essex Regiment.

"South Africa, 1902."

Hon. Colonel:—Warwick, F. R. C. G., Earl of.

Lt.-Colonel:—Colvin, C.H., D.S.O., hon. c. (Capt. Res. of Off.) (H).

Origin.

Descended from the forces of the Saxon Kingdom of Eastsex, the earliest Records of which appear in a Saxon Chronicle, A.D. 461 (B. Mus.).

At the Muster 30 Henry VIII. the Essex Hundreds furnished 849 men having "abilaments of war."

In 1588 Essex was represented at the assembly of "Milicia" to resist the Spanish Armada by 2000 trained men in "bands under Captaines." (Harleian MSS.)

1641, Feb. 12, The Earl of Warwick nominated by the House of Commons "as a person fit to be entrusted" with the organization of the Militia of Essex.

1644, Feb. 29, The County thanked by the Committee of both Kingdoms "for its forwardness in furnishing their proportion of forces upon the new ordinance of 12th July."

1697, By Militia Returns, Egerton MSS., Essex had then three Regiments of 24 Companies, 3070 foot with four Troops horse 250, total of both 3320. The Blew Regt. Col. Evans Lloyd. The Green Regt. (vacant). Col. . . . "Earl of Oxford's Regt."

1759, a Regt. was prepared for service as the 2nd or East Essex Militia Regt. of two Regts. for the quota to be furnished by the County under the order issued to Lords Lieutenants to complete and train their Militia; the Regt. afterwards (in 1854) became the Essex Rifles, and under 1881 organization, the 3rd Battn. of the Territorial Essex Regiment.

Embodiments.

Occasion.

Periods of Embodiment between 1759 and 1816	No Regimental Record.
Crimean War	1854 to 1856.
South African War ...	1899, Dec. 11, to 1900, Oct. 20.
South African War ...	1902, Mch. 10, to 1902, Oct. 6.

Services.

Besides those of early times, and during many centuries, in which the Constitutional Force of the Kingdom of Eastsex, and in later years of the County of Essex, took part, it is recorded that in 1591 the County furnished for the Earl of Essex's Army to aid the King of Navarre, 2 captains (Morgan and Dochray) with two Companies 300 men, and in 1596 a contingent for "succouring the Citidal of Calais besieged."—(State Papers Foreign and Domestic).

1598, a contingent for suppression of Rebellion in Ireland.

1601, Forces of the County in London to guard the Court.

1666, a levy by the King for threatened French and Dutch invasion.

Volunteered for Foreign Service during the South African War embodiment, and embarked for the seat of war. Strength 25 officers, one W.O., 549 N.C.O.'s and men, Colonel H. H. Stewart (3rd Innis. Fusiliers) commanding. On arrival Port Elizabeth April 17, 1902, proceeded to Kimberley, four companies under Major A. J. Galsworthy taking over the blockhouse line from Modder River to Winderton Road, afterwards furnishing troops for Barkley West and Schmidts Drift; Head Quarters and remaining four Companies being at Fourteen Streams, detaching one Company to Brussels siding for blockhouse duty between that place and Vryburg.

April 22.—Head Quarters with three Companies moved to Christiana on the Vaal River, taking over the forts and blockhouses at that place. July 9, 1902, Battalion concentrated at Modder River and entrained for Cape Town en route for home.

Extract from Garrison Orders, Christiana, July 7, 1902: "The Commandant desires to thank all ranks who have served under him during his tenure of command for their loyal support. During the short period the 3rd Essex Regiment has been stationed at Christiana he has noticed with pleasure that they have carried out their duties with zeal and promptness, and that the conduct of the Battalion has been exemplary."

Casualties.

Killed and died of disease, 5 N.C.O.'s and men.

Medals, *etc.*, received by Battalion.

South Africa 1902 with Clasps "Cape Colony," "Orange Free State," "Transvaal."

4th Battalion, The Essex Regiment.

Hon. Colonel :—Lockwood, A.R.M.
Lt.-Colonel :—Fleming, H.S., Maj. ret. pay (Maj. Res. of Off.).

Origin.

See 3rd Battn. prior to 1759, when completed for service as the 1st or Western Regiment, afterwards known as the West Essex Militia. In 1881 became the 4th Battn. of the Territorial "Essex Regiment."

Embodiments.

Occasion.

Seven Years War	...	1759, period unknown.
French ,,	...	1803 to 1816, Jan 10.
Crimean ,,	...	1854 to 1856, June 6.
South African ,,	...	1900, May 2, to 1901, July 2.

Services.

See 3rd Battalion prior to 1759.

The Luddite Riots in 1812, moved by forced marches in waggons to Nottingham, and remained in the disturbed districts until 1813.

Volunteered for and stationed in Ireland 1813-16.

3rd Battalion, The Sherwood Foresters (Nottinghamshire and Derbyshire Regiment).

Hon. Colonel :—Devonshire, Most Noble, S. C., Duke of, K.G.
Hon. Colonel : V. C. Roberts, Field Marshal, Rt. Hon. F. S., Earl, K.G., G.C.B., O.M., G.C.S.I., G.C.I.E., Col. Commdt. R. Art., I. Gds., (R), Kt. of Justice, Order of St. John of Jerusalem, etc.
Lt. Colonel :—p.s. Curzon. Hon. A. N.

Origin.

According to "Letters and Papers of the Reign of Henry VIII.," Derbyshire assembled in 1539 its harnessed men by virtue of Royal Commission issued 1st March, 30, Henry VIII. (see copy of certificate).

At the muster of trained men to resist the Spanish Armada invasion 1588, the County had (by Harleian MSS.) 400 trained men, besides horsemen 18 Launces, 50 Lighthorse, 12 Petronell.

In 1641, Feb. 12, the Earl of Rutland was appointed as a "fit person to be entrusted" with the organizing of the Militia of Derbyshire.

By Militia Returns 1697 (Egerton MSS.) the County of Derby had one Regiment of four Companies 524 foot, and horse 140, Colonelcy vacant.

In 1773, a Derbyshire Regiment was completed for service, and the quota of men to be found by the County.

In 1855 the Regiment became the 1st Derby Militia, a second regiment being raised as the 2nd or Chatsworth Rifles.

In the 1881 Territorial Reorganization of the Forces, the 1st. Derby Militia Regt. became the 5th Battn, and 2nd Derby the 3rd Battn. of the Territorial "Derbyshire Regiment."

In 1891 these two Battalions were amalgamated as the 3rd Battalion, and in 1903 the title of the Territorial Regiment was changed to "The Sherwood Foresters (Nottinghamshire and Derbyshire Regiment)."

Embodiments.

Occasion.

William of Orange's coming to the Throne	1689, Oct., to 1690, March.
American War	1778, period unknown.
European Disturbances	1803, Mar, to 1814, Sep.
,, ,,	1815, Nov., to 1816, Feb.
Indian Mutiny	1857 for 15 months.
South African War	1900, Jan. 23, to 1900, Dec. 4.

Services.

In 1666 (S.P. Dom. Chas. II.) a levy was made by the King on the Militia of Derbyshire to resist the threatened French and Dutch invasion.

According to Cox's Annals, the Militia Force of Derbyshire was assembled for "the coming of William of Orange to the Throne."

Volunteered for and stationed in Ireland 1813.

In 1814 volunteered for and furnished nine officers (Capt. John Leacroft, Lieuts. Brigg, Dakin, Gould, Latham, Emery, Carr, Lambert, Calcraft), and 290 other ranks for the 3rd Provisional Battn., Lt.-Colonel Sir Watkins Williams

Wynne, Bart. (Denbigh Militia) commanding, of the Militia Brigade under Lieut.-Col. Commanding Richard Marquis of Buckingham (Bucks Militia) which embarked at Portsmouth March 10th and 11th for France to join the Army of Wellington. "The fleet of transports sailed up the Garonne River to the village of Royan," and the Brigade eventually disembarked near Paulliac to join the Division of the Earl of Dalhousie, the three Battalions afterwards marching to Soisson, Cantenac, etc., arriving too late to take part in the last stand made by the French at Toulouse.

4th Battalion, The Sherwood Foresters (Nottinghamshire and Derbyshire Regiment).

"South Africa, 1900-01."

Hon.Colonel :—Portland, Most Noble, W. J. A. C. J., Duke of, K.G., G.C.V.O.

Lt. Colonel :—Wilkinson, G.A.E., D.S.O.

Origin.

Formed out of the Forces of the County, the earliest records of which date back to 1135, when soon afterwards they served under William de Percival, Lord of Nottingham, Nottinghamshire also appearing in the "Muster" March 24. 30, Henry VIII., as having furnished its trained men at the assembly of Militia in 1588, to resist the threatened attack by the Spanish Armada. By Militia Returns 1697 (Egerton MSS.) the County had then one Regiment composed of six companies 400 private soldiers, and two Troops of horse 120, total of both 520, John, D. of Newcastle, Colonel. In 1775 a regiment was completed and equipped for service as the Nottinghamshire Militia, its designation becoming in 1813 "The Royal Sherwood Forresters" or Nottinghamshire Regiment of Militia, and in 1881 the 4th Battn. of the Territorial Derbyshire Regiment, changed in 1903 to the Sherwood Foresters (Nottinghamshire and Derbyshire Regiment).

Embodiments.
　Occasion.

War with Scotland	... 1138,	period unknown
,, ,, ,,	... 1298	,, ,,
Wars with Scotland and France	... 1346	,, ,,
War with France	... 1356	,, ,,
Welsh Rebellion	... 1402	,, ,,
War with France	... 1415	,, ,,
Civil War	... 1642	,, ,,
American War	... 1778 to 1783.	
Revolutionary War, etc.	1793, Jan., to 1802.	
French War	... 1803, Aug., to 1814, Aug. 5.	
Crimean War	... 1854, Dec., to 1856, July.	
Indian Mutiny	... 1856, Oct., to 1859, March.	
South African War	... 1899, Dec. 11, to 1901, May 10.	

Services.

The Force of the County took part in the Battle of the Standard at Northallerton in Yorkshire 1138. The Battle of Falkirk 1298. Nevill's Cross at Durham, and Cressy in France 1346. The Battle of Poictiers in 1356 under Edward the Black Prince, against King John of France. The Welsh Rebellion in 1402.

The Battle of Agincourt in the North of France 1415, under Henry V. of England, it being recorded that the Nottinghamshire Archers took a very prominent part, and fought for the first time as "Sherwood Foresters." The Civil War, on the side of His Majesty King Charles the First, and were continually fighting between 1643-5 around Newark and Nottingham.

Volunteered for and stationed in Ireland 1803.

Volunteered for Foreign Service, and proceeded to South Africa in 1900. Strength embarked 32 officers, 1 W.O., 656 N.C.O.'s and men, Colonel N. L. Pearse commanding. On arrival Port Elizabeth Jan. 31, 1900, the left half Battalion was stationed at Cradock Siding, small detachments at Rosmead, Kroom Hoogte, Henning, and Steynsberg; the right half at Port Elizabeth furnishing detachments at Barkley and Swartzkop Bridges. May 22, the Battalion arrived at Zand River, and proceeded to Rhenoster River, stopping en route to put Roodevar Station in a state of defence. At daybreak, June 7th, the Battn. was attacked by the Boers, who were between 3,000 and 4,000 strong, and brought a heavy big gun and rifle fire on the camp from all sides. After a prolonged resistance, during which 2 officers, one W.O., and 26 N.C.O.'s and men were killed, 2 officers and 62 N.C.O.'s and men wounded, the Battalion surrendered on finding that the position taken up was untenable, and were marched away as prisoners. June 26, the rank and file were parted from the officers, the latter being taken on to Bethlehem and Fouriesburg, where on the 26th July they were released by the troops under General Hunter. July 5th, the rank and file were put over the Free State border into Natal. July 29, the Boer Forces under General Prinsloo surrendered, and the officers of Battn. were put in charge of the Boer prisoners. The rank and file of the Battalion in Natal having proceeded to Ladysmith, they were re-armed and clothed, and afterwards proceeded to Pretoria. Aug. 17, the officers rejoin their men at Pretoria. After the Regiment was inspected by Lord Roberts it was stationed on a range of hills outside of Pretoria. Sept 6, moved to Port Elizabeth until April 4, 1901, furnishing detachments at Cradock and Aberdeen. March 5, 1901, the Boers attacked Aberdeen but were repulsed.

Casualties.

Killed and died of disease, 4 officers (Major and Hon. Lt. Col. Baird-Douglas (attached), Captain E. B. Bailey, Lieut. R. H. Hall, Lieut. J. B. Horley), one W.O., 41 N.C.O.'s and men.

Mentioned in Despatches.

Major and Hon. Lt.-Col. G. A. E. Wilkinson.
Captain and Adjt. R. Brittan.
Captain G. H. W. Bernal.
Captain R. C. Fenwick.
Captain E. B. Bailey.
Lieut. and Qr.-Master N. McGuire (twice).
Sergt.-Major Taylor (twice).
Cr.-Sergt. Harwood (twice).
Cr.-Sergt. Walker.
Cr.-Sergt. Plowright.
Cr.-Sergt. Poulter.
Sergt.-Instr. of Musketry Norman.
Sergt. Hopkins.
Sergt. Allcock.
Sergt. Brendley.

Special Honours.

Major and Hon. Lt.-Col. G. A. E. Wilkinson, D.S.O.
Captain and Adjt. R. Brittan, D.S.O.

Captain G. H. W. Bernal, D.S.O.
Sergt.-Major Taylor, D.C. Medal.
Qr.-Mr.-Sergt. Harwood, D.C. Medal.
Cr.-Sergt. Walker, D.C. Medal.

Medals and Clasps Received by Battalion.

Queen's South African Medal with four Clasps, "Cape Colony," "Orange Free State," "Transvaal," "South Africa 1901."

3rd Battalion, The Loyal North Lancashire Regiment.

" Mediterranean."
"Mediterranean, 1900-01."
"South Africa, 1901-02."

Hon. Colonel :—V.C. Roberts, Field-Marshal, Rt. Hon. F. S., Earl, K.G., K.P., G.C.B., O.M., G.C.S.I., G.C.I.E., Col. Commdt. R. Art., Col. I. Gds. (R), Kt. of Justice, Order of St. John of Jerusalem.

Lt.-Colonel :—Pedder, J. H. W.

Origin.

Raised in 1797, as the second of five Supplementary Militia Regiments for Lancashire, under the Act of 37, Geo. III., C. 3, 22. In 1800, it was renumbered and retained on the establishment of regular Militia Regiments as the 3rd Royal Lancashire. In 1813 its designation became the Prince Regent's Own Regt. of Royal Lancashire Militia. In 1831 the name was changed to The Duke of Lancaster's Own Regt. of Militia. In 1858 the Regt. was affiliated to the 47th and 81st Regts. of the Line, and under Territorial Regimental Organization of the Forces in 1881, formed the 3rd and 4th Battns. of the Loyal North Lancashire Regiment.

In 1896 the two Battalions were amalgamated.

Embodiments.

   Occasion.

Revolutionary War, etc. 1798 to 1802.
European Disturbances 1803 to 1816, Jan.
Crimean War ... 1855 to 1856, July 7.
South African War ... 1899, Dec. 13 to 1902, March 15.

Services.

Volunteered for and stationed in Ireland 1813-15.

Volunteered for Foreign Service during the Crimean War, and formed part of the Garrison of Gibraltar April, 1855, to June, 1856, the word "Mediterranean" being borne on the Colour in recognition of this service.

Volunteered for Foreign Service during the South African War, and embarked Jan. 12, 1900 for Malta, proceeding from there March 2, 1901, to South Africa. Strength embarked, 21 officers, one W.O., 804 N.C.O.'s and men, Lt.-Colonel J. H. W. Pedder commanding. On arrival March 30, 1901, the Battalion was employed on the lines of communication from Port Elizabeth to Aliwal North, Lieut. Mackie distinguishing himself in the handling of a party of M.I. against a superior body of the Boers, and in endeavouring to bring in a wounded man. The Battn. re-embarked for England Feb. 13, 1902.

Casualties.

Killed and died of disease, etc., 3 N.C.O.'s and men.

Mentioned in Despatches.
Lt.-Colonel J. H. W. Pedder.
Capt. and Adjt. R. L. Stable.
Sergt.-Major R. Rowley.

Special Honours.
Capt. and Adjt. Stable, to be Brevet Major.
Lieut. Mackie, a Line Commission.
Sergt.-Major Rowley, D.C. Medal.

Medals, etc., received by Battalion.

Queen's South African Medal with Clasps 1901-1902.

3rd Battalion, The Northamptonshire Regiment.

"Mediterranean."
"South Africa, 1902."

Hon. Colonel:—Stopford Sackville, S. G., hon. c.
Lt.-Colonel:—Hill, J., C.B., hon. c.

Origin.

The Northampton and Rutland Militia Regt. became in 1881 the 3rd Battn. of the Northamptonshire Regiment.

In 1539, by "State Papers Foreign and Domestic of the Reign Henry VIII." Northamptonshire was represented April 31 at the great muster of armed and able men held throughout the kingdom by virtue of a Royal Commission, issued March I, 30, Henry VIII. (See copy of certificate.)

By Harleian MSS., 1588, Northampton furnished "600 Trained men besides Horsemen, Launces 190 and Lighthorse 80 reduced into bandes under Captaines" to resist invasion by the Spanish Armada.

In 1641, Feb. 12, when "persons fit to be entrusted" with organizing the Militia were nominated, Lord Spencer was appointed for Northamptonshire and the Earl of Essex for Rutland.

By Militia Returns, 1697, Egerton MSS., the Militia of Rutland comprised "one Company of 93 Foot and Horse one Troop of 53 men, Total of both 146."

When the Militia was reorganized under Act 30, Geo. II., a Regiment was completed for service in 1763 for the quota of men to be found by the County of Northampton, also a Regiment for Rutlandshire in 1761, which became Light Infantry 1810. In 1860 the Militia Forces of the two Counties were united as the Northamptonshire and Rutland Militia, and the Regiment divided into two Battalions in 1874, as the 1st and 2nd Battn. Northamptonshire and Rutland Regt., which became in 1881 the 3rd Battalion of the Territorial "Northamptonshire Regiment."

Embodiments.

 Occasion.

American War	1778, April, to 1787.
Revolutionary War, etc.	1793 to 1802.
European Disturbances	1803, March 25, to 1814, July 7.
Crimean War	1854, Aug., to 1856, July 18.
South African War	1900, Jan. 4, to 1900, Dec. 5.
,, ,, ,,	1902, Mar. 17, to 1902, Sept. 20.

Services.

By S.P. Dom., in 1666 the Militia of Northampton was drawn out by King Chas. II. owing to threatened invasion by the French and Dutch.

In 1780 the Northamptonshire Regt. took part in the suppression of the Gordon Riots in London, and was stationed at Lambeth Palace.

In 1792, the Regiment was engaged along with Sir John Carden's Dragoons in suppressing a serious mutiny among the "Loyal Irish Fencibles." The transport from Waterford to Jersey with this Corps put into Pill, near Bristol. The mutineers after preparing a gallows and threatening to hang two of their officers, who escaped by jumping overboard, forcibly landed and were surrounded by the Northamptons, who with fixed bayonets were ordered to withhold their fire till the last moment, the Mutineers not being disarmed and made prisoners until charged by the Dragoons led by Sir John Carden, whose horse was killed under him, and several wounded on both sides.

Volunteered for and stationed in Ireland 1811-13.

In 1814, furnished four officers (Captains Pettingall and Jones, Lieuts. Kingsbury and Glover) with 160 N.C.O.'s and Men for the 1st Provisional Battn. of the Militia Brigade under Colonel the Marquis of Buckingham (Bucks. Militia) which landed in France near Bordeaux to serve under the Duke of Wellington.

Volunteered for Foreign Service during the Crimean War, and proceeded to a Mediterranean garrison.

Volunteered for Foreign Service during the South African War, and embarked, strength 25 officers, 653 N.C.O.'s and Men, Colonel J. Hill commanding. On arrival Cape Town May 1, 1902, the Battalion proceeded direct to Victoria West Road, and occupied 88 miles of blockhouse line from there to Carnarvon at a right angle to the line of railway. In July and August the Battalion concentrated at Victoria West and moved to Stelenbosch, and in August re-embarked at Cape Town for England.

Casualties.

Killed and died of disease, etc., one man.

Special Honours.

Colonel J. Hill, C.B.

Medals, etc., received by Battalion.

Queen's South African with Clasps "South Africa" and "Cape Colony."

3rd Battalion, The Princess Charlotte of Wales's (Royal Berkshire Regiment).

"Mediterranean."

Hon. Colonel :—Abingdon, M.A., Earl of.
Lt.-Colonel :—Thornton, W. (H).

Origin.

The earliest notice of the Constitutional Force of Berkshire appears in the returns of the assembly at Tilbury 1588, by Queen Elizabeth, to resist invasion by the Spanish Armada. (See Abstracts of the nombers of everie sorte Barkeshire.) In 1640 the Berkshire Regiment was commanded by Sir Jacob Astley as Colonel. In 1641, Feb. 12, the Earl of Holland was appointed as "a person fit to be entrusted" with the organization of the County Militia, and a second Regiment was formed for Parliament in 1642 out of the Trained Bands, commanded by the Earl of Holland.

In 1697, by Militia Returns (Egerton MSS.), the "Berks Militia Regiment, The Duke of Norfolk as Colonel, and Paul Caulston, Esqr. Lieut.-Colonel, was composed of ten Companies 977 foot, and three Troops of horse 175, total of all 1,152."

When the Militia was reorganized under Act 30, Geo. II., a Regiment was completed for service and the quota of the County as the Berkshire Regiment, afterwards becoming a Royal Regiment, and in 1881 under Territorial Organization, the 3rd Battn. of "The Princess Charlotte of Wales's Royal Berkshire Regiment."

Embodiments.

Occasion.

Civil War	...	1640, period unknown.
Threatened Dutch Invasion	...	1666, period unknown.
Seven Years War	...	1759 to 1762, Oct.
American ,,	...	1778 to 1783, March.
Revolutionary War, etc.		1793, Dec. 18, to 1816, Mar. 14.
Crimean War	...	1855, Jan. 1, to 1856, July 4.
Indian Mutiny	...	1857, Sept. 30, to 1858, May 7.
South African War	...	1900, Feb. 19, to 1901, uly 13.

Services.

The assembly of the Force of the County at Tilbury 1588.

During the Civil War, took part in both battles of Newbury, it being recorded that on the first occasion the two Regiments of the County were fighting on different sides; also engaged at decisive battle of Worcester.

In 1666-7, formed part of the Force at the Isle of Wight for opposing the threatened French and Dutch Invasion.

Volunteered for and stationed in Ireland 1813-14.

Volunteered for foreign service during the Crimean War, and stationed at Corfu, in recognition of which service the word "Mediterranean" is borne on the colours.

3rd Battalion, The Queen's Own (Royal West Kent Regiment).

"Mediterranean, 1900-01."

Hon. Colonel:—Field Marshal H.R.H. Arthur W. P. A., Duke of Connaught and Strathearn, K.G., K.T., K.P., G.C.B., G.C.S.I., G.C.M.G., G.C.I.E., G.C.V.O., S. Gds., A.S. Corps., and Col.-in-Chief 6 Dns., High L.I., R. Dub. Fus., and Rifle Brig., Personal A.D.C. to the King, Insp.-Gen. of the Forces, Bailiff of Egle Order of St. John of Jerusalem, etc.

Lt.-Colonel:—Bailey, E. W. G.

Origin.

According to Regimental tradition, supported by local records, the Battalion claims to be descended from the Forces which existed in Kent when it formed the first kingdom of the Saxon Heptarchy, though according to Scarth's History of "Early Britain" the Tribal Forces of the Kentish District are referred to in 56, B.C.

By Harleian MSS., Kent "ffurnished 2,958 trayned men soarted wt weapons and reduced into bandes under Captaines, in Aprille ano. dom. 1588." to resist the Spanish Armada invasion.

In 1641, Feb., 12, the Earl of Leicester was appointed as a "fit person to be entrusted" with the Militia of Kent and City and County of Canterbury.

In State Papers Domestic, Aug. 16, 1644, the entry appears "that the 1000 men out of Kent continue a Regt."

By Militia Returns, 1697, Egerton MSS., Kent had (independent of the Cinque Ports) six Regts. for the Lath's of Sutton at Hone, St. Augustine, Aylesford, Shipway, Scray, and City of Canterbury, thirty-seven Companies 3,550 foot, and 4 Troops of horse 231, Colonels Sr. Stephen Leonard, Bart., Henry Oxenden, Esqr., Sir Philip Botcher, Bart., Sir Francis Head, and Henry Lee, Esqr.

When the Militia of England and Wales was reorganized under Act 30, Geo. II., a Regiment was completed for service, and the quota of men to be found by the County, as the Kent Regt. of Militia. In 1778 a second Regiment was formed, and the two Regiments were then called the East and West Kent Regiments, this Battalion being the latter, and became Light Infantry at a later date. In 1881 it became, under the Territorial Regimental Organization, the 3rd Battn. of "The Queen's Own (Royal West Kent Regiment)."

Embodiments.

Occasion.

Operations against the Covenanters	1650, period unknown.
Civil War, Chas. I.	Period unknown.
Seven Years War	1759, June, to 1762, Dec.
American War	1778, March, to 1783, March.
Revolutionary War, etc.	1792, Dec., to 1802, April.
European Disturbances	1803, March, to 1814, June.
" "	1815, June, to 1816, May.
Crimean War	1855, Jan., to 1856, July.
South African War	1899, Dec. 11, to 1901, June 10.

Services.

In 56 B.C., by Scarth's History, "The four Kings of the Kentish Tribes failed in an attack on the Naval Camp of the Romans when Cæsar was following Cassivelaunus to his stronghold at St. Albans."

In 1588, the Forces of Kent took part in the great Armada assembly.

In 1591, by "State Papers Domestic—the Constitutional Force of Kent" furnished 300 men with Captains Acton and Poore towards the 4000 men sent from five Counties and the City of London, to aid the French King against the Confederates of the League.

By S. P. Dom., 1596, Kent with four other Counties and City of London, provided its quota of the 6000 men to join the "Forces of the French King in succouring the Citadel of Calais then besieged by Spain."

By S. P. Dom., 1597, Apr. 30, The Sheriff of Kent was instructed to levy 600 men upon the coming of the Cardinal of Austria towards Boulogne.

By S. P. Dom., 1598, A levy was made on the Forces of Kent and six other Counties for 2000 men for service in Ireland—then in rebellion.

By S. P. Dom., 1599, The Queen requested 200 from Kent, Surrey, Sussex, and London for the War in the Low Countries. "The Earl Marshall to have £633 6s. 8d. to provide 100 horses and carriage."

In 1639, The Militia of Kent was employed by King Charles I. against the Covenanters. In 1645 there is an entry in State Papers Domestic, that the Forces of Kent including 80 horse, and 160 Dragoons, were sent to the Western Parts during the Civil War—the Horse rendezvous being at Romsey.

By S. P. Dom., 1666, the Militia of Kent was drawn out by King Charles II. for the threatened French and Dutch invasion, and in Sepr. of the same year a contingent was sent to London for duty during the great Fire.

Volunteered for Foreign service during the South African War, and stationed at Malta 1900-01.

3rd Battalion, The King's Own (Yorkshire Light Infantry).

"Mediterranean, 1901-02."

Hon. Colonel:—Aitkin, A., m.c.c

Lt.-Colonel:—p.s. Johnstone, M. G., D.S.O., Maj. ret. pay (Lt.-Col. Res. of Off.) hon. c. (T) (H).

Origin.

Formed into a Regiment about the middle of the seventeenth century, as one of three then organized for the West Riding of Yorkshire out of the local companies or armed bodies of the Wapentakes, which had existed in various forms from early times in that portion of the present County included in the Saxon Kingdom of Mercia, and associated with all the District fighting of early centuries.

From " Letters and Papers of the Reign of Henry VIII."

the West Riding of York, excluding York, had according to the certificates of the great Muster held in the spring of 1539, by virtue of a Royal Commission issued Mch. 1, 30 Henry VIII., 946 Archers, 1076 Billmen, 13 Spearmen, to serve the Lord their King.

In 1641, Feb. 12, the Earl of Essex was appointed as "a fit person to be entrusted" with the organization of the Militia of Yorkshire, and of the County of the City of York, and of the County of the Town of Kingstone-on-Hull.

By Militia Returns 1697 (Egerton MSS.), the West Riding of York is included as having three Regiments of six Companies each, 1592 foot, with three Troops of horse 213. Colonels Lord Fairfax, Sir Henry Goodrick, Bart., "Mich Wentworth Knt. (dead)."

In 1759 under Act. 30, Geo. II., and order issued to Lords Lieutenant of Counties to complete and train their Militia, three Regiments were completed for service and the quota of men to be furnished by the West Riding, known as the 1st West York or Lord Downes' Regt. (this Battn.), the 2nd West York or Sir Geo. Saville's Regt. (now the 3rd Battn. West Yorkshire Regt.), and the 3rd West York or Col. Thornton's Regt. (now the 3rd Battn. York and Lancaster Regt.). In 1763, the three Regiments were reorganized for the same quota of men to be found by the Riding into two Regiments, as the 1st or Southern (this Battn.) and the 2nd or Northern (now the 3rd Battn. West Yorkshire Regt.), the 3rd West York Regiment being absorbed.

In 1833 the 1st (or Southern Regt.) became Rifles, known as the 1st West York Rifles, and in 1881 under the Territorial organization, formed the 3rd Battalion of The King's Own Light Infantry, South Yorkshire Regt., changed later to "The King's Own Yorkshire Light Infantry."

Embodiments.

Occasion.

Seven Years War	1759, June, to 1762, Dec.
American War	1778, Mch., to 1783, Mch.
Revolutionary War. etc.	1793, Feb., to 1802, Apr.
French War	1803, Mch., to 1814, June.
French War	1815, June, to 1816, Feb.
Crimean War	1854, May, to 1856, June.
Indian Mutiny	1857, Oct., to 1861, Feb.
South African War	1900, May 5, to 1900, Oct. 17.
South African War	1901, May 6, to 1902, Mch. 2

Services.

Besides the services of the Constitutional Force in early days of what is now the West Riding, in connection with the many wars that raged, and battles fought in the District and other parts of Yorkshire between the year 633 and the middle of the fifteenth century, including the battles at Leeds, Northallerton, and other engagements about York, it is recorded that the reorganized 1st West Yorkshire Regiment of 1763, volunteered for service in Ireland during the Irish Rebellion 1798, and under Colonel The Earl Fitzwilliam, was one of the thirteen Militia Regiments immediately sent there on the passing of the Act which empowered the King to employ the English Militia in that Country for a limited time.

Volunteered for Foreign service during the South African War, and stationed at Malta and Gozo, June, 1901, to Feb., 1902.

3rd Battalion, The King's (Shropshire Light Infantry).

Hon. Colonel:—Meyrick, Sir T. C. Bt., C.B., hon. c.
Lt.-Colonel:—Cunliffe, E. S.

Origin.

Completed for Service 1762 as the Shropshire Militia Regiment, and quota of men to be furnished by the County—Colonel The Earl of Bath.

At the Assembly April, 1588, to resist the Spanish Armada, the County sent 600 "trayned and ffurnished" men, horsemen Launces 28, Lighthorse 165; Petroneles (numbers not legible in the Manuscript returns). Harleian MSS.

In 1641, Feb. 12, Lord Littleton, Lord Keeper of the Great Seal of England, was nominated "as a person fit to be entrusted with the Militia" reorganization of Salop. By Militia Returns 1697, Egerton MSS., the County had one Regt. of 8 Companies, 1050 men, 2 Troops 82 horse, Col. The Earl of Bradford.

Became in 1881 the 3rd Battn. of the Territorial "King's Own Shropshire Light Infantry Regiment."

Embodiments.
 Occasion.

Seven Years War	1763, Oct., to 1766.
American War	1778, Apr. 14, to 1783, Mch. 15.
French War, etc.	1793 to 1802, Apr. 14.
European Disturbances	1803, Mch., to 1815, Feb. 15.
Crimean War...	1854, Dec. 12, to 1856, May.
Indian Mutiny...	1857 to 1858, May.
South African War	1900, May 3, to 1901, July 11.

Services.

Volunteered for and stationed in Ireland 1812-14.

4th Battalion, The King's (Shropshire Light Infantry).

Hon. Colonel:—Hopton, Lt.-Gen. Sir E., K.C.B. (R).
Lt.-Colonel:—p.s. Bourne, G. C., hon. c.

Origin.

In 1881, the Herefordshire Militia Regiment became, under the Territorial Regimental organization of the Forces, the 4th Battn. of The King's Own Shropshire Light Infantry.

1539 (Letters and Papers of the Reign of Henry VIII.) see copy of the certificate addressed to the King of the numbers of Archers and Billmen in Herefordshire having "abilaments of war."

1641, Feb. 12, according to Rushworth Historical Collection, Lord Dacres was appointed as "a fit person to be entrusted" with the organizing of the Militia in Herefordshire.

In 1778 a Regt. was completed for service and quota of men to be found by Herefordshire, which between 1798 and 1803 was according to Woodhouse's Monthly Army List, described as the "Herefordshire Fusiliers," and in the Official War Office Army Lists, 1808-9, as the "Royal Herefordshire Militia."

In 1881 the "Herefordshire Militia" became as previously described.

Embodiments.

  Occasion.

Old Records Destroyed.

American War — Periods unknown; disembodied 1803.

Revolutionary War and European Disturbances — Periods unknown; disembodied 1816, May.

Crimean War ... 1854, Dec., to 1856, June.

South African War ... 1899, Dec. 12, to 1900, Nov. 1.

Services.

In 1666 (by State Papers Dom. Chas. II.), the Militia of Herefordshire was drawn out by the King owing to the threatened French and Dutch invasion.

1798, Volunteered for service in Ireland, and made a forced march from Gravesend to Milford Haven, "the Officers in Post chaises, the men in waggons," doing fifty miles a day, and arrived in Ireland to form part of the Force to which General Humbert surrendered, for which it received the thanks of Parliament and the distinction of bearing the Crowned Harp on the Regimental Colour.

In 1814, the Militia of Herefordshire furnished seven Officers (Lt.-Col. John Berington, Captains Lechmere and Evans, Lieuts. Freeman, Parker, Allen, and Ensign Gambier), with 210 N.C.O.'s and men for the 3rd Provisional Battn. of the Militia Brigade under Colonel the Duke of Buckingham, which landed in France to serve under the Duke of Wellington.

5th Battalion, The Duke of Cambridge's Own (Middlesex Regiment).

"South Africa, 1902."

Hon. Colonel:—p.s. Rolleston, V., hon. c. (Hon. Lt.-Col. in Army, 16 Oct., 1900), (T).

Lt.-Colonel:—Lynden-Bell, C. P. L., Capt. ret. pay (Capt. Res. of Off.).

Origin.

Raised 1853 under the title of the "Royal Elthorne" Regiment, after the 1st Division of the County Hundreds, and subsequently became Light Infantry. In 1860 the Regt.

was officially known as the "Royal Elthorne Regt. of Militia Light Infantry," with the distinctive badge of a Bugle and initials "R.E.M." on cap and appointments. Under the Territorial Regimental Organization of 1881, the Regt. became at first the 3rd Battn. and then 5th Battn. of the "Middlesex Regt." on its augmentation by two additional Line Battns. numbered as the 3rd and 4th.

Embodiments.

Occasion.

Crimean War	1855, Feb. 5, to 1856, June 12.
Indian Mutiny	1857, Oct. 1, to 1860, Mch. 31.
South African War	1900, May 4, to 1900, Oct. 15.
South African War	1902, Jan. 6, to 1902, Sept. 18.

Services.

Volunteered for Foreign service and embarked for South Africa, strength 27 Officers, 825 N.C.O.'s and men, Colonel V. Rolleston commdg.

On arrival at Cape Town Mch. 15, 1902, the Battn. proceeded to Vryburg; afterwards to Mafeking with detachments at Maribogo, Kraiapan, and Maritzani, the Head Quarters at a later date moving to the latter place, part of the Battn. taking over the Blockhouse duty on the Maritzani Line.

Head Quarters subsequently moved to Maribogo with detachments at Buluwayo and Crocodile Pool. Aug. 27, 1902, the whole Battn. having assembled at Mafeking, entrained for Cape Town and embarked 30 Aug., 1902, for England.

Casualties.

Killed and died of disease, etc., 8 N.C.O.'s and men.

Medals, etc., received by Battalion.

Queen's South African Medal with Clasps "Transvaal," "Cape Colony," and "1902."

6th Battalion, The Duke of Cambridge's Own (Middlesex Regiment).

"South Africa, 1900-02."

Hon. Colonel :—Kent, H., Maj.-Gen. (Hon. Lt.-Gen.).

Lt.-Colonel :—Chichester, R. P. D. S. (Capt. Res. of Off.) (H).

Origin.

Formed originally part of the Force of the Saxon Kingdom A.D. 871, in the time of King Alfred, and has borne on its colours, drums and appointments the three Saxon swords and five pointed Saxon Crowns.

At the assembly of the Constitutional Force of the County to resist invasion by the Spanish Armada, Middlesex appears by the certificate returned by ye Lieuftenant (Harleian MSS.) to have provided 10,000 furneshed men in Aprille ano dom. 1588, reduced into bandes under Captaines and soarted wt weapons, besides Horsemen 19 Launces, 65 Lighthorse, and some Petroneles.

In 1641, Feb. 12, the Earl of Holland was appointed as a "fit person to be entrusted" with the organizing of the Militia of Middlesex. By Militia Returns 1697 (Egerton MSS.) the County of Middlesex had three Regts. known as the "County," "Red," and "Blew" Regts., 26 Companies of foot 3641, Cols. Rd. Shoreditch, Esqr., The Hon. Phillip Howard, Esq., John Bond, Esqr., besides two troops of Horse 131, known as the County and Westminster Troops.

In 1778 a Regt. was completed for service as the 1st Middlesex (East) Regt. of Militia, which by W.O. Letter Apr. 24, 1804, was a Royal Regt., and under the Territorial Organization of 1881 became at first the 4th Battn. of the "Middlesex Regt." and afterwards the 6th Battn. on augmentation of the Territorial Regt. by two additional Line Battns. numbered as the 3rd and 4th.

Embodiments.

Occasion.

American War	1778 to 1783.
French War	1792 to 1795.
European Disturbances	1803 to 1816.
Crimean War	1854 to 1856.
South African War	1899, Dec. 19, to 1902, Apr. 1.

Services.

In 1591 (by State Papers Dom.) Mydellsex furnished 100 men under Captain Moshen of the 4000 sent to aid Henry of Navarre against King Philip and the Duke of Parma. By S.P.D. Middlesex provided its quota of 6000 men sent to join the Forces of the French King in succouring the Citadel of Calais besieged. By S.P.D. 1598 Middlesex with five other counties supplied 2000 men for service during Rebellion in Ireland.

In 1645, by S.P.D. June 10, the rendezvous of the Middlesex Militia was at Romsey on the 13th for service in the western parts during the Civil War.

In 1666 by S.P.D. Sept. 6, part of the Middlesex Force was on duty in London during the Great Fire of London.

Volunteered for Foreign service at the time of the South African War, and embarked for the seat of War Feb., 1900, 25 Officers, 512 N.C.O.'s and men, Colonel G. C. Helme, C.B., Commdg. On arrival at Cape Town Mch. 16, 1900, the Battn. proceeded to Piquetberg Road for the purpose of preventing the North Western Rebellion from spreading southwards into Cape Colony.

May 29th the danger being at an end, the Battn. moved to Green Point, Cape Town, as guard over Boer Prisoners of War. Jan. 4, 1901, in consequence of the enemy again trying to get South, the Battn. was sent to Piquetberg Road, with two Companies at Malmesbury, half the Battn. under Lt.-Col. Brenchley, being at Ceres with Maxim Gun Detachment, and a Company at Tulbagh Village.

Jan. 8th, Martial Law proclaimed, Colonel G. C. Helme, C.B., appointed Commandant of the District, and Captain Gillam, Station Commandant at Tulbagh Village, the Battn. subsequently furnished Detachments at Karoo Poort, Gydo Pass, Wellington, Porterville, Waterfall and Brede River Bridges, Clanwilliam and Calvinia.

May 29, 1901, Head Quarters moved to Matjesfontein, all Detachments being brought in except from Porterville and Calvinia, the Battn. then furnished Detachments for Blockhouses on the line from Matjesfontein to Fraserberg Road, and subsequently at Sutherland.

June 15, 1901, Col. G. C. Helme, C.B., appointed Commandant No. 7 area, comprising 7 Districts.

June 16, 1901, Lt.-Col. H. Brenchley appointed Station Commandant at Laingsberg.

Sep., 1901, Battn. furnished detachments at Worcester and Ceres, and in Oct. small Detachments at Hex River Pass, De Doorns, Twefontein and Triangle.

Feb. 22, 1902, Head Quarters and four Companies moved to Beaufort West.

Mch. 7, 1902, Head Quarters and six Companies moved to Cape Town en route for England, the remaining two Companies joining the Battn. after relief at Clanwilliam and Calvinia, these two places being at the time surrounded by the enemy.

Details of Fighting.

Aug. 22, 1901, Colonel G. C. Helme, C.B., Commandant of No. 7 Area when returning from Sutherland to Matjesfontein with personal escort of ten men 4th West York Regt., came in contact with 25 Boers at Orangefontein and attacked them at 500 yards distance, driving them off, the Boers leaving one badly wounded on the field. Sep. 7, 1901, Sutherland was attacked by 250 Boers. Firing lasted from 8.30 a.m. to 5.30 p.m. The defences were only completed 12 hours before the attack.

The enemy did not succeed in approaching nearer than 1000 yards, Captain Graves commanded the Troops, which consisted of two Companies 6th Middlesex, a small Town guard, and Troop of " District Mounted Troops."

Sep. 15, 1901, Captain Oldfield and 20 men of his Company captured from Calvinia 9 Boers who were endeavouring to take a Cossack Post on Kopje near.

Nov. 14, 1901, Captain Graves and his Company forming part of Lt.-Colonel Callwell's column, seized a kopje near Vogelfontein which had been occupied by the enemy, driving them off, the Boers leaving one wounded on the field. This same Company assisted at the capture of 8 Boers hidden in a cornfield on 22nd Sep. at Tentelbosch Hoek.

Casualties.

Killed and died of disease., etc., one W.O., 26 N.C.O.'s and men.

Mentioned in Despatches.

Colonel G. C. Helme, C.B.
Captain F. Sapte (Adjutant).
Captain W. A. Gillam.
Captain P. N. Graves.
Captain and Hon. Major G. E. Barker.
Lieutenant R. A. Slee.
Hon. Captain and Qr.-Mr. J. A. Walter.
Sergt.-Major W. Woollett.
Cr.-Sergt. A. E. Howell.

Cr.-Sergt. E. Pullen.
Cr.-Sergt. W. Taylor.
Cr.-Sergt. J. Fisher.
Sergt. J. Andrews.
Corporal J. Beaney.
Private J. Roberts.

Special Honours.
Colonel G. C. Helme, C.B.—and received C.M.G.
Captain F. Sapte, D.S.O.
Captain P. H. Graves, D.S.O.
Captain W. A. Gillam, D.S.O.
Sergt.-Major W. Woollett, D.C. Medal.
Cr.-Sergt. A. E. Howell, D.C. Medal.
Cr.-Sergt. W. Taylor, D.C. Medal.

Medals, etc., received by Battalion.

South African Medal and Clasp "Cape Colony," King's Medal and Clasps "1901" and "1902."

5th Battalion, The King's Royal Rifle Corps.

Hon. Colonel:—Sandwich, Col. E. G. H., Earl of, hon. c.

Major:—Pixley, A. D.

Origin.

In 1641, Feb. 12, Lord Mandeville was appointed as "a fit person to be entrusted" with the organizing of the Militia of the County of Hunts. By Militia Returns 1697, (Egerton MSS.), the Militia of the County of Huntingdon formed one Regiment of five Companies 390 foot, and one Troop horse 72, total of both 462. Col. Robt. Apreace, Esqr.

In 1759 under Act 30, George II., c. 25, a Regt. was completed for service and the quota of men to be provided by Huntingdonshire.

In 1881, the Huntingdon Militia Regt. became under the Territorial Regimental Organization of the Forces, the 5th Battn. of "The King's Royal Rifle Corps."

Embodiments.

Occasion.

South African War ... 1900, May 2, to 1900, Dec. 4.

Note.—No records are available of the embodied periods and services of the Huntingdonshire Regiment.

7th Battalion, The King's Royal Rifle Corps.

Hon. Colonel:—Hutton, Maj.-Gen., Sir E. T. H. K.C.M.G., C.B., p. s. c. (R).

Lt.-Colonel:—Milborne-Swinnerton-Pilkington, Sir E. T. R., Bt., Maj. ret. pay, hon. c. (H).

Origin.

In 1881 under the Territorial Regimental organization of the Forces, the 2nd Middlesex or Edmonton Royal Rifle Regt. of Militia became the 7th Battn. of The King's Royal Rifle Corps.

For records of the Constitutional Force of Middlesex prior to 1778, see 6th Battn. Middlesex Regt. formerly the 1st Middlesex Militia Regt.

In 1778 a Regt. was completed for service as the West Middlesex Militia. In 1804 became a Royal Regt. In 1852 the Royal West Middlesex Militia was made Light Infantry, and a Rifle Regiment in 1854 as the 2nd or Edmonton Royal Rifle Regt. of Middlesex Militia, attached in 1873 to the Rifle Depot at Winchester (60th Royal Rifles), under Brigade reorganization, and in 1881 became a Battn. of the King's Royal Rifle Corps.

Embodiments.

Occasion.

No Regimental Records 1778 to 1792.
Revolutionary War, etc. 1792 to 1801.
European Disturbances 1815, June 29, to 1816, Aug. 25.
South African War ... 1900, May 8, to 1900, Oct. 15.

Services.

In 1814, Mch. 25, the Regt. having volunteered for Foreign service, 21 Officers (Captains Banks, Evans, Sir Wm. Hatton, Bt., Lewis, Lieuts. Carton, Miles, Weir,

Alavoine, Grace, Austin (Paymaster), Parker (Assist.-Surg.), Myers, Abbott, Hester, Burchell, Luby (Assist.-Surg.), Ensigns Wilton, Brew (Adjt.), Miles (Qr.-Mr.), and Surgeon Wright), with 560 N.C.O.'s and men formed part of the 3rd Provisional Militia Battn. under command of Lt.-Colonel Edward Bayley (West Middlesex Regt.), of the Militia Brigade which embarked for France under command of Colonel the Marquis of Buckingham (Bucks Militia). The Force landed at a village opposite to Blaye in the Garonne River, and held Bordeaux and its neighbourhood for a time, afterwards proceeding to Toulouse where it arrived too late to take part in the final battle of the campaign.

8th Battalion, The King's Royal Rifle Corps.

Hon. Colonel :—Butler, Sir T. P., Bt.
Lt.-Colonel :—Millner, J. K., hon. c. (H).

Origin.

In 1793, a Regiment was completed for service as the Carlow Militia and quota of men to be provided by the County, which in 1881 became the 8th Battn. of the King's Royal Rifle Corps under the Territorial Regimental Organization of the Forces.

Embodiments.

Occasion.

South African War ... 1900, Jan. 23, to 1900, Nov. 1.

Note.—No records are available of the embodied periods and services of the Carlow Regiment.

9th Battalion, The King's Royal Rifle Corps.

"South Africa, 1900-01."

Hon. Colonel :—Fitz-Gerald, Sir R. U. P., Bt.

Lt.-Colonel :—Cooke-Collis, W., C.M.G., Lt.-Col. ret. pay, Col., A.D.C.

Origin.

According to Smith's History of the County and City of Cork, in 1584 the Militia of the County were as follows :—

The City of Cork	...	300 shot,	100 Billmen.
The Barony of Muskery	20 ,,	300	,,
Imokilly ...	... 12 ,,	80	,,
Condous ...	... 8 ,,	60	,,
Lord Barry's County	... 30 ,,	200	,,
Mac-Carty More	... 8 ,,	400	,,
In all ...	... 378 ,,	1140	,,

In 1681 "those in the County consisted of 1600 foot and 26 independent troops of horse."

"Anno 1691, Sir Richard Cox, Governor, increased the Militia of the County to three compleat regiments of foot besides horse, total 6000, notwithstanding many Protestants were dispersed."

At an array in 1746 "they do not much exceed those in 1691."

In 1793 the Militia of the County was reorganized, and three Regts. completed for service, one as the North Cork Militia for the quota of men levied on the N.R. of the County, which in 1852 became a Rifle Regiment.

In 1881, under the Territorial Regimental organization of the Forces, the North Cork Rifles Regiment became the 9th Battn. of The King's Royal Rifle Corps.

Embodiments.

Occasion.

Revolutionary War, etc.	1793 to 1816, Apr. 1, for periods almost continuous.
Crimean War	1854 to 1856, Aug. 29.
Indian Mutiny	1857, Sep. 15, to 1860, Feb. 28.
South African War ...	1899, Dec. 5, to 1901, July 31.

Services.

See "Cork Royal Garrison Artillery" for particulars of service of the County Forces in 1691.

The North Cork Regt. of Militia took an active part in the suppression of the Rebellion 1798. Among the many incidents connected with their service are recorded—

The engagement at Oulart Hill in Wexford, May 27th, when Lt.-Col. Foote, one Sergt., and three privates only escaped out of about 100 picked men who were at this desperate fight, Major Lombard, Captn. De Courcy, Lieuts. Williams, Ware, Barry, and Ensign Keogh being among the killed.

The defence of Enniscorthy Bridge, May 28th, by Captn. Snowe of the Regt. with eighty men, besides about 200 yeomen of Enniscorthy and adjoining baronies against a large force of the rebels, of whom 800 had firearms and 5000 armed with pikes led by "Father John." The assailants advanced to the attack along the road with a herd of cattle in front, according to ancient custom, which being goaded into madness, rushed into the lines of those defending the Bridge, who, losing men fast, had to give way fighting inch by inch desperately. As the rebels advanced they set fire to the houses, the battle going on under an arch of flame; when shelter was obtained volleys were sent with destructive effect into the exposed mass of men within ten paces of the guns, and Father John fell back to the fields outside. Foiled at the Bridge, and after two attempts to force a passage below, the Town was cleared and in possession of the Loyalists.

By Maxwell's History, one hundred of the North Cork formed part of the Force under General Dunn, which defended Athy, June 24th, and pursued the rebels, forcing them to retreat on Goresbridge. At Kilcomney Hill they were attacked by the Downshire Regimental Guns, and by General Asgill's troops in the rear, which caused them to break and run, many being cut down, the pursuit continuing for two hours with fatal effect. Father John Murphy was taken prisoner in an ale house at Goresbridge, and hanged in the Market Place, his head being fixed on the Market-house and his body burned.

Volunteered for Foreign service during the South African War, and embarked at Queenstown Jan. 13th, 1900. Strength 23 Officers, 622 other ranks, Colonel W. Cooke-Collis commdg.

On arrival at Cape Town Feb. 1st, the Battn. proceeded to Nauwpoort and took over the defence of the Western kopjes. Feb. 8, the Right half Battn. under Major W. Stopford moved to Thebus to take charge of the Railway line in that direction. Feb. 10th, Head Quarters with Left half Battn. proceeded to Arundel leaving "E" Company at Tweedale. Feb. 14th Maj.-Gen. Clement's Force relinquished Rensburg and falling back on Arundel the Left half Battn. took part in the action that ensued, and then moved back to Nauwpoort to share in the defence, the Militia Units there being brigaded under Colonel Cooke-Collis.

In March Head Quarters with three Companies were sent to Steynsburg, followed by "E" Company.

Mch. 13th, two Companies took over the duty of guarding the railway bridge at Kroomhoogte and Henning.

Apr. 2nd, the whole Battn. moved to Bethulie and on the 4th escorted a convoy of 100 ox waggons to Springfontein. Apr. 10th held the Reit River Bridge, the only bridge left intact by the Boers in the Orange Free State. May 7th proceeded to the Vet River to help the Engineers in making the deviation for the railway, the bridge having been destroyed. May 17th the Battn. moved to Rail Head (Virginia) and on completion of the railway deviation proceeded to Rhenoster. June 1st furnished two Companies as escort to convoy to the Rail Head at Leuespruit, and the escort being hard pressed by the Boers, the remainder of Battn. went out to its assistance, forcing the enemy to retire. In June, between the 2nd and 6th, the Battn. was a Wolverhoek and Steenpan, and from thence proceeded to guard the bridge at Taailbosch and take charge of 87 Boer prisoners, afterwards moving to Taailbosch Kop leaving two Companies to guard the bridge and detaching two others to Vilgoens Drift Station, the Head Quarters remaining at Taailbosch Kop having charge of the line Vereeniging to Wolverhoek, a task of great importance and responsibility, which required to be patrolled several times each night at uncertain hours, a distance of eleven miles, the Boers being very active in the District and many attempts defeated to wreck the line. The following circular memo was issued by the D.A.A.G. lines of communication on the subject of Officers using their ingenuity in devising means to stop this interference.

"That this can be done successfully is shown by the way a patrol of the 9th Battn. King's Royal Rifle Corps surprised a dozen Boers preparing to lay a mine south of Steenpan siding on the night of the 19th inst." In Army Orders, Pretoria, 28th June, 1901, the following Sergts, of the Battn. appear as specially brought to the notice of the Commander-in-Chief for gallantry in good leading in Action:

No. 2041 Sergt. W. McQue.
No. 2843 Sergt. W. Connor.

Copy of Order published by Brigr.-General G. G. Cunningham, C.B., D.S.O., on departure of the Battn. from Vereeniging, June 12th, 1901.

"The G.O.C. cannot let the 9th Battn. King's Royal Rifle Corps leave the command for home without placing on record the good work they have done, etc., etc. On arrival they at once proceeded to the front and joined the force in the Colesburg District, being engaged in the action of Feb. 14th, 1900. When the general advance took place the Battn. was employed in guarding the railway, and when visited by Field Marshal Lord Roberts, the Commander-in-Chief, he expressed his satisfaction with the Battn. To the lot of the Corps fell much arduous work when the efforts of De Wet to wreck the railway in Orange River Colony are remembered, etc., etc."

Embarked for England at Cape Town July 6th, 1901.

Casualties.

Killed and died of disease, etc., 3 Officers (Major L. A. de V. Mannsell, Captn. E. W. C. Dillon, Surgn. Lt.-Col. J. Creagh), and 22 N.C.O.'s and men.

Mentioned in Despatches.

Captain and Adjt. R. Byron.
Captain A. W. Clerke.
Captain W. H. Nichols.
Major and Qr.-Mr. W. Holmes.
Sergt.-Major D. Connell.
Qr.-Mr.-Sergt. T. Hogan.
Cr.-Sergt. T. Wallace.
Cr.-Sergt. W. Callaghan.
Sergt. W. Connor.

Special Honours.

Colonel W. Cooke-Collis, C.M.G.
Captain and Adjt. R. Byron, D.S.O.
Captain A. W. Clarke, D.S.O.
Sergt.-Major D. Connell, D.C. Medal.
Qr.-Mr.-Sergt. T. Hogan, D.C. Medal.

Medals, etc., received by Battalion.

Queen's South African with Clasps "**Cape Colony,**" "**Orange Free State,**" "**Transvaal,**" and "**South Africa, 1901.**"

3rd Battalion, The Duke of Edinburgh's (Wiltshire Regiment).

"Mediterranean."
"St. Helena, 1901-2."

Hon. Colonel: Methuen, Gen. P. S., Lord, G.C.B., K.C.V.O., C.M.G., S. Gds. s. (R).

Lt.-Colonel:—Barclay, R., hon. c.

Origin.

The "tithings lists of archers and billmen," March 1, 30, Henry VIII., representing the Constitutional Force of the County, appear in the "Letters and Papers of this Reign."

At the Spanish Armada assembly 1588, "Wiltsheire" had 1200 Trained men present, formed into companies, besides Horsemen Launces 25, Lighthorse 100.

In 1641, Feb. 12, the Earl of Pembroke was appointed as "a fit person to be entrusted" with the organization of the County Militia.

The Militia Returns of 1697 (Egerton MSS.) include Wiltshire as having four Regiments, 2,366 footmen, and 232 horse. The Red Regiment, Col. Sr. Thos. Nampesson; Blew Regiment, Col. Edward Webb; Green Regiment, Col. Henry Chivers; Yellow Regiment, Col. Henry Baintan.

In 1759, when the Militia of the Kingdom was reorganized, a Regiment was completed for service and the quota of men to be furnished by the County, as the Wiltshire Regt., which became a Royal Regiment in June 1841, and under the Territorial Organization of 1881, the 3rd Battn. of The Duke of Edinburgh's (Wiltshire Regiment).

Embodiments.

Occasion.

Civil War, Chas. I.	Period unknown.
Seven Years War ...	1759, June 30, to 1762, Dec. 15.
French War ...	1813, period unknown.
Crimean War ...	1854, June 10, to 1856, Sept. 17.
South African War ...	1900, Jan. 16, to 1902, Sept. 11.

Services.

Volunteered for Foreign Service 1814, four officers (Captain Kennier, Lieuts. Smith, Eastaugh, Terry) and 130 N.C.O.'s and men embarking at Portsmouth March 10th as part of the 2nd Battn of the three Provisional Battalions forming the Militia Brigade which landed in France near Bordeaux to serve under Wellington.

Volunteered for Foreign Service during the Crimean War, and stationed at the Ionian Islands, in recognition of which service "Mediterranean" is borne on the colour.

Volunteered for Foreign Service during the South African War, and stationed at St. Helena as guard over Boer prisoners of war, the Battalion suffering severely from an epidemic of enteric fever, five officers being invalided home, and deaths 13 N.C.O.'s and Men.

Honours.

Lt.-Colonel Commanding E. C. A. Sanford, C.M.G.
No. 5398 Pte. J. J. Cripps, D.C. Medal.

Medals, etc., received by Battalion.
Queen's South African Medal.

5th Battalion, The Manchester Regiment.

"South Africa, 1901-02."

Hon. Colonel :—Hamilton, Lt.-Gen. Sir I.S.M., K.C.B., D.S.O., Col. Cam'n. Highrs, S.

Lt.-Colonel :—Crosbie, H., hon. c. (Maj. Res. of Off.).

Origin.

Raised 1854 by Colonel Walbraham under authority of the Earl of Sefton as Lord Lieutenant, and as the 6th Royal Lancashire Militia Regiment. Formed in 1881 the 3rd and 4th Batts. of the Manchester Regiment, afterwards becoming the 5th and 6th upon augmentation of the Territorial Regiment by two additional Line Battalions numbered as the 3rd and 4th.

Embodiments.

Occasion.

Crimean War ... 1855, May 17, period not recorded.
South African War... 1900, May 3, to 1900, Oct. 20.
    ,,   ,,   ... 1901, May 6, to 1902, July 28.

Services.

Volunteered for Foreign Service and embarked for South Africa, strength 26 officers, 780 N.C.O.'s and men, Colonel H. Crosbie commanding. On arrival Cape Town 10th July, 1901, proceeded to Winburg, Orange River Colony, and employed on the lines of communication, building blockhouses, and making trenches, etc.

Casualties.

Killed and died of disease, etc., 1 officer, 21 N.C.O.'s and men.

Mentioned in Despatches.

Colonel H. Crosbie.
Captain and Adjt. J. C. Crawford.
Sergt.-Major J. Homneystreet.
Qr.-Mr.-Sergt. C. Joyce.

Medals, etc., received by Battalion.

South African with Clasps "Orange Free State," "Cape Colony," and 1901-2.

6th Battalion, The Manchester Regiment.

"South Africa, 1902."

Hon. Colonel :—Stanley, Rt. Hon. E. G. V., Lord, K.C.V.O., C.B.

Lt.-Colonel :—Johnson, H. A.

Origin.

Raised in 1854 as the 6th Royal Lancashire Militia Regt.

In 1881, under the Territorial Regimental Organization of the Forces, the Regiment formed the 3rd and 4th Battns. of The Manchester Regiment.

In 1900 this Regiment being augmented by two additional Line Battalions numbered as the 3rd and 4th, the two Militia Battalions became the 5th and 6th.

Embodiments.

Occasion.

(See 5th Battn. of the Regiment prior to 1881.)
South African War ... 1900, May 4, to 1900, Oct. 18.
    ,,   ,, ... 1902, Jan. 6, to 1902, Sept. 30.

Services.

Voluntered for Foreign Service during the South African War, and embarked for Cape Town Feb. 13th, 1902. Strength 20 officers, 645 other ranks, Colonel C. D. Leyden commanding.

On arrival, entrained March 6th for Norvals Pont on the Orange River to relieve the 3rd Battn. Norfolk Regiment on the blockhouse line between Jagersfontein and Achterlong Stations, a distance of thirty-six miles, and chain of forts, sangars, etc., around the Pont. Head Quarters being at Norvals Pont.

Apr. 14th, took over the additional blockhouse line occupied by the 3rd Gren. Guards, extending from Achterlong to Tweedale, a Garrison being also furnished at Colesburg Town to guard and escort Rebel prisoners. These various posts were held without molestation by the Boers until one month after the declaration of peace, when the Battn. concentrated at Norvals Pont, proceeded by rail to Port Elizabeth, and re-embarked Sept. 4th for England.

Casualties.

Killed and died of disease, etc., 8 N.C.O.'s and men.

Medals, *etc.*, received by Battalion.

Queen's South African Medal with Clasps "Cape Colony," "Orange Free State," and "South Africa 1902."

3rd Battalion, The Prince of Wales's (North Staffordshire Regiment).

"South Africa, 1902."

Hon. Colonel :—Buller, Sir M. E., Bt.
Lt.-Colonel :—p.s. Hall, G.C., hon. c.

Origin.

Raised 1853, as the 2nd King's Own Staffordshire Regt. of Militia, under Act of Parliament, 15, 16, Vict., cap. 90, for the increased quota of Militia to be found by the County divided into three Regiments known as the 1st, 2nd, and 3rd, the 2nd Regiment becoming in 1881 the 3rd Battn., Prince of Wales's (North Staffordshire Regt.) under Territorial Organization of the Forces.

Embodiments.

Occasion.

Crimean War ...	1854, Dec. 19, to 1856, June 16.
Indian Mutiny ...	1857, Sept. 28, to 1860, July 31.
South African War ...	1900, May 2, to 1900, Oct. 15.
,, ,, ...	1902, Feb. 10, to 1902, Sept. 23.

Services.

Volunteered for Foreign Service during South African War, strength embarked 27 officers, one W.O., and 525 N.C.O.'s and men. On arrival Cape Town March 26, 1902, proceeded to Vryburg and employed in fortifying the Town, then sent south to guard thirty-eight miles of railway, construct and occupy blockhouses at about half a mile apart, several attempts being made by the enemy to cross the line. On June 4th two of the blockhouses were heavily attacked by Van Zyl and driven off by the armoured train, one Company sent up the line being ambushed; the day after arrival at Vryburg some stock was captured which the Boers were attempting to drive across the line. A party of one hundred officers and men later on took part in the big drive of Boers to the North of Vryburg (which ended the war), 600 Boers surrendering and 20,000 head of stock being captured.

(It is recorded that the 2nd K.O. Staffordshire Militia gave 417 trained men to the Line during less than twelve months of the Indian Mutiny.)

Casualties in South Africa.

Killed and died of disease, etc., 10 N.C.O.'s and men.

Medals, *etc.*, received by Battalion.

Queen's South African Medal with Clasps "Cape Colony" and "South Africa 1902."

4th Battalion, The Prince of Wales's (North Staffordshire Regiment).

"South Africa, 1900-2."

Hon. Colonel :—Bill, C., hon. c.
Lt.-Colonel :—Mirehouse, R. W. B., C.M.G., hon. c.

Origin.

Raised 1853 as the 3rd Regiment of King's Own Staffordshire Militia to complete the quota of men required from the County, and soon afterwards designated the 3rd King's Own Stafford Rifles. In 1881, under Territorial Organization, became the 4th Battn. of The Prince of Wales's (North Staffordshire Regiment).

Embodiments.

    Occasion.

Crimean War	1854, Dec. 19, to 1876, May 26.
South African War	1900, Jan. 24, to 1902, June 11.

Services.

Volunteered for Foreign Service and embarked for South Africa, strength 24 officers, one W.O., 546 N.C.O.'s and men, Colonel R. W. B. Mirehouse commanding. On arrival Cape Town March 29, 1900, stationed at Green Point, Captains D. G. O. Saunders-Davies and F. H. Wedgwood with two Companies proceeding March 31st. to St. Helena in charge of General Cronje and Boer prisoners of war, captured at Paardeberg, rejoining the Battalion on completion of the duty.

June 9th, four Companies detached to Hermon, Wellington and Paarl. In Dec., Head Quarters moved to Frazerburg, Lt.-Col. F. R. Twemlow commanding, Colonel Mirehouse being at Beaufort West as commandant. June 25, 1901, a most determined attack was made by the combined commandoes of Malan, Smit and Reitz, together with some 40 men of Breeda's commando, numbering about four hundred. The town at this time was garrisoned by only 85 of the Staffords, 37 town guard, and 5 Cape Colony Cyclists Corps. Firing began at 5.30 a.m., when all Troops were at their posts. The attack was first made on a small post held by a Corporal and three men, eventually working round to the back of a sangar on a high ridge of kopjes dominating the town held by a Sergeant with 17 men of the Staffords, an unfinished blockhouse near aiding the enemy. Sergeant White and his men fought desperately for three hours before the position was rushed and captured by numerical strength. Captain Hawkshaw in Flagstaff sangar having refused Malan's message to surrender, the Boers then determined to capture a remaining small post on the ridge, this being rushed after all three men were wounded, so placing the enemy in possession of the ridge commanding Flagstaff position, upon which bullets literally rained. After two further messages from Malan to surrender, the Boers advanced down the main street preceded by a white flag, which prevented one sangar from firing, the Flagstaff sangar and Tower Hill still holding out, maintained a hot fire on the enemy, who were attempting to get round by the river bed. A sangar held by eight of the Townguard also held out for about eleven hours; the Prison garrisoned by the Townguard had likewise refused to surrender. Firing ceased at about 6 p.m., Malan sending in word to Captains Hawkshaw and Levett "that they ought to be thankful that their reinforcements were on the road." Killed and wounded in the engagement 12 N.C.O.'s and men, the Boer losses being approximately 6 killed and 18 wounded. The rebels aided the Boers by information and firing from the house tops. General French "complimented the garrison on their successful resistance, and thanked the troops for their splendid behaviour."

Feb., 1902, the Battalion occupied the blockhouses alternately with Cape Boys from Victoria Road to Carnarvon, a distance of 80 miles, until May 12, 1902, and entrained May 13, 1902, for Cape Town, where the Battalion embarked for home. General French addressed the Battalion before leaving, and accorded high praise for their "arduous and self-sacrificing labours throughout the Campaign."

(It is recorded that during the Crimean War the 3rd K.O. Stafford Rifles gave nearly one thousand trained men to the Regular Army.)

Casualties.

Killed and died of disease, etc., in South Africa, Captain R. N. Fane, Captain G. P. Bull, 2nd Lieut. J. M. Sharpe, and 25 N.C.O.'s and men.

Mentioned in Despatches.

Colonel R. W. B. Mirehouse.
Lt.-Colonel F. R. Twemlow.
Major E. S. Pipe-Wolferstan (twice).
Major C. Wedgwood (twice).
Captain G. P. Bull.

Sergeant-Major R. Katon.
Qr.-Master-Sergt. C. Preston.
Cr.-Sergeant J. Bradley.
Cr.-Sergeant W. H. Rowe (twice).
Cr.-Sergeant G. W. Tribe.
Cr.-Sergeant F. Brass.
Corporal E. Vaughan.

Special Honours.

Colonel R. W. B. Mirehouse, C.M.G.
Lt.-Colonel F. R. Twemlow, D.S.O.
Major C. Wedgwood, D.S.O.
Sergeant-Major R. Katon, D.C. Medal.
Qr.-Master Sergeant C. Preston, D.C. Medal.
Cr.-Sergeant W. H. Rowe, D.C. Medal.

Medals, *etc.*, received by Battalion.

Queen's Medal and Clasp Cape Colony.
King's Medal with Clasps inscribed "S.A. 1901," "S.A. 1902."

3rd Battalion, The York and Lancaster Regiment.

"South Africa, 1902."
Hon. Colonel :—Hardy, Major-Gen. F. (R).
Lt.-Colonel :—Groom, J.E., hon. c.

Origin.

See 3rd Battn. The Yorkshire Light Infantry.

When the Supplementary Militia Regiments which had been raised under Act 34, Geo. III., 1794, were disbanded in 1799, the 5th Regt. of the West Yorkshire (or third Supplementary Regt.) was retained to reform the 3rd West York regular Militia, which had been incorporated with the 1st and 2nd Regiments in 1762. It became Light Infantry in 1852, and under Territorial Organization of 1881, the 3rd Battn. of "The York and Lancaster Regiment."

Embodiments.

   Occasion.

Revolutionary War, etc.	1798, March 5, to 1802, April 22.
French War ...	1803, March 11 to 1814, June 24.
Crimean War ...	1854, May 26, to 1856, June 30.
Indian Mutiny ...	1857, Oct. 1, to 1860, May 2.
South African War ...	1899, Dec. 13, to 1900, Dec. 4.
,, ,, ...	1901, Dec. 9, to 1902, Sept. 23.

Services.

1798, July 19, called upon to suppress riots at Hull, for which service the following resolution of the Local Authorities was recorded and sent to the Regiment:

"That the thanks of the Magistrates be given to Colonel Sir George Cooke, Bart., for his readiness in assembling his Corps to suppress Riot of a serious nature in the Town, and that he be requested to represent to the Officers and Corps in general that they entertain a due sense of the advantages derived from their steady conduct on the occasion."

Volunteered for and stationed in Ireland 1812-14.

Volunteered for Foreign Service and embarked for South Africa, strength 29 officers, one W.O., 651 N.C.O.'s and men, Colonel J. G. Wilson, C.B., commanding. On arrival Cape Town Jan. 14, 1902, the Battalion proceeded to Kimberley, two Companies remaining there, two going on trek to Griquatown, one to Douglas, and one to Campbeltown, the remaining four Companies with Head Quarters moving by rail to Vryburg. From here, one Company was sent to Taungs, one to Pudimoe and a third to Kuruman. March 2, Col. Wilson joined Major Paris's Column proceeding from Vryburg to Lichtenburg, Lt.-General Lord Methuen being also with the Force. March 7, the Column was attacked by the Boers under General Delarey with disastrous results, Lord Methuen being seriously wounded, Colonel Wilson mortally, and all who remained alive on the field taken prisoners. April 15th, the Taungs and Pudimoe detachments rejoined Head Quarters at Vryburg, and on the 17th all moved South to Brussels, where blockhouses were occupied on the railway line with Brussels Fort as Head Quarters, remaining here for many weeks after peace was declared. The two Companies left at Kimberley in January were chiefly employed on blockhouse duty and escorting convoys into the Orange River Colony.

The Companies detached at Griquatown, etc., were quite cut off from the outside world, except on the occasional visit of an armed convoy.

Aug. 11, the Battalion assembled at Brussels and left on the 25th for Cape Town to embark for England.

Casualties.

Killed and died of disease, etc., Colonel J. G. Wilson, C.B., and 4 men.

Medals, etc., received by Battalion.

Queen's South African Medal with Clasps "South Africa 1902," "Cape Colony," "Transvaal," "Orange Free State."

3rd Battalion, The Durham Light Infantry.

"South Africa, 1900-01."

Hon. Colonel :—Surtees, C. F.

Lt.-Colonel :—p.s. Grimshawe, E. S. V., hon. c. (H).

Origin.

In 1272, a Force existed in the County vested in the Bishop of Durham as a County Palatine.

In 1346, the Force of the County was on active service, and at a Muster by order of King James I., 1615, the numbers liable to serve (8,291) are recorded, but not of those armed and organized for service.

In 1666 (State Papers Dom., Chas. II.), a levy was made on the County Militia by the King, owing to the threatened French and Dutch Invasion.

In 1685, the Regiment of the County was mustered, and numbered 885 foot under Sir Ralph Cole, Bart., as Colonel, with 300 horse, Nicholas Conyers, Esqr., Captain.

When the Militia Forces of England and Wales were reorganized under Act 30, Geo. II. a Regiment was completed for service in 1760 as the Durham Regiment of Militia. In 1853 the quota of the County being increased to 2,000, the County Regiment was divided into two Infantry Units, an Artillery Regiment being also formed, the original Unit being designated the 1st Durham, became Fusiliers in 1869, and 3rd Battalion of The Durham Light Infantry in 1881.

Embodiments.

Occasion.

War with Edward I. ... Dates not recorded.
War with Scotland ... 1346, dates not recorded.
American War ... 1778 to 1783.
Revolutionary War, etc. 1793, May, to 1802, May.
French War ... 1803, July 22, to 1814, Aug. 14.
„ „ ... 1815, July 14, to 1816, Feb. 28.
Crimean War ... 1854, Dec. 22, to 1856, May 22.
Threatened War ... 1885, Mar. 9, to 1885, Sept. 29.
South African War ... 1899, Dec. 5, to 1901, June 12.

Services.

Defence of Barnard Castle by Bishop Beck in defiance of Edward I., Battle of Neville's Cross 1346.

Volunteered for Foreign Service during South African War, and embarked for South Africa, strength 30 officers, 796 N.C.O.'s and men, Colonel R. B. Wilson commanding. On arrival East London, Feb. 3, 1900, employed in guarding lines of communication in Cape Colony and Orange Free State, escorting convoys and garrisoning De Wets Dorp for about six months, etc.

Casualties.

Killed and died of disease, etc., Col. R. B. Wilson, Lieut. F. H. A. Sowerby, Lieut. J. C. Williams, and 25 N.C.O.'s and men.

Mentioned in Despatches.

Col. R. B. Wilson.
Capt. S. G. Sowerby.
Capt. E. C. Sowerby.
Q.M.-Sergt. R. W. Storey.
Cr.-Sergt. T. Taft.
Sergt. T. Beeby (4th Battn.), attached.
Major E. S. V. Grimshawe.
Capt. E. C. Sowerby.
Sergt.-Major A. Anderton.
Cr.-Sergt. A. Chivers.
Sergt. T. Sweeney.

Special Honours.

Colonel R. B. Wilson, C.M.G.
Capt. and Hon. Maj. H. J. Sowerby, D.S.O.
Sergt. T. Beeby (attached), D.C. Medal.
Sergt. T. Sweeney, D.C. Medal.

Medals, etc., received by Battalion.

Queen's South African Medal with Clasps "Cape Colony," "Orange Free State," and "South Africa 1901."

4th Battalion, The Durham Light Infantry.

"South Africa, 1902."

Hon. Colonel :—Londonderry, Most Hon. C. S., Marq. of, K.G., G.C.V.O., C.B., Col. A.D.C.

Lt.-Colonel :—Darwin, C. W., Lt.-Col. ret. pay (Lt.-Col. Res. of Off), hon. c.

Origin.

Formed as the 2nd Durham Regiment of Militia in 1853, by division of the existing Militia Regiment of the County into two Infantry Regiments, the quota of Militia for Durham being 2,000 men. See Origin, 3rd Durham Light Infantry and its services prior to 1853. Became the 4th Battalion of the Territorial Durham Light Infantry Regiment in 1881.

Embodiments.

Occasion.

Crimean War	...	1855, Jan 1, to 1856, May 14.
South African War	...	1900, Jan. 23, to 1900, Dec. 4.
,, ,,	...	1901, Jan. 6, to 1902, Oct. 3.

Services.

Volunteered for Foreign Service and proceeded to South Africa, strength embarked 31 officers, one W.O., 820 N.C.O.'s and men, Colonel M. H. Lambert commanding. On arrival Cape Town Feb. 18, 1902, proceeded to Orange River Station, Cape Colony, and furnished detachments for Kimberley, Belmont, Modder River, Schmidts Drift, Barkley West, Daniels Kuil, Boshoff, Widnsorton Road, and Slip Klip Drift. The Battalion also taking over the blockhouses on the railway line from Orange River to Modder River, with one Company on the Orange River Bridge. A body of Mounted Infantry which was formed carried out convoy duty between Kimberley, Boshoff and Christiana. The Battalion re-embarked for England Sept. 3, 1902, at Port Elizabeth.

Casualties.

Killed and died of disease, etc., 16 men.

Honours.

Sergeant T. Beeby (attached to 3rd Battalion), D.C. Medal.

Medals, etc., received by Battalion.

Queen's South African Medal with Clasps "Cape Colony," "Orange Free State," "Transvaal," and "South Africa 1902."

3rd and 4th Battalions, The Highland Light Infantry.

(3rd Battalion, "South Africa, 1902.")

Hon. Colonel :—Field-Marshal H.R.H. Arthur W.P.A., Duke of Connaught and Strathearn, K.G., K.T., K.P., G.C.B., G.C.S.I., G.C.M.G., G.C.I.E.. G.C.V.O., G. Gds., A.S. Corps, and Col.-in-Chief 6 Dns., High L.I., R. Dub. Fus., and Rif. Brig., Personal A.D.C. to the King, Insp.-Gen. of the Forces, Bailiff of Egle Order of St. John of Jerusalem, etc., etc.

3rd Battn.—Lt.-Colonel :—Story, W. F., C.B., hon. c.

4th Battn. Hon. Lt.-Colonel :—Hamilton and Brandon, A. D., Duke of.

4th Battn.—Lt.-Colonel :—Robertson-Aikman, T. S. G. H., hon. c.

Origin.

A County Regiment of Lanark Militia existed in 1645.

In 1796 a Regiment was completed for service, which became a Royal Regiment in 1803.

In 1881 it became the 3rd Battn of the Territorial Highland Light Infantry Regiment, and was divided into two separate Units as the 3rd and 4th Battns. of the Regiment in 1883.

Embodiments.

Occasion.	
Revolutionary War,	1645, period unknown.
European Distrubances, etc.	1796 to 1801.
	1803, March, to 1814, Aug. 24.
Crimean War ...	1855, Feb. 6, to 1856 July 10.
3rd Battn. South African War	1899, Dec. 6, to 1900, Oct. 20.
,, ,,	1901, Dec. 9, to 1902, Sept. 25.
4th Battn. ,,	1900, May 2, to 1900, Oct. 15.

Services.

Embodied during disturbances in 1646. Volunteered for and served in Ireland 1811-13.

The 3rd Battalion having volunteered for Foreign Service, embarked for South Africa Dec., 1901, strength (including a portion of the 4th Battalion) 30 officers, one W.O., 978 N.C.O.'s and men.

On arrival Cape Town Jan. 14, 1902, Head Quarters with eight companies proceeded to Warrenton, two Companies under Major E. A. Everett remaining at Kimberley, afterwards proceeding to Bloemfontein to join Colonel Sitwell's column, and served in the Orange River Colony and Western Transvaal until the war ended. The right half Battalion performed blockhouse duty on the Western line of the railway between Kimberley and Vryburg, the remainder being employed with convoys between Warrenton and Christiana, except a detachment under Captain Hartley at Jacobsdal and Koffyfontein, the General Officers under whom the Regiment served in South Africa expressing "their appreciation of the work done, and the manner in which it was performed." After remaining for some time after the declaration of peace, the Battalion concentrated at Cape Town and re-embarked for England August 20, 1902.

Casualties.

Killed and died of disease, etc., 14 N.C.O.'s and men.

Mentioned in Despatches.

Captain and Adjt. G. T. B. Wilson.
Captain C. O. Greenwell, 4th Durham L.I. (attached).
Sergt.-Major J. Comb.
Cr.-Sergt. G. Bignall.

Medals, *etc.*, received by Battalion.

Queen's South African Medal with Clasps "Cape Colony," "Orange Free State," "Transvaal," "South Africa 1902."

3rd Battalion, Seaforth Highlanders (Ross-shire Buffs, The Duke of Albany's).

"Mediterranean, 1900-01."
Hon. Colonel :—p.s. Macleay, A. C., C.B., hon. c. (t).
Lt.-Colonel :—p.s. Henderson, J. H.

Origin.

One of the sixty Militia Regiments raised for the Revolutionary War, as the Ross, Sutherland, Caithness and Cromarty, of North British Militia.

In 1803 designated the 5th Ross, Caithness, Shetland and Cromarty. In 1854 became a Rifle Regt., and in 1860 the Highland Rifle Militia, until 1881, when, under Territorial Organization of the Forces, it became the 3rd Battn. Seaforth Highlanders (Ross-shire Buffs, The Duke of Albany's).

Embodiments.

   Occasion.

Revolutionary War, etc.	1798, April, 23, to 1802, May 1.
French War	1803, March 12, to 1814, Sept. 2.
,, ,,	1815, Aug. 1, to 1816, June 10.
Crimean War	1855, March 6, to 1856, June 23.
South African War	1889, Dec. 13, to 1901, June 11.

Services.

Volunteered for Foreign Service during South African War, and stationed in Egypt, occupying the Citadel Barracks at Cairo Feb., 1900, until May, 1901. Colonel Sir Hector Munro appointed A.D.C. to the King June, 1802.

3rd Battalion The Gordon Highlanders.

Hon. Colonel:—THE KING.
Lt.-Colonel:—Kintore, Rt. Hon. A. T., Earl of, G.C.M.G., Col., A.D.C.

Origin.

In 1881, under the Territorial Organization of the Forces of the Kingdom, the Royal Aberdeenshire Highlanders Regt. of Militia became the 3rd Battn. of "The Gordon Highlanders."

In 1649, Feb. 28, the quotas of men assigned by the Estates of the Scottish Parliament required the shire of Kincardine and Earl Marischal's part of Aberdeen to "raise and put out" 600 Foot and 200 Horse, the rest of Aberdeen and Sheriffdom of Banff 800 Foot and 480 Horse. In 1650, July 3, after King Charles II. had come to Scotland, the Estates of Parliament "appointed and ordained other proportions. For the horse, Aberdeen 186, (makes three troops at 62). For the foot, Kincardine and Marischal's part of Aberdeen 900 (one regiment). Rest of Aberdeen and Banff 1,200 (one regiment)."

In 1798, under reorganization of the Militia Force of Scotland, a Regiment was completed for service as the Aberdeenshire or 6th North British Militia Regt., Aberdeen being united with Banff for the quota of men to be furnished until 1802, when Aberdeenshire found the men for one complete Regiment. In 1855 it became a Royal Regiment, in 1858 Highlanders, and in 1881 part of the Territorial Gordon Highlanders Regiment.

Embodiments.

Occasion.

European Disturbances	1798, Oct. 6, to 1802, April 30.
French War	1803, April 21, to 1814, Sept. 23.
,, ,,	1815, July 25, to 1816, Feb. 24.
Crimean War	1855, Feb. 20, to 1856, May.
Indian Mutiny	1857, Nov. 12, to 1858, May 18.
South African War	1899, Dec. 6, to 1901, July 6.

Services.

1812, moved to Glasgow on particular service, for apprehended riots, etc., arising out of disturbances promoted by secret associations, as at Nottingham and in Yorkshire.

The Historical Records of this Regiment include the coincidence that it has formed part of the force detailed for the safety of each of the three capitals. In 1801 "the covering forces for Edinburgh," garrisoned the Tower of London in 1814, and stationed at Dublin 1858.

3rd Battalion, The Queen's Own Cameron Highlanders.

Hon. Colonel:—p.s. Mackintosh of Mackintosh, A. D., hon. c. (Hon. Lt.-Col. in Army 5 Dec. 1900).

Lt.-Colonel:—MacLeod, N., Capt. ret. pay, hon. c. (H).

Origin.

Raised 1803, as the Inverness, Banff, Elgin, and Nairn Militia, afterwards becoming the Highland Light Infantry Militia, and 3rd Battn. of The Queen's Own Cameron Highlanders in 1881 under Territorial Organization of the Forces.

Embodiments.

Occasion.

French War	1803 to 1814, Aug. 31.
French War	1815, June 29, to 1816, Jan. 16.
Crimean War	1855, Jan. 18, to 1856, May 26.
South African War	1899, Dec. 6, to 1900, Dec. 4.

3rd Battalion, The Royal Irish Rifles.

Hon. Colonel :—Londonderry, Most Hon. C. S., Marq. of, K.G., G.C.V.O., C.B., A.D.C.
Lt.-Colonel :—Findlay, F. (H).

Origin.

In 1881, the Royal North Down Rifles formed in 1793 as the North Downshire Militia Regt., for part of the quota of men to be found by the County, designated in 1800 the Royal North Downshire, afterwards known as the Royal North Down, and Royal North Down Rifles at a later date, became under the Territorial Organization of the Forces the 3rd Battn. of the Royal Irish Rifles Regiment.

Embodiments.

Occasion.

Revolutionary War ...	1793, period unknown.
European Disturbances	1802, to 1814, Oct.
European Disturbances	1815, Oct., to 1816, Mch. 24.
Crimean War	1855, Jan., to 1856, Aug. 13.
Indian Mutiny... ...	1857, Sep. 20, to 1859, Mch. 25.
South African War ...	1900, May 14, to 1900, Oct. 19.

Services.

N.B.—Records prior to 1855 destroyed by Fire. A service Company of 110 men, Captain W. R. McD. Parr formed part of the 5th Battalion Royal Irish Rifles for service in South Africa, 1901, and Pte. Owen was specially promoted Corporal for going out to be captured by the Boers for the purpose of bringing back information.

4th Battalion, The Royal Irish Rifles.

Hon. Colonel :—Macnaghten, Sir F. E., Bt., Col.
Lt.-Colonel :—Macartney-Filgate, E. J. P. F.

Origin.

Formed 1793, as the Antrim Regiment of Militia and became a Royal Regt. In 1881, under the Territorial organization of the Forces becoming the 4th Battn. of "The Royal Irish Rifles" Regiment.

Embodiments.

Occasion.

Revolutionary War, etc. 1793 to 1802.
European Disturbances 1803 to 1814.
                             1815 to 1816.
Crimean War ... ... 1854, Dec. 12, to 1856, Aug. 12.
Indian Mutiny... ... 1857, Sep. 24, to 1860, Mch. 10.
South African War ... 1900, May 10, to 1900, Nov. 1.

Services.

The Irish Rebellion of 1798, and took part in many of the battles which were fought in the South of Ireland.

Furnished a special service Company for South Africa, consisting of Captain E. M. G. McFerran, Lieuts. E. J. Fraser and P. S. Murray, with 107 N.C.O.'s and men, who embarked Apr. 29, 1901, with the 5th Battn. Royal Irish Rifles. On arrival stationed near Wolverhoek and employed on patrol duty, the Blockhouse system not having been then completed, while at this place an advanced post in charge of Lieut. Murray was attacked and the enemy beaten off.

July 1, 1901, an observation post furnished by the Gordon Highlanders Mounted Infantry was surprised, and a patrol from the service Company 4th Royal Irish Rifles became engaged with the enemy who retired with some loss. July 9th, the Company proceeded 150 miles south to the Vet River, the work being arduous in preventing the frequent and determined attempts made by the Boers to cross the line. July 20th the enemy endeavoured to get through the Blockhouse line at a bridge four miles South of the Vet River, Private Reavey, who was lying out on patrol with three native watchers being severely wounded, but held his post until reinforced, so defeating the attempt. Embarked at Cape Town for England July 30, 1902.

5th Battalion, The Royal Irish Rifles.

"South Africa, 1901-02."

Hon. Colonel :—Hill, Rt. Hon. Lord A. W.
Lt.-Colonel :—p.s. Wallace, R. H., C.B., hon. c. (H).

Origin.

Formed 1793 (under Act passed in the Irish Parliament 33 Geo. III.), as the Royal Downshire Regiment of Militia for part of the quota of men fixed for the County of Down,

Arthur 2nd Marquis of Downshire being the first Colonel, afterwards designated the Royal South Down. In 1857 became The Royal South Down Light Infantry, and in 1881 under Territorial organization, the 5th Battalion "The Royal Irish Rifles."

Embodiments.

Occasion.

Revolutionary War, etc.	1793, Aug. 31, to 1814, Oct. 10, for periods almost continuous.
French War	1815, July 14, to 1816, Mch. 18.
Crimean War	1855, Jan. 4, to 1856, Aug. 4.
Indian Mutiny... ...	1857, Sep. 21, to 1858, May 18.
South African War ...	1900, May 10, to 1902, July 24.

Services.

Took part in the suppression of the Irish Rebellion 1798. Engaged under Major Mathews with General Sir Charles Asgill's Force at Goresbridge—mentioned in Despatches, Kilkenny, June 26, 1798. (Musgrave's Hist. Irish Rebellion), "A few of the Downshire and Waterford Regts. held the bridge and checked the assailants, this gallant stand saving the garrison of the Castle." (Musgrave Memoirs) " General Dunn intending to attack the rebel camp, finding it abandoned, and failing to overtake the flying enemy, drove them into the hands of Major Mathews, Downshire Militia, who had marched with other details on the 24th to co-operate with Sir Chas. Asgill. On reaching Moy they found the rebels covering the heights of Doonane. Major Mathews held his ground, and in the morning, Sir Charles being then unable to co-operate, he marched to Goresbridge that night, and discovered the rebels on Kilcomery Hill. At daybreak the Downshire's Battalion Guns opened fire on the rebels, who made their dispositions to receive the Royalists. Sir Charles's Artillery was heard attacking them in their rear, soon completing their discomfiture, so that they broke, fled, and were cut down. Sep., 1798, Three hundred Downshire Militia formed part of Major-General Trench's Column operating in Killala District, when in the action it was officially reported Sep. 26th that the rebels had lost between five and six hundred men. It is also recorded by Musgrave, that the Downshire Militia from Maryborough appearing at Woif's Hill near Castlecomer, where a quiet industrious tradesman named Arthur Williams had been taken from the

Church by the rebels for execution, the whole rebel army made off to Doonane and thence to the ridge, bringing Williams along with them, and that here they put him on his knees and in the act of prayer ran him through with pikes and then shot his face almost off, though not an Orangeman.

Volunteered for and stationed in England 1813-14.

Volunteered for Foreign service and embarked for South Africa, Strength 11 Officers, 424 N.C.O.'s and men, with 4 Officers, 110 N.C.O.'s and men 3rd Royal Irish Rifles, and 3 Officers, 107 N.C.O.'s and men 4th Royal Irish Rifles attached, Colonel R. H. Wallace, 5th Royal Irish Rifles Commanding. On arrival at Cape Town April 28th, 1901, Head Quarters stationed at Wolverhoek in Orange River Colony with detachments at Kromellenboog, Vredefort Road, and Leusspruit to watch the Line by patrols. May 17th, one of these patrols kept a force of 100 Boers at bay for three-quarters of an hour, until their ammunition was exhausted and three being killed or badly wounded the remainder of the party surrendered. The G.O.C. mentioned the patrol in District Orders for its gallant though unsuccessful fight, and Corporal Heron was promoted Sergeant. The enemy lost six killed and five wounded. On the same night another patrol prevented the line from being blown up. In June and July, Blockhouses were erected at about a mile apart all down the line, thus reducing the Garrisons at Stations. July 25, Head Quarters were moved to Vredefort Road, and Colonel R. H. Wallace assumed command of No. 5 Sub-Section N. Section Lines of Communication. Colonel Garrett complimented Colonel Wallace on the behaviour of the Mounted Infantry Company in an engagement when 2 were wounded and 6 horses killed. They afterwards received the congratulations of the Commander-in-Chief for capturing 18 Boers in the action at Schoemans Drift, and in Mch., 1902, were complimented by General W. Kitchener for holding their ground in the open when engaged under him. Oct., 1901, Head Quarters were removed to Rhenoster River, and defences of the line strengthened, the system of organized "drives" commencing in December. The Blockhouses garrisoned by the 5th Royal Irish Rifles were often severely attacked but never taken, and only in one case did a small party of the enemy manage to break through under cover of darkness. An attempt was made to get remounts through at Vredefort Road, intended for Kemp's Commando, and 168 were captured. Congratulated by Major-General W. G. Knox.

Casualties.

Killed and died of disease, etc., Captain Leeds and 32 N.C.O.'s and men.

Mentioned in Despatches.

Colonel R. H. Wallace.
Captain C. G. Cole Hamilton.
Lieut. and Qr.-Mr. M. A. Henderson.
Cr.-Sergt. J. Conway.
Private S. Patterson.
Private A. Anderson.

Special Honours.

Colonel R. H. Wallace, C.B.
Captain C. G. Cole-Hamilton, D.S.O.
Sergt.-Major Gardiner, D.C. Medal.
Private A. Anderson, D.C. Medal.

Medals, etc., received by Battalion.

Queen's South Africa, with Clasps "Cape Colony," "Orange Free State," "Transvaal," "South Africa, 1901," "South Africa, 1902."

6th Battalion, The Royal Irish Rifles.

Hon. Colonel :—Rathdonnell, T. K., Lord.
Lt.-Colonel :—Jameson, H. W., hon. c.

Origin.

In 1793 when the Militia of Ireland was reorganized, a Regiment of nine Companies was completed for service and quota of men to be furnished under the Act by County Louth, officially called in 1855 the Louth Rifles, and which under the Territorial organization of 1881 became the 6th Battn. of The Royal Irish Rifles.

Embodiments.

Occasion.

Revolutionary War and European Disturbances.	Periods not recorded.
Crimean War	1855, Feb. 1, to 1856, July.
Indian Mutiny... ...	1857, Oct., to 1860, July 31.
South African War ...	1899, Dec. 6, to 1900, Oct. 17.

3rd Battalion, Princess Victoria's (Royal Irish Fusiliers).

Hon. Colonel :—Gosford, A. B. S., Earl of, K.P.
Lt.-Colonel :—Fitz-Gerald, W. C. (H).

Origin.

Formed 1793 as the Armagh Regiment; became Light Infantry in 1855, and 3rd Battn. Princess Victoria's (Royal Irish Fusiliers) in 1881 under the Territorial Organization.

Embodiments.

  Occasion.

Revolutionary War, etc. 1793, period unknown.
Crimean War ... ... 1855, Aug. 29, to 1856, Aug. 18.
South African War ... 1900, May 14, to 1900, Dec. 4.

Services.

Was actively engaged in the South and West of Ireland in 1798, until the suppression of the Rebellion, and repulsed the French at Ballanamuck, taking the Colours of the 70th Regt. of their Infantry, now in the Cathedral at Armagh.

4th Battalion Princess Victoria's (Royal Irish Fusiliers).

Hon. Colonel :—Saunderson, Rt. Hon. E. J., hon. c.
Lt.-Colonel :—p.s. Hodson, Sir R. A., hon. c. (H).

Origin.

In 1881 the Cavan Militia Regt. (completed for service in 1793 for the quota of men to be found by the County), became under Territorial Regimental organization the 4th Battn. of the Princess Victoria's Royal Irish Fusiliers Regt.

Embodiments.

  Occasion.

Revolutionary War and 1794, Mch. 25, to 1816, Mch. 13,
  European Disturb-   with two intervals of
  ances, etc. ...   about 8 and 10 months.
Crimean War ... ... 1855, Jan., to 1856, Aug.
South African War ... 1899, Dec. 5, to 1900, Oct. 19.

Services.

Served through the Rebellion 1798, the Regt. being engaged against the Rebels at the Battle of Arklow, June 9th, 1798, losing six men killed in action, and formed part of the army opposed to the Rebels at Vinegar Hill June 21st, 1798.

5th Battalion, Princess Victoria's (Royal Irish Fusiliers).

Hon. Colonel :—Rossmore, D. W. W., Lord.
Lt.-Colonel :—Leslie, J., hon. c.

Origin.

In 1881, the Monaghan Militia Regt. (which had been completed for service and the quota of men to be provided in 1793), became under Territorial Regimental Organization of the Forces the 5th Battn. of the Royal Irish Fusiliers Regiment.

Embodiments.

   Occasion.

Revolutionary War, etc.	1793 to 1802.
European Disturbances	1803 to 1814.
Crimean War	1855, Jan. 22, to 1856, Aug.
South African War ...	1900, May 8, to 1900, Oct. 20.

Services.

During the Rebellion of 1798, three Companies of the Regt. were engaged at the Battle of Antrim, and the Regt. took part in the Battle of Ballynahinchon, June 15th, 1798, the Adjutant (Evatt) being killed.

Volunteered for and stationed in England 1812-14.

3rd Battalion, The Connaught Rangers.

Hon. Colonel:—Knox, C. H. G.
Lt.-Colonel:—

Origin.

Formed at Castlebar, 1793, as the North Mayo Militia Regt. when two Units were organized for the County as the North and South Mayo. In 1881 the North Mayo became the 3rd Battn. of the Territorial Connaught Rangers Regiment, the South Regt. of Mayo Militia being amalgamated with the 3rd Battn., 1889.

Embodiments.
  Occasion.

Revolutionary War, etc. 1793, Oct., to 1802, May 14.
French War ... ... 1803, Apr. 6, to 1816, Mch. 26.
Crimean War ... ... 1855, Mch. 30, to 1856, July.
South African War ... 1900, Mch. 5, to 1901, July 5.

Services.

1797. Took part by forced marches in the operations to oppose the intended French landing at Bantry Bay, and served during the Rebellion, the light Company being engaged in 1798 against the rebels at Vinegar Hill.

Volunteered for and stationed in England 1813-14. In 1820 the Staff of the Regiment was engaged in suppressing the Whiteboy riots against rebels armed with forks, pikes and firearms, securing a large number of prisoners.

4th Battalion, The Connaught Rangers.

Hon. Colonel:—Daly, J. A., hon. c.
Lt.-Colonel:—p.s. Lopdell, J. R.

Origin.

In 1881 The Galway Regt. of Militia which was completed for service for the Revolutionary War, became, under the Territorial Regimental organization of the Forces, the 4th Battn. of "The Connaught Rangers."

Embodiments.
  Occasion.

Note.—No Regimental Records exist of the embodied periods nor services of the Galway Regt.

South African War ... 1900, May 7, to 1900, Oct. 17.

5th Battalion, The Connaught Rangers.

Hon. Colonel :—Kirkwood, T. Y. L., hon. c.
Lt.-Colonel :—Hammond, D. T., Capt. ret. pay (Maj. res. of Off.), hon. c. (H).

Origin.

In 1881, under Territorial organization of the Forces, the Roscommon Regt. of Militia (formed in 1793 for the quota of men to be found by the County) became the 5th Battn. of the Connaught Rangers Regiment.

Embodiments.

Occasion.

Revolutionary War and European Disturbances	1793 to 1816, Apr., for periods almost continuous.
Crimean War ...	1855, Jan. 23, to 1856, Aug. 25.
Indian Mutiny...	1857, Sep. 19, to 1858, June 8.
South African War ...	1899, Dec. 6, to 1900, Oct. 17.

Services.

Took part in the suppression of the 1798 Rebellion, and assisted in disarming the Baronies of Omakilly, Kinatalion, Barrymore, Fermoy, and East and West of Carberry in the County of Cork. On the conclusion of hostilities, the Regiment offered to serve with their Officers in any part of Europe, and the reply received by His Excellency the Lord Lieutenant, dated Whitehall, 17th February, 1799, is kept on record as being of both Regimental and general interest :—

"I have the honour to receive your Excellency's letter etc., of Roscommon Regt. of Militia offering in a very spirited manner to extend their services to any part of Europe. I have laid before the King this very commendable and strong proof of zeal and safety of the Empire and of loyalty and attachment to his sacred person, and received His Majesty's command to direct your Excellency to signify the high sense His Majesty entertains of their public spirited conduct at this important crisis."

Volunteered for and stationed in England for two periods during the 1793 to 1816 embodiments.

3rd Battalion, Princess Louise's (Argyll and Sutherland Highlanders.

"South Africa, 1902."

Hon. Colonel :—

Lt.-Colonel :—Scott-Plummer, J. W. (t).

Origin.

A Regiment of Stirlingshire Militia existed in 1639, and also in 1745, which became the Fifeshire Regiment on the reorganization of the Scottish Forces in 1797. In 1801 it was called the Stirling, Dumbarton, Clackmannan, and Kinross Militia, until after the Crimean War, when it was specially designated "Loyal Infantry," and subsequently the Highland Borderers Light Infantry, which in 1881 under Territorial organization became the 3rd Battn. of " The Argyll and Sutherland Highlanders Regiment."

Embodiments.

Occasion.

The Covenanters Rebellion	1689, period unknown.
Jacobite Rebellion ...	1745, period unknown.
Revolutionary War, etc.	1797 to 1814, for periods almost continuous.
Crimean War	1855 to 1856.
Indian Mutiny	1857, Nov. 2, to 1860.
South African War ...	1900, Jan. 23, to 1900, Dec. 4.
South African War ...	1902, Jan. 6, to 1902, Sep. 23.

Services.

Served as the Stirlingshire Militia both for and against the Covenanters in 1639, and in the defence of Stirling Castle against the Jacobites during the 1745 rebellion.

Volunteered for Foreign service during the South African War, and embarked strength 25 Officers, one W.O., 899 N.C.O.'s and men, Colonel the Duke of Montrose, K. T., A.D.C., commdg. On arrival at Cape Town Feb. 19th, 1902, three Companies proceeded to De Aar, one to Fraserburg, one to Sutherland and the remaining three to Simonstown. Between the time of arrival in South Africa until leaving, the Battn. was never united. It was employed at various times on Blockhouse duty from De Aar to Victoria Road, and on the cross country line from Victoria Road to

Calvinia. On the conclusion of the war twelve hundred rebels surrendered in this District, which explains the hard work experienced by the Battn. and its being subjected to much sniping. At times when on the branch line, the men were frequently on half rations, it being difficult to get up supplies so far from the main line. Colonel the Duke of Montrose was appointed to command a column for covering the construction of Blockhouse-line from Carnarvon to Calvinia, part of the Battn. being employed on this work. General Sir J. French issued the following Order: "I think progress made on the Blockhouse line has been most satisfactory," and on completion of the work to Calvinia, Colonel Hickman, commdg. Western District, Cape Colony, telegraphed "Congratulate you, most excellent."

The Battn. re-embarked for England at Cape Town in Sep., 1902.

Casualties.

Killed and died of disease, etc., 2nd Lieut. S. Cuthbert and 8 men.

Medals, *etc.*, received by Battalion.

Queen's South African, 1902, with Clasps "South Africa, 1902," and "Cape Colony."

4th Battalion, Princess Louise's (Argyll and Sutherland Highlanders.

"South Africa, 1900-01."

Hon. Colonel:—Blythswood, A. C., Lord, Col. (Vols.), A.D.C.

Lt.-Colonel:—Campbell, M. D., D.S.O., hon. c. (H).

Origin.

In 1881 the Royal Renfrew Militia (Prince of Wales') became under the Territorial Regimental Organization of the Forces, the 4th Battn. of The Argyll and Sutherland Highlanders Regt. By the County Records, 1745, a "Company of Militia" was sent from Paisley for service against the Pretender. It was inspected by the Earl of Hume, and fought at the Battle of Falkirk, Jan. 17th, 1746, the Colours carried at this Battle being unfurled in the County Buildings at Paisley on Kings' and Queens' Birthdays until 1856, when the last shreds were destroyed. *It is also recorded that a County Regt. served from 1793 until the close of the long war in 1815. By a letter Dec. 20th, 1796, from the Duke of Gloucester to Colonel Mure of Caldwell, the Regt. was known as the "West Lowland Fencibles." In 1798, Sept. 4th, they were described by General Sir Ralph Abercrombie for service in Ireland, as the "West Lowlanders." In 1803, Nov. 3, they were serving as the "Renfrewshire Militia" which subsequently became a Royal Regt. (Prince of Wales'), and in 1881 as already recorded.

Embodiments.

   Occasion.

European Disturbances, etc.... ... ... } 1793 to 1815, for periods almost continuous.

Crimean War ... ... 1 year, 167 days, dates not recorded.

South African War ... 1899, Dec. 5, to 1901, Aug. 6.

Services.

Volunteered for and served in Ireland 1798.

Volunteered for Foreign service Dec., 1899, and embarked for South Africa Jan. 18th, 1900, strength 29 Officers, 800 N.C.O.'s and men, Colonel A. Douglas-Dick Commdg. On arrival at Cape Town Feb. 13th, the Battn. went up country to Naauwpoort, and marched from there by half Battns. to Arundel and Rensburg, to take up the lines of communication of General Clements' Command, and continued to follow his line of advance as far as Norvals Pont. While at Colesburg on the way up six Companies took part with a Battery of F. A., and some Colonials, in a demonstration against the enemy about Colesburg Road to prevent them returning into Cape Colony out of which they had been driven.

The object having been attained by destruction of the Bridge by the Boers the 4th Argylls were withdrawn to the lines of communication. At Norvals Pont the left half Battn. occupied a position on the North bank of the Orange River, and the right half on the South bank. Mch. 22nd, their positions were reversed, Head Quarters being on the North side. Apr. 5th, the Battn. concentrated at Springfontein and took up positions under General Gatacre. Apr. 22nd, the Battn. escorted a Convoy of 100 waggons with details of different Regts., numbering over 2000 accompanying it, and on completion of the duty furnished detachments for various places. May 1st, Head Quarters with all detachments proceeded to Bloemfontein, and on the 17th by route march to Kroonstad, arriving on the 23rd, and employed in the defence of the town. At this time De Wet was continually blowing up the railway line both North and South and in preventing this destruction the Battn. was often in contact with the enemy. No guns or mounted troops having been left at Kroonstad the defence of the district was difficult. On June 22nd, when reinforcements had arrived including Artillery and Cavalry, the Battn. entrained to Honing Spruit, the Artillery and mounted troops by route march, to relieve that place which had been attacked by De Wet, but on the appearance of the Force he made off. On Nov. 1st, a detachment of the Battn. joined the Force of General Sir Archibald Hunter at Ventersburg and came into action, Captain W. A. Gordon, Sergt. Mitchell and Pte. Hart being specially brought to notice. In Dec. a mounted Infantry troop was formed, and did good service under Captn. Cuninghame around Kroonstad with small flying column, on convoy duties, and in the general defence of the neighbourhood. Between Aug. 1st, 1900, and May 31st, 1901, a detachment of 200 N.C.O.'s and men of the Battn. under Lt.-Col. H. D. Campbell was stationed at a Siding fourteen miles to the North of Kroonstad, and constantly in touch with the enemy, the communications between the two places being frequently interrupted. On Dec. 29th, 1900, half Battn. under Captain W. Mure was attached to Colonel Munro's Column and proceeded to Lindley, being constantly under fire while on the march. On arrival it became part of General Boye's Brigade, and moved to Senekal, taking part in several small engagements. May 4th, 1901, two Companies left Kroonstad under Major Pyne Coffin, marching to Lace Diamond Mines and other places West of the Line, where the Force was constantly engaged with the enemy. The Battn. left Kroonstad July 3rd, and re-embarked at Cape Town July 18th, 1901, for England.

Casualties.

Killed and died of disease, etc., 23 N.C.O.'s and men.

Mentioned in Despatches.
Colonel A. C. Douglas-Dick.
Lt.-Colonel M. D. Campbell.
Captain W. Mure.
Captain B. A. Cuninghame.
Lieut. and Qr.-Mr. R. C. Williamson.

Sergt. I. of M. M. McLachlan.
Cr.-Sergt. W. Jackson.
Cr.-Sergt. J. Mackie.
Sergt. J. Mitchell.
Sergt. A. Goodbrand.
Sergt. J. Wallace.

Special Honours.

Colonel A. C. Douglas-Dick, C.B.
Lt.-Colonel M. D. Campbell, D.S.O.
Lieut. and Qr.-Mr. R. C. Williams, The hon. rank of Captain.
Cr.-Sergt. J. Mackie, D.C. Medal.
Cr.-Sergt. J. Mitchell, D.C. Medal.

Medals, etc., received by Battalion.

Queen's South African with Clasps "Cape Colony," "Orange River Colony," and "South Africa, 1901."

3rd Battalion, The Prince of Wales's Leinster Regiment (Royal Canadians).

"South Africa, 1900-02."

Hon. Colonel:—Cosby, R. G., hon. c.
Lt.-Colonel:—Barry, W. E. A. (Hon. Capt. in Army, 20th Oct., 1900), (H) (T).

Origin.

About 1793, the "Parsonstown Loyal Independents" Volunteer Corps, formed at Birr, King's County, in 1776, Sir W. Parsons being Colonel, was converted into the 98th Regt. of Militia under the designation of the "King's County Royal Rifles," which became in 1881 under the Territorial organization of the Forces, the 3rd Battn. of the Leinster Regt. (Royal Canadians).

Embodiments.

Occasion.

American War, etc. ...	1776 to 1782.
Crimean War	1855, Apr. 16, to 1856, July 28.
South African War ...	1900, Jan. 18, to 1902, May 26.

Services.

Volunteered for Foreign service during the South African War, and embarked Mch. 7th, 1900, for the seat of War, strength 18 Officers, one W.O., 475 N.C.O.'s and men, Colonel J. H. G. Smyth, commdg.

On arrival at Table Bay, Mch. 27th, 1900, the Transport was ordered to East London, and on Apr. 2nd the Battn. disembarked and encamped on the Western side, arrangements being at once made to protect a section of the line of communication between Tylden and Bushmans Hoek, the left half Battn. was pushed forward to Sterkstroom. On Apr. 7th the Battn. was held in readiness to proceed by rail to Bethulie to repel an attack made on that place.

Aug. 8th, 1900, moved to Stormberg with Head Quarters at the Railway Station, and formed a chain of outposts on the adjacent hills in order to connect the junction with Steynsberg on the West, and Burgersdorp on the North, detachments being stationed at Bamboo Bridges and Wandersboom.

The left half Battn. was afterwards moved to Aliwal North and commenced earthworks for the protection of Orange River Bridge in addition to furnishing escorts for convoys into Orange Free State.

During Sepr. the enemy was very active on the Orange River, and on the 26th a party under Captn. Sheppard was detached to Albert Junction where the line branches to Bethulie and Aliwal North, to watch the River.

On Oct. 2nd, the Boers being reported marching on Stormberg and only ten miles off, the Garrison was reinforced by Cape Police, and strong inlying Picquet told off, every precaution being taken to protect the junction, and all that could be spared sent out to intercept the enemy. On the next day the Boers were driven back across the Orange River. During Oct., Nov., and Dec., the men were under arms night and day, owing to the harassing tactics of the Boers, who had established themselves in the Zurberg Mountains and "Wilcop" within striking distance of the Junction, frequent attempts being made to destroy the Railway Lines.

Early in 1901, Col. Luttman Johnson was directed to construct Blockhouses for defence of the Junction.

On Mch. 20th, 1901, the party guarding Driefontein Drift on the Orange River was attacked by a strong force of the enemy between 9 a.m. and 11.30, a detached party of the 3rd Leinsters succeeding in outflanking the Boers and driving them from a strong kopje position.

On Apr. 18th, the Boers held up a train at "Twist Neet," between Moltens and Stormberg, after looting the waggons and setting fire to them, a party of about 120 of the 3rd Leinsters under Captn. Sheppard, with Sergt.-Major Haddick and Cr.-Sergt. Cannon, succeeded in driving off the enemy and saving part of the train, 8 natives being killed and 6 Boers taken prisoners.

Apr. 30th, the Battn. proceeded to Kimberley and a squadron of Mounted Infantry was formed under Captn. Arnott and Lieut. Stoney, which was employed in scouting duties and as escort to convoys. Although frequently attacked they had only one man killed and Lieut. Stoney severely wounded. A detachment of 100 men under Major Barry was attached to the Kimberley column for six months, earning the encomiums of their superior officers.

About this time the Blockhouse system having been established between Modder River and Warrenton, the Battn. was detailed to furnish the garrisons on this line, and men for the armoured train under Lieut. Dent between Modder River and Mafeking, also detachments at Smiths Drift, Danils Kieul in Griqualand West, Jacobsdaal, etc. Oct. 9th, the remainder of the Battn. moved to Modder River, for protection of the Bridge (which had been blown up in the early stages of the War), and duty in the Blockhouses between Enslin and Spyfontein, Colonel Luttman Johnson being appointed Commandant of the District. The duty was so heavy that the Band and Regimental Staff had to take their turn in the Blockhouses, and even then the garrisons in some consisted only of three men who had to work by day on the railway line and keep watch by night.

May 6th, 1902, the Battn. re-embarked for home.

Casualties.

Killed and died of disease, etc., Captn. C. Biddulph, 25 N.C.O.'s and men.

Mentioned in Despatches.

Colonel J. H. G. Smyth.
Lt.-Colonel F. Luttman Johnson.
Major W. E. A. Barry (twice).
Captain P. E. S. Reeves.
Captain and Qr.-Mr. J. W. Gallehawk (twice).
Sergt.-Major R. J. Haddick.
Qr.-Mr.-Sergt. B. Boyle.
Cr.-Sergt. P. Flanagan.
Pte. P. Cleary.

Special Honours.

Colonel J. H. G. Smyth, C.M.G.
Lt.-Colonel F. Luttman Johnson, D.S.O.
Captain P. E. S. Reeves, D.S.O.
Sergt.-Major R. J. Haddick, D.C. Medal.
Qr.-Mr.-Sergt. B. Boyle, D.C. Medal.
Cr.-Sergt. P. Flanagan, D.C. Medal.

Medals, etc., received by Battalion.

Queen's South African, with Clasps "Cape Colony," "Orange Free State," and "Transvaal." King's South African, with Clasps "South Africa, 1901," "South Africa, 1902."

4th Battalion, The Prince of Wales's Leinster Regiment (Royal Canadians).

Hon. Colonel :—Brooke, G. H., Adjt. ret. pay.
Lt.-Colonel :—Castletown, B. E. B., Lord, C.M.G.

Origin.

When the Militia Force of Ireland was reorganized in 1793, a Regiment was completed for service and the quota of men to be found by Queen's County, as the Queen's County Militia, which subsequently became a Royal Regiment, and was in 1854 a Rifle Corps known as the Royal Queen's County Rifles. In 1881, under Territorial Organization of the Forces into Regiments, it formed the 4th Battalion of the Prince of Wales's Leinster Regiment (Royal Canadians).

Embodiments.

Occasion.

Revolutionary War and European Disturbances } Periods not recorded, except disembodied in 1816, Mar. 23.
Crimean War ... 1854, Dec. 14, to 1856, Aug. 4.
South African War ... 1900, May 8, to 1901, July 6.

5th Battalion, The Prince of Wales's Leinster Regiment (Royal Canadians).

Hon. Colonel:—Pepper, C., hon. c. (Hon. Lt.-Col. in Army).

Lt.-Colonel:—Everard, N. T., hon. c.

Origin.

Formed as the Royal Meath Militia in 1793, and became in 1881 the 5th Battalion of the Territorial Prince of Wales's Leinster Regiment (Royal Canadians).

Embodiments.

Occasion.

Revolutionary War, etc 1793 to 1802, March.
European Disturbances 1803 to 1814, Aug.
    etc. 1815, May, to 1816.
Crimean War ... 1854 to 1856.
South African War ... 1900, May 2, to 1900, Oct. 19.

Services.

Served through the suppression of the Irish Rebellion, 1798, and sent to the relief of the Royalists in Wexford, where a company, being surprised by the Rebels, was cut to pieces at the Three Rocks on May 31st; the captain, 2 subalterns, 4 sergeants and 94 men killed. The Regt. was afterwards engaged at Vinegar Hill, Ross, Fokes, and other battles during the continuance of the Rebellion.

Volunteered for and stationed in England 1811-13.

3rd Battalion, The Royal Munster Fusiliers.

"South Africa, 1900-02."

Hon. Colonel:—Warren, Sir A. R., Bart, hon. c.

Lt.-Colonel:—O'Donovan, M. W. (The O'Donovan), hon. c.

Origin.

One of the sixty Regiments raised for the Revolutionary War in 1793, as the South Cork Militia, known at a later date as the South Cork Light Infantry Militia, and became in 1881 the 3rd Battn. Royal Munster Fusiliers Regiment under Territorial Organization.

Embodiments.

Occasion.

Revolutionary War, etc. 1794 to 1802.
European Disturbances 1803 to 1816.
Crimean War ... 1854 to 1856.
South African War ... 1899, Dec. 5, to 1902, Mar. 31.

Services.

In 1796 took part in the forced march from Limerick to Bantry Bay to resist the French Invasion, and was employed in the suppression of the Irish Rebellion 1798.

Volunteered for Foreign Service during South African War, and embarked for South Africa, strength 24 officers, 416 N.C.O.'s and men, Colonel F. W. Bell commanding. On arrival Feb., 1900, stationed at Stormberg, Aliwal North, Vryburg, Mafeking, Orange River, etc., and was on trek with General Sir H. Settle's Column in the Western Transvaal, afterwards being stationed at Orange River, occupying the blockhouses along the railway towards Kimberley until re-embarked for home March, 1902.

Casualties.

Killed and died of disease, etc., Lieut. P. C. Shaw and 5 N.C.O.'s and men.

Mentioned in Despatches.

Lt.-Col. The O'Donovan.
Major and Adjt. J. Longridge.
Captain B. U. S. Domnill.
Lieut. S. D. Nash.
Lieut. and Qr.-Mr. W. H. Forsdick.

Special Honours.

Major and Adjt. T. Longridge, D.S.O.
Lieut. and Qr.-Mr. W. H. Forsdick, granted the hon. rank of Captain.

Medals, etc., received by Battalion.

Queen's South African Medal with Clasps "Cape Colony," "Orange Free State," and "Transvaal."

King's Medal with Clasps "South Africa 1901," and "South Africa 1902."

4th Battalion, The Royal Munster Fusiliers.

Hon. Colonel:—Kenmare, V.C., Earl of, C.V.O.
Lt.-Colonel:—Sugrue, J. M. (H).

Origin.

Formed as the Kerry Regiment of Militia in 1793, the Force of the County having previously been the 1st Munster Volunteer Regiment of Foot. In 1881 the Regiment became the 4th Battn. of "The Royal Munster Fusiliers" under Territorial Organization of the Forces.

Embodiments.
 Occasion.

Revolutionary War, etc. 1793 to 1815.
Crimean War ... 1855, Jan. 10, to 1856, June.
Indian Mutiny ... 1857, Nov. 2, to 1860, July 31.
South African War ... 1900, May 4, to 1900, Oct. 18.

Services.

In 1798 the Regiment was moved to Castlebar, and took part in the operations which resulted in the surrender of the French invading Force during the Rebellion, the execution of the rebel leader Blake, and action at Killala on Sept. 23, 1798.

5th Battalion, The Royal Munster Fusiliers.

"Mediterranean, 1901."

Hon. Colonel:—Dunraven and Mountreal, Rt. Hon. W. T., Earl of, K.P., C.M.G. (Hon. Capt. in Army).
Lt-Colonel:—Massy-Westropp, J., C.M.G., hon. c.

Origin.

Formed in 1793 as one of the 38 Regiments to be raised in Ireland under the Militia Act 33, Geo. III., and one of the six to which the title of Royal was granted. At first designated the Royal Limerick County Regiment of Militia, in 1876 The Royal Limerick Fusilier Regt., and in 1881 The 5th Battn. Royal Munster Fusiliers under the Territorial Regimental Organization.

Embodiments.

> *Occasion.*
> Revolutionary War, etc. 1793 to 1802.
> European Disturbances 1803, Dec., to 1814, July 25.
> ,,   ,,   1815 to 1816, April.
> Crimean War   ... 1854, Dec., to 1856, Aug. 11.
> Indian Mutiny   ... 1857, Sept., to 1860, Feb.
> South African War ... 1900, May 10, to 1901, Oct. 8.

Services.

Took part in the suppression of the Irish Rebellion, 1798, and defeat of the French Invasion, a private named James Damery was publicly thanked and received a reward of forty pounds for bringing to bay and capturing a gang of rebels near Castle Island, Co. Kerry.

Volunteered for Foreign Service during the South African War, and stationed at Malta and Gozo.

3rd Battalion, The Royal Dublin Fusiliers.

Hon. Colonel :—Lawless, Hon. E., hon. c.

Lt.-Colonel :—O'Neil, W. H. S., D.S.O., Maj. ret. pay (Maj. Res. of off), hon. c., (S) (H).

Origin.

Raised as the Kildare Militia Regiment about the year 1780. Became Rifles in 1855, and in 1881 the 3rd Battn. Royal Dublin Fusiliers under the Territorial Organization.

Embodiments.

> *Occasion.*
> Revolutionary War, etc., 1793, period unknown.
> French War   ... 1802 to 1814.
> ,,   ,,   ... 1815 to 1816.
> Crimean War   ... 1855, Mar. 5, to 1856, July 21.
> South African War ... 1900, May 4, to 1900, Oct. 18.

Services.

Took part in the suppression of the Irish Rebellion 1798.

4th Battalion, The Royal Dublin Fusiliers.

"South Africa, 1902."
Hon. Colonel:—p.s. Seton, R.E.
Lt.-Colonel:—Pearse, E., Maj. ret. pay, hon. c.

Origin.

In 1881 The Queen's Own Royal Dublin City Militia Regiment became, under Territorial Regimental Organization of the Forces, the 4th Battalion of "The Royal Dublin Fusiliers."

By local tradition, the Battalion represents the Regiment of Militia which was raised in 1660 for service within the City of Dublin, two Regiments being raised in Dublin, one for defence within and the other without the City, commonly known as the City Guards. In 1793 a Regiment was completed for service in Dublin, which subsequently became a Royal Regiment (confirmed by Horseguards Order dated Jan. 26, 1813), Queen's Own being afterwards added, and in 1881 the Regiment became a Battalion of the Territorial Regiment, as already recorded.

Embodiments.

Occasion.

Irish Rebellion, etc. ...	Period not recorded.
European Disturbances	——— to 1814, Aug. 6.
Indian Mutiny ...	1857, Sept 21, to 1860, Mar. 1.
South African War ...	1900, May 3, to 1900, Dec. 4.
,, ,, ...	1902, Mar. 10, to 1902, Oct. 4.

Services.

Served through the whole of the 1798 Rebellion, and the Colours carried were placed, Dec. 16, 1879, over the central door of St. Patrick's Cathedral, Dublin.

Volunteered for Foreign Service during the South African War, and embarked March 27, 1902, strength 23 officers, one W.O., 546 N.C.O.'s and men, Colonel Elford Pearse commanding. Arrived Table Bay April 14th, and disembarked at Port Elizabeth April 17th, proceeded up country at once to Kroonstad, where the Battalion took over the railway blockhouse line to Honingspruit, Serfontein, Roodeval, etc., Head Quarters being at Honingspruit; also the Refuge Camps, etc., Colonel Pearse being appointed Commandant Sub. Sec., No. 3, L. of C., O.R. Colony. The Battalion was at first occupied in putting up barbed wire fences and in other ways strengthening the line, Roodival, the most northern station, being several times subjected to night firing, and other parts fired on, but no party of Boers succeeded in getting through.

In May, 1902, General Bruce Hamilton conducted a big "drive" from Wolverhoek, Frankfort, and Vrede to the Kroonstad-Lindley Line, the blockhouses of Battalion guarding the right flank. At the end of the "drive" over 800 Boers were captured, none getting through the portion of line occupied by the Battalion. On June 1st., the conclusion of Peace was communicated. Between June 1 and July 2 the Battalion was employed dismantling barbed wire fences, filling in trenches, and breaking up forts, etc., which entailed much labour. July 3, the Battalion having concentrated, marched to Jordan Siding, destroyed the fort, etc., at that place, proceeded on to Kroonstad, and took part in the Coronation Review, 9th Aug., 1902.

On 29th Aug. it moved by rail to Cape Town, and re-embarked Sept. 11, 1902, for home.

Casualties.

Killed and died of disease, etc., 4 N.C.O.'s and men.

Medals, etc., received by Battalion.

Queen's South African Medal with Clasps "Cape Colony," "Orange Free State," "South Africa 1902."

5th Battalion, The Royal Dublin Fusiliers.

"South Africa, 1900-02."

Hon. Colonel :—Meath, Rt. Hon. R., Earl of, K.P., (t).
Lt.-Colonel :—p.s. Finlay, H. T., hon. c. (H).

Origin.

In 1881 the Dublin County Militia, which had been re-organized under the Act of 1793, and was originally raised in 1666 for duty without the City, and "sometimes referred to (with another regiment for duty within the City) as the Guards of the City in the Assembly rolls," became the 5th Battn. of the Territorial Royal Dublin Fusilier Regiment.

Embodiments.

Occasion.

Revolutionary War, etc. Dates not recorded.
Crimean War ... 1854, Dec. 18, to 1856, Aug. 11.
South African War ... 1899, Dec. 5, to 1902, Feb. 25.

Services.

Took part in the suppression of the 1798 Irish Rebellion, Colonel Lord Mountjoy being among the killed at the battle of New Ross, the Regiment being also engaged at the battle of Vinegar Hill.

Volunteered for Foreign Service during the South African War, and embarked, strength 24 officers, 499 N.C.O.'s and men, Colonel E. C. Gernon commanding. On arrival South Africa March 14, 1900, the Battalion proceeded to Kimberley and joined the 1st Div. Lieut.-General Lord Methuen, being afterwards broken up and employed in guarding various places, escorting convoys, protecting the railway line, etc., in Cape Colony, Orange River Colony and Transvaal. Amongst the most important places held were Berkley West with the bridge over the Vaal, until the Mafeking Relief Column had passed through.

Windsorton Road on the lines of communication near Fourteen Streams, Boshof and Rooidam previous to and during the severe fighting at these places.

Mafeking just after the British occupation of Pretoria.

Warrenton and Fourteen Streams, where the duties were very responsible and arduous owing to the presence of Boers in the vicinity.

Jacobsdal, where parties of the enemy were frequently encountered.

Colonel Finlay assumed the command of the Battalion on 19th June, 1901.

Casualties.

Killed and died of disease, etc., 15 N.C.O.'s and men.

Mentioned in Despatches.

Colonel H. T. Finlay.
Major Sir F. W. Shaw, Bart.
Hon. Major P. la Touche, Capt. A. T. MacDermott.
Lieut. Adjt. Watson.
Lieut. G. B. C. Irvine.
Captain and Qr.-Mr. R. Baker (twice).
Sergt.-Major F. A. Whalen.

Qr.-Mr.-Sergt. B. F. Bruen.
Cr.-Sergt. D. Ryan.
Cr.-Sergt. P. Moore.
Cr.-Sergt. M. Dunne.
Sergt. C. Christie (twice).
Sergt. B. Thompson.

Special Honours.

Major Sir F. W. Shaw, Bart., D.S.O.
Captain and Qr.-Mr. R. Baker, D.S.O.
Sergt.-Major F. A. Whalen, D.C. Medal.
Qr.-Mr.-Sergt. B. F. Bruen, D.C. Medal.
Cr.-Sergt. M. Dunne, D.C. Medal.

Medals, etc., received by Battalion.

Queen's S.A. Medal with Clasps "Cape Colony," "Transvaal," "Orange Free State," and "Wittenberg."

King's S.A. Medal with Clasps "S.A. 1901" and "S.A. 1902."

5th Battalion, The Rifle Brigade (The Prince Consort's Own).

"South Africa, 1902."

Hon. Colonel :—Maxwell, G. S. (H).

Lt.-Colonel :—p.s. Serjeant, Wm. C. Eldon, C.B., hon. c. (Hon. Lt.-Col. in Army) (Maj. Res. of Off.), Kt. of Grace, Order of St. John of Jerusalem, formerly of the 1st Mounted Rifles (Methuen's Horse) and commanding detachment "the Pioneer Regt." Bechuanaland Field Force 1884-5. and Second in Command "The Cape Boys' Corps," Matabeleland Relief Force 1896.

Origin.

In 1642, a Regiment of Tower Hamlets Militia was formed by Sergt. Major-General Philip Skippon of the London Militia (President of the Council of War under the Earl of Essex) from the Trained Bands of the County of the Tower Hamlets disbanded under Act Chas. I.

In 1694 the Regt. was divided into two Regiments, this being the 2nd or Queen's Own Tower Hamlets Militia, both Regts. continuing to be, until 1840, under the general command of His Majesty's Constable of the Tower, or Lieutenant of the Tower Hamlets, "for the service and preservation of that Royal Fortress," vide 13 and 14 Chas. II., 23 and 27 Geo. II., and subsequent Acts relating thereto.

In the Militia Returns 1697 (Egerton MSS.) the Force of the Tower Hamlets comprised two Regiments commanded by Col. Lord Lucas and Col. Sir Henry Johnson—no details being given, but with the following footnote: "Lord Lucas having perused the lists of each Captain in these two Regiments, finds he may modestly and safely engage and promise his Majesty 2,000 able and effective men duly qualifyed and fitt to serve him on any occasion."

In 1793 this Battalion completed for service as the "2nd or Queen's Own Tower Hamlets Militia," and was subsequently designated "The Queen's Own Light Infantry."

In 1874 the Regiment was named "The Queen's Own Royal Tower Hamlets Militia," and in 1881, under Territorial organization, the 5th Battalion The Rifle Brigade (Prince Consort's Own).

Embodiments.

Occasion.

Civil War	Sept., 1642, until the termination of the War.
European Disturbances and French War	1797, June 27, to 1814, June 14. 1814, July 3, to 1816, May 7.
Crimean War	1854, Mar. 1, to 1857.
Egyptian War	1885, Mar. 9, to 1885, Sep. 1.
South African War	1900, May 1, to 1900, Oct. 20.
South African War	1901, Dec. 9, to 1902, Oct. 3.

Services.

Took part under Sir William Waller 1643, in the storming and capture of Basing House. Engagements at Alton and Farnham. Present in most of the important actions during this war. Lord Clarendon, in his History, Bk. VIII. p. 347, and Rapin, the French Military Historian, Tome VIII., p. 426, bear testimony to its valiant services under General Philip Skippon at the battle of Newbury, etc.

Stationed in Ireland from Nov., 1814, till 30th April, 1816.

Volunteered for Foreign service during the South African War, embarked at Woolwich 21st Dec., 1901, strength 27 Officers, 743 N.C.O.'s and Riflemen, Colonel W. C. E. Serjeant Commanding. Arrived Cape Town 14th Jan., 1901, and proceeded to Kroonstadt the same day, dropping two Companies under Major Hon. W. D. Cairns, to strengthen Kroonstadt Defences, and the taking over Stations, Posts and Blockhouses from near Kroonstadt to Serfontein, with Head Quarters at Honingspruit. On the night of 23rd Jan., the C.O. took out a party of 18 marksmen and engaged the enemy who for several nights had been sniping Head Quarters; the enemy retired via Malans Kopje to Liverpool Farm, thence to Paardeberg; next day their casualties were ascertained to have been one man killed and eight wounded. On 24th Jan. took over Blockhouses from Serfontein to Roodeval, thus occupying about 44 miles of line. At this time the enemy were very numerous on both sides of the line, sniping by day and continually attacking by night, often several of the Blockhouses simultaneously, the want of mounted troops much hampering the defence.

Jan. 27th a determined attack by the Boers was made in force on Honingspruit Station and Blockhouses below, which was repulsed after two hours' fighting. The Battalion was successful in preventing any Boers from getting through the Section (44 miles) during the big De Wet drives 4th to 8th February, 1902, and during its entire occupation of this line. Feb. 16th the Battalion proceeded to Kroonstadt for duty on the defences, and providing reinforcements at threatened points. Feb. 28th, a detachment under 2nd Lieut. J. A. Yates took part in repelling a fierce attack on Honingspruit, and on the next day two attacks on the line held by the 5th Royal Irish Rifles. March 6th, moved to Lace Mines for occupation of thirty-three miles of the Kroonstadt—Lace Mines—Valsch River Blockhouse line, some of the Blockhouses being subjected to nightly attacks, and attempts to cross the line. The Valsch river bed running parallel to the Blockhouse line for many miles, the enemy, at times in considerable numbers, were able to remain in concealment a few hundred yards off, and mounted men were much wanted at the Head Quarters Station for protection of the cattle and aggressive operations. March 16th, a considerable number of sheep and cattle were captured from the enemy at Rhenoster Kopje, distant about two and a half miles. March 21st a bold attack in force on No. 15 Blockhouse was repulsed. March 22nd a party of Boers 150 strong under Commandant Nagel attacked No. 10 Blockhouse, and cutting the fence, succeeded in crossing. March 27th this same party on attempting to return South was prevented doing so with a loss to them of two killed and five wounded. April 2nd an attack by fifty Boers on Lace Mines was repulsed. April 14th a general attack by six to seven hundred of the enemy was delivered simultaneously at several points, the engagement lasted from 7.30 p.m. to 1.30 a.m.; there was evidence next day that the Boers had been repulsed with loss. April 18th they were again driven off with more casualties. The Battalion system was to place small parties under cover of Scherms between the Blockhouses which on this line were sometimes one thousand to fifteen hundred yards apart, and out of eighty-five attacks made on lines occupied by the Battalion while in South Africa, only three crossings were effected by the enemy. June 27th, 1902, Battalion concentrated at Kroonstadt leaving on 2nd September, 1902, for East London, and embarked on the 8th September in S.S. "Avondale Castle" for England. It is noteworthy, that during the entire period of active operation in South Africa, the duties of Adjutant were performed by a Militia Officer, Captain de Vernon—and that, consequent on the withdrawal of Reservists and trained men for Line service before the Regiment proceeded to South Africa, nearly five hundred of the men of the Battalion had not passed through the Militia trained course of Musketry ere they were called upon to defend their posts.

Casualties.

Killed and died of disease, etc., Lieut. T. W. Sergeant and 23 N.C.O.'s and Riflemen.

Wounded in action, Lieut. R. B. Gosset and 6 Riflemen.

Mentioned in Despatches.

Captain and Actg. Adjt. F. V. de L. G. de Vernon.
Cr.-Sergt. (Actg. Sergt.-Major) H. Poutard.
Corporal T. McGrath.

Special Honours.

Colonel Wm. C. Eldon Serjeant, C.B. promoted Major Res. of Officers, and thanked by the Commander-in-Chief.

Medals, etc., received by Battalion.

Queen's Medal with Clasps "Cape Colony," "Orange Free State," and "South Africa, 1902."

6th Battalion, The Rifle Brigade (The Prince Consort's Own).

Hon. Colonel :—Dopping, J. H., hon. c.
Lt.-Colonel :—Nugent, G. L. J. J. G., hon. c.

Origin.

The Prince of Wales's Royal Longford Militia formed in 1793 as one of the Regts. for the Revolutionary War, its designation being changed to Royal Longford Rifles in 1854, Light Infantry in 1855, and united with the West Meath Regt. of Militia (also raised for the Revolutionary War), became in 1881 the 6th Battn. "The Rifle Brigade (The Prince Consort's Own)," under Territorial organization of the Forces.

Embodiments.

Occasion.

Revolutionary War, etc. 1793, June 6, to 1802, May 12.
European Disturbances 1803, Ap. 6, to 1814, Oct. 10.
1815, July 13, to 1816, Ap. 15.
Crimean War ... ... 1854, Dec. 26, to 1856, Aug. 18.
South African War ... 1899, Dec. 5, to 1900, Dec. 3.

Services.

Took part in the forced march and concentration of Troops under General Crosbie, 1796, to oppose the attempted French invasion at Bantry Bay.

Served through the suppression of the Irish Rebellion, taking part in the unfortunate battle of Castlebar, Aug. 26th, 1798, losing four Officers and fifty-four N.C.O.'s and men killed—a party of the Regiment under its Colonel the Earl of Grannard, holding the bridge at Castlebar for a time, to cover the retreat of the Royal Forces. Formed the advanced guard, and assisted under General Lake, in storming the Rebel position at the battle of Vinegar Hill, the Regt. having also been in contact with the Rebels at Kilcavan Hill.

Volunteered for and stationed in England 1813-14.

7th Battalion, The Rifle Brigade (The Prince Consort's Own).

Hon. Colonel :—Somerset, Sir A. P. F. C., K.C.B
Lt.-Colonel :—Hardinge, H. C., Visct., hon. c.

Origin.

In 1881, the 1st King's Own Royal Tower Hamlets Militia became the 7th Battn. The Rifle Brigade (The Prince Consort's Own), under Territorial Organization of the Forces.

See 5th Battn. Rifle Brigade for the Origin, Services, etc., prior to 1694, when this Battn. became the 1st or King's Own Tower Hamlets Militia Regt. In 1793 the Regt. was completed for service as 1st or King's Own Tower Hamlets Militia, and at a later date became " The King's Own Light Infantry." In 1874 the Regt. was known as " The King's Own Royal Tower Hamlets Militia," and in 1881 as already recorded.

Embodiments.

Since 1694.

Occasion.

Revolutionary War, etc.	1797, Feb., to 1802, May.
European Disturbances, etc....	1803, Apr., to 1814, June.
	1815, June, to 1816, Feb.
Crimean War... ...	1855, Mch., to 1855, Oct.
Indian Mutiny... ...	1857, Nov., to 1860, June.
South African War ...	1900, May 4, to 1900, Oct. 18.

Services.

See 5th Battalion Rifle Brigade for those of the Tower Hamlets Regt. prior to 1694, and role of the King's Own Tower Hamlets Regt. in connection with the Tower until 1840.

Volunteered for and was one of the twenty-eight English and Scotch Regts. stationed in Ireland for two years each after the passing of the Interchange Act, 51 Geo. III.

THE CHANNEL ISLANDS MILITIA.

We are unable to deal with this Force in the same form as Regiments of the United Kingdom.

The antiquity, almost continuous service for long periods of years without being actually embodied, and special services, are such, however, as entitle it to a place among others who have contributed to the History of England.

We find by a most comprehensive sketch of the Royal Guernsey Militia compiled by Colonel J. Percy Groves (late Royal Guernsey Artillery) that in 347 there were Military Chiefs in the Island appointed by the Romans, and that in 578 Jersey and Guernsey furnished bodies of armed men to fight the Bretons, whilst in the 9th century the landed proprietors were liable for military service, and were organized under Centeniers, Vingteniers, and Dixeniers. During the 11th century the Guernsey Militia, aided by the Normans, repelled an invasion from the coasts of the Bay of Biscay.

In 1146 the Militia served under an oath of fidelity and in 1161 under direct oath.

In the 13th century one fifth of the Revenue was devoted to the Militia, and twenty years later bows and arrows were supplied from the Tower by order of King Henry III. In the 13th century several invasions by the French were defeated.

In 1331, pikes and cross-bows were in use, and the Militia turned out when required for exercise, etc.

In 1338 Castle Cornet and the Islands of Guernsey, Sark, Alderney, were in possession of the French. At this time a body of the Militia signally defeated the invaders at Les Hubits, and tradition has it that in recognition of this, King Charles II., about three centuries later, allowed the Militia of two parishes to wear "Royal Livery" blue facings and silver lace, the 3rd Regt. Guernsey Militia, of which they formed part, becoming a Royal Regiment in 1831.

In 1372 there was an "armed array" of the inhabitants under mandate of King Edward III., these Forces in the following year encountering the invasion of Sir Owen (or Evans) of Wales.

According to Hollinshed's Chronicles—

"The French King sent 4,000 men under the guidance of one Yvans, a banished Welsh Gentleman, which landing in the Isle of Guernsey was encountered by the Captayn of that isle, called Sir Edmund Rous, who with 800 of his own souldiers, together with them of the isle, boldlie gave battell, but in the end were discomfitted, and 400 of them slaine, so that Sir Edmund fled to the Castell of Cornett and was there besieged by Yvans till the French King sent to him to come back from thence."

Groves records that in 1467 a party of Militia from St. Martin's accompanied Sir Richard Harliston's Force which proceeded to the relief of Jersey, then in the hands of the French, and took a prominent part in the re-capture of Mont Orgueil Castle.

About 1550 the law exempted long-bows, cross-bows and all weapons from arrest for debt. Some twenty years later Queen Elizabeth granted "six pieces of Artillery and two culverins" for the defence of Guernsey.

At this period, and for at least two centuries later, every Guernsey man was bound by law to furnish himself with "arms and equipment according to the value of his lands and goods."

Heylin, referring to the Militia in his Survey of Guernsey and Jersey (1629), observes that "their trained band consists of only 1,200, and these God knows poorly weaponed. Nevertheless, these poorly weaponed and unpaid Militiamen did on many occasions yeoman service in defence of their sea-girt home."

In 1719 (though not embodied) the Militia furnished the Guards of Castle Cornet and Harbour of St. Peter Port.

In 1750 there was a Troop of Horse Militia in Guernsey. besides 1,800 Foot, the Batteries and field guns being manned by men selected from the Infantry, previously in 1682 the Company cannon in each parish were served by invalids.

In 1755 two Artillery companies were formed out of officers and men from the Infantry, other companies being added at later dates to complete the Royal Guernsey Artillery Militia Regt.

Ansted, writing in 1765, says: "The feudal character of the Channel Islands customs is nowhere more clearly shown than in the establishment of the Militia. Every male between the ages of seventeen and sixty-five in Jersey, and sixteen and sixty in the other Islands, is bound to render man-service to the Crown. The extent of this service in law being that each should provide himself with arms and ammunition, attend drill when required, keep watch and guard round the Islands by night and day, repair bulwarks, and keep the garrison when no troops of the line are available, and perform all other services for defence."

During the following wars :—

Seven Years War	...	1756 to 1763.
French War	...	1778 to 1783.
European Disturbances		1793 to 1802.
,, ,,		1803 to 1815

the Militia of the Channel Islands is said to have had a hard time of it.

Though not regularly embodied, the force was held ready at any moment to repel attack, while guards, watches and patrols (which lasted for many years, as the routine by day and night) were urged never to relax their vigilance. Richards says in "Her Majesty's Army": "Almost every war with France has witnessed an attack on Jersey."

"In 1781 a serious attack was made, which for a time threatened to wrest the old Norman possession of Jersey from the Crown of England. The French Commander, the Baron de Rullecour, succeeded in surprising the Governor and extorting submission from him and the leading inhabitants. Fortunately, however, Major Pierson, of the 78th Regt., rallied the Militia, and with the small body of regulars inflicted on the jubilant French a complete and unexpected defeat in the Royal Square of St. Helier. The French Commander was killed, but so, unfortunately, was the gallant Pierson, who led the attack. In recognition of this achievement the Jersey Infantry Regiments bear the distinction "Jersey 1781."

In 1799 an invasion of Jersey was attempted by Count de Nassau with 3000 men and repulsed by a wing of the 78th Highlanders assisted by the Militia.

In 1813 the Guard duties were very arduous consequent on an outbreak of plague at Malta, many posts being occupied to prevent any landing of persons, and strong nightly guards were also mounted by the Guernsey Militia at Hougue a la Pere and Mont Crevett "to interpose and make prisoners of troublesome foreign soldiers (in British pay) quartered in the Island as a depôt, who were prohibited by law from being quartered in England."

In 1835 the troop of Light Dragoons was disbanded.

In 1838 a proportion of guns, officers and gunners of the Artillery were attached to each Infantry Regiment.

In 1876 the Artillery was reduced to two Garrison and two Field Batteries.

In 1878 there was another reorganization, and in 1881 Field Batteries were abolished, since which date many other changes affecting the Channel Islands Militia have been made. In future, under the new law, Engineers and Medical Corps are to be formed.

EXISTING REGIMENTS.

Royal Jersey Artillery.

Lt.-Colonel :—Le Cornu, Col., C.P., C.B., A.D.C. (X).

1st or West Battalion.
(Light Infantry).
"Jersey 1781."

Lt.-Colonel :—

2nd or East Battalion.
(Light Infantry).
"Jersey 1781."

Lt.-Colonel :—Stewart, G.P., Maj. ret. pay (Res. of Off) (X) S.

3rd or South Battalion.
(Light Infantry).
"Jersey 1781."

Lt.-Colonel :—

Royal Guernsey Militia.

Lt.-Colonel :—Yates, H. T. S., Col. ret. pay.

1st Battalion.
(Light Infantry).

Lt.-Colonel :—Frere, W. A. J., hon. c.

2nd Battalion.
(Light Infantry).

Lt.-Colonel :— Macartney, J., hon. c.

Royal Alderney Artillery.

Lt.-Colonel :—de Jersey, Bt., Coll. W. G., ret. pay (Lt. Col. Res. of Off.).

With this epitomized History of the "Constitutional Force" now before us, we are in a position to understand and appreciate an Institution of the Country founded in the days of early Britain, which through storm and sunshine has played an important part in the history of England.

We find it resembling a great Military Play in many acts, with the people as players, staged in different centuries to meet the ever changing requirements of the age, and at its best on those numerous occasions when the players have appeared before the curtain.

An eminent statesman is reported to have said to an appreciative Scottish audience a few years since:

"Come the three corners of the world in arms,
We shall shock them, naught will make us rue,
If England to itself do rest but true."

If we apply England's Military experience of many centuries to the foregoing lines of warning, confidence, and resource, it would appear to be impossible not to realise the absolute necessity of an efficient, expansile, and territorial "Constitutional Force" in touch with the People, in which will re-appear on urgency occasions the same patriotic zeal that brightened the outgoing of the 18th and incoming of the 19th centuries, the Crimean War period, and South African Campaign.

Then would the Sovereign be able to adopt with confidence and success, Admiral Lord Nelson's memorable signal, in effect, that "all are expected to do their duty," and declare those words of Pope,

"He serves me best who serves me most."

In conclusion, there has to be recognised with grateful thanks the valuable information so freely given by all whom it has been necessary to consult, and to say, that, without the help of historians and others who, during centuries, have been contributing to the literary wealth of the Country, together with the Press whose researches are ever bringing to light facts and incidents relating to the "Constitutional Force," it would have been an impossible task to complete this work.

It should likewise be placed upon record that Commanding Officers of the entire Militia Force have, without exception, taken a zealous interest in furnishing all possible details in connection with their Regiments, towards making this History of value to the State for purposes of reference.

THE OLDEST SERVICE PAPER
74th YEAR OF PUBLICATION.

PUBLISHED EVERY THURSDAY PRICE SIXPENCE.

Since the "UNITED SERVICE GAZETTE" came under entirely new proprietorship and editorial control in April, 1905, every effort has been made and no expense spared to restore this old established paper to its original position as the *premier* Service Journal. That the efforts have not been unsuccessful has been proved by the continually increasing demand for the "U.S.G.," and the very large subscription list, which includes the most prominent officers in both Navy and Army.

THE NOTES ON MILITIA AFFAIRS

which are a regular feature of the Journal, have done much towards obtaining a just and proper recognition of the old Constitutional Force, while its advocacy of a separate department at the War Office for the Militia, will, it is hoped, secure the desired end.

EVERYONE INTERESTED IN THE MILITIA

is invited to assist in furthering the aims of the Force by supporting the "UNITED SERVICE GAZETTE," and thus contribute to its power as the representative Journal of the Old Constitutional Force.

Being published on Wednesday evening (for Thursday), it is therefore two days ahead of its contemporaries.

THE TERMS OF SUBSCRIPTION ARE:—

	United Kingdom.			Abroad.		
	£	s.	d.	£	s.	d.
3 months		7	6		8	0
6 months		14	6		15	6
12 months	1	8	6	1	10	6

Payable by P.O.O. or Cheque to the Proprietors:—

UNITED SERVICE GAZETTE:—
Offices 43 & 44, Temple Chambers, London, E.C.

Specimen Copy free on receipt of postcard.

THE BROAD ARROW

THE Naval and Military Gazette.

EVERY SATURDAY.   [Established 1833.]   PRICE 6D.

A Review and Journal devoted to the Regular Army, The Royal Navy, The Militia, Imperial Yeomanry, and The Volunteer Force.

RECOGNISED AS THE BEST MILITARY PAPER,
Which in addition to its advocacy of all other branches of the Imperial Forces, has for forty years specially devoted its attention to the Militia, being the first Service paper to represent the cause of the Old Constitutional Force.

It contains early and exclusive Intelligence and Articles and Comments on current Service topics written by Officers of experience, who have made Military Affairs their special study. It has a reputation for accuracy combined with considerable literary merit.

TERMS OF SUBSCRIPTIONS.
For the United Kingdom...   ...   ... £1 8 0
For the Colonies and Foreign
                    Countries, &c. £1 10 6
PAYABLE IN ADVANCE.

On Sale at all the principal Railway Bookstalls and Newsagents throughout the United Kingdom.

Editorial and Publishing Offices:
TEMPLE HOUSE, TEMPLE AVENUE, LONDON, E.C.

www.ingramcontent.com/pod-product-compliance
Lightning Source LLC
Chambersburg PA
CBHW062136160426
43191CB00014B/2300